L

Education

Library of Congress Classification
2012

Prepared by the Policy and Standards Division
Library Services

LIBRARY OF CONGRESS
LIBRARY OF CONGRESS Cataloging Distribution Service
Washington, D.C.

This edition cumulates all additions and changes to class L through List 2012/01, dated January 16, 2012. Additions and changes made subsequent to that date are published in lists posted on the World Wide Web at

<http://www.loc.gov/aba/cataloging/classification/weeklylists/>

and are also available in *Classification Web*, the online Web-based edition of the Library of Congress Classification.

Library of Congress Cataloging-in-Publication Data

Library of Congress.
  Library of Congress classification. L. Education / prepared by the Policy and Standards Division, Library Services.
      pages cm
  "This edition cumulates all additions and changes to Class L through List 2012/01, dated January 16, 2012. Additions and changes made subsequent to that date are published in lists posted on the World Wide Web ... and are also available in Classification Web, the online Web-based edition of the Library of Congress Classification"--Title page verso.
  Includes index.
  ISBN 978-0-8444-9539-2
  1. Classification, Library of Congress. 2. Classification--Books--Education. I. Library of Congress. Policy and Standards Division. II. Title. III. Title: Education.

Z696.U5L 2012   025.4'637--dc23   2012006490

For sale by the Library of Congress Cataloging Distribution Service,
101 Independence Avenue, S.E., Washington, DC 20541-4912.
Product catalog available on the Web at **www.loc.gov/cds**

PREFACE

The first edition of Class L, Education, was published in 1910, the second in 1928. The third edition appeared in 1951, incorporating additions and changes through 1949. The third edition was reprinted in 1960 with additions and changes through September 1959 and again in 1966 with additions and changes through 1965. The fourth edition was published in 1984. The 1995, 1998, and 2005 editions cumulated additions and changes that were made since the publication of the previous editions. This 2012 edition includes additions and changes made since the 2008 edition was published.

In editions of the Library of Congress classification schedules published since 2004, classification numbers or spans of numbers that appear in parentheses are formerly valid numbers that are now obsolete. Numbers or spans that appear in angle brackets are optional numbers that have never been used at the Library of Congress but are provided for other libraries that wish to use them. In most cases, a parenthesized or angle-bracketed number is accompanied by a "see" reference directing the user to the actual number that the Library of Congress currently uses, or a note explaining Library of Congress practice.

Access to the online version of the full Library of Congress Classification is available on the World Wide Web by subscription to Classification Web. Details about ordering and pricing may be obtained from the Cataloging Distribution Service at

<http://www.loc.gov/cds/>

New or revised numbers and captions are added to the L.C. Classification schedules as a result of development proposals made by the cataloging staff of the Library of Congress and cooperating institutions. Upon approval of these proposals by the editorial meeting of the Policy and Standards Division, new classification records are created or existing records are revised in the master classification database. Lists of newly approved or revised classification numbers and captions are posted on the World Wide Web at

<http://www.loc.gov/aba/cataloging/classification/weeklylists/>

The Policy and Standards Division is responsible for coordinating the overall intellectual and editorial content of class L and its various subclasses. Kent Griffiths and Ethel Tillman, assistant editors of classification schedules, create new classification records and their associated index terms, and maintain the master database.

Barbara B. Tillett, Chief
Policy and Standards Division

October 2011

OUTLINE

OUTLINE

Individual institutions
Asia - Continued

OUTLINE

Education (General)

    Periodicals. Societies

        Class here, by imprint of country or larger geographic region as indicated, all periodicals and serials of a general character

        For works relating to the education of a specific region or country see LA190+

        Cf. LB5 Serial collections

Official documents, reports, etc.
United States
By state
Arizona -- Continued

120	General
121.A-Z	Local, A-Z
	Arkansas
122	General
123.A-Z	Local, A-Z
	California
124	General
125.A-Z	Local, A-Z
	Colorado
126	General
127.A-Z	Local, A-Z
	Connecticut
128	General
129.A-Z	Local, A-Z
	Dakota (Territory)
130	General
131.A-Z	Local, A-Z
	Delaware
132	General
133.A-Z	Local, A-Z
	District of Columbia
134	General, including Washington
135.A-Z	Local (other than Washington), A-Z
	e.g.
135.G3	Georgetown
	Florida
136	General
137.A-Z	Local, A-Z
	Georgia
138	General
139.A-Z	Local, A-Z
	Hawaii see L777+
	Idaho
140	General
141.A-Z	Local, A-Z
	Illinois
142	General
143.A-Z	Local, A-Z
	Indiana
146	General
147.A-Z	Local, A-Z
	Iowa
148	General

Official documents, reports, etc.
United States
By state
Iowa -- Continued

149.A-Z	Local, A-Z
	Kansas
150	General
151.A-Z	Local, A-Z
	Kentucky
152	General
153.A-Z	Local, A-Z
	Louisiana
154	General
155.A-Z	Local, A-Z
	Maine
156	General
157.A-Z	Local, A-Z
	Maryland
158	General
159.A-Z	Local, A-Z
	Massachusetts
160	General
161.A-Z	Local, A-Z
	Michigan
162	General
163.A-Z	Local, A-Z
	Minnesota
164	General
165.A-Z	Local, A-Z
	Mississippi
166	General
167.A-Z	Local, A-Z
	Missouri
168	General
169.A-Z	Local, A-Z
	Montana
170	General
171.A-Z	Local, A-Z
	Nebraska
172	General
173.A-Z	Local, A-Z
	Nevada
174	General
175.A-Z	Local, A-Z
	New Hampshire
176	General
177.A-Z	Local, A-Z

Official documents, reports, etc.
United States
By state -- Continued
New Jersey
178   General
179.A-Z   Local, A-Z
New Mexico
180   General
181.A-Z   Local, A-Z
New York
182   General
183.A-Z   Local, A-Z
North Carolina
184   General
185.A-Z   Local, A-Z
North Dakota
186   General
187.A-Z   Local, A-Z
Ohio
188   General
189.A-Z   Local, A-Z
Oklahoma
190   General
191.A-Z   Local, A-Z
Oregon
192   General
193.A-Z   Local, A-Z
Pennsylvania
194   General
195.A-Z   Local, A-Z
Rhode Island
196   General
197.A-Z   Local, A-Z
South Carolina
198   General
199.A-Z   Local, A-Z
South Dakota
200   General
201.A-Z   Local, A-Z
Tennessee
202   General
203.A-Z   Local, A-Z
Texas
204   General
205.A-Z   Local, A-Z
Utah
206   General

	Official documents, reports, etc.
	United States
	By state
	Utah -- Continued
207.A-Z	Local, A-Z
	Vermont
208	General
209.A-Z	Local, A-Z
	Virginia
210	General
211.A-Z	Local, A-Z
	Washington
212	General
213.A-Z	Local, A-Z
	West Virginia
214	General
215.A-Z	Local, A-Z
	Wisconsin
216	General
217.A-Z	Local, A-Z
	Wyoming
218	General
219.A-Z	Local, A-Z
	Other countries
221-223	Canada (Table L17)
227-229	Mexico (Table L17)
	Central America
231-233	Belize (Table L17)
234-236	Costa Rica (Table L17)
237-239	Guatemala (Table L17)
240-242	Honduras (Table L17)
243-245	Nicaragua (Table L17)
	Panama
246	General
247.A-Z	Local (provinces, counties, cities, etc.), A-Z
	El Salvador
248	General
249.A-Z	Local (provinces, counties, cities, etc.), A-Z
	West Indies
251-253	Bahamas (Table L17)
254-256	Cuba (Table L17)
257-259	Haiti (Table L17)
261-263	Jamaica (Table L17)
264-266	Puerto Rico (Table L17)

Official documents, reports, etc.
  Other countries
    Europe
      Austria-Hungary -- Continued
        Hungary
381   General
383.A-Z   Local, A-Z
          Czech Republic. Czechoslovakia. Bohemia
385   General
387.A-Z   Local, A-Z
388.A-Z   Other states, provinces, etc., A-Z
        France
391   General
392   Musée pédagogique
392.A3   Mémoires et documents scolaires
394   Departments
              For Seine see L396.P4+
396.A-Z   Local, A-Z
                e.g.
396.B7   Bordeaux (Aquitaine)
396.P4-.P7   Paris (Département de la Seine)
        Germany
              Including West Germany
401   General
403   Prussia
404   Saxony
405   Bavaria
406   Württemberg
406.5   Baden
407.A-Z   Other states, provinces, etc., A-Z
409.A-Z   Cities, A-Z
        East Germany
410.A2   General
410.A3-Z   Local (if necessary)
        Greece
411   General
416.A-Z   Local, A-Z
        Italy
421   General works
426.A-Z   Local, A-Z
        Netherlands (Low Countries)
          Belgium
431   General
436.A-Z   Local, A-Z
          Netherlands (Holland)
441   General
446.A-Z   Local, A-Z

Official documents, reports, etc.
 Other countries
  Asia -- Continued
   Afghanistan

561	General
562.A-Z	Local (provinces, counties, cities, etc.), A-Z
	Arabia
563	General
564.A-Z	Local (provinces, counties, cities, etc.), A-Z
	China
571	General
572.A-Z	Provinces, A-Z
573.A-Z	Cities, A-Z
573.35	Macau
	Taiwan
574	General
575.A-Z	Local (provinces, counties, cities, etc.), A-Z
	India
	Including the Republic of India
577	General
578.A-Z	Provinces, etc., A-Z
	Pakistan
578.5	General
578.6.A-Z	Local, A-Z
579.A-Z	Cities, A-Z
	Indochina
	Malaysia
583	General
	Malay States, Federated
584.M3	General
584.M32A-.M32Z	Local, A-Z
	Singapore
584.S5	General
584.S52A-.S52Z	Local, A-Z
	Straits Settlements
584.S7	General
584.S72A-.S72Z	Local, A-Z
	French
585	General
	Cambodia
586.C2	General
586.C22A-.C22Z	Local, A-Z
	Cochin China
586.C7	General
586.C72A-.C72Z	Local, A-Z
	Tongking (Tonkin)
586.T7	General

Official documents, reports, etc.
Other countries
Asia
Indochina
French
Tongking (Tonkin) -- Continued

586.T72A-.T72Z	Local, A-Z
	Vietnam
586.V5	General
586.V52A-.V52Z	Local, A-Z
	Thailand
591	General
592.A-Z	Local (provinces, counties, cities, etc.), A-Z
	Indonesia
597	General
598.A-Z	Local (provinces, counties, cities, etc.), A-Z
	North Borneo
599	General
600.A-Z	Local (provinces, counties, cities, etc.), A-Z
	Philippines
601	General
602.A-Z	Local (provinces, counties, cities, etc.), A-Z
	Sarawak
605	General
606.A-Z	Local (provinces, counties, cities, etc.), A-Z
	Japan
611	General
612.A-Z	Local (provinces, counties, cities, etc.), A-Z
	Korea
613	General
614.A-Z	Local (provinces, counties, cities, etc.), A-Z
	Iran
615	General
616.A-Z	Local (provinces, counties, cities, etc.), A-Z
	Siberia (Russia)
617	General
618.A-Z	Local (provinces, counties, cities, etc.), A-Z
	Central Asia
619	General
	Kazakhstan
620.A2	General
620.A3-Z	Local (if necessary)
	Kyrgyzstan
621.A2	General
621.A3-Z	Local (if necessary)
	Tajikistan
622.A2	General

	Official documents, reports, etc.
	Other countries
	Asia
	Central Asia
	Tajikistan -- Continued
622.A3-Z	Local (if necessary)
	Turkmenistan
623.A2	General
623.A3-Z	Local (if necessary)
	Uzbekistan
623.5.A2	General
623.5.A3-Z	Local (if necessary)
	Caucasus
624	General
	Azerbaijan
624.3.A2	General
624.3.A3-Z	Local (if necessary)
	Georgia (Republic)
624.5.A2	General
624.5.A3-Z	Local (if necessary)
	Armenia
624.7.A2	General
624.7.A3-Z	Local (if necessary)
	Cyprus
625	General
626.A-Z	Local (provinces, counties, cities, etc.), A-Z
	Iraq
627	General
628.A-Z	Local (provinces, counties, cities, etc.), A-Z
	Lebanon
629	General
630.A-Z	Local (provinces, counties, cities, etc.), A-Z
	Israel. Palestine
631	General
631.A-Z	Local (provinces, counties, cities, etc.), A-Z
	Jordan
633	General
634.A-Z	Local (provinces, counties, cities, etc.), A-Z
	Syria
641	General
642.A-Z	Local (provinces, counties, cities, etc.), A-Z
	Yemen
645	General
646.A-Z	Local (provinces, counties, cities, etc.), A-Z
649	Arab countries
	Africa
	Ethiopia

	Official documents, reports, etc.
	Other countries
	Africa
	Ethiopia -- Continued
651	General
652.A-Z	Local (provinces, counties, cities, etc.), A-Z
	British Africa
	Botswana
	Formerly Bechuanaland
658.A2	General
658.A3-Z	Local (if necessary)
	Union of South Africa
660.A2	General
660.A3-Z	Local (if necessary)
	Cape of Good Hope (Cape Colony)
661	General
662.A-Z	Local (provinces, counties, cities, etc.), A-Z
	Central Africa Protectorate. Nyasaland. Malawi
663	General
664.A-Z	Local (provinces, counties, cities, etc.), A-Z
	East Africa and East Africa Protectorate. Kenya Colony and Protectorate
665	General
666.A-Z	Local (provinces, counties, cities, etc.), A-Z
	Natal
667	General
668.A-Z	Local (provinces, counties, cities, etc.), A-Z
	Orange Free State (Orange River Colony)
669	General
670.A-Z	Local (provinces, counties, cities, etc.), A-Z
	Rhodesia
671	General
	Zambia
672.N6	General
672.N62A-.N62Z	Local, A-Z
	Zimbabwe
672.S6	General
672.S62A-.S62Z	Local, A-Z
672.5.A-Z	Local, A-Z
	Transvaal (South African Republic)
673	General
674.A-Z	Local (provinces, counties, cities, etc.), A-Z
675.A-Z	West African countries, A-Z

Under each:

.x	*General*
.x2A-.x2Z	*Local, A-Z*

	Official documents, reports, etc.
	Other countries
	Africa
	British Africa -- Continued
677.A-Z	All other countries, A-Z
	Under each:
	.x *General*
	.x2A-.x2Z *Local, A-Z*
	Rwanda
679	General
680.A-Z	Local (provinces, counties, cities, etc.), A-Z
	Congo (Democratic Republic). Zaire
681	General
682.A-Z	Local (provinces, counties, cities, etc.), A-Z
	Egypt
686	General
687.A-Z	Local (provinces, counties, cities, etc.), A-Z
	Algeria and Tunis
691	General
692.A-Z	Local (provinces, counties, cities, etc.), A-Z
	French Equatorial Africa
694	General
695.A-Z	Local (provinces, counties, cities, etc.), A-Z
	Madagascar
697	General
698.A-Z	Local (provinces, counties, cities, etc.), A-Z
	Senegambia
701	General
702.A-Z	Local (provinces, counties, cities, etc.), A-Z
	Sudan
704	General
705.A-Z	Local (provinces, counties, cities, etc.), A-Z
	German Africa (Former)
	Including Tanzania, Cameroon, Southwest Africa
707	General
708.A-Z	Local (provinces, counties, cities, etc.), A-Z
	Italian Africa
	Including Eritrea, Somaliland
711	General
712.A-Z	Local (provinces, counties, cities, etc.), A-Z
	Liberia
714	General
715.A-Z	Local (provinces, counties, cities, etc.), A-Z
	Morocco
716	General
717.A-Z	Local (provinces, counties, cities, etc.), A-Z
	Orange River Colony see L669+

	Official documents, reports, etc.
	Other countries
	Africa -- Continued
	Portuguese Africa
721	General
722.A-Z	Local (provinces, counties, cities, etc.), A-Z
	South African Republic see L673+
	Spanish Africa
	Including Canary Islands, Rio de Oro
731	General
732.A-Z	Local (provinces, counties, cities, etc.), A-Z
	Tripoli
741	General
742.A-Z	Local (provinces, counties, cities, etc.), A-Z
	Australia and New Zealand
750	Commonwealth of Australia
	New South Wales
751	General
752.A-Z	Local (provinces, counties, cities, etc.), A-Z
	New Zealand
754	General
755.A-Z	Local (provinces, counties, cities, etc.), A-Z
	Northern Territory
757	General
758.A-Z	Local (provinces, counties, cities, etc.), A-Z
	Queensland
761	General
762.A-Z	Local (provinces, counties, cities, etc.), A-Z
	South Australia
764	General
765.A-Z	Local (provinces, counties, cities, etc.), A-Z
	Tasmania
767	General
768.A-Z	Local (provinces, counties, cities, etc.), A-Z
	Victoria
771	General
772.A-Z	Local (provinces, counties, cities, etc.), A-Z
	Western Australia
774	General
775.A-Z	Local (provinces, counties, cities, etc.), A-Z
	Pacific islands
	Hawaii
777	General
778.A-Z	Local, A-Z

Official documents, reports, etc.
  Other countries
    Pacific islands -- Continued

791.A-Z	Other groups, A-Z

Under each:

.x	*General*
.x2A-.x2Z	*Local, A-Z*

Educational exhibitions and museums
  Including private collections
  Cf. LB3291+ School museums
  Cf. LC6691 Traveling educational exhibits

797	General works

By region or country
  Class here general reports of exhibitions only
  For special reports on exhibits of particular countries, e.g., German educational exhibit at the St. Louis Exposition, see LA
  For reports on exhibits illustrating particular subjects, see LB-LC, or subdivision "Study and teaching" under other subjects in Classes B-K, M-Z

United States

801	General
803.A-Z	Local, A-Z

Canada

805	General works
806.A-Z	Local, A-Z

Mexico

808	General works
809.A-Z	Local, A-Z

Central America

811	General works
812.A-Z	Local, A-Z

West Indies

814	General works
815.A-Z	Local, A-Z

South America

816	General works
817.A-Z	Local, A-Z

Europe

818	General works

Great Britain

819	General works
820	England
821	Ireland
823	Scotland
825	Wales
826.A-Z	Local, A-Z

Educational exhibitions and museums
By region or country
Europe -- Continued
Austria-Hungary

828	General works
829	Czech Republic. Czechoslovakia. Bohemia
830	Hungary
831.A-Z	Local, A-Z

France

833	General works
835.A-Z	Local, A-Z

Germany

837	General works
839.A-Z	Local, A-Z

Greece

841	General works
842.A-Z	Local, A-Z

Italy

844	General works
845.A-Z	Local, A-Z

Low countries

847	General works
848	Belgium
849	Netherlands

Russia. Soviet Union

851	General works
852	Finland
853	Poland
854.A-Z	Local, A-Z

Scandinavia

855	Denmark
859	Iceland
861	Norway
863	Sweden

Spain and Portugal
Spain

865	General works
866.A-Z	Local, A-Z

Portugal

867	General works
868.A-Z	Local, A-Z

Switzerland

869	General works
870.A-Z	Local, A-Z

Turkey and the Balkan states

873	General works
874.A-Z	Local, A-Z

Educational exhibitions and museums
 By region or country
  Europe
   Turkey and the Balkan states -- Continued
    Bulgaria
875   General works
876.A-Z   Local, A-Z
(877)   Montenegro
        see L883
     Romania
879   General works
880.A-Z   Local, A-Z
(881-882)   Serbia
        see L883
     Yugoslavia. Serbia. Montenegro
883   General works
884.A-Z   Local, A-Z
885.A-Z   Other European regions or countries, A-Z
    Asia
887   General works
888.A-Z   Local, A-Z
889   Arab countries
    Africa
890   General works
891.A-Z   Local, A-Z
    Australia and New Zealand
893   General works
894.A-Z   Local, A-Z
    Pacific islands
897   General works
898.A-Z   Local, A-Z
   School fairs
899.A2   General works
899.A6-Z   By place
   Directories of educational institutions
      Including directories for all levels and types of education, e.g.,
         adult education, and directories of teachers, students, etc.
      Cf. LA203 Directories of foreign students in the United
         States
      Cf. LB1042.7+ Directories of audiovisual education
         personnel
      Cf. LB2283 Directories of employment of teachers in
         foreign countries
      Cf. LB2376 Directories of international exchange students
      Cf. LB2803.A1 Directories of school officials
900   General

Directories of educational institutions -- Continued
United States
Including directories of the United States and Canada
901   General
903.A-Z   By region or state, A-Z
                   Under each state:
                   .x   *General*
                   .x3A-.x3Z   *Counties, A-Z*
                   .x5A-.x5Z   *Cities, A-Z*
Other countries
Canada
For directories of the United States and Canada see
L901+
905   General
906.A-Z   Local, A-Z
Mexico
907   General
908.A-Z   Local, A-Z
Central America
909   General
910.A-Z   Local, A-Z
West Indies
911   General
912.A-Z   Local, A-Z
South America
913   General
914.A-Z   Local, A-Z
Europe
914.5   General
Great Britain
915   General
916.A-Z   Local, A-Z
Scotland
917   General
918.A-Z   Local, A-Z
Ireland
919   General
920.A-Z   Local, A-Z
Austria
921   General
922.A-Z   Local, A-Z
923   Czech Republic
924   Slovakia
925   Hungary
France
927   General
928.A-Z   Local, A-Z

	Directories of educational institutions
	Other countries
	Europe
	Switzerland -- Continued
954.A-Z	Local, A-Z
	Turkey and the Balkan states
955	General
956.A-Z	Local, A-Z
957.A-Z	Other European countries, A-Z
	Asia
960	General works
961.A-Z	By region or country, A-Z
	e.g.
961.A4	Armenia
961.A6	Azerbaijan
961.C6	China
961.G4	Georgia (Republic)
961.I4	India
961.K4	Kazakhstan
961.K6	Kyrgyzstan
961.P4	Philippines
961.T4	Tajikistan
961.T6	Turkmenistan
961.U4	Uzbekistan
967	Arab countries
968	Islamic countries
	Africa
970	General works
971.A-Z	By region or country, A-Z
973.A-Z	Indian Ocean islands, A-Z
	Australia
981	General
982.A-Z	Local, A-Z
	New Zealand
985	General
986.A-Z	Local, A-Z
991.A-Z	Pacific islands, A-Z
995	Electronic information resources
	Including computer network resources, the Internet, digital libraries, etc.

LA

	History of higher education
	Modern -- Continued
	General see LA173+
179	1500-1800
181	1801-1960
183	1961-1990
184	1991-
186	Student life
	For political activity see LB3610
	By region or country see LA201+
	Individual institutions
	see LD-LG
	By region or country
190-198.7	America (Table L1a)
	United States
201	Periodicals. Collections
	Directories
	Institutions see L901+
	Personnel see LB2803+
203	Foreign students
	Biography see LA2301+
	History
205	General works
206	Early to 1865
209	1865-1945
209.2	1945-
210	Description. Organization. Policy
	Class here general works only
	For specific policies, see the policy, e.g., Discrimination in education, LC212+
	Public or common-school education
	History
212	General works
	By period
215	To 1865
216	1865-1965
217	1965-1990
217.2	1990-
219	Elementary or primary education
222	Secondary education
	Higher education
225	Encyclopedic works
226	General works
	By period
227	Early to 1800
227.1	1800-1945
227.2	1945-1965

By region or country
United States
Higher education
By period -- Continued
227.3   1965-1990
227.4   1990-
228   Addresses, essays, lectures. Pamphlets
               Individual institutions see LD1+
228.5   Graduate education
229   Student life
230   Miscellaneous
                 Including student mobility
230.5.A-Z   By region, A-Z
230.5.N4   New England
               By state
231-233   Alabama (Table L18)
234-236   Alaska (Table L18)
237-239   Arizona (Table L18)
240-242   Arkansas (Table L18)
243-245   California (Table L18)
246-248   Colorado (Table L18)
249-251   Connecticut (Table L18)
252-254   Delaware (Table L18)
255-257   District of Columbia (Table L18)
258-260   Florida (Table L18)
261-263   Georgia (Table L18)
                 Hawaii
263.2   General
263.25   Higher education
263.3.A-Z   Counties or regions, A-Z
263.4.A-Z   Cities, A-Z
264-266   Idaho (Table L18)
267-269   Illinois (Table L18)
283-285   Indiana (Table L18)
286-288   Iowa (Table L18)
289-291   Kansas (Table L18)
292-294   Kentucky (Table L18)
295-297   Louisiana (Table L18)
298-300   Maine (Table L18)
301-303   Maryland (Table L18)
304-306   Massachusetts (Table L18)
307-309   Michigan (Table L18)
310-312   Minnesota (Table L18)
313-315   Mississippi (Table L18)
316-318   Missouri (Table L18)
319-321   Montana (Table L18)
322-324   Nebraska (Table L18)

LA

By region or country
  United States
    By state -- Continued

325-327	Nevada (Table L18)
328-330	New Hampshire (Table L18)
331-333	New Jersey (Table L18)
334-336	New Mexico (Table L18)
337-339	New York (Table L18)
340-342	North Carolina (Table L18)
343-345	North Dakota (Table L18)
346-348	Ohio (Table L18)
349-351	Oklahoma (Table L18)
352-354	Oregon (Table L18)
355-357	Pennsylvania (Table L18)
358-360	Rhode Island (Table L18)
361-363	South Carolina (Table L18)
364-366	South Dakota (Table L18)
367-369	Tennessee (Table L18)
370-372	Texas (Table L18)
373-375	Utah (Table L18)
376-378	Vermont (Table L18)
379-381	Virginia (Table L18)
382-384	Washington (Table L18)
385-387	West Virginia (Table L18)
388-390	Wisconsin (Table L18)
391-393	Wyoming (Table L18)
396	Insular possessions (General)
	For special islands see LA500+
398	American education outside the United States
	Individual institutions see LD1+
	Canada
410-417.7	General (Table L1b)
418.A-Z	Provinces, A-Z
419.A-Z	Cities, A-Z
	Mexico
420-428.7	General (Table L1a)
429.A-Z	States and districts, A-Z
430.A-Z	Cities, A-Z
	Central America
435-438.7	General (Table L2a)
440-444	Belize (Table L2)
445-449	Costa Rica (Table L2)
450-454	Guatemala (Table L2)
455-459	Honduras (Table L2)
460-464	Nicaragua (Table L2)
465-469	Panama (Table L2)
469.5	Panama Canal Zone

By region or country
Europe
Great Britain
General, and England
History
20th century -- Continued

631.8	General works
631.82	1944-2000
631.83	21st century
632	General works

Class here works by contemporary writers on current situation, etc.

633	Elementary education
	Secondary education
634	History
635	General works. Present situation
	Higher education
	History
636	General, and general modern
636.3	Early and medieval
636.4	16th century
636.5	17th-18th centuries
636.7	19th century
636.8	20th century
636.82	21st century
637	General works. Present situation
637.7	General special

Including student life
Local: England

638.A-Z	Counties, shires, etc., A-Z
639.A-Z	Cities, A-Z

e.g.

639.L8	London

Individual institutions see LF13.92+

640-649	Northern Ireland (Table L1)
650-659	Scotland (Table L1)
660-669	Wales (Table L1)
669.5	Colonies (General)
	Ireland. Irish Republic
669.6	Collections
	General works. History and present situation
669.61	General
669.62	Primary education. Secondary education
669.63	Higher education
669.64.A-Z	Local, A-Z
670-679	Austria-Hungary (Former). Austria (Table L1)
680-687.7	Hungary (Table L1b)

	By region or country
	Europe
	Austria-Hungary (Former). Austria -- Continued
688.A-Z	Other states, A-Z
688.B7	Bohemia
688.C95	Czechoslovakia. Czech Republic
688.S56	Slovakia
689.A-Z	Cities, A-Z
	e.g.
689.V5	Vienna
	France
690	Collections
	History
691	General, and general modern
691.3	Early and medieval
691.4	16th century. Period of the Reformation
691.5	Early modern. 17th-18th centuries
691.7	19th century
691.8	20th century
691.82	1965-2000
691.83	21st century
692	General works
	Class here works by contemporary writers on current situation, etc.
	Primary and elementary education (Schools)
	History
693.A2	Sources. Documents
693.A4	Exhibitions (Reports, etc.)
693.A5-Z	General works
694	General works. Present situation
	Secondary education (Schools)
	History
695.A2	Sources. Documents
695.A4	Exhibitions (Reports, etc.)
695.A5-Z	General works
696	General works. Present situation
	Higher education
697	Sources. Documents
698	History
699	General works. Present situation
707	General special
	Including student life
	Local
713.A-Z	Provinces and departments, A-Z
715.A-Z	Cities, A-Z
	e.g.
715.P3	Paris

	By region or country
	Europe
	France -- Continued
716	Colonies (General)
	Including French-speaking countries
	Individual institutions see LF1711+
718	French education outside of France
	Germany
720	Periodicals. Collections
	History
721	General works
	Early and medieval
721.3.A2	Sources. Documents
721.3.A4	Exhibitions (Reports, etc.)
721.3.A5-Z	General works
	16th century. Period of the Reformation
721.4.A2	Sources. Documents
721.4.A4	Exhibitions (Reports, etc.)
721.4.A5-Z	General works
	Early modern. 17th and 18th centuries
721.5.A2	Sources. Documents
721.5.A4	Exhibitions (Reports, etc.)
721.5.A5-Z	General works
	19th century
721.7.A2	Sources. Documents
721.7.A4	Exhibitions (Reports, etc.)
721.7.A5-Z	General works
	20th century
721.8	General works
	1933-1945
721.81.A2	Sources. Documents
721.81.A4	Exhibitions (Reports, etc.)
721.81.A5-Z	General works
721.82	1945-1990
	Including Germany (West)
	1990-2000
721.83.A2	Sources. Documents
721.83.A4	Exhibitions (Reports, etc.)
721.83.A5-Z	General works
721.85	21st century
722	General works. Present situation, etc.
722.7	General special
	e.g. Student activities
	Primary and elementary education (Schools)
	History
723.A2	Sources and documents
723.A4	Exhibitions (Reports, etc.)

By region or country
Europe
Germany
Primary and elementary education (Schools)
History -- Continued

723.A5-Z	General works
724	General works. Present situation
724.7	General special
	e.g. Student activities

Secondary education (Schools)
History

725.A2	Sources and documents
725.A4	Exhibitions (Reports, etc.)
725.A5-Z	General works
726	General works. Present situation
726.7	General special
	For student life see LA729.A1+

Higher or university education (Colleges and universities)
History

727.A2	Sources and documents
727.A4	Exhibitions (Reports, etc.)
727.A5-Z	General works
728	General works. Present situation
728.7	General special
	For student life see LA729.A1+

Student life. Deutsche Burschenschaft

729.A1-.A29	Periodicals. Collections
729.A3	General works
729.A4	Early
729.A5-Z	1870-1990
729.2	1990-

Individual schools and colleges
    see LF2401.62+

730-739	Prussia (Table L1)
740-749	Saxony (Table L1)
750-759	Bavaria (Table L1)
760-769	Württemberg (Table L1)
770.A-Z	Other states and provinces, A-Z
	e.g.
770.A4	Alsace

Germany (East)

771	Periodicals. Collections
	General works. History and present situation
772	General
773	Primary education. Secondary education
774	Higher education

	By region or country
	Europe
	Germany
	Germany (East)
	General works. History and present situation -- Continued
774.7	General special
	e.g. Student life
775.A-Z	Cities, A-Z
	e.g.
775.B5	Berlin
777	German colonies (General)
	For individual colonies see LA1830+; LA2270.A+
779	German education outside of Germany
	Individual institutions see LF2401.62+
780-789	Greece (Table L1)
	For education in Ancient Greece see LA75
789.5	Greek education outside of Greece
	Italy
790	Periodicals. Collections
	History
	General, and general modern
791.A2	Sources. Documents
791.A4	Exhibitions (Reports, etc.)
791.A5-Z	General works
	Early and medieval
791.3.A2	Sources. Documents
791.3.A4	Exhibitions (Reports, etc.)
791.3.A5-Z	General works
	16th century. Period of the Reformation
791.4.A2	Sources. Documents
791.4.A4	Exhibitions (Reports, etc.)
791.4.A5-Z	General works
	Early modern. 17th and 18th centuries
791.5.A2	Sources. Documents
791.5.A4	Exhibitions (Reports, etc.)
791.5.A5-Z	General works
	19th century
791.7.A2	Sources. Documents
791.7.A4	Exhibitions (Reports, etc.)
791.7.A5-Z	General works
	20th century
791.8.A2	Sources. Documents
791.8.A4	Exhibitions (Reports, etc.)
791.8.A5-Z	General works
	1945-2000
791.82.A2	Sources. Documents

	By region or country
	Europe
	Italy
	History
	20th century
	1945-2000 -- Continued
791.82.A4	Exhibitions (Reports, etc.)
791.82.A5-Z	General works
	21st century
791.83.A2	Sources. Documents
791.83.A4	Exhibitions (Reports, etc.)
791.83.A5-Z	General works
792	General works. Present situation, etc.
792.7	General special
	e.g. Student activities
	Primary and elementary education (Schools)
	History
793.A2	Sources and documents
793.A4	Exhibitions (Reports, etc.)
793.A5-Z	General works
794	General works. Present situation
794.7	General special
	e.g. Student activities
	Secondary education (Schools)
	History
795.A2	Sources and documents
795.A4	Exhibitions (Reports, etc.)
795.A5-Z	General works
796	General works. Present situation
796.7	General special
	e.g. Student activities
	Higher education
797	History
797.5	General works. Present situation
797.7	Student life
	Local
798.A-Z	Provinces and districts, A-Z
799.A-Z	Cities, A-Z
	e. g.
799.G3	Genoa
799.5	Italian education outside of Italy
	Individual institutions see LF3248+
	San Marino
799.6	Periodicals. Collections
799.61	General
799.62	Elementary and secondary education
799.63	Higher education

LA

	By region or country
	Asia -- Continued
1050-1059	General (Table L1)
1080-1084	Afghanistan (Table L2)
(1100-1104)	Arabia
	see LA1436+
1130-1134	China (Table L2 modified)
	General works. History and present situation
1131	General
1131.8	To 1912
1131.81	1912-1949
1131.82	1949-
1135-1139	Taiwan (Table L2 modified)
	General works. History and present situation
1136	General
1136.8	To 1945
1136.81	1945-
1140-1144	East Asia. Far East (Table L2)
	South Asia
1144.4	Collected works
	General works. History and present situation
1144.5	General
1144.6	Elementary education. Secondary education
1144.7	Higher education
1145-1149	Sri Lanka (Table L2)
1150-1154	India (Table L2)
	Including the Republic of India
1155-1159	Pakistan (Table L2)
1160-1164	Nepal (Table L2)
	Bhutan
1164.2	Periodicals. Collections
1164.3	General works
1164.4	Elementary and secondary education
1164.5	Higher education
1164.6.A-Z	Local, A-Z
1165-1169	Bangladesh (Table L2)
	Indochina
1170-1174	French Indochina (Table L2)
1180-1184	Annam. Vietnam (Table L2)
1185-1189	Vietnam (Democractic Republic, 1946-) (Table L2)
1190-1194	Cambodia (Table L2)
1200-1204	Cochin China (Table L2)
1205-1209	Laos (Table L2)
1210-1214	Tongking (Tonkin) (Table L2)
1220-1224	Thailand (Table L2)
1235-1239	Malaysia (Table L2)
1239.5	Singapore

	By region or country
	Asia
	Indochina -- Continued
1240-1244	Burma. Myanmar (Table L2)
1250-1254	Southeast Asia (Table L2)
1270-1274	Indonesia (Table L2)
1280-1284	Brunei (Table L2)
1290-1299	Philippines (Table L1)
1310-1319	Japan (Table L1)
1330-1334	Korea (Table L2)
1335-1339	Korea (North) (Table L2)
1340-1344	Mongolia (Table L2)
1350-1354	Iran (Table L2)
1360-1363.7	Portuguese possessions (Goa, Macau) (Table L2a)
	Former Soviet areas of Asia
1370-1373.7	General (Table L2a)
	Central Asia
1380-1383.7	General (Table L2a)
	Kazakhstan
1385	Periodicals. Collections
1385.2	General works
1385.3	Elementary and secondary education
1385.4	Higher education
1385.5.A-Z	Local, A-Z
	Kyrgyzstan
1386	Periodicals. Collections
1386.2	General works
1386.3	Elementary and secondary education
1386.4	Higher education
1386.5.A-Z	Local, A-Z
	Tajikistan
1387	Periodicals. Collections
1387.2	General works
1387.3	Elementary and secondary education
1387.4	Higher education
1387.5.A-Z	Local, A-Z
	Turkmenistan
1388	Periodicals. Collections
1388.2	General works
1388.3	Elementary and secondary education
1388.4	Higher education
1388.5.A-Z	Local, A-Z
	Uzbekistan
1389	Periodicals. Collections
1389.2	General works
1389.3	Elementary and secondary education
1389.4	Higher education

	By region or country
	Asia
	Former Soviet areas of Asia
	Central Asia
	Uzbekistan -- Continued
1389.5.A-Z	Local, A-Z
1390-1394	Siberia (Russia) (Table L2)
	Caucasus
1395-1398.7	General (Table L2 modified)
1400-1404	Azerbaijan (Table L2)
1405-1409	Georgia (Republic) (Table L2)
1425-1429	Armenia (Table L2)
	Middle East (Near East). The Levant
1430	Periodicals. Collections
1430.2	General works
1430.3	Elementary education. Secondary education
1430.4	Higher education
	Arabian Peninsula
1431	Periodicals. Collections
1431.2	General works
1431.3	Elementary education. Secondary education
1431.4	Higher education
1432	Bahrain
1433	Kuwait
1434	Oman
1435	Qatar
	Saudi Arabia
1436	Periodicals. Collections
1436.2	General works
1436.3	Elementary education. Secondary education
1436.4	Higher education
1437	United Arab Emirates
1438	Yemen
1440-1444	Israel. Palestine (Table L2)
1444.5	West Bank
1444.6	Gaza Strip
1455-1459	Syria (Table L2)
1460-1464	Lebanon (Table L2)
1465-1469	Iraq (Table L2)
1470-1474	Jordan (Table L2)
1480-1484	Cyprus (Table L2)
1490-1493.7	Arab countries (Table L2a)
1495-1498.7	Islamic countries (Table L2a)
	Africa
1500-1503.7	General (Table L2a)
1515-1519	Ethiopia (Table L2)
1520-1524	Eritrea (Table L2)

	By region or country
	Africa -- Continued
	British and former British possessions
1530-1533.7	General (Table L2a)
	South Africa
1535	Periodicals. Collections
	General works. History and present situation
1536	General
1537	Primary education. Secondary education
1538	Higher education
1539	General special
1544.A-Z	Local, A-Z
1544.O73	Orange Free State
1544.T73	Transvaal
	Individual schools and colleges see LG405+
	Educational biography see LA2301+
1545-1549	Lesotho (Table L2)
1550-1554	Malawi (Table L2)
	East Africa
1555-1558.7	General (Table L2a)
1560-1564	Kenya (Table L2)
1565-1569	Uganda (Table L2)
1590-1594	Zimbabwe. Southern Rhodesia (Table L2)
1595-1599	Zambia (Table L2)
1600-1604	Botswana (Table L2)
1605-1609	Swaziland (Table L2)
	British West Africa
1610-1613.7	General (Table L2a)
1620-1624	Gambia (Table L2)
1625-1629	Ghana (Table L2)
1630-1634	Nigeria (Table L2)
1640-1644	Sierra Leone (Table L2)
1645-1649	Egypt (Table L2)
1650-1654	Sudan (Table L2)
	French Africa
1660-1664	General (Table L2)
1670-1674	Algeria (Table L2)
1680-1683.7	French Equatorial Africa (Table L2a)
1785	Central African Republic. Ubangi-Shari
1786	Chad
1787	Congo (Brazzaville)
1788	Gabon
1790-1794	Madagascar (Table L2)
1800-1804	Senegambia (Table L2)
1810-1814	Mali. French Sudan (Table L2)
1815-1819	Tunisia (Table L2)
1821.A-Z	Other, A-Z

	By region or country
	Africa -- Continued
	German Africa (Former)
1830-1833.7	General (Table L2a)
1840-1844	Tanzania. Tanganyika (Table L2)
	Burundi see LA2090.B9
	Rwanda see LA2090.R95
1850-1854	Cameroon (Table L2)
1860-1864	Namibia. Southwest Africa (Table L2)
	Italian Africa
1880-1883.7	General (Table L2a)
1890-1894	Eritrea (Table L2)
	Libya see LA2070+
1900-1904	Somalia (Table L2)
1910-1914	Congo (Democratic Republic). Zaire. Belgian Congo (Table L2)
1920-1924	Liberia (Table L2)
1940-1944	Morocco (Table L2)
(1960-1964)	Orange Free State
	see LA1544.O73
	Portuguese Africa
1980-1983.7	General (Table L2a)
1985-1989	Mozambique (Table L2)
1990-1994	Angola (Table L2)
1995-1999	Guinea-Bissau (Table L2)
2000-2004	Sao Tome and Principe (Table L2)
(2010-2014)	Transvaal (South Africa)
	see LA1544.T73
	Spanish Africa
2030-2033.7	General (Table L2a)
2040-2044	Canaries (Table L2)
2050-2054	Rio de Oro (Table L2)
2060.A-Z	Other, A-Z
2070-2074	Libya (Table L2)
2090.A-Z	Other regions or countries of Africa, A-Z
2090.B46	Benin
2090.B9	Burundi
2090.R95	Rwanda
2094.A-Z	Atlantic Ocean islands, A-Z
2095.A-Z	Indian Ocean islands, A-Z
	Australia and New Zealand
2100-2108.7	General (Table L1a)
2110-2119	New South Wales (Table L1)
2120-2129	New Zealand (Table L1)
2130-2139	Queensland (Table L1)
2140-2149	South Australia (Table L1)
2150-2159	Tasmania (Table L1)

	By region or country
	Australia and New Zealand -- Continued
2160-2169	Victoria (Table L1)
2170-2179	Western Australia (Table L1)
2180-2189	Australian Capital Territory (Table L1)
	Pacific islands
2200-2203.7	General (Table L2a)
	Hawaii see LA263.2+
2270.A-Z	Other, A-Z
	e.g.
2270.S3	American Samoa
	Arctic regions
	General works. History and present situation
2277	General works
2277.3	Primary education. Secondary education
2277.5	Higher education
2280-2284	Greenland (Table L2)
	Developing countries see LC2601+
	Biography
	Mainly for collections. Class here only such individual biography
	as cannot be classed in LB51+
2301	General collections
2303	Minor collections
	By region or country
	America
	United States
2311	General
2315.A-Z	By region or state, A-Z
2317.A-Z	Individual biography, A-Z
	Canada
2321	General
2325.A-Z	Individual biography, A-Z
	Mexico
2331	General
2335.A-Z	Individual biography, A-Z
	Central America
2341	General works
2343.A-Z	By region or country, A-Z
	Under each country:
	.x *Collective*
	.x2 *Individual, A-Z*
	West Indies
2351	General works
2353.A-Z	Special. By island or group of islands, A-Z
	Under each country:
	.x *Collective*
	.x2 *Individual, A-Z*

	Biography	
	By region or country -- Continued	
	Bermuda	
2355	General works	
2356.A-Z	Individual biography, A-Z	
	South America	
	Including Latin America in general	
2361	General works	
2365.A-Z	By region or country, A-Z	
	Under each country:	
	.x	*Collective*
	.x2	*Individual, A-Z*
	Europe	
2371	General works	
2375.A-Z	By region or country, A-Z	
	Under each country:	
	.x	*Collective*
	.x2	*Individual, A-Z*
	Asia	
2381	General works	
2383.A-Z	By region or country, A-Z	
	Under each country:	
	.x	*Collective*
	.x2	*Individual, A-Z*
	e.g.	
2383.I6-.I62	India	
2383.I65-.I652	Indonesia	
2385	Arab countries	
	Africa	
2387	General works	
2388.A-Z	By region or country, A-Z	
	Under each country:	
	.x	*Collective*
	.x2	*Individual, A-Z*
	Australia	
2391	General works	
2392.A-Z	Individual, A-Z	
	New Zealand	
2393	General works	
2394.A-Z	Individual, A-Z	
	Pacific islands	
2395	General works	
2396.A-Z	Special. By island or group of islands, A-Z	
	Under each:	
	.x	*Collective*
	.x2	*Individual, A-Z*

LB

Theory and practice of education
Including philosophy
Collected writings
Including essays, monographs, papers
Several authors
5   Serial collections
7   Minor collections
Including selections, extracts, etc.
Individual authors see LB51+
General works
14   Early to 1800
14.5   1801-1960
14.6   1961-1990
14.7   1991-
15   Encyclopedias and dictionaries
For encyclopedic works see LB17
17   Modern comprehensive works. Systematic encyclopedias. Handbooks
Compends (Theory, philosophy of education, etc.) see LB51+; LB175.A+
41   Addresses, essays, lectures. Pamphlets
Including value, aims, relations of education, etc.
For theory, methods, etc. see LB1027; LB1033; LB1045
41.5   Forecasting
Including forecasts
Educational sociology see LC189+
Right to education see LC213
43   Comparative education
For comparative education studies on specific subjects, see the subjects
45   Educational anthropology
Cf. LB1125 Child study
Systems of individual educators and writers
For analyses and comparisons of various systems see LA31+
General pre-Christian
51.A-Z   Chinese educators and writers, A-Z
Subarrange each by Table L14
55.A-Z   Hindu educators and writers, A-Z
Subarrange each by Table L14
61.A-Z   Egyptian educators and writers, A-Z
Subarrange each by Table L14
65.A-Z   Assyro-Babylonian educators and writers, A-Z
Subarrange each by Table L14
71.A-Z   Phenician educators and writers, A-Z
Subarrange each by Table L14
Cf. LC701+ Jewish education

Systems of individual educators and writers
General pre-Christian -- Continued

75.A-Z	Jewish educators and writers, A-Z
	Subarrange each by Table L14
81.A-Z	Persian educators and writers, A-Z
	Subarrange each by Table L14
85.A-Z	Greek educators and writers, A-Z
	Subarrange each educator by Table L14
	Aristotle
85.A69	Collected works. By date
85.A69A-.A69Z	Individual works. By title
85.A7	Biography and criticism
	Plato
85.P69	Collected works. By date
85.P69A-.P69Z	Individual works. By title
85.P7	Biography and criticism
85.P8-.P82	Plutarch (Table L14)
91.A-Z	Roman educators and writers, A-Z
	Subarrange each by Table L14
91.Q7-.Q72	Quintilian (Table L14)
95.A-Z	Other ancient, A-Z
	Subarrange each by Table L14
125.A-Z	Early Christian and medieval educators and writers, A-Z
	Subarrange each by Table L14
	For general works see LA96
125.A4-.A42	Alcuin (Table L14)
125.T5-.T52	Thomas Aquinas (Table L14)
125.V5-.V52	Vincent de Beau (Table L14)
175.A-Z	Renaissance. Humanists
	Subarrange each by Table L14
	For general works see LA106
175.E6-.E62	Erasmus (Table L14)
175.P6-.P62	Platter, Thomas (Table L14)
175.V45-.V452	Vegius, Mapheus (Table L14)
175.V6-.V62	Vives, Juan Luis (Table L14)
175.W6-.W62	Wimpheling, Jakob (Table L14)
275.A-Z	Reformation
	Subarrange each by Table L14
	For general works see LA106
	Luther, Martin
275.L75	Collected works. By date
275.L75A-.L75Z	Individual works. By title
275.L8	Biography and criticism
	Zwingli, Ulrich
275.Z7	Collected works. By date
275.Z7A-.Z7Z	Individual works. By title
275.Z8	Biography and criticism

	Systems of individual educators and writers -- Continued
375.A-Z	Counter-Reformation
	Subarrange each by Table L14
	For general works see LC493
	Loyola, Ignacio de
375.L59	Collected works. By date
375.L59A-.L59Z	Individual works. By title
375.L6	Biography and criticism
	16th and 17th centuries
	For general works see LA116+
472	Collections
475.A-Z	Individual educators, A-Z
	Subarrange each by Table L14
475.A7-.A72	Ascham, Roger (Table L14)
475.C5-.C52	Cheever, Ezekiel (Table L14)
	Comenius, Johann Amos
	For criticism of Comenius' literary work, see PG5037.C6
475.C59	Collected works. By date
475.C59A-.C59Z	Individual works. By title
475.C6	Biography and criticism
475.F8-.F82	Francke, August Hermann (Table L14)
475.L2-.L22	La Salle, Jean Baptiste de, Saint (Table L14)
	Cf. BX4700.L3 La Salle as a saint
	Locke, John
475.L6	Collected works. By date
475.L6A-.L6Z	Individual works. By title
475.L7	Biography and criticism
	Loyola, Ignacio de see LB375.L59+
	Luther, Martin see LB275.L75+
475.M6-.M62	Montaigne, Michel Eyquem de (Table L14)
475.M8-.M82	Mulcaster, Richard (Table L14)
475.R7-.R72	Rollin, Charles (Table L14)
	Vives, Juan Luis see LB175.V6+
475.Y45-.Y452	Yen, Yüan (Table L14)
501-575	Eighteenth century to ca. 1789
	For general works see LA121+
	Rousseau
	Cf. B2130+ Philosophy
510	Collected works
	Special works
	Émile
511	Original. By date
512.A-Z	Translations. By language, A-Z, and date
512.5	Concordances
517	Biography
518	Criticism
519	Special. Miscellaneous minor

	Systems of individual educators and writers
	Eighteenth century to ca. 1789 -- Continued
575.A-Z	Other educators, A-Z
	Subarrange each by Table L14
	e. g.
575.B4-.B42	Basedow, Johann Bernard (Table L14)
575.C2-.C22	Campe, Joachim Heinrich (Table L14)
575.G4-.G42	Genlis, Stéphanie Félicité Ducrest de Saint-Aubin (Table L14)
	Salzmann, Christian Gothilf
575.S29	Collected works. By date
575.S29A-.S29Z	Individual works. By title
575.S3	Biography and criticism
575.V4-.V42	Verney, Luis Antonio (Table L14)
	Nineteenth century (1776/89-1870)
	For general works see LA126+; LB1025+
	Foreign educators
621-629	Pestalozzi
621	Collected works. Selections. By date
622.A-Z	Translations (General). By language, A-Z, and date
	Special works
	Lienhard and Gertrud
624	Original. By date
624.5.A-Z	Translations (General). By language, A-Z, and date
	Wie Gertrud ihre Kinder lehrt
625	Original. By date
625.5.A-Z	Translations. By language, A-Z, and date
626.A-Z	Other, A-Z
	e.g.
626.A6	An die unschuld, den ernst und den edelmut meines vaterlands
626.B8	Buch der mütter
626.F5	Figuren zu meinem ABC-buch
626.K5	Kinderlehre der Wohnstubeh
627	Biography
628	Criticism
629	Special. Miscellaneous minor
	Froebel
	Cf. B2986.F6+ Philosophy
631	Collected works on education. Selected works
632.A-Z	Translations. By language, A-Z
	Individual works see LB1153+
637.A2	Autobiography
637.A3-Z	Biography
	Criticism
	Cf. LB1162 Kindergarten theories
638	General works

	Systems of individual educators and writers
	Nineteenth century (1776/89-1870)
	Foreign educators
	Froebel
	Criticism -- Continued
639	Special. Miscellaneous minor
	Herbart
	Cf. B3000+ Philosophy
641.A-Z	Collected works on education. Selected works. By editor, A-Z
642.A-Z	Translations. By language, A-Z, and date
	Individual works
	Aesthetische Darstellung der Welt
643	Original. By date
643.5.A-Z	Translations. By language, A-Z, and date
	Allgemeine Pädagogik
644	Original. By date
644.5.A-Z	Translations. By language, A-Z, and date
	Umriss pädagogischer Vorlesungen
645	Original. By date
645.5.A-Z	Translations. By language, A-Z, and date
646.A-Z	Other, A-Z
647	Biography
	Criticism
648	General works
649	Special. Miscellaneous minor
675.A-Z	Other foreign educators, A-Z
	Subarrange each by Table L14 unless otherwise provided for e.g.
675.D8-.D82	Dupanloup, Félix Antoine Philibert (Table L14)
675.L2-.L22	Lancaster, Joseph (Table L14)
675.N3-.N32	Necker de Saussure, Albertine-Adrienne. (Table L14)
675.R4-.R42	Richter, Johann Paul Friedrich (Table L14)
	Sailer, Johann Michael
675.S14	Collected works. By date
675.S14A-.S14Z	Individual works. By title
675.S15	Biography and criticism
	Spencer, Herbert
	Texts
675.S7	English and American. By date
675.S71-.S78	Translations. By language (alphabetically)
675.S72	French. By date
675.S79	Criticism
695.A-Z	American educators, A-Z
	Subarrange each by Table L14 unless otherwise provided for e.g.
695.A3-.A32	Alcott, Amos Bronson (Table L14)

Systems of individual educators and writers

Nineteenth century (1776/89-1870)

American educators, A-Z -- Continued

Mann, Horace

Collected works

Including life and works

695.M2	General
695.M23-.M24	Collected essays
695.M25-.M34	Individual works or essays
	Biography. Criticism
695.M35	General
695.M37	Drama. Fiction. Poetry
695.M39	Minor works. Pamphlets

1871-1950

For general works see LA126+; LB1025+

775.A-Z	Foreign educators, A-Z

Subarrange each by Table L14 unless otherwise provided for
e.g.

Fukuzawa, Yukichi

Cf. LG271.K44 Kei-o Gijuku Daigaku

775.F8	Collected works. Selections
775.F81-.F819	Individual works
775.F82A2-.F82A29	Autobiography
775.F82A3-.F82Z	Biography. Criticism
	Gentile, Giovanni
775.G39	Collected works. By date
775.G39A-.G39Z	Individual works. By title
775.G42	Biography and criticism
	Montessori, Maria

Cf. LB1029.M75 Montessori method of education

775.M68	Collected works
775.M682	Selections
775.M7-.M79	Separate works
	e. g.
775.M76	Il metodo della pedagogia scientifica (Il scoperta del bambino)
775.M8	Biography. Criticism
	Spranger, Edward
775.S6799	Collected works. By date
775.S6799A-.S6799Z	Individual works. By title
775.S68	Biography and criticism
875.A-Z	American educators, A-Z

Subarrange each by Table L14 unless otherwise provided for
e.g.

Dewey, John

875.D34-.D49	Works
875.D5	Biography. Criticism

Systems of individual educators and writers

1871-1950

American educators, A-Z -- Continued

Eliot, Charles William

Class here general educational writings

For biography see LD2148

875.E43	Collected works. By date
875.E43A-.E43Z	Individual works. By title
875.E5	Biography and criticism
875.H25-.H252	Harris, William Torrey (Table L14)

Class here general works, biography, criticism

1951-

880.A-Z	Foreign educators, A-Z

Subarrange each by Table L14

Class here general works, biography, criticism

885.A-Z	American educators, A-Z

Subarrange each by Table L14

Teaching (Principles and practice)

For analysis and comparisons of various systems see
LA31+

For systems (theories, etc.) of individual educators see
LB51+

Collections see LB5+

Documents see L111+

History see LA1+; LB51+

General works

1025	To 1964
1025.2	1965-1990
1025.3	1991-
1026	Experimental studies in educational theory and practice
1027	General special

Religious aspects

1027.2	General works
1027.22	Buddhism
1027.223	Christianity
1027.23	Active learning
1027.25	Activity programs
1027.28	Classroom observation
1027.3	Experimental methods
1027.4	Lesson planning
1027.415	Microlearning
1027.42	Problem-based learning
1027.43	Project method
1027.44	Questioning
1027.47	Training

For occupational training see HD5715+

For training of employees see HF5549.5.T7

Teaching (Principles and practice) -- Continued
Student guidance and counseling. Personnel service
1027.5 General works
1027.55 School psychology
1027.6 Electronic data processing. Computer-assisted counseling
1027.7 Home rooms
Student aspirations
Class here works on general educational and occupational aspirations
For vocational interests see HF5381.5
1027.8 General works
By region or country see LA201+
1027.9 Choice of school
Educational research. Regional educational laboratories
Cf. LB2326.3 Higher education
Cf. LB2806.25 Research in administration
1028 General works
1028.2 Management
1028.24 Action research
1028.25.A-Z By region or country, A-Z
1028.26 Information services
Including information retrieval systems
1028.27.A-Z By region or country, A-Z
1028.3 Technology. Educational technology
Instructional systems
1028.35 General works
1028.38 Instructional systems design
1028.4 Media programs
Computers in education. Electronic data processing
Cf. LB1027.6 Student counseling
Cf. LB2806.17 School administration
Cf. LB2846.4 School records and reports
1028.43 General works
1028.46 Computer managed instruction
Computer assisted instruction. Programmed instruction
Including the use of teaching machines in general
Cf. LC4024 Children with disabilities
Cf. LB1140.35.C64 Computers in preschool education
Cf. LC33 Computers in self-education and self-culture
1028.5 General works
1028.55 Interactive multimedia. Hypermedia
1028.6 Authorship
Computer programming
1028.65 General works
1028.66 Authoring programs
1028.68 Computer programs

Teaching (Principles and practice)
  Instructional systems
    Computers in education. Electronic data processing
      Computer assisted instruction. Programmed instruction --
        Continued

1028.7	Catalogs of software, programmed instruction materials, etc.
1028.73	Intelligent tutoring systems
1028.75	Interactive video
	Including programs
1028.8	Resource programs
	Cf. LC4023 Audiovisual aids for children with disabilities
1029.A-Z	Other kinds of instruction, A-Z
1029.A13	4MAT system
1029.A22	Acceleration in education
1029.B55	Biographical methods
1029.C37	Case method
	Collective education see LC1025+
1029.C53	Combination of grades
1029.C55	Concentrated study
(1029.C6)	Cooperative education
	see LC1049+
1029.D4	Departmental system
1029.D5	Dictation method
1029.D55	Differentiated teaching staff
1029.F7	Free schools
1029.G3	Educational games
	Cf. LB1140.35.E36 Preschool education
1029.G55	Global method
1029.J4	Jena plan
1029.L3	Laboratory plan (Dalton, etc.)
1029.L43	Learning contracts
1029.L6	Looping
1029.M7	Monitorial system
1029.M75	Montessori method of education
1029.N6	Nongraded schools
1029.O3	Object teaching
	Cf. LB1519+ Primary education
1029.O6	Open plan schools
1029.P53	Platoon schools
1029.P67	Portfolios
1029.R35	Reggio Emilia approach
1029.R4	Remedial teaching
1029.S5	Simulated environment
1029.S53	Simulation and gaming methods
1029.T4	Teaching teams

	Teaching (Principles and practice)
	Instructional systems
	Other kinds of instruction, A-Z -- Continued
1029.T6	Educational toys
	Cf. GV1218.5+ Games and amusements
	Cf. TT174+ Handicrafts
1029.U6	Unit method
1029.W34	Waldorf method
1031	Individual instruction
1031.4	Mastery learning
1031.5	Peer-group tutoring of students
1032	Group work
	Classification of pupils. Ability grouping see LB3061+
1033	Teacher-student relationships
1033.5	Communication in education. Authorship
	Including nonverbal communication
1034	Interaction analysis in education
1037	Popular works
1037.5	Pictorial works
1038	Schedules of recitations, etc.
	School schedules see LB3032+
1039	Recitations
	Quizzes and question books see LB1761
1042	Stories and storytelling
	Cf. GR1+ Folklore
	Cf. LB1179 Kindergarten
	Cf. LC6635 Reading circles and correspondence clubs
	Cf. PZ7 Juvenile literature
	Cf. Z718.3 Storytelling in libraries
	Audiovisual education. Audiovisual materials
	For audiovisual aids for children with disabilities see LC4023
	Cf. HD9810+ Instructional materials
	Cf. LC1048.A7 Vocational education
	Cf. LC4605 Children with mental disabilities
1042.5	Dictionaries. Terminology
	Directories
1042.7	General works
	By region or country
	United States
1042.72	General works
1042.74.A-Z	By region or state, A-Z
1042.76.A-Z	Other regions or countries, A-Z
	General and United States
1043.A-.Z8	General works
1043.Z9	Catalogs
	For catalogs of specific media, see the medium in
	LB1043.5+ ; LB1044.2+ ; and LB1044.7+

Teaching (Principles and practice)

Audiovisual education. Audiovisual materials -- Continued

1043.2.A-Z	Other regions or countries, A-Z

Under each:

.xA-.xZ8	*General works*
.xZ9-.xZ99	*Catalogs*

> *For catalogs of specific media, see the medium in LB1043.55 and subsequent numbers; LB1044.3 and subsequent numbers; and LB1044.72 and subsequent numbers*
>
> *Subarrange by main entry*

1043.4	Authorship of scripts, captions, etc., for audiovisual materials
	Visual aids. Visual instruction
1043.5	General works
1043.55	Blackboards
	Cf. LB3265.B5 School equipment
	Cf. NC865 Blackboard drawing
1043.58	Bulletin boards
1043.6	Displays
1043.62	Flannelgraphs
1043.64	Posters (Table L27)
1043.67	Pictures (Table L27)
1043.7	Slides. Transparencies (Table L27)
1043.8	Filmstrips (Table L27)
1043.9	Microforms (Table L27)
1043.93	Self-adhesive vinyl film
1044	Motion pictures (Table L27)
	Including sound films
	Cf. TR892.7 Cinematography
	Auditory aids
1044.2	General works
1044.3	Phonographs. Phonograph records (Table L27)
1044.4	Audiocassettes. Phonotapes (Table L27)
	Radio
1044.5	General works and United States
1044.6.A-Z	Other countries, A-Z
1044.65	Telephone
	Television. Television programs
	Cf. LB1028.75 Interactive video programs
1044.7	General works (Table L27)
1044.72	Cable television (Table L27)
1044.75	Video tape recorders. Video tapes. Video discs (Table L27)

	Teaching (Principles and practice)
	Audiovisual education. Audiovisual materials -- Continued
1044.8	Broadcasting (Radio and television)
	Class here general works on educational radio or television from the standpoint of the broadcaster, e.g., production, programming, public relations
1044.84	Telecommunications
	Satellites in education
1044.86	General works
	By region or country
	United States
1044.866	General works
1044.867.A-Z	By region or state, A-Z
1044.868.A-Z	Other regions or countries, A-Z
1044.87	Computer network resources
1044.875	Computer conferencing
	For Internet videoconferencing see LB1044.9.V53
1044.88	Teaching aids and devices
1044.9.A-Z	Special, A-Z
1044.9.C59	Comic books, strips, etc.
1044.9.F73	Free material
1044.9.I44	Illustrated periodicals
1044.9.N4	Newspapers
1044.9.P3	Paperbacks
1044.9.P47	Periodicals. Serial publications
1044.9.P49	Picture books
	Serial publications see LB1044.9.P47
1044.9.T38	Teleconferencing
1044.9.T4	Teletype
1044.9.V53	Videoconferencing
	Including Internet videoconferencing
1045	Minor works
	Including pedagogical "don'ts," "helps," etc.
	Cf. LB41 Addresses, essays, lectures
1046	Practice, laboratory methods, etc.
1047	Fieldwork. Excursions. Museums
	Including vacation activities
	For vacation schools see LC5701+
	Cf. LB2394 Higher education
1047.3	Report writing. Research
	Cf. LB2369 Higher education
	Study and study environments
1047.5	Supervised study
1048	Home work and home study
1048.5	Parent participation

Teaching (Principles and practice)
    Study and study environments -- Continued

1049	Methods of study
	e.g., McMurry, How to study
	Cf. LB1601+ Elementary education
	Cf. LB2395+ Higher education
	Cf. LC5225.M47 Adult education
1049.5	Study environment and facilities
	Reading (General)
	Cf. BF456.R2 Psychology of reading
	Cf. LB1525+ Reading (Primary education)
	Cf. LB1573 Reading (Elementary education)
	Cf. LB1632 Reading (Secondary education)
	Cf. LC5225.R4 Reading (Adult education)
	Cf. LC6601+ Group reading
	Cf. Z1003+ Choice of books
1049.9	Periodicals. Societies
1049.95	Congresses
1049.98	Dictionaries and encyclopedias
1050	General works
1050.2	General special
	Special teaching methods
	Code emphasis and linguistic approaches
1050.22	General works
	Adapted alphabets
1050.25	Initial teaching alphabet
1050.27	Reading color aids
1050.3	Cloze procedure
1050.33	Miscue analysis
1050.34	Phonic method. Phonetic method
1050.35	Analytic and language experience approaches. Whole word method
1050.36	Basal reading instruction
1050.365	Direct instruction approach
1050.37	Programmed instruction. Reading machines. Computer-assisted instruction
1050.375	Captioned media
1050.377	Guided reading
1050.38	Individualized reading instruction
1050.4	Reading games
	Diagnosis, evaluation, prediction, improvement techniques
	Cf. LB1050.3 Cloze procedure
	Cf. LB1050.33 Miscue analysis
1050.42	General works
1050.43	Reading readiness
1050.44	Word recognition
1050.45	Comprehension

Teaching (Principles and practice)

Reading (General)

Diagnosis, evaluation, prediction, improvement techniques

-- Continued

1050.455	Content area reading
1050.46	Ability testing
1050.5	Reading disability. Remedial teaching

        Including dyslexia as a reading disability

        For education of dyslexic children see LC4708+

1050.53	Developmental reading
1050.54	Rapid reading. Speed reading
1050.55	Silent reading
1050.58	Supplementary reading
1050.6	Research
1050.7	Collections of tests, examinations
1050.75.A-Z	Individual tests. By name, A-Z
1050.75.D43	Degrees of Reading Power tests
1050.75.Q34	Qualitative Reading Inventory
1050.75.R43	Reading Skills Competency Tests
1050.75.T48	Test of Early Reading Ability

Educational psychology

        For history of educational psychology see BF81+

        For history of the psychology of learning see BF318

        For teachers' psychology see LB2840+

        Cf. LB125.A+ Systems of individual educators

        Cf. LB1115 Child study

        Cf. QP351+ Physiological psychology

1050.9	Dictionaries and encyclopedias
1051	General works
1053	Popular works
1055	Addresses, essays, lectures. Pamphlets
1057	Nervous system

        Cf. QP351+ Physiology of the nervous system

1059	Formal discipline. Transfer of training
	Learning

        Cf. BF318 Psychology

        Cf. LC5225.L42 Adult learning

        Cf. QP408 Physiology

1060	General works
1060.2	Behavior. Behavior modification
1061	Habit
1062	Imagination. Abstraction. Creative thinking. Concept learning

        Cf. BF723.C7 Creative ability (Child psychology)

        Cf. LB1590.3+ Study and teaching of thinking skills

1062.5	Judgment. Decision making
1062.6	Performance. Competence. Academic achievement

Educational psychology

Learning -- Continued

Memory

Cf. BD181.7 Philosophy

Cf. BF370+ Psychology

1063	General works
1064	Paired-association
1064.5	Time
1065	Interest. Attention. Motivation

Cf. BF501+ Psychology

Cf. LB3025 Rewards

Apperception

1067	General works
1067.5	Visual learning
1068	Visual literacy
1069	Suggestion and imitation
1071	Will
1072	Affective education
1073	Emotion
1075	Fatigue

Cf. LB3431 School hygiene

1076	Rest
1077	Sleep-learning
1083	Individuality
1084	Group behavior
1085	Ethics
1088	Pathological aspects
1090	Alienation. Disaffection
1091	School phobia
1092	Psychoanalysis and education

Child study

Cf. GN63 Anthropology

Cf. HQ750+ Eugenics

Cf. HQ768+ Care and training of children

Cf. HV9051+ Juvenile offender

Cf. LB3421+ Physical measurement

Cf. RJ1+ Pediatrics

1101	Periodicals
1103	Societies, documents, etc.
1105	Collections
1115	General works
1117	General special

e.g., Personality adjustments and development, behavior
characteristics, attitudes, habit, reasoning

1118	Child biography

Cf. HQ779 Baby diaries

1119	Addresses, essays, lectures. Pamphlets

	Child study -- Continued
	Psychological studies
	Cf. LB3421+ School hygiene
1121	General works
1123	Left-and-right-handedness
1124	Behavioral assessment of children
1125	Anthropological studies
	Cf. LB3421+ School hygiene
	Psychical development
	Including intelligence tests and testing, aptitude tests, measurement in education (Achievement tests), interest tests, prognosis, character tests
	Cf. BF721+ Child psychology
	Cf. LC1031+ Competency test (Competency-based education)
1131	General works
1131.5	Collections of tests
1131.75.A-Z	Individual tests. By name, A-Z
1131.75.C46	Children's Skills Test
1131.75.C64	College Major Interest Inventory
1131.75.S76	Student Self-Concept Scale
1131.75.S78	Student Talent and Risk Profile
1131.75.W47	Wechsler Intelligence Scale for Children
1131.75.W66	Woodcock-Johnson Psycho-Educational Battery
1132	Readiness for school
1133	School age. Relation between age of entry and school progress
	Cf. LC129+ Compulsory education
1134	Learning ability
	Cf. LC4704+ Children with learning disabilities
1135	Adolescence
	Cf. BF724 Psychology
	Cf. HQ35 Sociology
1137	Play, games, etc.
	Cf. BF717 Psychology of play
	Cf. GN454+ Games of primitive people
	Cf. LB1140.35.P55 Preschool education
	Cf. LB1177 Kindergarten
	Cf. LB3031 Recreation in school management and discipline
	Drama and education, educational theaters, etc. see PN3151+
	Educational puppetry see PN1979.E4
1139.A-Z	Special, A-Z
	Cf. BF456.A+ Psychology of reading, spelling, etc.
1139.A3	Aesthetics
1139.C6	Collecting activity

	Early childhood education
	Individual areas of study, A-Z -- Continued
1139.5.L35	Language arts
1139.5.L58	Literature
(1139.5.M67)	Moral education
	see LB1139.35.M67
	Nature study see LB1139.5.S35
1139.5.R43	Reading
1139.5.S35	Science. Nature study
1139.5.S64	Social sciences. Civics. History
	Preschool education. Nursery schools
1140.A1	Periodicals, societies, etc.
1140.A13	Congresses
1140.A15	Dictionaries and encyclopedias
1140.A18	Research
	General works
1140.A2	Through 1964
1140.2	1965-
1140.22	Addresses, essays, lectures
	By region or country
	United States
1140.23	General works
1140.24.A-Z	By region or state, A-Z
1140.245.A-Z	By city, A-Z
1140.25.A-Z	Other regions or countries, A-Z
	Nursery school administration and supervision see LB2822.7
	Teaching personnel see LB2832+
	Methodology
1140.3	General works
1140.35.A-Z	Special aspects and methods, A-Z
1140.35.A93	Audiovisual aids
1140.35.C64	Computers
1140.35.C74	Creative activities and seat work
	Cf. LB1537+ Primary school occupations
1140.35.E36	Educational games
	Cf. LB1029.G3 Educational games in teaching
	principles and practice
1140.35.G74	Group work in preschool education
	Cf. LB1032 Group work in education
1140.35.O63	Open plan methods
	Cf. LB1029.O6 Open plan schools
1140.35.P37	Parent participation
1140.35.P53	Picture books
1140.35.P55	Play
	Cf. LB1137 Play in child development
1140.35.S76	Stories. Storytelling
	Storytelling see LB1140.35.S76

Preschool education. Nursery schools
  Methodology
    Special aspects and methods, A-Z -- Continued

1140.35.T68	Toys
1140.4	Curricula
1140.5.A-Z	Individual areas of study, A-Z
	Arithmetic see QA135+
1140.5.A7	Art. The arts
1140.5.H4	Health
	History see LB1140.5.S6
1140.5.L3	Language arts
1140.5.P4	Penmanship
1140.5.R4	Reading
1140.5.S35	Science. Nature study
1140.5.S6	Social sciences. History

Kindergarten

1141	Periodicals. Societies
1143	Collections
(1145)	Yearbooks
	see LB1141
1147	Congresses

  Theory
    Froebel
      Collected works on education. Selected works see LB631
      Individual works

1153	Menschenerziehung (Education of man)
1153.5	Mutter-und-Koselieder (Mother and nursery songs)
1154	Mottoes and commentaries
1155	Songs and music
1156	Briefwechsel mit kinder (Letters on the kindergarten)
1157	Pädagogik des Kindergartens
1158	Pt. II. Education by development
1159	Pt. III. Third and last volume of Pädagogik
1160.A-Z	Other, A-Z
1162	Criticism and outlines of Froebel's kindergarten theories
1165.A-Z	Other writers, A-Z
1167	General special

      e.g. Kindergarten in relation to the health, mental hygiene,
        citizenship, etc., of a child; effect on a child's progress
        through the grades

  Method
    For Montessori method see LB1029.M75

1169	General

    Special: Occupations, gifts, melodies, etc.

1171	Periodicals. Collections
1173	Occupations
1175	Gifts (and occupations)

Kindergarten
  Method
    Special: Occupations, gifts, melodies, etc. -- Continued

1177   Melodies, songs and plays, games
        Cf. LB1137 Child study
        Cf. LB3031 School management and discipline
        Cf. MT920 Music

1179   Stories
        Cf. LB1042 Teaching (Principles and practice)
    Branches of study
      Including curriculum

1180   General works
1181   Language. Speech
      Reading
1181.2   General works
        Special teaching methods
          Code emphasis and linguistic approaches
1181.25   General works
          Adapted alphabets
1181.28   General works
1181.3   Initial teaching alphabet
1181.33   Analytic and language experience approaches
        Diagnosis, evaluation, prediction, improvement
          techniques
1181.35   Reading readiness
1181.4   Word recognition
1182   Social sciences. History
1185   Nature study
1186   Numbers
1186.5   Penmanship
1187   Art: Drawing, color, etc.
      Cf. NC625 Study and teaching of drawing
1188   Color
    Needlework, sewing see TT708
1195   Miscellaneous
1197   Addresses, essays, lectures. Pamphlets
  History and statistics of kindergarten and infant schools
1199   General
    By region or country
1201   America
      North America
1203   General works
        United States
1205   General works
1206   Laws and legislation
1235.A-.W   States, A-W
1238.A-Z   Cities, A-Z

Kindergarten
  History and statistics of kindergarten and infant schools
    By region or country
      North America -- Continued

1241-1243	Canada (Table L17)
1244-1246	Mexico (Table L17)
	Central America
1247	General works
	Belize
1248.A1-.A3	General
1248.A5-Z	Local
	Costa Rica
1249.A1-.A3	General
1249.A5-Z	Local
	Guatemala
1252.A1-.A3	General
1252.A5-Z	Local
	Honduras
1255.A1-.A3	General
1255.A5-Z	Local
	Nicaragua
1257.A1-.A3	General
1257.A5-Z	Local
	Panama
1259.A1-.A3	General
1259.A5-Z	Local
	Panama Canal Zone
1261.A1-.A3	General
1261.A5-Z	Local
	El Salvador
1262.A1-.A3	General
1262.A5-Z	Local
	West Indies
1265	General works
	Bahamas
1268.A1-.A3	General
1268.A5-Z	Local
	Cuba
1271.A1-.A3	General
1271.A5-Z	Local
	Haiti
1274.A1-.A3	General
1274.A5-Z	Local
	Santo Domingo. Dominican Republic
1276.A1-.A3	General
1276.A3-Z	Local
	Jamaica

Kindergarten
History and statistics of kindergarten and infant schools
By region or country
North America
West Indies
Jamaica -- Continued

1277.A1-.A3	General
1277.A3-Z	Local
	Puerto Rico
1280.A1-.A3	General
1280.A3-Z	Local
	Virgin Islands of the United States
1283.A1-.A3	General
1283.A5-Z	Local
1285.A-Z	Other, A-Z
	South America
1286	General works
1289-1291	Argentina (Table L17)
1292-1294	Bolivia (Table L17)
1295-1297	Brazil (Table L17)
1298-1300	Chile (Table L17)
1301-1303	Colombia (Table L17)
1304-1306	Ecuador (Table L17)
	Guianas
	Guyana
1307.A1-.A3	General
1307.A5-Z	Local
	Suriname
1308.A1-.A3	General
1308.A5-Z	Local
	French Guiana
1309.A1-.A3	General
1309.A5-Z	Local
1310-1312	Paraguay (Table L17)
1313-1315	Peru (Table L17)
1316-1318	Uruguay (Table L17)
1319-1321	Venezuela (Table L17)
	Europe
1322	General works
1328-1330	Great Britain (Table L17)
1336-1338	Austria (Table L17)
1339-1341	France (Table L17)
1342-1344	Germany (Table L17)
1345-1347	Greece (Table L17)
1348-1350	Italy (Table L17)
	Low Countries
1354-1356	Belgium (Table L17)

Kindergarten
  History and statistics of kindergarten and infant schools
    By region or country
      Europe
        Low Countries -- Continued

1357-1359	Netherlands (Table L17)
1360-1362	Russia. Former Soviet Union (Table L17)
	Scandinavia
1365	General works
1366-1368	Denmark (Table L17)
1372-1374	Norway (Table L17)
1375-1377	Sweden (Table L17)
1378-1380	Spain (Table L17)
1381-1383	Portugal (Table L17)
1384-1386	Switzerland (Table L17)
	Turkey and the Balkan states
1387-1389	Turkey (Table L17)
1390-1392	Bulgaria (Table L17)
1393-1395	Montenegro (Table L17)
1396-1398	Romania (Table L17)
1399-1401	Yugoslavia (Table L17)
1402.A-Z	Other European regions or countries, A-Z
	Asia
1403	General works
1405-1407	China (Table L17)
1408-1410	India (Table L17)
	Including Republic of India
	Pakistan
1410.5.A1-.A3	General
1410.5.A5-Z	Local
	Indochina
1411	General works
	French Indochina
1414.A1-.A3	General
1414.A5-Z	Local
1416.A-Z	Other divisions, A-Z
1417	Indonesia
1420-1422	Dutch East Indies (Table L17)
	Including Republic of Indonesia
1423-1425	Philippines (Table L17)
1426-1428	Japan (Table L17)
1429-1431	Iran (Table L17)
	Iraq
1431.5.A1-.A3	General
1431.5.A5-Z	Local
1432-1434	Former Soviet Union in Asia (Table L17)
1435-1437	Turkey in Asia (Table L17)

	Kindergarten
	History and statistics of kindergarten and infant schools
	By region or country
	Asia -- Continued
1438.A-Z	Other divisions of Asia, A-Z
1439	Arab countries
1440	Islamic countries
	Africa
1441	General works
	Egypt
1444.A1-.A3	General
1444.A5-Z	Local
	British Africa
1446-1448	South Africa (Table L17)
1449.A-Z	Other divisions, A-Z
	French Africa
1450.A1-.A3	General
1450.A5-Z	Local
	German Africa (Former)
1453.A1-.A3	General
1453.A5-Z	Local
	Italian Africa
1454.A1-.A3	General
1454.A5-Z	Local
	Portuguese Africa
1456.A1-.A3	General
1456.A5-Z	Local
	Spanish Africa
1457.A1-.A3	General
1457.A5-Z	Local
1459.A-Z	Other divisions of Africa, A-Z
1462-1464	Australia and New Zealand (Table L17)
	Pacific islands
1489.A1-.A3	General
1489.A5-Z	Local, A-Z
(1496-1499)	Training of kindergarten teachers
	see LB1733
	Primary education
1501	Periodicals. Societies
1503	Collections
	General works
1507	Principles and practice
1511	Practice
1513	General special
	Special
1515	By name of system
	For Montessori method see LB1029.M75

	Primary education -- Continued
	Object lessons
1519	Through 1900
1520	1901-
	Branches of study
1523	General works. Curriculum
	Special
1524	Speech
	Reading
1525	General works
	Special teaching methods
	Code emphasis and linguistic approaches
1525.24	General works
	Adapted alphabetics
1525.25	General works
1525.26	Initial teaching alphabet
1525.3	Phonic method. Phonetic method
1525.34	Analytic and language experience approaches
1525.35	Basal reading instruction
1525.354	Direct instruction approach
	Including DISTAR programs
1525.36	Primer use in reading instruction
	Cf. PE1117+ English readers
	Other aids and devices
1525.4	General works
1525.5	Programmed instruction. Reading machines
1525.55	Reading games
1525.56	Individualized reading instruction
	Diagnosis, evaluation, prediction, improvement techniques
	Reading readiness
1525.6	General works
1525.65	Alphabet
1525.7	Comprehension
1525.75	Ability testing
1525.76	Reading disability. Remedial teaching
1525.77	Developmental reading
1525.8	Supplementary reading
1526	Spelling
1527	Literature and stories
	Language and composition
1528	General works
1528.5	Vocabulary
1529.A-Z	By region or country, A-Z
1530	Social studies. History
	For local United States history see F1+
	Cf. D16.2+ Study and teaching of history

	Primary education
	Branches of study
	Special -- Continued
1531	Geography
	Cf. G72+ Study and teaching of geography
1532	Nature study. Science
	Cf. Q181+ Study and teaching of science
	Cf. QH50.5+ Study and teaching of natural science
	Arithmetic see QA135+
1536	Penmanship
	Cf. Z43+ Writing
	Activity programs
1537	General works
	Art see N361
	Construction
1541	General works
1542	Paper and cardboard work
1543	Weaving and basketry
1544	Modeling
1547	Addresses, essays, lectures. Pamphlets
	Elementary or public school education. Elementary school teaching
	Periodicals and societies see L11
	Collections see LB5+
1555	General works
1556	Juvenile works
	By region or country
	United States
1556.5	General works
1556.6.A-Z	By region or state, A-Z
1556.7.A-Z	Other regions or countries, A-Z
1557	Outlines. Syllabi
	Manuals of instruction, etc. Courses of study
	United States
	General works see LB1570
1561.A-.W	By state, A-W
1563.A-Z	By city, A-Z
	Other regions or countries
1564.A-Z	By region or country, A-Z
1565.A-Z	By city, A-Z
(1566)	Suburban schools
	see LC5145+
(1567-1568)	Rural schools. Rural education. Education of children in rural areas
	see LC5146+
1569	Addresses, essays, lectures. Pamphlets
	Course of studies. Curriculum

	Elementary or public school education. Elementary school teaching
	Course of studies. Curriculum -- Continued
1570	General works and United States (General)
	For curriculum planning see LB2806.15
	By state see LB1561.A+
	By city see LB1563.A+
1571	By grade (First to seventh, etc.)
	Other regions or countries see LB1564+
	Special branches
	Class here works on the study and teaching of special topics at the elementary level or the elementary and secondary levels combined, if the topics have been specifically provided for below
	Class works on the study and teaching of subjects not specifically provided for below under special subjects in Classes B-Z, e.g., QB61+, Astronomy (Study and teaching)
1572	Speech. Oral communication
	Cf. LB3454 Speech defects
	Reading
	Class here methods of teaching ("Manuals," "Companions," etc.) for readers at various levels; for the readers themselves, see PE
	Cf. LB1050.5 Remedial teaching
1572.8	Periodicals. Societies. Serials
1572.9	Congresses
1573	General works
	Special teaching methods
	Code emphasis and linguistic approaches
	Adapted alphabets
1573.25	Initial teaching alphabet
1573.27	Uniform alphabet
1573.28	Reading color aids
1573.3	Phonetic methods
	Analytic and language-experience approaches
1573.33	General works
1573.35	Global method
1573.37	Whole word method
1573.38	Basal reading instruction
	Other aids and devices
1573.39	General works
1573.4	Program instruction. Reading machines
1573.45	Individualized reading instruction
1573.5	Oral reading
	Diagnosis, evaluation, prediction, improvement techniques
1573.6	Word recognition

Elementary or public school education. Elementary school teaching

Special branches

Reading

Diagnosis, evaluation, prediction, improvement techniques -- Continued

1573.7	Comprehension
1573.75	Content area reading
1573.8	Developmental reading
1574	Spelling
1574.5	Vocabulary

Literature

For drama, dramatization see PN3175+

1575	General works
1575.5.A-Z	By region or country, A-Z

Class here methods of teaching practiced in particular countries, not the study of literature of those countries

Language, grammar, composition, etc.

The teaching of the mother tongue

1575.8	General works
1575.9	Textbooks

English

Cf. LB1631+ Secondary education

1576	General works
1576.7	Computers in English language teaching
1577.A-Z	Other languages, A-Z

The teaching of language other than the mother tongue

1578	General works

By language

see classes P - PM

1580.A-Z	By region or country, A-Z

Class here methods of teaching practiced in particular countries, not the study of language, etc. of those countries

1580.5	Education

History

For use of maps see GA151

Cf. D16.2+ Study and teaching of history

1581	General works
1582.A-Z	By region or country, A-Z

Class here methods of teaching practiced in particular countries, not the study of the history of those countries

1583	Local history and geography

For United States see F1+

Cf. G72+ Study and teaching of geography

1583.5	Current events

Elementary or public school education. Elementary school teaching

Special branches -- Continued

1583.8	Folklore
	Including the use of folklore as a teaching method
	Social sciences. Civics
1584	General and United States
1584.5.A-Z	Other regions or countries, A-Z
1584.7	Computers in social science teaching
1584.75	Economics
	Nature study. Science
	Cf. GF26+ Study and teaching of human ecology (Environmental education)
	Cf. Q181+ Study and teaching of science
	Cf. QH50.5+ Study and teaching of natural history
	Cf. QH315+ Study and teaching of biology
	Cf. QK51+ Study and teaching of botany
	Cf. QL51+ Study and teaching of zoology
1585	General works
	By region or country
1585.3	United States
1585.5.A-Z	Other regions or countries, A-Z
1585.7	Computers in science teaching
	Physiology, hygiene and health education
	Cf. HQ57.3+ Sex education
	Cf. HV5060+ Alcohol education
	Cf. LB1140.5.H4 Preschool education
	Cf. LC4613 Children with mental disabilities
	Cf. QP39+ Study and teaching of physiology
1587.A3	General works
1587.A4-Z	Special topics, A-Z
1587.H8	Human genetics
1587.N8	Nutrition
1587.P37	Parent participation
1588.A-Z	By region or country, A-Z
	Mathematics (General) see QA11+
	Mathematics (Elementary) see QA135+
1590	Penmanship
	Religion see BV1460+
	Thinking skills
	Including cognition, abstraction, and categorization
1590.3	General works
1590.5	Creative thinking

	Elementary or public school education. Elementary school teaching
	Special branches -- Continued
	The arts
	Cf. LB1187 Kindergarten
	Cf. LB1541+ Primary education
	Cf. N350+ Elementary art study
	Cf. NC610+ Drawing
	Cf. PN1701+ Drama (Study and teaching)
	Cf. PN1979.E4 Educational puppetry
	Cf. PN3157+ Children as actors
1591	General works
1591.5.A-Z	By region or country, A-Z
1592	Activity programs
	Home economics see TX1+
1593	Industrial arts
	Industrial and vocational education
	Cf. LC1043 Vocational education in general
	Cf. LC1081 Industrial education in general
	Cf. T61+ Technical education
	Cf. TT161+ Arts and crafts
1594	General works
1594.5	Aeronautics
	Manual training
1595	General works
1596.A-Z	By region or country, A-Z
	Methods and lessons
1598	General works
1599.A-Z	Special, A-Z
1599.K6	Knife work
1599.2	Printing
	Agricultural training see SB51+
	Use of library resources see Z711+; Z1037+
	Methods of study
1601	General works
1601.3	Independent study
1601.5	Note-taking
1602	Recollections and reminiscences of school days, etc.
	Cf. LB2397 Higher education
	Secondary education. High school teaching
	Periodicals and societies see L11+
	Documents (Serial) see L111+
1603	Collections
1607	General works
	By region or country
	United States
1607.5	General works

	Secondary education. High school teaching
	By region or country
	United States -- Continued
1607.52.A-Z	By region or state, A-Z
1607.53.A-Z	Other regions or countries, A-Z
1609	Outlines. Syllabi
	Manuals of instruction
	United States
	General works see LB1607
1613.A-.W	By state, A-W
1615.A-Z	By city, A-Z
	Individual schools see LD1+
	Other regions or countries
1617.A-Z	By region or country, A-Z
1619.A-Z	By city, A-Z
	Individual American schools see LE1+
	Individual European schools see LF1+
	Individual Asian, African, etc. schools see LG1+
1620	General special
	e.g., Coeducation, teacher load, size of high school, and efficiency
	Student guidance and counseling. Personnel service
1620.4	General works
	By region or country
	United States
1620.5	General works
1620.52.A-Z	By region or state, A-Z
1620.53.A-Z	Other regions or countries, A-Z
1620.6	High school orientation
1620.7	Home rooms
1621	Rural high schools
	Junior high schools. Middle schools. Intermediate schools. Middle school teaching
1623	General works
	By region or country
	United States
1623.5	General works
1623.52.A-Z	By region or state, A-Z
1623.53.A-Z	Other regions or countries, A-Z
1625	Addresses, essays, lectures. Pamphlets
1626	Relation between elementary and secondary education
	Entrance requirements
	Cf. LB3051 School examinations
1627	General works
1627.4.A-Z	By region or country, A-Z
1627.7	Transfer of credits
	Graduation requirements see LB3065

	Secondary education. High school teaching -- Continued
	Curriculum
1628	General
	Study courses prescribed in United States
1628.5	General
1629.A-Z	By state or city, A-Z
1629.5.A-Z	Study courses prescribed in other regions or countries. By region, country, or city, A-Z
	Elective system
1629.6	General works
1629.65.A-Z	By region or country, A-Z
1629.7	By grade (eighth to twelfth, etc.)
1629.8	Honor courses
	Individual branches
	Prefer subdivision "Study and teaching" under the subject in Classes B-Z except English LB1631
	For works on the study and teaching of special topics at both the elementary and secondary levels combined, see LB1572+ if specifically provided for in those numbers
	Language
(1630)	General
	see P - PM
	English and composition (as the mother tongue only)
1631	General works
1631.3	Computers in English language teaching
1631.5	Examinations
1632	Reading
	Modern languages
(1633)	General works
(1634.A-Z)	Special languages, A-Z
	Ancient languages
(1637)	General works
	Special
(1638.A-Z)	By language, A-Z
(1639.A-Z)	By region or country, A-Z
	History
(1641)	General works
(1642.A-Z)	By region or country, A-Z
(1643)	Social sciences
	see H62+
(1644)	Political science
	see class J
(1645-1646)	Mathematics
	see QA11 QA451
(1647-1665)	Science
	see class Q

LB

Secondary education. High school teaching
　　Individual branches -- Continued
(1675)　　　　Industrial training
　　　　　　　　see T61+
(1676)　　　　Home economics
　　　　　　　　see TX
(1677-1680)　　Manual training
　　　　　　　　see LB1595+ TT165+
(1681)　　　　Agriculture
　　　　　　　　see S531+
(1694)　　　　Philosophy
　　　　　　　　see classes B-BJ
　　　　　　　Art see N363; NC635
　　　　　　　Athletics see GV345
　　　　　　　Service learning see LC220.5
1695　　　　Postgraduate work
　　　　　　　　Cf. LC1039+ Post-compulsory education
　　　　　　Surveys of high school graduates
1695.5　　　General works
　　　　　　By region or country
　　　　　　　United States
1695.6　　　　General works
1695.7.A-Z　　By region or state, A-Z
1695.8.A-Z　　Other regions or countries, A-Z
　　　　　　Foreign high school student exchanges
　　　　　　　United States
1696　　　　　General works
1696.3.A-Z　　With individual regions or countries, A-Z
1696.6.A-Z　　Other regions or countries, A-Z
　　　　　　　　For works involving two countries, class with country
　　　　　　　　　appearing first alphabetically
　　　Education and training of teachers and administrators
　　　　　　Cf. LB2153+ Model schools (Elementary). Laboratory
　　　　　　　schools
　　　　　　Cf. LB2157.A3 Student teaching. Student teachers
1705　　　　Collections
1707　　　　General works
　　　　　　By region or country
　　　　　　　United States
1715　　　　　General works
1716.A-Z　　　By region or state, A-Z
1719.A-Z　　　Other American regions or countries, A-Z
　　　　　　　Europe
1723　　　　　General
1725.A-Z　　　By region or country, A-Z
1727.A-Z　　　Other regions or countries, A-Z
　　　　　　Reading as an aid to education, culture, etc. see Z1003+

Education and training of teachers and administrators --
Continued

1728	Assessment. Portfolios
1729	Teacher orientation
1731	In-service training of teachers
1731.4	Mentors
1731.5	Microteaching
1731.6	Observation (Educational methods)
1731.75	Training of student counselors
	Special training
	For training teachers of minorities see LC2685
	For training teachers of gifted children see LC3993.25
	Cf. LB1775 Teaching as a profession
1732	General works
1732.3	Early childhood teachers
1732.5	Nursery school teachers
1733	Kindergarten teachers
	Elementary teachers
	General works see LB1715+
1734.5	Teacher assistant training
1735	Rural schools
1735.5	Middle school teachers
1736	Manual training. Vocational instruction
	Secondary teachers
1737.A3	General works
1737.A5-Z	By region or country, A-Z
	Instructors in teachers' colleges. Normal school teachers
1737.5.A3	General works
1737.5.A5-Z	By region or country, A-Z
1738	College and university instructors
1738.5	School administrators and school supervisors
	Adult education see LC5225.T4
	Church education see LC379; LC501+; LC561+
	Other special subjects, see the subject
	e. g. Training of teachers of elementary and secondary
	mathematics, see QA11
1739	Outlines of normal courses, manuals, etc.
	Class here general works only
	For individual schools see LB1805+
1740	Summer sessions
	Class here general works only
	For individual schools see LB1805+
1741	Addresses, essays, lectures. Pamphlets
	Academic degrees in education
1741.5	Masters
1742	Doctorate
1743	Teachers' workshops

LB

	Education and training of teachers and administrators -- Continued
1745	Teachers' centers
	Teachers' institutes, meetings, etc.
	For proceedings and transactions of institutes see LB1811+
1751	General works
	Plans and outlines of institute courses
1753.A-.W	United States. By state, A-W
1755.A-Z	Other regions or countries, A-Z
1761	Question books, etc.
	Teachers' examinations
1761.5	General works
	Pre-Professional Skills Tests see LB2367.75
	By region or country
	United States
1762	General works
1763.A-.W	By state, A-W
1764.A-Z	By city, A-Z
1765.A-Z	Other regions or countries, A-Z
	Subarrange each by Table L19
1766.A-Z	Individual tests. By name, A-Z
1766.C74	CSET: Multiple Subjects
1766.M64	Multiple Subjects Assessment for Teachers
1766.P73	Principles of Learning and Teaching Test
1766.P76	Program for Licensing Assessments for Colorado Educators
	Certification of administrators
	Including superintendents and principals
1767	General works
	By region or country
	United States
1768	General works
1769.A-Z	By region or state, A-Z
1770.A-Z	Other regions or countries, A-Z
	Certification of teachers
1771	General works and United States
1772.A-.W	United States. By state, A-W
1773.A-Z	Other regions or countries, A-Z
	Subarrange each by Table L19
1775	Professional aspects of teaching and school administration. Vocational guidance
	Cf. LB1732+ Special training of teachers
	By region or country
	United States
1775.2	General works
1775.3.A-Z	By region or state, A-Z

	Education and training of teachers and administrators
	Professional aspects of teaching and school administration.
	Vocational guidance
	By region or country -- Continued
1775.4.A-Z	Other regions or countries, A-Z
	Subarrange each by Table L19
1775.5	Preschool and kindergarten teachers
1775.6	Early childhood teachers and educators
1775.8	Primary school teachers and educators
1776	Elementary school teachers
	By region or country
	United States
1776.2	General works
1776.3.A-Z	By region or state, A-Z
1776.4.A-Z	Other regions or countries, A-Z
	Subarrange each by Table L19
1776.5	Middle school teachers
1777	Secondary school teachers
	By region or country
	United States
1777.2	General works
1777.3.A-Z	By region or state, A-Z
1777.4.A-Z	Other regions or countries, A-Z
	Subarrange each by Table L19
1777.5	School administrators and school supervisors
1778	College and university teachers
	By region or country
	United States
1778.2	General works
1778.3.A-Z	By region or state, A-Z
1778.4.A-Z	Other regions or countries, A-Z
	Subarrange each by Table L19
1778.45	Academic couples
1778.5	College administrators
1779	Professional ethics
	Supply and demand, turnover see LB2833+
1780	Teacher placement
	Including placement services by institutions and teachers' agencies, advice on how to apply for a position
	Cf. HD5860+ Employment agencies
	Salaries and pensions see LB2842+
	Selection and appointment, contractual status see LB2835+
(1781)	The teacher in literature
	see class P
1782	Teachers' wives

Education and training of teachers and administrators
Professional aspects of teaching and school administration.
Vocational guidance -- Continued

(1785)	Fiction
	see class P
	State teachers colleges. Normal schools. Teachers' institutes
1805	General works
	United States
1811	General works
	By state
1821-1823	Alabama (Table L16)
1824-1826	Alaska (Table L16)
1827-1829	Arizona (Table L16)
1833-1835	Arkansas (Table L16)
1836-1838	California (Table L16)
1839-1841	Colorado (Table L16)
1842-1844	Connecticut (Table L16)
1845-1847	Delaware (Table L16)
1848-1850	District of Columbia (Table L16)
1851-1853	Florida (Table L16)
1854-1856	Georgia (Table L16)
1857-1859	Idaho (Table L16)
1860-1862	Illinois (Table L16)
1863-1865	Indian Territory (Table L16)
1866-1868	Indiana (Table L16)
1869-1871	Iowa (Table L16)
1872-1874	Kansas (Table L16)
1875-1877	Kentucky (Table L16)
1878-1880	Louisiana (Table L16)
1881-1883	Maine (Table L16)
1884-1886	Maryland (Table L16)
1887-1889	Massachusetts (Table L16)
1890-1892	Michigan (Table L16)
1893-1895	Minnesota (Table L16)
1896-1898	Mississippi (Table L16)
1899-1901	Missouri (Table L16)
1902-1904	Montana (Table L16)
1905-1907	Nebraska (Table L16)
1908-1910	Nevada (Table L16)
1911-1913	New Hampshire (Table L16)
1914-1916	New Jersey (Table L16)
1917-1919	New Mexico (Table L16)
1920-1922	New York (Table L16)
1926-1928	North Carolina (Table L16)
1929-1931	North Dakota (Table L16)
1932-1934	Ohio (Table L16)
1935-1937	Oklahoma (Table L16)

Education and training of teachers and administrators
State teachers colleges. Normal schools. Teachers' institutes
United States
By state -- Continued

1941-1943	Oregon (Table L16)
1944-1946	Pennsylvania (Table L16)
1947-1949	Rhode Island (Table L16)
1953-1955	South Carolina (Table L16)
1956-1958	South Dakota (Table L16)
1959-1961	Tennessee (Table L16)
1962-1964	Texas (Table L16)
1965-1967	Utah (Table L16)
1968-1970	Vermont (Table L16)
1971-1973	Virginia (Table L16)
1974-1976	Washington (Table L16)
1977-1979	West Virginia (Table L16)
1980-1982	Wisconsin (Table L16)
1983-1985	Wyoming (Table L16)
1987.A-Z	Non-contiguous possessions, A-Z

Canada

1991	General works
1995.A-Z	By province, A-Z
1997.A-Z	By school, A-Z
1998.A-Z	Meetings and institutes. By place, A-Z

Mexico

2001	General works
2002.A-Z	By state, A-Z
2003.A-Z	By institution, A-Z

Central America

2005	General works

By country
Belize

2006	General works
2007.A-Z	Individual colleges, schools, institutions. By place, A-Z

Costa Rica

2008	General works
2009.A-Z	Individual colleges, schools, institutions. By place, A-Z

Guatemala

2010	General works
2011.A-Z	Individual colleges, schools, institutions. By place, A-Z

Honduras

2012	General works
2013.A-Z	Individual colleges, schools, institutions. By place, A-Z

Education and training of teachers and administrators
  State teachers colleges. Normal schools. Teachers' institutes
    Central America
      By country -- Continued
        Nicaragua

2014	General works
2015.A-Z	Individual colleges, schools, institutions. By place, A-Z

        Panama

2016	General works
2017.A-Z	Individual colleges, schools, institutions. By place, A-Z

        El Salvador

2018	General works
2019.A-Z	Individual colleges, schools, institutions. By place, A-Z

    West Indies

2020	General works

      By island or group of islands
        Bahamas

2021	General works
2022.A-Z	Individual colleges, schools, institutions. By place, A-Z

        Cuba

2023	General works
2024.A-Z	Individual colleges, schools, institutions. By place, A-Z

        Haiti

2025	General works
2026.A-Z	Individual colleges, schools, institutions. By place, A-Z

        Jamaica

2027	General works
2028.A-Z	Individual colleges, schools, institutions. By place, A-Z

        Puerto Rico

2029	General works
2030.A-Z	Individual colleges, schools, institutions. By place, A-Z
2031.A-Z	Other, A-Z

          Under each:

.x	*General works*
.x2A-.x2Z	*Individual colleges, schools, institutions. By place, A-Z*

        Bermudas

2032.A2	General works
2032.A3-Z	Individual colleges, schools, institutions. By place, A-Z

Education and training of teachers and administrators

State teachers colleges. Normal schools. Teachers' institutes

-- Continued

South America

2035	General works
	By country
	Argentina
2037	General works
2038.Z-Z	Individual colleges, schools, institutions. By place, A-Z
	Bolivia
2039	General works
2040.A-Z	Individual colleges, schools, institutions. By place, A-Z
	Brazil
2041	General works
2042.A-Z	Individual colleges, schools, institutions. By place, A-Z
	Chile
2043	General works
2044.A-Z	Individual colleges, schools, institutions. By place, A-Z
	Colombia
2045	General works
2046.A-Z	Individual colleges, schools, institutions. By place, A-Z
	Ecuador
2047	General works
2048.A-Z	Individual colleges, schools, institutions. By place, A-Z
	Guianas
	Guyana
2049.2	General works
2049.3.A-Z	Individual colleges, schools, institutions. By place, A-Z
	French Guiana
2049.4	General works
2049.5.A-Z	Individual colleges, schools, institutions. By place, A-Z
	Suriname
2049.6	General works
2049.7.A-Z	Individual colleges, schools, institutions. By place, A-Z
	Paraguay
2051	General works
2052.A-Z	Individual colleges, schools, institutions. By place, A-Z

Education and training of teachers and administrators
State teachers colleges. Normal schools. Teachers' institutes
South America
By country -- Continued
Peru
2053 General works
2054.A-Z Individual colleges, schools, institutions. By place, A-Z
Uruguay
2055 General works
2056.A-Z Individual colleges, schools, institutions. By place, A-Z
Venezuela
2057 General works
2058.A-Z Individual colleges, schools, institutions. By place, A-Z
Europe
2059 General works
By region or country
Great Britain
2060 General works
England and Wales
2061 General works
2062.A-2067.Z Individual colleges, schools, institutions. By place, A-Z
Ireland
2063 General works
2064.A-Z Individual colleges, schools, institutions. By place, A-Z
Scotland
2065 General works
2066.A-Z Individual colleges, schools, institutions. By place, A-Z
Wales
2067 General works
2068.A-Z Individual colleges, schools, institutions. By place, A-Z
Austria
2069 General works
2070.A-Z Individual colleges, schools, institutions. By place, A-Z
Hungary
2073 General works
2074.A-Z Individual colleges, schools, institutions. By place, A-Z
Belgium see LB2089+
France

Education and training of teachers and administrators
State teachers colleges. Normal schools. Teachers' institutes
Europe
By region or country
France -- Continued

2075	General works
2076.A-Z	Country divisions, A-Z
2077.A-Z	Individual schools. By place, A-Z
2078.A-Z	Meetings and institutes. By place, A-Z

Germany

2079	General works
2080.A-Z	Country divisions, A-Z
2081.A-Z	Individual schools. By place, A-Z
2082.A-Z	Meetings and institutes. By place, A-Z

Greece

2083.A2	General works
2083.A3-Z	Individual colleges, schools, institutions. By place, A-Z

Italy

2085	General works
2086.A-Z	Country divisions, A-Z
2087.A-Z	Individual schools. By place, A-Z
2088.A-Z	Meetings and institutes. By place, A-Z

Low countries
Belgium

2089	General works
2090.A-Z	Country divisions, A-Z
2091.A-Z	Individual schools. By place, A-Z
2092.A-Z	Meetings and institutes. By place, A-Z

Netherlands

2093	General works
2094.A-Z	Country divisions, A-Z
2095.A-Z	Individual schools. By place, A-Z
2096.A-Z	Meetings and institutes. By place, A-Z

Russia. Former Soviet Union

2097	General works
2098.A-Z	Country divisions, A-Z
2098.5.A-Z	Individual schools. By place, A-Z

Poland

2099	General works
2099.5.A-Z	Individual colleges, schools, institutions. By place, A-Z

Finland

2100	General works
2100.5.A-Z	Individual colleges, schools, institutions. By place, A-Z

Scandinavia

Education and training of teachers and administrators
State teachers colleges. Normal schools. Teachers' institutes
Europe
By region or country
Scandinavia -- Continued

2101	General works
	Denmark
2102	General works
2103.A-Z	Individual colleges, schools, institutions. By place, A-Z
	Iceland
2103.5.A2	General works
2103.5.A3-Z	Individual colleges, schools, institutions. By place, A-Z
	Norway
2104	General works
2105.A-Z	Individual colleges, schools, institutions. By place, A-Z
	Sweden
2106	General works
2107.A-Z	Individual colleges, schools, institutions. By place, A-Z
	Spain
2108	General works
2109.A-Z	Individual colleges, schools, institutions. By place, A-Z
	Portugal
2110	General works
2111.A-Z	Individual colleges, schools, institutions. By place, A-Z
	Switzerland
2112	General works
2113.A-Z	Cantons, A-Z
2114.A-Z	Institutions, A-Z
	Turkey and the Balkan states
	Turkey
2115	General works
2116.A-Z	Individual colleges, schools, institutions. By place, A-Z
	Bulgaria
2117	General works
2118.A-Z	Individual colleges, schools, institutions. By place, A-Z
	Romania
2119	General works
2120.A-Z	Individual colleges, schools, institutions. By place, A-Z

Education and training of teachers and administrators
State teachers colleges. Normal schools. Teachers' institutes
Europe
By region or country
Turkey and the Balkan states -- Continued
Yugoslavia

2121	General works
2122.A-Z	Individual colleges, schools, institutions. By place, A-Z
2124.A-Z	Other regions or countries of Europe, A-Z

Under each country:

.x	*General works*
.x2A-.x2Z	*Individual colleges, schools, institutions. By place, A-Z*

Asia

2125	General works
2126.A-Z	Countries, A-Z
2127.A-Z	Institutions. By place, A-Z
2128.A-Z	Meetings and institutes. By place, A-Z

Arab countries

2129.A2	General works
2129.A3-Z	Individual colleges, schools, institutions. By place, A-Z

Africa

2130	General works
2131.A-Z	Countries, A-Z
2132.A-Z	Institutions, A-Z
2133.A-Z	Meetings and institutes. By place, A-Z

Australia and New Zealand

2135	General works

New South Wales

2136	General works
2137.A-Z	Individual colleges, schools, institutions. By place, A-Z

New Zealand

2138	General works
2139.A-Z	Individual colleges, schools, institutions. By place, A-Z

North Australia

2140	General works
2141.A-Z	Individual colleges, schools, institutions. By place, A-Z

Queensland

2142	General works
2143.A-Z	Individual colleges, schools, institutions. By place, A-Z

Tasmania

2144	General works
2145.A-Z	Individual colleges, schools, institutions. By place, A-Z

Victoria

2146	General works
2147.A-Z	Individual colleges, schools, institutions. By place, A-Z

Education and training of teachers and administrators
State teachers colleges. Normal schools. Teachers' institutes
Australia and New Zealand -- Continued
Western Australia

2148	General works
2149.A-Z	Individual colleges, schools, institutions. By place, A-Z

Pacific islands

2150	General works
2151.A-Z	Individual colleges, schools, institutions. By place, A-Z

Model schools. Laboratory schools

2153	General works

United States

2154.A3	General works
2154.A5-Z	By city, A-Z
2155.A-Z	Other regions or countries, A-Z

Student teachers. Student teaching

2157.A3	General works
2157.A4-Z	By region or country, A-Z

Teacher training in secondary schools
Including normal courses and teacher-training departments

2159	General works

United States

2160.A3	General works
2160.A4A-.A4W	By state, A-W
2160.A5-Z	By city
2161.A-Z	Other regions or countries, A-Z

Teacher training in universities and colleges
Including schools and colleges of education, university and
college departments of education, courses in education
For training of teachers for special classes of persons
see LC379
Cf. LB2157.A3+ Student teachers

2165	General works, and United States
2167.A-.W	United States. By state, A-W
2169.A-Z	Other American countries, A-Z

Europe

2171	General works
2173.A-Z	By region or country, A-Z
2175.A-Z	Other regions or countries, A-Z

Individual universities. By region or country

2193	United States
	Assign first Cutter number for the institution, by place, and second Cutter number for the author
2195	Canada
	Assign first Cutter number for the institution, by place, and second Cutter number for the author

Education and training of teachers and administrators
Teacher training in universities and colleges
Individual universities. By region or country -- Continued

2196	Mexico
	Assign first Cutter number for the institution, by place, and second Cutter number for the author
	Central America
2197	Belize
	Assign first Cutter number for the institution, by place, and second Cutter number for the author
2198	Costa Rica
	Assign first Cutter number for the institution, by place, and second Cutter number for the author
2199	Guatemala
	Assign first Cutter number for the institution, by place, and second Cutter number for the author
2200	Honduras
	Assign first Cutter number for the institution, by place, and second Cutter number for the author
2201	Nicaragua
	Assign first Cutter number for the institution, by place, and second Cutter number for the author
2202	Panama
	Assign first Cutter number for the institution, by place, and second Cutter number for the author
2203	Salvador
	Assign first Cutter number for the institution, by place, and second Cutter number for the author
	West Indies
2205	Cuba
	Assign first Cutter number for the institution, by place, and second Cutter number for the author
2206	Haiti
	Assign first Cutter number for the institution, by place, and second Cutter number for the author
2206.5	Santo Domingo. Dominican Republic
	Assign first Cutter number for the institution, by place, and second Cutter number for the author
2207	Jamaica
	Assign first Cutter number for the institution, by place, and second Cutter number for the author
2208	Puerto Rico
	Assign first Cutter number for the institution, by place, and second Cutter number for the author
2208.5	Virgin Islands of the United States
	Assign first Cutter number for the institution, by place, and second Cutter number for the author

Education and training of teachers and administrators
Teacher training in universities and colleges
Individual universities. By region or country
West Indies -- Continued
2209.A-Z   Other, A-Z
Assign first cutter for country, second cutter for institution,
by place
South America
2211   Argentina
Assign first Cutter number for the institution, by place,
and second Cutter number for the author
2212   Bolivia
Assign first Cutter number for the institution, by place,
and second Cutter number for the author
2213   Brazil
Assign first Cutter number for the institution, by place,
and second Cutter number for the author
2214   Chile
Assign first Cutter number for the institution, by place,
and second Cutter number for the author
2215   Colombia
Assign first Cutter number for the institution, by place,
and second Cutter number for the author
2216   Ecuador
Assign first Cutter number for the institution, by place,
and second Cutter number for the author
2217   Guianas
Assign first Cutter number for the institution, by place,
and second Cutter number for the author
2218   Paraguay
Assign first Cutter number for the institution, by place,
and second Cutter number for the author
2219   Peru
Assign first Cutter number for the institution, by place,
and second Cutter number for the author
2220   Uruguay
Assign first Cutter number for the institution, by place,
and second Cutter number for the author
2221   Venezuela
Assign first Cutter number for the institution, by place,
and second Cutter number for the author
Europe
2224   England and Wales
Assign first Cutter number for the institution, by place,
and second Cutter number for the author

LB

Education and training of teachers and administrators
Teacher training in universities and colleges
Individual universities. By region or country
Europe -- Continued

2225	Scotland
	Assign first Cutter number for the institution, by place, and second Cutter number for the author
2226	Ireland
	Assign first Cutter number for the institution, by place, and second Cutter number for the author
2227	Austria-Hungary (Former). Austria. Czechoslovakia
	Assign first Cutter number for the institution, by place, and second Cutter number for the author
2228	France
	Assign first Cutter number for the institution, by place, and second Cutter number for the author
2229	Germany
	Assign first Cutter number for the institution, by place, and second Cutter number for the author
2230	Greece
	Assign first Cutter number for the institution, by place, and second Cutter number for the author
2231	Italy
	Assign first Cutter number for the institution, by place, and second Cutter number for the author
	Low Countries
2233	Belgium
	Assign first Cutter number for the institution, by place, and second Cutter number for the author
2234	Netherlands
	Assign first Cutter number for the institution, by place, and second Cutter number for the author
2234.5	Luxemburg
	Assign first Cutter number for the institution, by place, and second Cutter number for the author
2235	Russia. Former Soviet Union
	Assign first Cutter number for the institution, by place, and second Cutter number for the author
	Scandinavia
2237	Denmark
	Assign first Cutter number for the institution, by place, and second Cutter number for the author
2238	Iceland
	Assign first Cutter number for the institution, by place, and second Cutter number for the author

Education and training of teachers and administrators
Teacher training in universities and colleges
Individual universities. By region or country
Europe
Scandinavia -- Continued

2239	Norway
	Assign first Cutter number for the institution, by place, and second Cutter number for the author
2240	Sweden
	Assign first Cutter number for the institution, by place, and second Cutter number for the author
2241	Spain
	Assign first Cutter number for the institution, by place, and second Cutter number for the author
2242	Portugal
	Assign first Cutter number for the institution, by place, and second Cutter number for the author
2243	Switzerland
	Assign first Cutter number for the institution, by place, and second Cutter number for the author
	Turkey and the Balkan states
2244	Turkey
	Assign first Cutter number for the institution, by place, and second Cutter number for the author
2245	Bulgaria
	Assign first Cutter number for the institution, by place, and second Cutter number for the author
2246	Montenegro
	Assign first Cutter number for the institution, by place, and second Cutter number for the author
2247	Romania
	Assign first Cutter number for the institution, by place, and second Cutter number for the author
2248	Serbia
	Assign first Cutter number for the institution, by place, and second Cutter number for the author
2248.5	Yugoslavia
	Assign first Cutter number for the institution, by place, and second Cutter number for the author
2249.A-Z	Other European regions or countries, A-Z
	Assign first cutter for country, second cutter for institution, by place
	Asia
2250	China
	Assign first Cutter number for the institution, by place, and second Cutter number for the author

Education and training of teachers and administrators
Teacher training in universities and colleges
Individual universities. By region or country
Asia -- Continued

2251	India. Pakistan
	Assign first Cutter number for the institution, by place, and second Cutter number for the author
2252	Indochina
	Assign first Cutter number for the institution, by place, and second Cutter number for the author
2254	Indonesia
	Assign first Cutter number for the institution, by place, and second Cutter number for the author
2255	Dutch East Indies
	Assign first Cutter number for the institution, by place, and second Cutter number for the author
	Including Republic of Indonesia
2256	Philippines
	Assign first Cutter number for the institution, by place, and second Cutter number for the author
2257	Japan
	Assign first Cutter number for the institution, by place, and second Cutter number for the author
2258	Iran
	Assign first Cutter number for the institution, by place, and second Cutter number for the author
2259	Former Soviet Union in Asia
	Assign first Cutter number for the institution, by place, and second Cutter number for the author
2260	Turkey in Asia
	Assign first Cutter number for the institution, by place, and second Cutter number for the author
2261.A-Z	Other Asian regions or countries, A-Z
	Assign first cutter for country, second cutter for institution, by place
2262	Arab countries
	Assign first Cutter number for the institution, by place, and second Cutter number for the author
	Africa
2263	Egypt
	Assign first Cutter number for the institution, by place, and second Cutter number for the author
2264	British Africa
	Assign first Cutter number for the institution, by place, and second Cutter number for the author

LB

Education and training of teachers and administrators
Teacher training in universities and colleges
Individual universities. By region or country
Arab countries -- Continued

2265	French Africa
	Assign first Cutter number for the institution, by place, and second Cutter number for the author
2266	German Africa (Former)
	Assign first Cutter number for the institution, by place, and second Cutter number for the author
2266.5	Italian Africa (Former)
	Assign first Cutter number for the institution, by place, and second Cutter number for the author
2267	Portuguese Africa (Former)
	Assign first Cutter number for the institution, by place, and second Cutter number for the author
2268.A-Z	Other African states, A-Z
2268.L5	Liberia
	Assign second Cutter number for the institution, by place
2268.M6	Morocco
	Assign second Cutter number for the institution, by place
2269	Australia
	Assign first Cutter number for the institution, by place, and second Cutter number for the author
2271	New Zealand
	Assign first Cutter number for the institution, by place, and second Cutter number for the author
2278.A-Z	Pacific islands, A-Z
	Assign first Cutter number for the country, and second Cutter number for the institution, by place

International exchange of teachers
Including international exchange of educational personnel in general
Cf. LB2376 International exchange of college students

2283	General works
	Including United States exchanges in general and directories of employment of teachers in foreign countries
2285.A-Z	U.S. exchanges with other regions or countries, A-Z
2286.A-Z	Exchanges by other countries, A-Z

Higher education
For individual institutions, see LD-LG
Cf. LA173+ History of higher education (General)
Cf. LA225+ History of higher education (United States)
Cf. LC165+ Higher education and the state
Cf. LC1551+ Higher education of women

Higher education -- Continued

2300	Periodicals
2301	Associations, conferences, congresses, etc.
2305	Collections
(2310)	Yearbooks
	see LB2300
	General works
2319	Early works through 1800
2321	1801-1964
2322	1965-1990
2322.2	1991-
2324	General special
2325	Addresses, essays, lectures. Pamphlets
2326	Facetiae, satire, etc.
	Cf. PN6231.C6 Collections of college wit and humor
2326.3	Research
	Institutions of higher education
	Use for general works only. For special topics, prefer LB2331.7-LB2411, e.g., Trustees, see LB2342.5
2326.4	General works
	Two year institutions
	For general works only. For special topics, prefer LB2331.7-2411, e.g., Trustees, see LB2342.5
2326.7	General works
2327	Junior colleges (Private)
	For general works only. For special topics, prefer LB2331.7-2411, e.g., Trustees, see LB2342.5
2328	Community colleges. Junior colleges (Public)
	For general works only. For special topics, prefer LB2331.7-2411, e.g., Trustees, see LB2342.5
2328.15.A-Z	By region or country, A-Z
	Subarrange each by Table L19
	Four year institutions. Universities and colleges
	For general works only. For special topics, prefer LB2331.7-2411, e.g., Trustees, see LB2342.5
2328.2	General works
	Small colleges and universities
	For general works only. For special topics, prefer LB2331.7-2411, e.g., Trustees, see LB2342.5
2328.3	General works
2328.32.A-Z	By region or country, A-Z
	Urban universities and colleges
	For general works only. For special topics, prefer LB2331.7-LB2411, e. g. Trustees, see LB2342.5
2328.4	General works
2328.42.A-Z	By region or country, A-Z

Higher education
Institutions of higher education
Four year institutions. Universities and colleges --
Continued
Private universities and colleges
For general works only. For special topics, prefer
LB2331.7-2411, e.g., Trustees, see LB2342.5

2328.5	General works
2328.52.A-Z	By region or country, A-Z

Public universities and colleges
For general works only. For special topics, prefer
LB2331.7-2411, e.g., Trustees, see LB2342.5

2328.6	General works
2328.62.A-Z	By region or country, A-Z
2329	Municipal

For general works only. For special topics, prefer
LB2331.7-LB2411, e.g., Trustees, see LB2342.5

2329.5	State

For general works only. For special topics, prefer
LB2331.7-2411, e.g., Trustees, see LB2342.5

2329.8.A-Z	By region or country, A-Z
2330	International universities and colleges

For general works only. For special topics, prefer
LB2331.7+ e. g., Trustees, LB2342.5

Special aspects of higher education
College teaching

2331	General works
2331.2	Developmental studies programs. Remedial teaching
2331.4	University autonomy

University public services

2331.43	General works

By region or country
United States

2331.44	General works
2331.45.A-Z	By region or state, A-Z
2331.46.A-Z	Other regions or countries, A-Z
2331.5	Inter-institutional cooperation
2331.53	College-school cooperation
2331.56	Parent participation

Accreditation

2331.6	General works
2331.615.A-Z	By region or country, A-Z

Subarrange each by Table L19
Evaluation and ranking of universities and colleges

2331.62	General works

By region or country
United States

Higher education

Special aspects of higher education

Evaluation and ranking of universities and colleges

By region or country

United States -- Continued

2331.63	General works
2331.64.A-Z	By region or state, A-Z
2331.65.A-Z	Other regions or countries, A-Z

Personnel management

Including works on academic employees in general

2331.66	General works
2331.67.A-Z	Special topics, A-Z
2331.67.D57	Disabled employees
2331.67.H4	Health services

Including employee assistance programs

2331.67.S44	Selection and appointment

By region or country

United States

2331.68	General works
2331.683.A-Z	By region or state, A-Z
2331.685.A-Z	Other regions or countries, A-Z
2331.69	Administrative personnel

By region or country

United States

2331.692	General works
2331.6924.A-Z	By region or state, A-Z
2331.6926.A-Z	Other regions or countries, A-Z
2331.694	Supply and demand

By region or country

United States

2331.6942	General works
2331.69424.A-Z	By region or state, A-Z
2331.69426.A-Z	Other regions or countries, A-Z
2331.695	Selection and appointment

By region or country

United States

2331.6952	General works
2331.69524.A-Z	By region or state, A-Z
2331.69526.A-Z	Other regions or countries, A-Z
2331.696	Efficiency. Rating

By region or country

United States

2331.6962	General works
2331.69624.A-Z	By region or state, A-Z
2331.69626.A-Z	Other regions or countries, A-Z
2331.697	Salaries. Pensions

By region or country

Higher education
  Special aspects of higher education
    Personnel management
      Administrative personnel
        Salaries. Pensions
          By region or country -- Continued
            United States

2331.6972	General works
2331.69724.A-Z	By region or state, A-Z
2331.69726.A-Z	Other regions or countries, A-Z

      Teaching personnel
        Cf. LB1738 Training for university and college instruction
        Cf. LB1778 University and college teaching as a profession

2331.7	General works
	By region or country
	United States
2331.72	General works
2331.73.A-Z	By region or state, A-Z
2331.74.A-Z	Other regions or countries, A-Z

        Academic freedom see LC72
      Women

2332.3	General works
	By region or country
	United States
2332.32	General works
2332.33.A-Z	By region or state, A-Z
2332.34.A-Z	Other regions or countries, A-Z
2332.6	Faculty integration
	Selection and appointment
2332.7	General works
	By region or country
	United States
2332.72	General works
2332.73.A-Z	By region or state, A-Z
2332.74.A-Z	Other regions or countries, A-Z
2333	Efficiency. Rating

        Including academic success and failure
      Psychology

2333.2	General works
2333.3	Job stress
	Salaries. Pensions. Fringe benefits. Incentive awards

        Including retirement systems
        Cf. LB2842+ School teachers

2333.5	General works
	By region or country

Higher education
  Special aspects of higher education
    Personnel management
      Teaching personnel
        Salaries. Pensions. Fringe benefits. Incentive awards
          By region or country -- Continued
          United States

2334	General works
2334.3.A-Z	By region or state, A-Z
2335.A-Z	Other regions or countries, A-Z
2335.3	Supply and demand. Turnover
2335.35	Workload
2335.4	Teaching assistants
2335.5	Non-professional personnel
2335.7	Tenure. Dismissal
2335.8	Leaves of absence. Sabbatical leave

      Labor disputes. Strikes. Lockouts
        College teachers

2335.84	General works
2335.845.A-Z	By region or country, A-Z
	Subarrange each by Table L19

      Trade unions
        College teachers

2335.86	General works
2335.865.A-Z	By region or country, A-Z
	Subarrange each by Table L19

      Collective bargaining
        College employees

2335.87	General works
2335.875.A-Z	By region or country, A-Z
	Subarrange each by Table L19

        College teachers

2335.88	General works
2335.885.A-Z	By region or country, A-Z
	Subarrange each by Table L19

      Collective labor agreements
        see class K
      Endowments, trusts, etc.
        Cf. LC241+ Foundations, endowments, funds (General)

2335.95	General works

      By region or country
        United States

2336	General works
2336.3.A-Z	By region or state, A-Z
2337.A-Z	Other regions or countries, A-Z

    Student financial aid
      Including scholarships, fellowships, and loans

	Higher education
	Student financial aid -- Continued
2337.2	Directories
2337.3	General works
	By region or country
	United States
2337.4	General works
2337.5.A-Z	By region or state, A-Z
2337.6.A-Z	Other regions or countries, A-Z
	Scholarships and fellowships
	Cf. LB2376 International exchange of college students
	Cf. LB2848+ School administration
2338	General works, and United States
2339.A-Z	Other regions or countries, A-Z
	Student loan funds
2340	General works
	By region or country
	United States
2340.2	General works
2340.3.A-Z	By region or state, A-Z
2340.4.A-Z	Other regions or countries, A-Z
	Financial aid administration
2340.5	General works
2340.8	Administrative personnel
	Prepaid tuition plans
2340.9	General works
	By region or country
	United States
2340.94	General works
2340.95.A-Z	By region or state, A-Z
2340.96.A-Z	Other regions or countries, A-Z
	Supervision and administration
	Including duties of presidents, deans, registrars, faculty participation in administration, collegiate registration; public relations; record forms, etc.
2341	General works, and United States
	State supervision
2341.5	General works
2341.6.A-.W	By state, A-W
2341.6.C3	California
	For the administration of specific systems, see the system, e.g., LD729.5+, California State University and Colleges
2341.6.N7	New York
	Including New York (State). State University (i.e. State University of New York, an administrative body only)
2341.8.A-Z	Other regions or countries, A-Z

	Higher education -- Continued
	Business management
2341.92	General works
2341.93.A-Z	By region or country, A-Z
	National associations
2341.94	General works
2341.95.A-Z	By region or country, A-Z

Under each country:

.x	*General works*
.x2A-.x2Z	*Particular associations, A-Z*

2341.98	Finance. Income and expenditure. Accounting
	Including tuition and fees
	By region or country
	United States
2342	General works
2342.15.A-Z	By region or state, A-Z
2342.2.A-Z	Other regions or countries, A-Z
	Federal aid for higher education
2342.3	General works
2342.4.A-Z	By region or country, A-Z
	Subarrange each by Table L19
2342.5	Trustees
(2342.7)	Personnel management
	see LB2331.66+
2342.75	Communications systems. Telecommunication
2342.77	Information resources management
	Public relations
2342.8	General works
2342.82	College publicity. Recruiting
	College publications
	Cf. LB3621+ Student journalism and publications
	Cf. LD1+ Publications of individual institutions
	Cf. LH1+ Student publications themselves
	Cf. Z231.5.U6 University presses
	Cf. Z286.S37 Scholarly publishing
	Cf. Z6944.S3 Scholarly periodicals
2342.85	General works
2342.86	College catalogs
	Cf. LD1+ Publications of individual institutions
	Student affairs services. Student personnel administration
2342.9	General works
	By region or country
	United States
2342.92	General works
2342.93.A-Z	By region or state, A-Z
2342.94.A-Z	Other regions or countries, A-Z
2343	Student guidance and counseling

Higher education
Student affairs services. Student personnel administration --
Continued

2343.25	Campus-based child care
	College orientation. College freshmen
2343.3	General works
	By region or country
	United States
2343.32	General works
2343.33.A-Z	By region or state, A-Z
2343.34.A-Z	Other regions or countries, A-Z
2343.4	College student development programs
2343.5	Employment bureaus. College placement services
2343.6	Commuting students
2344	Discipline
	Cf. HV8290+ Campus police
2345	Campus violence
2346	Self-government of students. College student government
2346.3	Class size
2347	School year
	For summer school see LC5701+
2349	Standardization
2350	Relation between higher and secondary education
2350.3	Campus visits
2350.5	Choice of college
	Admissions and entrance requirements
	Including selection, prediction, and placement policies
2351	General works
	By region or country
	United States
2351.2	General works
2351.3.A-Z	By region or state, A-Z
2351.4.A-Z	Other regions or countries, A-Z
	Open admission
2351.45	General works
	By region or country
	United States
2351.46	General works
2351.47.A-Z	By region or state, A-Z
2351.48.A-Z	Other regions or countries, A-Z
	College applications
2351.5	General works
2351.52.A-Z	By region or country, A-Z
2351.6	College admission officers
	Entrance examinations
	Including college, college department, private, and state achievement tests

	Higher education
	Admissions and entrance requirements
	Entrance examinations -- Continued
2353	General works
	By region or country
	United States
2353.2	General works
2353.24.A-Z	By region or state, A-Z
2353.26.A-Z	Other regions or countries, A-Z
2353.28	Anecdotes, facetiae, satire, etc.
	College-administered entrance examinations
2353.3	General works
	By region or country
	United States
2353.32	General works
2353.34.A-Z	By region or state, A-Z
	For individual institutions see LD1+
2353.36.A-Z	Other regions or countries, A-Z
	For individual institutions, see LE - LG
	National entrance examinations
2353.4	General works
	By region or country
	United States
2353.42	General works
	American College Testing Program (ACT)
	Including history, organization, policies and programs
2353.44	General works
2353.46	Scores
	Including analysis, prediction, interpretation
2353.48	Examinations. Academic test handbooks and study guides
	Including the Proficiency Examination Program (PEP) and ACT Assessment
	College Entrance Examination Board (CEEB). Educational Testing Service (ETS)
	Including history, organization, policies and programs
	For specific programs, see the subject
2353.5	General works
2353.52	Scores
	Including analysis, prediction, interpretation
2353.54	Examinations. Academic test handbooks and study guides
	Admissions Testing Program (ATP)
2353.55	General works
2353.56	PSAT. Preliminary SAT
2353.57	SAT
	Including the various formats

Higher education
  Admissions and entrance requirements
    Entrance examinations
      National entrance examinations
        By region or country
          United States
            College Entrance Examination Board (CEEB).
              Educational Testing Service (ETS)
              Admissions Testing Program (ATP) -- Continued

2353.6	Achievement tests
	Including subject specialty and supplementary achievement tests
	For examinations in specific subject areas, see the subject areas in classes A-Z
2353.62	Advanced Placement Program (APP)
2353.64	College Scholarship Service (CSS)
	For programs and services see LB2338+
2353.66	National Merit Scholarship Qualifying Test (NMSQT)
	Sponsored by National Merit Scholarship Corporation, Evanston, Illinois
	College level examinations
	Including tests for college placement, college credit and job related evaluation usages demonstrating scales of comparative competence for independent study, correspondence courses, nonformal education, and experimental learning
2353.67	General works
2353.68	College-Level Examination Program (CLEP)
	Cf. LB2353.5+ College Entrance Examination Board and its other tests
	Comparative guidance (CGP) and placement program see LB2343
2353.7.A-Z	Other examinations. By name, A-Z
2353.7.C64	College Level Academic Skills Test
2353.7.C85	CUNY Skills Assessment Test
2353.7.D43	The Defense Activity for Non-Traditional Educational Support (DANTES) examination
2353.7.F56	Florida College Basic Skills Exit Test
2353.7.S45	Selective Service College Qualification Test (SSCQT)
2353.7.T37	Texas Higher Education Assessment Test (THEA)
	Formerly Texas Academic Skills Program Test (TASP)

	Higher education
	Admissions and entrance requirements
	Entrance examinations
	National entrance examinations
	By region or country -- Continued
2353.8.A-Z	Other regions or countries, A-Z

Under each country:

	.x	*General works*
	.x2	*Special examinations. By name, A-Z*

2355	Admission by certificate. Certification policies
2357.A-Z	Requirements in special subjects, A-Z
2357.E5	English
2357.L3	Latin
2359	Other special subjects
2359.5	College credits
2360	Transfer of students. Transfer of credits
	Academic departments. Subject organization
	Cf. LB2341+ Supervision and administration
2360.2	General works
	By region or country
	United States
2360.3	General works
2360.35.A-Z	By region or state, A-Z
2360.4.A-Z	Other regions or countries, A-Z
	Curriculum
	Including college majors
2361	General works
	By region or country
	United States
2361.5	General works
2361.6.A-Z	By region or state, A-Z
2362.A-Z	Other regions or countries, A-Z
2363	Elective system
2364	Honor courses
(2365)	The role of special subjects
	see the specific subject
(2365.C5)	Children's literature
	see PB-PT
(2365.C58)	Civics
	see J+
(2365.E5)	English
	see PE
(2365.H6)	History
	see D+
(2365.H8)	Humanities
	see AZ

Higher education

Curriculum

The role of special subjects -- Continued

(2365.I5)	Insurance	
	see HG	
(2365.I6)	International relations	
	see JZ	
(2365.I8)	Italian	
	see PC	
(2365.J3)	Japanese studies	
	see PL	
(2365.L38)	Language arts	
	see P	
(2365.L4)	Languages (Modern)	
	see PB	
(2365.L5)	Latin	
	see PA	
(2365.M3)	Mathematics	
	see QA	
(2365.R4)	Reading	
	see LB2395.3	
	Religion	
	see BL-BX	
(2365.S6)	Social sciences	
	see H+	
(2365.T45)	Theology	
	see BT	

College examinations

Including examination methods, term and semester examinations, comprehensive examinations and graduate school methods

Cf. LB2395 Study methods

Cf. LB3050+ Educational tests, measurements, evaluations and examinations

2366	General works
	By region or country
	United States
2366.2	General works
2366.4.A-Z	By region or state, A-Z
2367.A-Z	Other regions or countries, A-Z
2367.2	Academic Profile (Test)
2367.25	College Basic Academic Subjects Examination
2367.27	Collegiate Learning Assessment
2367.3	General Intellectual Skills Assessment
2367.4	Graduate record exam
2367.6	Miller Analogies Test (MAT)
2367.75	Pre-Professional Skills Test

Higher education -- Continued

2368	Grading and promotion
	Including rating of college students, grading and marking and the pass-fail grading system
2369	Preparation of theses
	Including research and thesis writing; also the preparation of papers and reports
	Cf. LB1047.3 Teaching (Principles and practice)
	Graduate education
	Including graduate study and work, graduate schools and courses in general
2371	General works
	By region or country
	United States
2371.4	General works
2371.5.A-Z	By region or state, A-Z
2371.6.A-Z	Other regions or countries, A-Z
2372.A-Z	The role of special subjects, A-Z
2372.E3	Education
2372.3	Research institutes, centers, laboratories
	Exchange of students and scholars. Foreign study
	Including directories and the guidance and counseling of exchange students
	For foreign high school student exchanges see LB1696+
	Cf. LB2283+ Exchange of teachers
	Cf. LB2338+ Scholarships and fellowships
2375	General works
	United States
	American students in foreign countries
	Including students from an individual state of the U.S.
2376	General works
2376.3.A-Z	American students in specfic regions or countries, A-Z
	Foreign students in the United States
	Including students studying in a specific state of the U.S.
2376.4	General works
2376.5.A-Z	Students from specific regions or countries, A-Z

Higher education

Exchange of students and scholars. Foreign study --
Continued

2376.6.A-Z	Other regions or countries, A-Z

For works involving only two countries, class with the country appearing first alphabetically. If one of the two countries is the United States, class in LB2376+

Under each:

.x	*Students from the region or country studying abroad*
	Including students studying in specific countries
	e.g. LB2376.6.C6, Chinese students in foreign countries; Chinese students in Italy
.x2	*Foreign students studying in the region or country*
	Including students from specific countries
	e.g. LB2376.6.C62, Students from foreign countries studying in China; students from Italy studying in China
(2377-2378)	These numbers are no longer valid

Works formerly classed in these numbers are now classed in LB2375+

Returned students

2378.3	General works
2378.5.A-Z	By region or country, A-Z
2379	Academic protocol, etiquette, etc.

Academic degrees

Class here requirements, regulations, etc., including dictionaries, guides

For graduate degrees in a special subject, see the subject, e. g. Medical degrees, see class R

2381	General works
2383	B.A.
2385	M.A.
2386	Ph.D.
2387	Honorary degrees
2388	Fraudulent degrees. Diploma mills
2389	Academic costume, regalia, etc.

Cf. LB3630 School colors

By region or country

United States

2390	General works
2390.5.A-Z	By region or state, A-Z

Higher education
 Academic degrees
  By region or country -- Continued

2391.A-Z	Other regions or countries, A-Z
2393	Lectures in college teaching
2393.5	Seminars
2394	Fieldwork

     Cf. LB1047 Teaching
  Methods of study

2395	General works
2395.2	Independent study
2395.25	Note-taking
2395.3	Reading skills
2395.35	Thinking skills. Creative thinking
2395.4	Time management

     Cf. LB3607.8 General time management for students

2395.7	Technology. Information technology

     Including use of computers

2396	Tutoring
2397	Recollections and reminiscences of college days, etc.

     General (reflections, meditations) only
     For individual institutions, see LD-LG
   College life in literature
    see PN-PT
   College humor see PN6231.C6
   Athletics see GV345
   Student-athletes see LC2580.6

2411	Alumni and alumni associations (General)

     For individual American institutions see LD1+
     For magazines and papers see LH1+
   Surveys of college graduates
     Cf. HD6277+ Employment of college graduates

2420	General works

   By region or country
    United States

2424	General works
2426.A-Z	By region or state, A-Z
2430.A-Z	Other regions or countries, A-Z

  Educational consultants and consulting

2799	General works

   By region or country

2799.2	United States
2799.3.A-Z	Other regions or countries, A-Z

  School administration and organization
   Including school supervision
   Cf. LB1705+ Education and training
   General

	School administration and organization
	General -- Continued
	Manuals, regulations, etc.
2801.A1	General works
	United States
2801.A2	General works
2801.A3-Z	Regions, states, counties, and districts, A-Z
	e.g.
2801.O7	Oregon
2801.O7M3	Marion County
2801.O7M379	District, No. 79
2802.A-Z	Cities, A-Z
	Directories and lists of school officials
2803.A1	General works
	United States
2803.A2	Official. By date
2803.A3	General nonofficial
2803.A4-Z	Regions or states, A-Z

Under each state:

.x	*General*
.x2A-.x2Z	*Counties, A-Z*
.x3A-.x3Z	*Cities, A-Z*

Cf. L901+ Directories of educational institutions

2803.2.A-Z	Other regions or countries, A-Z

Under each country:

.xA2	*Official. By date*
.xA3-.xA39	*General nonofficial*
.xA4-.Z	*Local, A-Z*

*e.g. Japan, LB2803.2.J3A2 (Official. By date); .J3A3-39
(General nonofficial); .J3T6, Tokyo*

2804	Associations
	e.g., National Association of School Superintendents
2805	General works and United States
2805.5	Outlines. Syllabi
2806	General special
2806.14	Centralization
2806.15	Curriculum planning
2806.17	Electronic data processing
2806.2	Performance contracts in education
2806.22	Educational accountability
2806.24	Educational productivity
2806.25	Research in administration
2806.3	School management teams
2806.35	School-based management
2806.36	Privatization in education. Charter schools
2806.4	School supervision
	Cf. LB1777.5 School supervisors

	School administration and organization
	General -- Continued
2806.45	Teacher participation in administration
2806.5	National supervision of education
	Including Federal department of education
2807	United States Office of Education
	Formerly United States Bureau of Education
	Including establishment, organization, history, relations, etc.
	For reports see L111.A3+
	State boards. Departments of public instruction. School control
2809.A2	General works
2809.A3-Z	By region or state, A-Z
	State supervision see LB2809.A+
2810	Accreditation
	By region or country
	United States
2810.3	General works
2810.4.A-Z	By region or state, A-Z
2810.5.A-Z	Other regions or countries, A-Z
2813	County school systems. County supervision
2815	Township school systems. Township supervision
	District school systems. District supervision
2817	General works
	By region or country
	United States
2817.3	General works
2817.4.A-Z	By region or state, A-Z
2817.5.A-Z	Other regions or countries, A-Z
2818	Magnet schools. Magnet centers
	City school systems. City supervision
2819	General works
2820	Community schools. Neighborhood schools
	University and college administration see LB2341+
	High school administration. High school supervision
	Including junior high and middle schools
2822	General works
	By region or country
	United States
2822.2	General works
2822.25.A-Z	By region or state, A-Z
2822.3.A-Z	Other regions or countries, A-Z
2822.5	Elementary school administration. Elementary school supervision
	Early childhood school administration. Early childhood school supervision
2822.6	General works

	School administration and organization
	General
	Early childhood school administration. Early childhood school supervision -- Continued
2822.7	Nursery school administration. Nursery school supervision
2822.75	Educational evaluation
	School improvement programs
2822.8	General works
	By region or country
	United States
2822.82	General works
2822.83.A-Z	By region or state, A-Z
2822.84.A-Z	Other regions or countries, A-Z
2822.9	School autonomy
2823	School surveys
2823.2	School closings
	Business management
2823.5	General works
	School finance. Taxation, bonds, etc.
	Cf. LC184+ Taxation of schools and colleges
2824	General and comparative
	Prefer individual country
	By region or country
	United States
2825	General works
2826.A-.W	By state, A-W
	Including counties
2826.5.A-Z	By city, A-Z
2826.6.A-Z	Other regions or countries, A-Z
2827	Land grants
	Federal aid to private schools
2827.3	General works
	By region or country
	United States
2827.4	General works
2827.5.A-Z	By region or state, A-Z
2827.6.A-Z	Other regions or countries, A-Z
	State aid to private schools
	United States
2828	General works
2828.5.A-.W	States, A-W
2828.6.A-Z	Other regions or countries, A-Z
	Educational vouchers
2828.7	General works
	By region or country
	United States

LB

School administration and organization
General
Personnel management
Administrative personnel
By region or country -- Continued
United States

2831.62	General works
2831.624.A-Z	By region or state, A-Z
2831.626.A-Z	Other regions or countries, A-Z
2831.63	General special
	Training of see LB1738.5
2831.64	Supply and demand. Turnover
	By region or country
	United States
2831.642	General works
2831.644.A-Z	By region or state, A-Z
2831.646.A-Z	Other regions or countries, A-Z
	Selection and appointment. Contractual status
	Including tenure and dismissal
2831.65	General works
	By region or country
	United States
2831.652	General works
2831.654.A-Z	By region or state, A-Z
2831.656.A-Z	Other regions or countries, A-Z
2831.658	Time management
	Certification see LB1767+
	Efficiency. Rating
2831.66	General works
	By region or country
	United States
2831.662	General works
2831.664.A-Z	By region or state, A-Z
2831.666.A-Z	Other regions or countries, A-Z
	Salaries. Pensions
2831.67	General works
	By region or country
	United States
2831.672	General works
2831.674.A-Z	By region or state, A-Z
2831.676.A-Z	Other regions or countries, A-Z
2831.7-.776	Superintendents (Table L26)
2831.8-.876	Administrators (Table L26)
	Including supervisors, directors, and coordinators
2831.9-.976	Principals (Elementary and/or Secondary) (Table L26)
	Including assistant principals
2831.99.A-Z	Other administrative personnel, A-Z

School administration and organization
General
Personnel management -- Continued
Teaching personnel
Cf. LB2331.7+ College teachers
Cf. LB3013.5 Visiting teachers
Cf. LB3013.6 School psychologists
2832 General works
By region or country
United States
2832.2 General works
2832.3.A-Z By region or state, A-Z
2832.4.A-Z Other regions or countries, A-Z
Supply and demand. Turnover. Transfer. Mobility
2833 General works
By region or country
United States
2833.2 General works
2833.3.A-.W By state, A-W
2833.4.A-Z Other regions or countries, A-Z
Selection and appointment. Contractual status
2835 General works
By region or country
United States
2835.25 General works
2835.26.A-Z By region or state, A-Z
2835.28.A-Z Other regions or countries, A-Z
Subarrange each by Table L19
2835.3 Loyalty oaths
2836 Tenure. Dismissal
2837 Women teachers
Including married women
Cf. LB2843.W7 Salaries of women
Certification see LB1771+
Training see LB1705+
Efficiency. Rating
Including self-rating
Cf. LB2333 Higher education
2838 General works
2838.3 Incentive awards, prizes, etc.
2838.8 Time management
2839 Promotion
Psychology
Cf. LB2333.2+ Higher education
2840 General works
2840.2 Job stress. Teacher burnout

School administration and organization
General
Personnel management
Teaching personnel -- Continued
Salaries. Pensions. Fringe benefits. Incentive awards
Including retirement systems
Cf. LB2333.5+ Higher education
General works, and United States

2842	Early through 1964
2842.2	1965-1990
2842.22	1991-
2842.4.A-Z	By region or state, A-Z
2843.A-Z	Special, A-Z
2843.L4	Leaves of absence
	Including leave regulations, sabbatical leave plans
2843.P3	Part-time teachers
2843.V5	Visiting teachers
2843.W7	Women teachers
	Cf. LB2837 Women as teachers
2844.A-Z	Other regions or countries, A-Z
2844.1.A-Z	Other topics, A-Z
2844.1.A8	Assistants
2844.1.C54	Child sexual abuse by teachers
2844.1.C6	Communism
	First year teachers see LB2844.1.N4
2844.1.G39	Gay teachers
2844.1.H35	Handicapped teachers. Teachers with disabilities
	Language arts teachers see LB2844.1.R4
2844.1.N4	New teachers. First year teachers
2844.1.O8	Out-of-school activities
2844.1.P3	Part-time teachers
2844.1.P4	Peace Corps
2844.1.P6	Political activity
2844.1.P67	Preschool teachers
2844.1.P7	Probationary teachers
2844.1.R4	Reading teachers. Language arts teachers
2844.1.R5	Retired teachers. Retirement
	Retirement see LB2844.1.R5
2844.1.S6	Social origins
2844.1.S8	Substitute teachers
2844.1.S86	Supplementary employment
	Teachers with disabilities see LB2844.1.H35
2844.1.V6	Volunteer workers
2844.1.W4	Welfare funds for teachers
2844.1.W6	Workload

Nonprofessional personnel
Cf. LB3235 Care of school buildings, janitor service

School administration and organization
General
Personnel management
Nonprofessional personnel -- Continued

2844.2	General works
2844.4	School secretaries
	Labor disputes. Strikes. Lockouts
	Teachers
2844.46	General works
2844.47.A-Z	By region or country, A-Z
	Subarrange each by Table L19
	Trade unions
	Teachers' unions
2844.52	General works
2844.53.A-Z	By region or country, A-Z
	Subarrange each by Table L19
	Collective bargaining
2844.56	General works
2844.57.A-Z	By region or country, A-Z
	Subarrange each by Table L19
	Teachers
2844.58	General works
2844.59.A-Z	By region or country, A-Z
	Subarrange each by Table L19
	School administrators
	Including supervisors, superintendents, school boards and principals
2844.62	General works
2844.63.A-Z	By region or country, A-Z
	Subarrange each by Table L19
	Collective labor agreements
	see class K
2845	Inspection of schools
	Cf. LB3411 Medical inspection
	School records and reports
2845.7	General works
2846	Educational statistics. Educational indicators. Graphics methods
	Including methods of forecasting school population
	Cf. LC130 Enrollment. Registration of school children. School census
2846.4	Electronic data processing
2847	Public relations. Advertising. Marketing
	Scholarships and fellowships
	Cf. LB2338+ Higher education
2848	General works, United States
2849.A-Z	Other regions or countries, A-Z

	School administration and organization
	General -- Continued
	School textbooks see LB3045+
2861	Centralization of schools (Rural)
2862	Decentralization of schools (Urban)
	Transportation of students
	Cf. LC214.5 Busing for integration
2864	General works
2864.2	Students with disabilities
	School safety
	Cf. LB3013.3+ Violence in schools
2864.5	General works
2864.6.A-Z	Special, A-Z
2864.6.A25	Accidents
2864.6.A78	Art rooms
2864.6.C54	Chemicals
2865	School safety patrols. School crossing guards
2866	School security. Campus security
	Cf. HV8290+ Campus police
2866.5	School crisis management
	Other regions or countries
	Canada
2890	General
2891.A-Z	Local, A-Z
	Latin America
2891.5	General works
	Mexico
2892	General
2893.A-Z	Local, A-Z
	Central America
2894	General
2895.A-Z	Local, A-Z
	West Indies
2896	General
2897.A-Z	Local, A-Z
	South America
2898	General works
	Argentina
2898.21	General
2898.22.A-Z	Local, A-Z
	Bolivia
2898.23	General
2898.24.A-Z	Local, A-Z
	Brazil
2898.25	General
2898.26.A-Z	Local, A-Z
	Chile

	School administration and organization
	Other regions or countries
	Latin America
	South America
	Chile -- Continued
2898.27	General
2898.28.A-Z	Local, A-Z
	Colombia
2898.29	General
2898.30.A-Z	Local, A-Z
	Ecuador
2898.31	General
2898.32.A-Z	Local, A-Z
	Guianas
2898.33	Guyana
2898.34	Suriname
2898.35	French Guiana
	Paraguay
2898.36	General
2898.37.A-Z	Local, A-Z
	Peru
2898.38	General
2898.39.A-Z	Local, A-Z
	Uruguay
2898.40	General
2898.41.A-Z	Local, A-Z
	Venezuela
2898.42	General
2898.43.A-Z	Local, A-Z
	Europe
2900	General works
2900.5	Great Britain
	England and Wales
2901	General
2902.A-Z	Local, A-Z
	Scotland
2903	General
2904.A-Z	Local, A-Z
	Ireland
2905	General
2906.A-Z	Local, A-Z
	Austria
2907	General
2908.A-Z	Local, A-Z
	France
2909	General
2910.A-Z	Local, A-Z

School administration and organization
Other regions or countries
Europe -- Continued
Germany
Including West Germany

2911	General
2912.A-Z	Local, A-Z
	East Germany
2913	General
2914.A-Z	Local, A-Z
	Greece
2915	General
2916.A-Z	Local, A-Z
	Italy
2917	General
2918.A-Z	Local, A-Z
	Low countries
	Belgium
2919	General
2920.A-Z	Local, A-Z
	Netherlands
2921	General
2922.A-Z	Local, A-Z
	Russia. Soviet Union
2923	General
2924.A-Z	Local, A-Z
	Scandinavia
2924.5	General works
	Denmark
2925	General
2926.A-Z	Local, A-Z
2927	Iceland
	Norway
2928	General
2929.A-Z	Local, A-Z
	Sweden
2930	General
2931.A-Z	Local, A-Z
	Spain
2932	General
2933.A-Z	Local, A-Z
	Portugal
2934	General
2935.A-Z	Local, A-Z
	Switzerland
2936	General
2937.A-Z	Local, A-Z

School administration and organization
Other regions or countries
Europe -- Continued
Turkey and the Balkan states
Turkey

2938	General
2939.A-Z	Local, A-Z
2940	Bulgaria
2941	Montenegro
2942	Romania
2943	Yugoslavia
2944.A-Z	Other regions or countries of Europe

Asia

2944.5	General works

China

2945	General
2946.A-Z	Local, A-Z

Taiwan

2946.3	General
2946.4.A-Z	Local, A-Z

India

2947	General
2948.A-Z	Local, A-Z

Sri Lanka

2948.3	General
2948.4.A-Z	Local, A-Z

Bangladesh

2948.5	General
2948.6.A-Z	Local, A-Z

Pakistan

2948.7	General
2948.8.A-Z	Local, A-Z

Indochina
French Indochina

2949	General
2950.A-Z	Local, A-Z

Thailand

2952.5	General
2952.6.A-Z	Local, A-Z

Indonesia

2953	General
2954.A-Z	Local, A-Z

Philippines

2955	General
2956.A-Z	Local, A-Z

Japan

2957	General

School administration and organization
Other regions or countries
Asia
Japan -- Continued
2958.A-Z   Local, A-Z
                   Iran
2959   General
2960.A-Z   Local, A-Z
                   Soviet Union in Asia
2961   General
2962.A-Z   Local, A-Z
                   Turkey in Asia
2963   General
2964.A-Z   Local, A-Z
2965.A-Z   Other divisions of Asia, A-Z
2966   Arab countries
               Africa
                 Egypt
2967   General
2968.A-Z   Local, A-Z
                 British possessions (Former)
2969   General works
2970.A-Z   By region or country, A-Z
2970.K4   Kenya
                 French possessions (Former)
2971   General
2972.A-Z   Local, A-Z
                 German possessions (Former)
2973   General
2974.A-Z   Local, A-Z
                 Portuguese possessions
2975   General
2976.Z-Z   Local, A-Z
2977.A-Z   Other divisions of Africa, A-Z
                     Subarrange each by Table L19
               Australia and New Zealand
2979   General
                 New South Wales
2981   General
2982.A-Z   Local, A-Z
                 New Zealand
2983   General
2984.A-Z   Local, A-Z
                 North Australia
2985   General
2986.A-Z   Local, A-Z
                 Queensland

	School administration and organization
	Other regions or countries
	Australia and New Zealand
	Queensland -- Continued
2987	General
2988.A-Z	Local, A-Z
	South Australia
2989	General
2990.A-Z	Local, A-Z
	Tasmania
2991	General
2992.A-Z	Local, A-Z
	Victoria
2993	General
2994.A-Z	Local, A-Z
	Western Australia
2995	General
2996.A-Z	Local, A-Z
2997.A-Z	Pacific islands, A-Z
	School management and discipline
3011	General works
3011.5	General special
	School discipline
	Cf. LB3089+ Student suspension
3012	General works
	By region or country
	United States
3012.2	General works
3012.3.A-Z	By region or state, A-Z
3012.4.A-Z	Other regions or countries, A-Z
3012.5	School size
	Admissions and entrance requirements
	Including selection, prediction, and placement policies
3012.6	General works
	By region or country
	United States
3012.7	General works
3012.8.A-Z	By region or state, A-Z
3012.9.A-Z	Other regions or countries, A-Z
	Classroom management
3013	General works
3013.2	Class size
3013.25	Classroom stress
	Violence in schools
	Including bullying in schools
	Cf. HV6250.4.S78 Crimes against students
	Cf. LB3249 Vandalism

School administration and organization
School management and discipline
Violence in schools -- Continued

3013.3	General works
	By region or country
	United States
3013.32	General works
3013.33.A-Z	By region or state, A-Z
3013.34.A-Z	Other regions or countries, A-Z
	School social work
3013.4	General works
3013.5	Visiting teachers. School social workers
3013.55	School-linked services
3013.6	School psychologists
	Special systems, Departmental, Monitorial, etc. see LB1029.A+
3014	Minor works
3015	Opening exercises
	Including assembly and auditorium activities, programs
3019	Friday afternoon exercises
3020	Commencement exercises, etc.
3021	Student honor
	For official lists see Z5817
	Cf. LB3092+ Self-government
3024	Dress codes
3025	Rewards and punishments
	Cf. LB3089+ Suspension, expulsion
3031	Amusements and games. Recreation
	Cf. BF717 Psychology of play
	Cf. GV1+ Sports and games
	Cf. LB1137 Child study
	School schedules
3032	General works
3032.2	Block scheduling
3032.5	Electronic data processing
3033	School hours. Recesses
3033.5	School week
3034	School year
3041	Vacations
	Educational media
3044	General works
3044.5	Industrial propaganda in educational media
	Instructional materials centers
3044.7	General works
	By region or country
	United States
3044.72	General works

	School administration and organization
	School management and discipline
	Educational media
	Instructional materials centers
	By region or country
	United States -- Continued
3044.73.A-Z	By region or state, A-Z
3044.74.A-Z	Other regions or countries
	Classroom learning centers
3044.8	General works
	By region or country
	United States
3044.82	General works
3044.83.A-Z	By region or state, A-Z
3044.84.A-Z	Other regions or countries, A-Z
	Textbooks
3045	General works
3045.5	Authorship
	Bias in textbooks
3045.6	General works
3045.62	Antisemitism
3045.64	Racism
3045.66	Sexism
3045.7	Censorship
3045.8	Readability
3045.84	Religion in textbooks
	By region or country
	United States
3047	General works
3047.5.A-Z	By region or state, A-Z
3048.A-Z	Other regions or countries, A-Z
	Educational tests, measurements, evaluations and examinations
	For competency-based educational examinations see LC1034+
	Cf. LB2366+ College examinations
3050	Periodicals. Societies. Serials
3050.5	Congresses
3051	General works, and United States
3052.A-.W	By state, A-W
3053.A-Z	By city, A-Z
	Other American countries
3054.A-Z	By region or country, A-Z
3055.A-Z	By city, A-Z
	Europe
3056.A2	General works
3056.A3-Z	By region or country, A-Z

School administration and organization
School management and discipline
Educational tests, measurements, evaluations and
examinations
Europe -- Continued

3057.A-Z	By city, A-Z
3058.A-Z	Other regions or countries, A-Z
3059.A-Z	Other cities, A-Z
3059.5	Addresses, essays, lectures
3060	Anecdotes, facetiae, satire, etc.

Cf. PN6231.S3 Schools (Humor)
Individual levels of testing
Cf. LB1132 Preschool testing

3060.217	Early childhood testing
3060.22	Elementary school testing
3060.24	Secondary school entrance testing
3060.26	Secondary school testing
3060.27	School-to-work assessment

High school graduation examinations. School leaving
exams
Including high school equivalency examinations

3060.28	General works
3060.285.A-Z	By region or country, A-Z

Special types of evaluations, measurements, tests and
examinations
Achievement tests and examinations

3060.3	General works
3060.32.A-Z	Special types of achievement tests, A-Z
3060.32.C65	Computer adaptive testing
3060.32.C74	Criterion-referenced tests

Degrees of Reading Power tests see
LB1050.75.D43

3060.32.D65	Domain-referenced tests
3060.32.M85	Multiple choice examinations

Including true-false examinations

3060.32.N67	Norm-referenced tests
3060.32.O35	Objective tests
3060.32.S35	Scholastic aptitude tests

Cf. LB2353.57 Scholastic Assessment Test for
college entrance

3060.33.A-Z	Particular tests, A-Z

ACT Assessment see LB2353.48

3060.33.C34	California Basic Educational Skills Tests
3060.33.C35	California High School Exit Exam
3060.33.C36	California High School Proficiency Examination
3060.33.C65	Comprehensive Scales of Student Abilities
3060.33.C69	Courtis Standard Tests

School administration and organization
School management and discipline
Educational tests, measurements, evaluations and
examinations
Special types of evaluations, measurements, tests and
examinations
Particular tests, A-Z -- Continued

3060.33.D45	Detroit Tests of Learning Aptitude
3060.33.E27	Early Learning Skills Analysis
3060.33.F54	Florida Comprehensive Assessment Test
3060.33.F55	Florida State Student Assessment Test II
3060.33.G45	General Educational Development Tests. GED tests
3060.33.G47	Georgia High School Graduation Test
3060.33.H35	Hammill Multiability Achievement Test
3060.33.H54	High School Proficiency Test
3060.33.I53	Independent School Entrance Examination
3060.33.I68	Iowa Tests of Basic Skills
3060.33.K38	Kaufman Test of Educational Achievement
3060.33.M36	Massachusetts Comprehensive Assessment System
3060.33.M46	Metropolitan Achievement Tests
3060.33.M54	Miller-Yoder Language Comprehension Tests
3060.33.M57	Missouri Mastery and Achievement Tests
3060.33.N65	North Carolina Competency Test
3060.33.P43	Peabody Individual Achievement Test-Revised
3060.33.P75	Project Talent
3060.33.S34	Scaled Curriculum Achievement Levels Tests
3060.33.S42	Secondary School Admission Test
3060.33.T43	Test of Auditory Reasoning and Processing Skills
3060.33.T46	Tests of Achievement and Proficiency
3060.33.T47	Texas Assessment of Knowledge and Skills
	Formerly Texas Assessment of Academic Skills
3060.33.T48	Texas Educational Assessment of Minimum Skills
3060.33.V57	Virginia Standards of Learning Tests
3060.33.W38	Washington Assessment of Student Learning Test (WASL)
3060.33.W47	Wechsler Individual Achievement Test
3060.33.W66	Woodcock-Munoz Language survey
3060.37	Grading and marking
	Including pass-fail grading system
3060.45	Listening comprehension tests
	Special topics
	Technology in testing
3060.5	General works
3060.53	Audiovisual aids and materials
3060.55	Data processing
3060.57	Test taking skills
	Including study handbooks

School administration and organization
School management and discipline
Educational tests, measurements, evaluations and
examinations
Special topics -- Continued

3060.6	Test anxiety
3060.62	Test bias
3060.65	Test construction
	Test evaluation
3060.68	General works
3060.7	Test validity
3060.75	Test reliability
3060.77	Test scoring
3060.8	Test interpretation
	National and local norms
	Including standards
3060.82	General works
	By region or country
	United States
3060.83	General works
3060.85.A-Z	By region or state, A-Z
3060.87.A-Z	Other regions or countries, A-Z
	Classification of pupils. Ability grouping. Age grouping
3061	General works
3061.3	Mixed ability grouping
3061.5	School grade placement
	Including equivalency evaluation of school credits
3061.8	Track system
	Segregation in education see LC212.5+
3063	Grading and promotion
	Including equivalency evaluation of school credits
	Transfer of students
3064	General works
	By region or country
	United States
3064.2	General works
3064.3.A-Z	By region or state, A-Z
3064.4.A-Z	Other regions or countries, A-Z
3065	Graduation
	For exercises see LB3020
	Coeducation
	Cf. LC1601 Education of women
3065.5	General works
	By region or country
	United States
3066	General works
3066.4.A-Z	By region or state, A-Z

School administration and organization
School management and discipline
Coeducation
By region or country -- Continued
3067.A-Z   Other regions or countries, A-Z
3067.3   Single-sex schools
By region or country
United States
3067.4   General works
3067.5.A-Z   By region or state, A-Z
3067.7.A-Z   Other regions or countries, A-Z
Prize competitions
3068   General works
3069.A-Z   Documents. Reports, etc. By country, A-Z

Under each country:

.x	*General*
.x2A-.x2Z	*By state, A-Z*
.x3	*Special contests*

Forms, blanks, etc.
3071   General
3073   Tables
School age see LB1133; LC130
Attendance service. Absenteeism. Truancy
Cf. LC142+ Attendance
Cf. LC4801+ Truants, incorrigibles, etc.
3081   General works
3085   Tardiness
3087   Anecdotes, facetiae, satire, etc.
Cf. PN6231.C6 Schools (Humor)
Suspension. Expulsion
3089   General works
By region or country
United States
3089.2   General works
3089.3.A-Z   By region or state, A-Z
3089.4.A-Z   Other regions or countries, A-Z
Compulsory education see LC129+
Self-government of pupils
Including student participation and cooperation, student
councils
Cf. LB3021 Student honor
3092   General works
School city, school republic, etc.
3093   General works
3095.A-Z   Local, A-Z
School architecture and equipment. School physical facilities.
Campus planning

	School architecture and equipment. School physical facilities. Campus planning -- Continued
3201	Periodicals. Societies
3203	Congresses
3205	General works
3209	General special
3215	Pamphlets, etc.
	By region or country
	United States
3218.A1A-.A1Z	General works
3218.A5-.W	By state, A-W
3219.A-Z	Other regions or countries, A-Z
3220	School sites
3221	Architecture, and school building plans
3222	Specifications
3222.3	Access for people with disabilities. Barrier-free design
3222.5	Joint occupancy of buildings. Multiple use of buildings
3222.7	High-rise school buildings
	University and college physical facilities. Campus planning
	For individual institutions, see LD+
	For university and college architecture see NA6600+
3223	General works
	By region or country
	United States
3223.3	General works
3223.4.A-.W	By state, A-W
3223.5.A-Z	Other regions or countries, A-Z
3224	Classroom utilization
3225	Teachers' dwellings
	Dormitories. Residence halls. Student housing
3226	Periodicals. Societies
3227	General works
	By region or country
	United States
3227.5	General works
3227.6.A-Z	By region or state, A-Z
3228.A-Z	Other regions or countries, A-Z
3229	Furniture, equipment, etc.
3231	Sanitation
	Cf. TH6515.S4 Plumbing
3233	Cleaning and disinfecting
3235	Care of buildings. Janitor services, etc.
	Cf. TX339 Home economics
	Environmental technologies of school buildings. School and physical environment
	Cf. LB3401+ School hygiene
3241	General works

School architecture and equipment. School physical facilities.
    Campus planning
Environmental technologies of school buildings. School and
    physical environment -- Continued
    By region or country
      United States

3241.2	General works
3241.3.A-Z	By region or state, A-Z
3241.4.A-Z	Other regions or countries, A-Z

         Under each country:

.x	*General works*
.x2A-.x2Z	*Local, A-Z*

3241.5	Acoustics

        Cf. NA2800 Architectural acoustics

3242	Heating
3243	Lighting
3244	Ventilation. Air conditioning

      Fire prevention see TH9445.S3

3249	Vandalism
3250	Damages from disasters

    School grounds. School playgrounds
        Cf. GV421+ Playgrounds (General)

3251	General works
3253	Parking
3257	Schoolroom decoration

    School equipment, apparatus, etc.
        Cf. LB3229 Dormitories

3261	General works
3263	Exhibits
3265.A-Z	Special, A-Z
3265.B5	Blackboards
3265.C3	Carpeting
3265.C5	Charts
3265.C55	Computers
3265.C6	Copying machines
3265.D5	Desks

    Lists and catalogs of supplies, etc.

3275	General, and United States (Official)
3276.A-.W	United States. States, A-W
3277.A-Z	United States. Cities, A-Z
3278.A-Z	Other regions or countries, A-Z
3280	Directories of firms
3281	Catalogs of manufacturers, dealers, etc.

    School museums
        For educational museums see L797+

3291	General works
3295.A-Z	Special. By place, A-Z

School architecture and equipment. School physical facilities.
Campus planning -- Continued
School libraries see Z675.S3; Z718

(3300)	Collections, serials, etc.
(3302)	General works
(3304)	General special
	By country
	United States
(3307)	General works
(3308.A-.W)	States, A-W
(3309.A-Z)	Cities, A-Z
(3310.A-Z)	Other countries, A-Z
3325.A-Z	Special, A-Z
3325.A6	Art rooms
3325.A8	Auditoriums
3325.B6	Boarding schools
3325.B8	Business education
	Children with disabilities see LB3325.H3
3325.C5	Classrooms
3325.F65	Foreign language rooms
3325.G4	Geography rooms
3325.G74	Greenhouses
3325.H3	Handicapped children. Children with disabilities
3325.H6	Home economics
3325.K5	Kindergartens
	Laboratories see LB3325.S35
3325.M3	Manual training
3325.M35	Mathematics classrooms
3325.M8	Multipurpose rooms
3325.M84	Music rooms
3325.N8	Nursery schools
3325.O35	Office layout
3325.P4	Personnel service facilities
3325.P7	Primary schools
3325.S35	Science rooms. Laboratories
3325.T9	Typing rooms
	Vocational educational facilities see LC1048.F3
	School hygiene. School health services
3401	Periodicals. Societies
3403	Congresses
3405	General works
(3407)	General special
	see the specific subject
3408	Addresses, essays, lectures. Pamphlets, etc.
3409.A-Z	By region or country, A-Z
	For public documents see LB3411+
	United States

School hygiene. School health services
By region or country, A-Z
United States -- Continued

3409.U5	General works
3409.U6A-.U6W	By state, A-W
3409.U7A-.U7Z	By city, A-Z
3410	School health personnel
	Medical inspection of schools
3411	General works, and United States
3412.A-.W	United States. States, A-W
	For cities, class with the state
3413.A-Z	Other regions or countries, A-Z
3415	Health of teachers
	Diseases

Class here works on the administrative aspects of managing diseases in schools
For medical works on the prevention and control of diseases in schools see RA643+

3416	General works
3418.A-Z	Special diseases, A-Z
3418.A35	AIDS (Disease)

School safety see LB2864.5+
Physical measurements. Anthropometry
Including growth, height, and weight of school children
Cf. GN51+ Anthropology
Cf. HQ771+ Child study
Cf. LB1121+ Child study

3421	General works
	By region or country
	United States
3423.A2	General works
3423.A4-.W	States, A-W
	Class cities with the states
3425.A-Z	Other regions or countries, A-Z

Under each country:
.x	General works
.x2A-.x2Z	Local, A-Z

3427	Posture
3430	Mental hygiene. Mental health services
	Cf. RC451.4.S7 Psychopathology of students
	Cf. RJ499+ Child psychiatry
3430.5	Student assistance programs
3431	Strain and overpressure. Mental capacity
	Cf. LB1075 Fatigue
	Reproductive health concerns
3432	General works
3432.5	Birth control programs

	School hygiene. School health services
	Open-air schools
	By region or country
	United States -- Continued
3490	General works
3491.A-.W	By state, A-W
3492.A-Z	By city, A-Z
	Including individual schools
3495.A-Z	Other regions or countries, A-Z
	Hygiene in universities and colleges
	Including safety measures and accident prevention
	Cf. RC451.4.S7 College psychiatric programs
3497	General works
	By region or country
	United States
3497.3	General works
3497.5.A-Z	By region or state, A-Z
3498.A-Z	Individual institutions, A-Z
3499.A-Z	Other regions or countries, A-Z

Under each country:

.x	General works
.x2A-.x2Z	Individual institutions, A-Z

	School gardens see SB55+
	Playgrounds (Public) see GV421+
	Playgrounds (School) see LB3251+
	Special days
3525	General works, and United States
	Including state manuals
	Arbor Day see SD363+
	Bird Day see QL676
3531	Flag Day
	Cf. JC346 Flags of the United States, their symbolism, etc.
	Cf. JK1761 National holidays of the United States
3533	Hundredth Day of School
3541	State Day, etc.
3545.A-Z	Other regions or countries, A-Z
	Birthdays anniversaries, etc.
	Prefer classification with biography
	United States
(3551)	General works
(3552.A-Z)	By name of person, A-Z
	Cf. JK1761 National holidays of the United States
(3554.A-Z)	Other countries, etc., A-Z
	National educational festivals
3560	General works
	United States

	Special days
	National educational festivals
	United States -- Continued
3562	General works
3563.A-.W	By state, A-W
	America other than United States
3565.A2	General works
3565.A3-Z	Individual countries
	Other countries
	Europe
3567.A2	General works
3567.A3-Z	Individual countries
	Asia
3569.A2	General works
3569.A3-Z	Individual countries
	Africa
3571.A2	General works
3571.A3-Z	Individual countries
	Australia and New Zealand
3573.A2	General works
3573.A3-Z	Individual countries
	Pacific islands, A-Z
3575.A2	General works
3575.A3-Z	Individual countries
	School life. Student manners and customs
	Class here general works only
	Including extracurricular activities; student leadership, relationships, etc.; and student clubs
	For individual institutions, see LD+
	For individual countries see LA1+
	For preparatory school student life see LC58.7
	For student magazines and papers see LH1+
	For fraternities and sororities see LJ1+
3602	Associations, conferences, congresses, etc.
	Cf. BV970.A1+ School and college religious societies, movements, etc.
	Cf. LJ1+ Student fraternities and societies
3604	Dictionaries
3605	General works
3607	General special
	Including dormitory life, banquets, club programs, student cooperatives, ephebic oath
	For student etiquette see BJ1850+
3607.8	Time management
	Cf. LB2395.4 Management of college students' study time
3608	Recreation. Use of leisure time

	School life. Student manners and customs -- Continued
3609	Moral, religious, and physical life of students. Student conduct and behavior
	Cf. BV4376 Campus ministry
	Cf. HQ35.2 College students and sex
3610	Political activity
3611	Self-support
	Social and economic status see LC202+
3612	Student cooperatives
3613.A-Z	Other special, A-Z
3613.M3	Married students
3614	Interscholastic and international correspondence. "Pen pals"
3615	Pamphlets, etc.
3618	Class reunions
	Including arrangements for publicity, invitations, entertainment, publications, etc.
	School journalism. Student publications
	Including editing, publishing, etc.
3620	General works
	Specific types of publications
3621	Student newspapers and periodicals
	For individual publications, see LD+
3621.25	School yearbooks
	By levels in school
3621.3	Elementary school
3621.4	Junior high school
3621.5	High school
	College
	For individual publications, see LD+
3621.6	General works
3621.65	College student newspapers and periodicals
3621.67	College yearbooks
3622	Trade publications. Stock control, etc.
	College records, diaries, etc.
3623	Men's
3625	Women's
3630	School colors, insignia, etc.
	For university, college, and school heraldry (General), see CR200+ (Tables I-II, subdivisions 8-9, 4)
	For heraldry of individual institutions, see LD+
	For heraldry of student fraternities and societies, see LJ53
3633	School mascots
3635	Cheers and cheer leading
3640	Student unions. College community centers

	Special aspects of education
	Forms of education
8	General works
15	Conversation and culture
	Self-education. Self-culture
25	Periodicals
	Treatises. Essays, etc.
30	Early works through 1800
31	1801-1964
32	1965-
33	Computers in self-education and self-culture
	After-school programs. After-school education
34	General works
	By region or country
	United States
34.4	General works
34.5.A-Z	By region or state, A-Z
34.8.A-Z	Other regions or countries, A-Z
	Subarrange each by Table L19
(37-38)	Domestic education
	see LC40+
	Home schooling
40	General works
40.5.A-Z	Special topics, A-Z
40.5.C66	Computer-assisted instruction
	Including Web-based instruction
40.5.C87	Curricula
40.5.R47	Research
41	Education by tutors, governesses, etc.
	Cf. LB1031.5 Peer-tutoring of students
(43)	Visiting teachers. "Home teachers"
	For education of children and youth with diabilities by visiting teachers see LC4001+
	For visiting teachers in school social work see LB3013.5
(44-44.3)	Workshop classes
	see LC6562+
	Nonformal education
	Cf. LC1496+ Women
45	Periodicals. Societies. Serials
45.2	Congresses
45.3	General works
	By region or country
	United States
45.4	General works
45.5.A-Z	By region or state, A-Z
45.8.A-Z	Other regions or countries, A-Z
	Subarrange each by Table L19

	Forms of education -- Continued
	Alternative education. Alternative schools
46	Periodicals. Societies. Serials
46.2	Congresses
46.3	General works
	By region or country
	United States
46.4	General works
46.5.A-Z	By region or state, A-Z
46.8.A-Z	Other regions or countries, A-Z
	Subarrange each by Table L19
	International schools
	Class here works on schools with student bodies consisting
	mainly of non-citizens, such as children of embassy officials
46.9	General works
	By region or country
	United States
46.92	General works
46.93.A-Z	By region or state, A-Z
46.94.A-Z	Other regions or countries, A-Z
	Subarrange each by Table L19
	Private school education
47	General works
	By region or country
	United States
49	General works
50.A-.W	By state, A-W
	Canada
51	General works
51.2.A-Z	Provinces, A-Z
52.A-Z	Other American regions or countries, A-Z
53.A-Z	Europe, A-Z
54.A-Z	Asia, A-Z
54.3	Arab countries
55.A-Z	Africa, A-Z
	Australia
56	General works
56.3.A-Z	Local, A-Z
	New Zealand
56.6	General works
56.9.A-Z	Local, A-Z
57.A-Z	Pacific islands, A-Z
57.5	Developing countries
	Preparatory schools. Preparatory school education
	Cf. LD+ Individual institutions
58	General works
	By region or country

	Forms of education
	Private school education
	Preparatory schools. Preparatory school education
	By region or country -- Continued
	United States
58.4	General works
58.5.A-Z	By region or state, A-Z
58.6.A-Z	Other regions or countries, A-Z
	Subarrange each by Table L19
58.7	School life. Student manners and customs
58.75	Cram schools
59	Public school education
	Cf. LA1+ History of education
	Cf. LB1+ Theory and practice of education
	Preparation for examinations see LB3060.57
	Social aspects of education
	Economic aspects of education
65	General works
	By region or country
	United States
66	General works
66.5.A-Z	By region or state, A-Z
67.A-Z	Other regions or countries, A-Z
	Secondary education
67.5	General works
	By region or country
	United States
67.52	General works
67.55.A-Z	By region or state, A-Z
67.58.A-Z	Other regions or countries, A-Z
	Higher education
67.6	General works
	By region or country
	United States
67.62	General works
67.65.A-Z	By region or state, A-Z
67.68.A-Z	Other regions or countries, A-Z
	Educational sociology see LC189+
	Demographic aspects of education
68	General works
	By region or country
	United States
69	General works
69.5.A-Z	By region or state, A-Z
70.A-Z	Other regions or countries, A-Z
	Education and the state
	Including political aspects of education

LC

	Social aspects of education
	Education and the state -- Continued
71	General works
	By region or country see LC89+
71.2	Educational planning
	By region or country see LC89+
71.3	Control of curriculum
	By region or country see LC89+
	Academic freedom
	Including freedom of teaching
72	General works
	By region or country
	United States
72.2	General works
72.3.A-Z	By region or state, A-Z
72.5.A-Z	Other regions or countries, A-Z
(73-87)	Popular education
	see LC196+
	By region or country
	United States
89	General works
90.A-Z	By region or state, A-Z
	Canada
91	General works
91.2.A-Z	Provinces, A-Z
	Other American regions or countries
92.A2	Latin America (General)
92.A3-Z	By region or country, A-Z
	Europe
93.A2	General works
93.A3-Z	By region or country, A-Z
	Asia
94.A2	General works
94.A3-Z	By region or country, A-Z
94.3	Arab countries
	Africa
95.A2	General works
95.A3-Z	By region or country, A-Z
95.5.A-Z	Indian Ocean islands, A-Z
	Australia
96	General works
96.3.A-Z	Local, A-Z
	New Zealand
96.6	General works
96.9.A-Z	Local, A-Z
	Pacific islands
96.95	General works

	Social aspects of education
	Education and the state
	By region or country
	Pacific islands -- Continued
96.97.A-Z	By island or group of islands, A-Z
98	Developing countries
	Cf. LC2601+ Education in developing countries
	Public school question. Secularization. Religious instruction in the public schools
	Class here controversial works only
	For pedagogical works see LC401+
	Cf. LB3045.84 Religion in textbooks
107	General works
109	General special
111-120.4	By region or country (Table L22)
	Compulsory education
129	General works
130	Enrollment. Registration of school children. School census
131-139	By region or country (Table L23)
	Attendance. Dropouts
	Cf. LB3081+ Attendance service. Truancy
142	General works
	United States
143	General works
144.A-.W	States, A-W
145.A-Z	Other regions or countries, A-Z
	Elementary school attendance
145.4	General works
145.5	Dropouts
	By region or country
	United States
145.6	General works
145.7.A-Z	By region or state, A-Z
145.8.A-Z	Other regions or countries, A-Z
	High school attendance and enrollment
146	General works
146.5	Dropouts
	By region or country
	United States
146.6	General works
146.7.A-Z	By region or state, A-Z
146.8.A-Z	Other regions or countries, A-Z
	College attendance and enrollment
148	General works
148.13	Auditing of courses
148.15	Dropouts

Social aspects of education
Education and the state
Literacy. Illiteracy
By region or country
New Zealand -- Continued

159.9.A-Z	Local, A-Z
160.A-Z	Pacific islands, A-Z

Subarrange each by Table L19

Arctic regions

160.4	Greenland
161	Developing countries

Higher education and the state

Including political aspects of higher education

165	Congresses
171	General works

By region or country
United States

173	General works
174	National university (University of the United States)
175.A-.W	States, A-W

Canada

176	General works
176.2.A-Z	Provinces, A-Z
177.A-Z	Other American regions or countries, A-Z

Europe

177.2	General works
178.A-Z	By region or country, A-Z
179.A-Z	Asia, A-Z
179.5	Arab countries
180.A-Z	Africa, A-Z

Australia

181	General works
181.3.A-Z	States, A-Z
181.6	New Zealand
182.A-Z	Pacific islands, A-Z

Taxation of schools and colleges

Cf. LB2824+ School finance, taxation, etc.

184	General works

United States

185	General works
186.A-.W	States, A-W
187.A-Z	Individual institutions, A-Z
188.A-Z	Other regions or countries, A-Z

Educational sociology

189	Education and social philosophy

Social aspects of education
Educational sociology -- Continued
Education and society
Cf. LC1090 International education
Cf. LC1099+ Multicultural education

189.8	Periodicals. Societies. Serials
189.85	Congresses
189.9	Collected works (nonserial)
189.95	Dictionaries. Terminology
191	General works
191.2	Addresses, essays, lectures
	By region or country
	United States
191.4	General works
191.6.A-Z	By region or state, A-Z
191.8.A-Z	Other regions or countries, A-Z

Under each country:
	.x	*General works*
	.x2A-.x2Z	*By province, state, etc., A-Z*

Higher education
191.9	General works
	By region or country
	United States
191.94	General works
191.96.A-Z	By region or state, A-Z
191.98.A-Z	Other regions or countries, A-Z

Under each country:
	.x	*General works*
	.x2A-.x2Z	*By province, state, etc., A-Z*

192	Social change
192.2	Social problems
192.3	Social psychology
192.4	Socialization
192.6	Homosexuality and education
	Popular education. Critical pedagogy
196	General works
196.5.A-Z	By region or country, A-Z
197	Feminism and education
198	Social services and the schools
201	Education and heredity
	Education and native language
	Cf. LC3701+ Bilingual education
201.5	General works
	By region or country
	United States
201.6	General works
201.65.A-Z	By region or state, A-Z

	Social aspects of education
	Educational sociology
	Education and native language
	By region or country -- Continued
201.7.A-Z	Other regions or countries, A-Z
	Education and social background. Students' socio-economic status
	For education and social background of special classes of persons, including minority groups see LC1390+
202	Periodicals. Societies
202.5	Congresses
203	General works
204	General special
	By region or country
	United States
205	General works
205.5.A-Z	By region or state, A-Z
206.A-Z	Other regions or countries, A-Z
	By level
208	Preschool and elementary school students
208.4	Secondary school students
208.8	College students
	School social environment
210	General works
	By region or country
	United States
210.5	General works
210.6.A-Z	By region or state, A-Z
210.8.A-Z	Other regions or countries, A-Z
	Subarrange each by Table L19
	Education and crime see HV6166; HV8875+; HV9081; HV9285
	Discrimination in education
	For discrimination against special groups of persons, see the group, e.g. LC1401+ Women
212	General works
	By region or country
	United States
212.2	General works
212.22.A-Z	By region or state, A-Z
212.23.A-Z	By city, A-Z
212.3.A-Z	Other regions or countries, A-Z
	Subarrange each by Table L21
	Discrimination in higher education
212.4	General works
	By region or country
	United States

Social aspects of education
Educational sociology
Discrimination in education
Discrimination in higher education
By region or country
United States -- Continued
212.42   General works
212.422.A-Z   By region or state, A-Z
212.423.A-Z   By city, A-Z
212.43.A-Z   Other regions or countries, A-Z
                    Subarrange each by Table L21
Segregation in education. Racial separation
                    For segregation of specific minority or ethnic groups, see
                        the group, e.g. LC2701+, Blacks
212.5   General works
By region or country
United States
212.52   General works
212.522.A-Z   By region or state, A-Z
212.523.A-Z   By city, A-Z
212.53.A-Z   Other regions or countries, A-Z
                    Subarrange each by Table L21
212.6   De facto segregation in education
By region or country
United States
212.62   General works
212.622.A-Z   By region or state, A-Z
212.623.A-Z   By city, A-Z
212.63.A-Z   Other regions or countries, A-Z
                    Subarrange each by Table L21
212.7   Segregation in higher education
By region or country
United States
212.72   General works
212.722.A-Z   By region or state, A-Z
212.723.A-Z   By city, A-Z
212.73.A-Z   Other regions or countries, A-Z
                    Subarrange each by Table L21
Sex discrimination in education. Sexual harassment.
Homophobia
212.8   General works
By region or country
United States
212.82   General works
212.822.A-Z   By region or state, A-Z
212.823.A-Z   By city, A-Z

	Social aspects of education
	Educational sociology
	Discrimination in education
	Sex discrimination in education. Sexual harassment. Homophobia
	By region or country -- Continued
212.83.A-Z	Other regions or countries, A-Z
	Subarrange each by Table L21
	Sex discrimination in higher education. Sexual harassment. Homophobia
212.86	General works
	By region or country
	United States
212.862	General works
212.8622.A-Z	By region or state, A-Z
212.8623.A-Z	By city, A-Z
212.863.A-Z	Other regions or countries, A-Z
	Subarrange each by Table L21
	Sex differences in education
212.9	General works
	By region or country
	United States
212.92	General works
212.922.A-Z	By region or state, A-Z
212.923.A-Z	By city, A-Z
212.93.A-Z	Other regions or countries, A-Z
	Subarrange each by Table L21
213	Educational equalization. Right to education. Compensatory education
	By region or country
	United States
213.2	General works
213.22.A-Z	By region or state, A-Z
213.23.A-Z	By city, A-Z
213.3.A-Z	Other regions or countries, A-Z
	Subarrange each by Table L21
	Affirmative action programs in education
213.5	General works
	By region or country
	United States
213.52	General works
213.522.A-Z	By region or state, A-Z
213.523.A-Z	By city, A-Z
213.53.A-Z	Other regions or countries, A-Z
	Subarrange each by Table L21
	School integration
214	General works

Social aspects of education
  Educational sociology
    Educational equalization. Right to education.
      Compensatory education
     School integration -- Continued
      By region or country
       United States

214.2	General works
214.22.A-Z	By region or state, A-Z
214.23.A-Z	By city, A-Z
214.3.A-Z	Other regions or countries, A-Z

        Subarrange each by Table L21
     Special means of integration
      Magnet schools see LB2818

214.5	Transportation. Busing

      By region or country
       United States

214.52	General works
214.522.A-Z	By region or state, A-Z
214.523.A-Z	By city, A-Z
214.53.A-Z	Other regions or countries, A-Z

        Subarrange each by Table L21
Communities and schools
  Cf. LB2820 Community school administration

215	General works
216	General special

    Including the school and civilian mobilization
  Special types of communities

217	Rural
218	Village
219	Urban
220	Citizens advisory committees
220.5	Service learning

  By region or country
   United States

221	General works
221.2.A-Z	By region or state, A-Z
221.3.A-Z	By city, A-Z
221.4.A-Z	Other regions or countries, A-Z

   Subarrange each by Table L21

223	Schools as community centers

  Cf. HN41+ Community centers, social centers in
    general
  Cf. LB3640 University and college community centers
Home and school
  Cf. LB1048.5 Parent participation in the study
    environment

	Social aspects of education
	Community and the school
	Home and school -- Continued
225	General works
	By region or country
	United States
225.3	General works
225.32.A-Z	By region or state, A-Z

Under each state:

.x	*General works*
.x2A-.x2Z	*Local, A-Z*

225.33.A-Z	Other regions or countries, A-Z
	Subarrange each by Table L21
225.5	Parent-teacher conferences. Conference reporting to parents
	Parent-teacher relationships
226	General works
	By region or country
	United States
226.6	General works
226.65.A-Z	By region or state, A-Z
226.7.A-Z	Other regions or countries, A-Z
227	Teachers and community
	Parent-teacher associations. Home and school associations
230	General works
	By region or country
	United States
231	General works
232.A-.W	By state, A-W
233.A-Z	By city, A-Z
235.A-Z	Other regions or countries, A-Z
	Subarrange each by Table L21
	College-university and the community
237	General works
	By region or country
	United States
238	General works
238.2.A-Z	By region or state, A-Z
238.3.A-Z	By city, A-Z
238.4.A-Z	Other regions or countries, A-Z
	Subarrange each by Table L21
239	Place-based education
	Foundations, endowments, funds
	Cf. LB2335.95+ Higher education
241	General works
242.A-Z	International foundations, A-Z

	Moral and religious education
	Moral education. Character building
	By region or country -- Continued
	Africa
315.8	General works
316.A-Z	By region or country, A-Z
317	Australia
317.6	New Zealand
318.A-Z	Pacific Islands, A-Z
	Religion and education. Education under church control
	For religious education see BL - BX
321	Collections
331	General works
341	Addresses, essays, lectures. Pamphlets
	Christian education. Church education
	Periodicals and societies see BV1460+
	Conventions and conferences, etc. see BV1463
	General history see LA95
	Individual countries and sects see LC427+
	General works
	Early through 1870
361	American and English works
362	French works
363	German works
364	Italian works
365	Spanish works
366	Other works
	1871-
368	American and English works
369	French works
370	German works
371	Italian works
372	Spanish works
373	Other works
375	General special
377	The parochial school system
	Class here general works only
	For Catholic see LC501+
	For Protestant see LC531
378	Student life
379	Training of teachers
	Class here general works only
	For Catholic see LC501+
	For Protestant see LC531
	Pedagogy of religious instruction: The Sunday school see BV1533+
383	Church and higher education

Moral and religious education
  Religion and education. Education under church control
    Christian education. Church education
      General special -- Continued
        Religious instruction in universities and colleges see
          BV1610+
      The Bible and religious instruction in the public schools
        Class here pedagogical literature only
        For controversial works see LC107+

401	General works
	By region or country
	United States
405	General works
406.A-.W	States, A-W
407.A-Z	Cities, A-Z
	Canada
408	General works
408.2.A-Z	Provinces, A-Z
408.3.A-Z	Cities, A-Z
409.A-Z	Other American regions or countries, A-Z
410.A-Z	Europe, A-Z
411.A-Z	Asia, A-Z
411.3	Arab countries
412.A-Z	Africa, A-Z
	Australia
413	General works
413.3.A-Z	Local, A-Z
	New Zealand
413.6	General works
413.9.A-Z	Local, A-Z
414.A-Z	Pacific islands, A-Z
421	Addresses, essays, lectures. Pamphlets
	By country (Church education)
	Cf. LC377 The parochial school system
	United States
427	General works
428	Special aspects
428.5.A-Z	By region or state, A-Z
429	Canada
430.A-Z	Other American regions or countries, A-Z
431.A-Z	Europe, A-Z
432.A-Z	Asia, A-Z
432.3	Arab countries
433.A-Z	Africa, A-Z
434	Australia
434.6	New Zealand
435.A-Z	Pacific islands, A-Z

	Moral and religious education
	Religion and education. Education under church control
	Christian education. Church education -- Continued
	Coptic Church
440	General works
441.A-Z	By region or country, A-Z
	Armenian Church
442	General works
443.A-Z	By region or country, A-Z
	Orthodox Eastern Church
446	General works
	By region or country
	United States
451	General works
452.A-Z	By region or state, A-Z
453.A-Z	By city, A-Z
454.A-Z	Other regions or countries, A-Z
	Roman Catholic
461	Periodicals. Societies
465	Conferences
468	Exhibitions
471	History
473	General works
485	General special
487	Catholic colleges (General)
	For individual institutions, see LD+
	For by region or country see LC501+
	Parochial school system
	General works see LC377
	By region or country see LC501+
	Student life
	General works see LC378
	By region or country see LC501+
	Training of teachers
	General works see LC379
	By region or country see LC501+
	Religious orders
490	General works
493	Jesuits
495.A-Z	Other special, A-Z
495.D7	Dominican
495.F7	Franciscan
	By region or country
	For individual institutions, see LD+
	United States
501	General works
502.A-Z	By region or state, A-Z

	Moral and religious education
	Religion and education. Education under church control
	Christian education. Church education
	Roman Catholic
	By region or country
	United States -- Continued
503.A-Z	By city, A-Z
	Canada
504	General works
504.2.A-Z	Provinces, A-Z
504.3.A-Z	Cities, A-Z
505.A-Z	Other American regions or countries
505.A2A-.A2Z	Latin America (General)
505.A3-Z	By region or country, A-Z
	Subarrange each by Table L19
	Europe
506.A2A-.A2Z	General works
506.A3-Z	By region or country, A-Z
	Subarrange each by Table L19
507.A-Z	Asia
507.A2A-.A2Z	General works
507.A3-Z	By region or country, A-Z
	Subarrange each by Table L19
507.3	Arab countries
	Africa
508.A2A-.A2Z	General works
508.A3-Z	By region or country, A-Z
	Subarrange each by Table L19
	Australia
509	General works
509.3.A-Z	Local, A-Z
	New Zealand
509.6	General works
509.9.A-Z	Local, A-Z
510.A-Z	Pacific islands, A-Z
	Subarrange each by Table L19
	Arctic regions
510.4	Greenland
	Individual institutions
	see LD - LG
515	Jansenist (Port Royal)
	Protestant
	Periodicals and societies see BV1460+
	Conferences see BV1463
531	General works
533	General special

	Moral and religious education
	Religion and education. Education under church control
	Christian education. Church education
	Protestant
	By denomination
	Other denominations, A-Z -- Continued
586.M4	Mennonites
586.M6	Mormons
586.N4	New Jerusalem Church
	Including Swedenborgian schools
586.R3	Reformed Church
586.S48	Seventh-Day Adventists
586.U5	Unitarian
	Young Men's Christian Association see BV1130+
	By region or country
	United States
621	General works
622.A-Z	By region or state, A-Z
622.2.A-Z	By city, A-Z
	Canada
623	General works
623.2.A-Z	Provinces, A-Z
623.3.A-Z	Cities, A-Z
	Other American regions or countries
624.A1	Latin America (General)
624.A3-Z	By region or country, A-Z
	Subarrange each by Table L20
	Europe
625.A1	General works
625.A3-Z	By region or country, A-Z
	Subarrange each by Table L20
	Asia
626.A1	General works
626.A3-Z	By region or country, A-Z
	Subarrange each by Table L20
626.3	Arab countries
	Africa
627.A1	General works
627.A3-Z	By region or country, A-Z
	Subarrange each by Table L20
	Australia
628	General works
628.3.A-Z	Local, A-Z
	New Zealand
628.6	General works
628.9.A-Z	Local, A-Z

	Moral and religious education
	Religion and education. Education under church control
	Christian education. Church education
	Protestant
	By region or country -- Continued
629.A-Z	Pacific islands, A-Z
	Subarrange each by Table L20
	Individual institutions
	see LD-LG
	Jewish education
	Cf. BM70+ Study and teaching of Judaism
	Cf. LC3551+ Education of Jews
701	Periodicals. Societies
	History see LA47; LA102
715	General works
719	General special
	Special types of schools (General education)
	For religious education see BM109.A+
720	Day nursery. Kindergarten. Foundation School
721	Heder
722	Talmud Torah
723	Yeshivah ketanah. Day school
724	Yiddish school. "Folk-shule"
	By region or country
	United States
741	General works
742.A-Z	By region or state, A-Z
743.A-Z	By city, A-Z
	Canada
744	General works
744.2.A-Z	Provinces, A-Z
744.3.A-Z	Cities, A-Z
	Other American regions or countries
745.A2	Latin America (General)
745.A3-Z	By region or country, A-Z
	Subarrange each by Table L19
	Europe
746.A2	General works
746.A3-Z	By region or country, A-Z
	Subarrange each by Table L19
	Asia
747.A2	General works
747.A3-Z	By region or country, A-Z
	Subarrange each by Table L19
747.3	Arab countries
	Africa
748.A2	General works

	Moral and religious education
	Religion and education. Education under church control
	Jewish education
	By region or country
	Africa -- Continued
748.A3-Z	By region or country, A-Z
	Subarrange each by Table L19
	Australia
749	General works
749.3.A-Z	Local, A-Z
	New Zealand
749.6	General works
749.9.A-Z	Local, A-Z
750.A-Z	Pacific islands, A-Z
	Subarrange each by Table L19
	Arctic regions
750.4	Greenland
	Individual institutions. By place
771.A-Z	United States, A-Z
775.A-Z	Other, A-Z
	Islamic education
901	Periodicals
902	Societies
903	General works
904	General special
905.A-Z	Special topics, A-Z
905.T42	Teachers
	History
	Medieval see LA99
906	Modern
	By region or country
910.A-Z	Asia, A-Z
910.3	Arab countries
911.A-Z	Africa, A-Z
912.A-Z	Europe, A-Z
913.A-Z	America, A-Z
914.A-Z	Pacific islands, A-Z
915.A-Z	Individual institutions. By place, A-Z
	Buddhist education
921	Periodicals
922	Societies
923	General works
924	General special
925.A-Z	Special topics, A-Z
926	History
927.A-Z	By division, sect, etc., A-Z
927.S5	Shin

	Moral and religious education
	Religion and education. Education under church control
	Buddhist education
	By division, sect, etc., A-Z -- Continued
927.S6	Sōka Gakkai
927.T4	Tendai
	By region or country
	Prefer classification by division, sect, etc.
	Burma. Myanmar
928.A1	General works
928.A2-Z	Special institutions. By place, A-Z
	Japan
929.A1	General works
929.A2-Z	Special institutions. By place, A-Z
929.3.A-Z	Other Asian regions or countries, etc., A-Z

Under each country:

.x	General works
.x2A-.x2Z	Special institutions. By place, A-Z

929.7.A-Z	Other regions or countries, etc., A-Z

Under each country:

.x	General works
.x2A-.x2Z	Special institutions. By place, A-Z

951.A-Z	Other, A-Z
	Types of education
	General education
980	General works
	By region or country
	United States
985	General works
986.A-Z	By region or state, A-Z
988.A-Z	Other regions or countries, A-Z
	Holistic education
990	General works
	By region or country
	United States
995	General works
996.A-Z	By region or state, A-Z
998.A-Z	Other regions or countries, A-Z
	Humanistic education. Liberal education
	General works
1001	Early through 1800
	1801-1870
1003	American and English works
1004	French works
1005	German works
1006	Italian works
1007	Spanish works

	Types of education
	Humanistic education. Liberal education
	General works
	1801-1870 -- Continued
1008	Other works
	1871-
1011	American and English works
1012	French works
1013	German works
1014	Italian works
1015	Spanish works
1016	Other works
1021	General special
	Computer-assisted instruction
1022	General works
	By region or country
	United States
1022.2	General works
1022.22.A-Z	By region or state, A-Z
1022.25.A-Z	Other regions or countries, A-Z
	By region or country
	United States
1023	General works
1023.5.A-Z	By region or state, A-Z
1024.A-Z	Other regions or countries, A-Z
	Collective education
1025	General works
	By region or country
1026	United States
1027.A-Z	Other regions or countries, A-Z
	Subarrange each by Table L19
1030	Communist education
	For by country see LA1+
	Competency-based education
1031	General works
	By region or country
	United States
1032	General works
1032.5.A-Z	By region or state, A-Z
1033.5.A-Z	Other regions or countries, A-Z
	Subarrange each by Table L19
	Competency tests
1034	General works
1034.5.A-Z	Individual tests. By name, A-Z
1034.5.N38	National Competency Tests
1034.5.O45	Ohio Graduation Test
	Basic education. Basic skills education

Types of education
  Basic education. Basic skills education -- Continued

1035	General works
1035.2	Elementary and public school education
1035.4	Secondary education
1035.5	Higher education
	By region or country
	United States
1035.6	General works
1035.7.A-Z	By region or state, A-Z
1035.8.A-Z	Other regions or countries, A-Z
	Subarrange each by Table L19
	Community education
1036	General works
	By region or country
	United States
1036.5	General works
1036.6.A-Z	By region or state, A-Z
1036.8.A-Z	Other regions or countries, A-Z
	Subarrange each by Table L19
	Career education
	Cf. HF5381+ Vocational guidance
	Cf. LB1027.8+ Student occupational aspirations
1037	General works
	By region or country
	United States
1037.5	General works
1037.6.A-Z	By region or state, A-Z
1037.8.A-Z	Other regions or countries, A-Z
	Subarrange each by Table L19
	Outdoor education
	Including adventure education
1038	General works
	By region or country
	United States
1038.5	General works
1038.6.A-Z	By region or country, A-Z
1038.8.A-Z	Other regions or countries, A-Z
	Subarrange each by Table L19
	Post-compulsory education
1039	General works
	By region or country
	United States
1039.5	General works
1039.6.A-Z	By region or state, A-Z
1039.8.A-Z	Other regions or countries, A-Z
	Subarrange each by Table L19

	Types of education -- Continued
	Vocational education (General)
	Including proprietary schools
	Cf. HD5715+ Occupational training and retraining
	Cf. HF5549.5.T7 Employee training (Personnel management)
	Cf. LB1594+ Elementary schools
	Cf. LC1081+ Industrial education
	Cf. LC1500+ Education of women
	Cf. LC2780+ Vocational education of Blacks
	Cf. T61+ Technical education
1041	Periodicals. Societies
1042	Congresses
1042.5	Philosophy
1043	General works
1044	General special
	By region or country
	United States
1045	General works
1046.A-Z	By region or state, A-Z
1046.5.A-Z	By city, A-Z
1047.A-Z	Other regions or countries, A-Z
	Administration
1047.8	General works
	By region or country
	United States
1047.82	General works
1047.822.A-Z	By region or state, A-Z
1047.825.A-Z	Other regions or countries, A-Z
	Teaching personnel
1047.85	General works
1047.89	Salaries. Pensions
1048.A-Z	Special topics, A-Z
1048.A7	Audiovisual aids
1048.C57	Computers
1048.C6	Costs
	Counseling see LC1048.P47
1048.C87	Curriculum
1048.D76	Dropouts
1048.E92	Examinations
1048.F3	Facilities planning
1048.P47	Personnel service. Counseling
1048.S7	Standards
1048.T54	Time management
1048.V63	Vocational evaluation
	Cooperative education
1049	General works

	Types of education
	Cooperative education -- Continued
	By region or country
	United States
1049.5	General works
1049.6.A-Z	By region or state, A-Z
1049.8.A-Z	Other regions or countries, A-Z
	Subarrange each by Table L19
	Professional education
	Cf. LC2785 Professional education of Blacks
	General works
	Early through 1870
1051	American and English works
1052	French works
1053	German works
1054	Italian works
1055	Spanish works
1056	Other works
	1871-
1059	American and English works
1060	French works
1061	German works
1062	Italian works
1063	Spanish works
1064	Other works
	Examinations
1070	United States
1071.A-Z	Other regions or countries, A-Z
1072.A-Z	Special topics, A-Z
	Certification see LC1072.S73
1072.C56	Continuing education
1072.C6	Costs
1072.I58	Interns. Internship programs
	Internship programs see LC1072.I58
	Licensure see LC1072.S73
1072.P57	Planning
1072.P73	Practicums
1072.S73	Standards. Certification. Licensure
	Special professions and occupations
	see slasses B+ e.g. Agriculture, see S531; Commerce, see HF1101 etc.; Law, see class K

	Types of education -- Continued
	Industrial education (General)
	Cf. LB1594+ Industrial training in elementary schools
	Cf. LB1595+ Manual training in elementary schools
	Cf. LC1041+ Vocational education
	Cf. LC2780.5 Industrial education of blacks
	Cf. T61+ Technology: Study and teaching
	Cf. TT161+ Manual training (Arts and crafts)
1081	General works
	Industry and education. Business and education
1085	General works
	By region or country
	United States
1085.2	General works
1085.3.A-Z	By region or state, A-Z
1085.4.A-Z	Other regions or countries, A-Z
	High technology and education
1087	General works
	By region or country
	United States
1087.2	General works
1087.3.A-Z	By region or state, A-Z
1087.4.A-Z	Other regions or countries, A-Z
	Political education
	For education of princes see JC393
	Cf. LC4929 "Upper-class" education
1090	International
	Cf. JZ5534 Peace education
1091	Citizenship
1095	Transnational education
	Multicultural education (General)
1099	General works
	By region or country
	United States
1099.3	General works
1099.4.A-Z	By region or state, A-Z
1099.5.A-Z	Other regions or countries, A-Z
	Special education see LC3950+
1100	Transformative learning
	Inclusive education
	Including Mainstreaming in education
1200	General works
	By region or country
	United States
1201	General works
1202.A-Z	By region or state, A-Z
1203.A-Z	Other regions or countries, A-Z

LC

Education of special classes of persons
  Men. Boys
    Cf. HQ775 Care of boys
    Cf. LD7501.A+ Special schools

1390	General works. Principles and practice
1392	Early childhood education
1393	Elementary and public school education
1394	Secondary education
1394.5	Vocational education
1395	Higher education
	Special topics
	Language arts
1396.4	General works
1396.5	Reading
	By region or country
	United States
1397	General works
1397.5.A-Z	By region or state, A-Z
1398.A-Z	Other regions or countries, A-Z
	Women. Girls
1401	Periodicals. Societies
1402	Congresses
1405	Collections
1411	Handbooks
	General works. Principles and practice
	Cf. HQ1101+ Women, feminism
	Early through 1870
	General works
1421	American and English
1422	French
1423	German
1424	Italian
1425	Spanish
1426.A-Z	Other, A-Z
	Letters and lectures to schoolgirls
1441	American and English
1442	French
1443	German
1444	Italian
1446.A-Z	Other, A-Z
	Textbooks
1461	American and English
1462	French
1463	German
1464	Italian
1465	Spanish
1466.A-Z	Other, A-Z

	Education of special classes of persons
	Women. Girls
	General works. Principles and practice -- Continued
	1871-
1481	American and English
1482	French
1483	German
1484	Italian
1485	Spanish
1486.A-Z	Other, A-Z
	Nonformal education
1496	General works
	By region or country
	United States
1496.3	General works
1496.4.A-Z	By region or state, A-Z
1496.5.A-Z	Other regions or countries, A-Z
	Vocational education
1500	General works
	By region or country
	United States
1503	General works
1504.A-.W	By state, A-W
1505.A-Z	By city, A-Z
1506.A-Z	Other regions or countries, A-Z
	Higher education
1551	Periodicals. Societies. Collections
1557	Handbooks
1567	General works
	By region or country
	United States
1568	General works
1569.A-.W	By state, A-W
1570.A-Z	By city, A-Z
1571.A-Z	Other regions or countries, A-Z
1601	Coeducation
1605	Segregation
1620	Deans of women
1621	Health, hygiene, and sex in the education of women
1626	College women and marriage
1651	College women and life
	Adult education
1660	General works
	By region or country
	United States
1663	General works
1664.A-.W	By state, A-W

Education of special classes of persons
  Women. Girls
    Adult education
      By region or country
        United States -- Continued

1665.A-Z	By city, A-Z
1666.A-Z	Other regions or countries, A-Z
1671	Addresses, essays, lectures. Pamphlets
	History
1701	General
1707	General special
	Including education of women during the Middle Ages
	By region or country
1751-1759	United States (Table L15)
1761-1769	Canada (Table L15)
1771-1779	Mexico (Table L15)
	Central America
1781	General works
1786	Belize
1791	Costa Rica
1801	Guatemala
1811	Honduras
1821	Nicaragua
1831	Panama
1836	Panama Canal
1841	El Salvador
	West Indies
1851	General works
1856	Bahamas
1861	Cuba
1871	Haiti
1876	Santo Domingo. Dominican Republic
1881	Jamaica
1891	Puerto Rico
1896	Virgin Islands of the United States
1901.A-Z	British West Indies, A-Z
1907.A-Z	Dutch West Indies, A-Z
1909.A-Z	French West Indies, A-Z
	South America
1911-1917	General works (Table L15a)
1921-1929	Argentina (Table L15)
1931-1939	Bolivia (Table L15)
1941-1949	Brazil (Table L15)
1951-1959	Chile (Table L15)
1961-1969	Colombia (Table L15)
1971-1979	Ecuador (Table L15)
	Guianas

Education of special classes of persons
Women. Girls
History
By region or country
South America
Guianas -- Continued
Guyana

1981	General works
1982.A-Z	Local, A-Z
	Suriname
1983	General works
1984.A-Z	Local, A-Z
	French Guiana
1985	General works
1986.A-Z	Local, A-Z
1991-1999	Paraguay (Table L15)
2001-2009	Peru (Table L15)
2011-2019	Uruguay (Table L15)
2021-2029	Venezuela (Table L15)
	Europe
2031-2037	General works (Table L15a)
	Great Britain (Table L15a)
2041-2047	General works (Table L15a)
2051-2059	England and Wales (Table L15)
2061-2069	Scotland (Table L15)
2071-2079	Ireland (Table L15)
2081-2089	Austria-Hungary (Former). Austria (Table L15)
2091-2099	France (Table L15)
2101-2109	Germany (Table L15)
2111-2119	Greece (Table L15)
2121-2129	Italy (Table L15)
	Low Countries
2131-2137	General works (Table L15a)
2141-2149	Belgium (Table L15)
2151-2159	Netherlands (Table L15)
2161-2169	Russia. Former Soviet Union (Table L15)
	Scandinavia
2180	General works
2181-2189	Denmark (Table L15)
2191-2199	Iceland (Table L15)
2201-2209	Norway (Table L15)
2211-2219	Sweden (Table L15)
2221-2229	Spain (Table L15)
2231-2239	Portugal (Table L15)
2241-2249	Switzerland (Table L15)
	Turkey and the Balkan states
2251-2259	Turkey (Table L15)

Education of special classes of persons
Women. Girls
History
By region or country
Europe
Turkey and the Balkan states -- Continued

2261-2269	Bulgaria (Table L15)
2281-2289	Romania (Table L15)
2291-2299	Yugoslavia (Table L15)
2300.A-Z	Other European regions or countries, A-Z

Asia

2301-2307	General works (Table L15a)
2311-2319	China (Table L15)
2321-2329	India (Table L15)
2330	Pakistan
2331-2339	Indochina (Table L15a)
2341-2349	Indonesia (Table L15)
2351-2359	Philippines (Table L15)
2361-2369	Japan (Table L15)
2371-2379	Iran (Table L15)
2381-2389	Russia in Asia. Siberia (Table L15)
2391-2399	Turkey in Asia (Table L15)
2410.A-Z	Other divisions of Asia, A-Z
2410.3	Arab countries
2410.5	Islamic countries

Africa

2411-2417	General works (Table L15a)
2421-2429	Egypt (Table L15)
2431-2437	British Africa (Former) (Table L15a)
2441	French Africa (Former)
2451	German Africa (Former)
2456	Italian Africa (Former)
2461	Portuguese Africa (Former)
(2471.A-Z)	Other regions or countries, A-Z
	see LC2472+

North Africa
Including Northwest Africa

2472	General works
2472.2	Morocco
2472.3	Algeria
2472.4	Tunisia
2472.5	Libya
	Egypt see LC2421+
2472.7	Sudan

Northeast Africa

2473	General works
2473.2	Ethiopia

Education of special classes of persons
  Women. Girls
    History
      By region or country
        Africa
          Northeast Africa -- Continued

2473.3	Eritrea
2473.4	Somalia
2473.5	Djibouti. French Territory of the Afars and Issas

          Southeast Africa
            Including East Africa

2474	General works
2474.2	Kenya
2474.3	Uganda
2474.4	Rwanda
2474.5	Burundi
2474.6	Tanzania. Tanganiyika. Zanzibar
2474.7	Mozambique
2474.8	Madagascar. Malagasy Republic

          Southern Africa

2475	General works
2475.2	South Africa
2475.3	Rhodesia

            Including Zimbabwe (Southern Rhodesia)

2475.4	Zambia. Northern Rhodesia
2475.5	Lesotho. Basutoland
2475.6	Swaziland
2475.7	Botswana. Bechuanaland
2475.8	Malawi. Nyasaland
2475.9	Namibia. Southwest Africa

          Central Africa

2476	General works
2476.2	Angola
2476.3	Zaire. Congo (Democratic Republic)
2476.4	Equatorial Guinea
2476.45	Sao Tome and Principe

           French-speaking Equatorial Africa

2476.5	General works
2476.6	Gabon
2476.7	Congo (Brazzaville). Middle Congo
2476.8	Central African Republic. Ubangi-Shari
2476.85	Chad
2476.9	Cameroon

          West Africa. West Coast

2477	General works
2477.2	Sahel

           French-speaking West Africa

Education of special classes of persons
  Women. Girls
    History
      By region or country
        Africa
          West Africa. West Coast
            French-speaking West Africa -- Continued

2477.3	General works
2477.4	Benin. Dahomey
2477.45	Togo
2477.5	Niger
2477.55	Côte d'Ivoire. Ivory Coast
2477.6	Guinea
2477.65	Mali
2477.7	Burkina Faso. Upper Volta
2477.75	Senegal
2477.8	Mauritania
2477.85	Nigeria
2477.9	Ghana
2477.95	Sierra Leone
2478	Gambia
2478.2	Liberia
2478.3	Guinea-Bissau. Portuguese Guinea
2478.4	Western Sahara. Spanish Sahara
2480.A-Z	Indian Ocean islands, A-Z
2481-2489	Australia (Table L15)
2491-2499	New Zealand (Table L15)
2571.A-Z	Pacific islands, A-Z
2572	Developing countries

Individual schools and colleges
  see LD - LG
Gays. Lesbians. Bisexuals

2574	General works
2574.5	Secondary education
2574.6	Higher education

By region or country
  United States

2575	General works
2575.5.A-Z	By region or state, A-Z
2576.A-Z	Other regions or countries, A-Z

Subarrange each by Table L19
Student-athletes

2580	General works
2580.5	Secondary education
2580.6	Higher education

By region or country
  United States

	Education of special classes of persons
	Student-athletes
	By region or country
	United States -- Continued
2581	General works
2581.5.A-Z	By region or state, A-Z
2582.A-Z	Other regions or countries, A-Z
	Subarrange each by Table L19
	Education in developing countries
	Cf. LC45+ Non-formal education
	Cf. LC98 Education and state
2601	Periodicals. Collections
2603	Congresses
2605	General works
2607	General special
2608	Elementary and public school education
2609	Secondary education
2610	Higher education
2611	Teacher training
	Education of immigrants or ethnic and linguistic minorities as a whole see LC3701+
	American Indians. Indians of North America see E97+
	Asian Americans. Asians in the United States
	For specific groups of Asian Americans see LC3071+
2630	Periodicals. Societies
2631	Congresses. Conferences, etc.
2632	General works
2633	General special
2633.3	Elementary and public school education
2633.4	Secondary education
2633.6	Higher education
2635	Teacher training
	Special topics
	Language arts
2636.4	General works
2636.5	Reading
	Local
2637.A-Z	By region or state, A-Z
2638.A-Z	By city, A-Z
	Latin Americans. Hispanic Americans
	Including Latin Americans in the United States
	For specific groups of Latin Americans see LC2680+
2667	Periodicals. Societies
2668	Congresses. Conferences
2669	General works
2670	General special
2670.3	Elementary and public school education

Education of special classes of persons
Latin Americans. Hispanic Americans -- Continued

2670.4	Secondary education
2670.6	Higher education
2671	Teacher training
	Special topics
2672.4	Language arts
	Local
2674.A-Z	By region or state, A-Z
2675.A-Z	By city, A-Z
	Mexican Americans. Mexicans in the United States
2680	Periodicals. Societies
2681	Congresses. Conferences, etc.
2682	General works
2683	General special
2683.3	Elementary and public school education
2683.4	Secondary education
2683.6	Higher education
2685	Teacher training
	Special topics
	Language arts
2686.4	General works
2686.5	Reading
	Local
2687.A-Z	By region or state, A-Z
2688.A-Z	By city, A-Z
	Puerto Ricans. Puerto Ricans in the United States
2690	Periodicals. Societies
2691	Congresses. Conferences, etc.
2692	General works
2693	General special
2693.3	Elementary and public school education
2693.4	Secondary education
2693.6	Higher education
2695	Teacher training
	Language arts
	Special topics
2696.4	General works
2696.5	Reading
	Local
2697.A-Z	By region or state, A-Z
2698.A-Z	By city, A-Z

LC

Education of special classes of persons -- Continued
Blacks. African Americans
Class here works for countries in which blacks are not the
controlling element in the population
For works for countries in which blacks are the controlling
element, see LA190+ e.g. LA1565+ Uganda
Cf. LC212.5+ Segregation in education (General)

2699	General works
	By region or country
	United States
2701	Periodicals. Collections
2703	Societies
2707	Educational funds and charities
2717	General works
2725	Teachers' handbooks, etc.
2731	General special
2741	History
2751	Moral and religious education
2761	Private school education
2765	Preschool education
	Elementary and public school education
2771	General works
	Special topics, A-Z
2778.L34	Language arts
2778.R4	Reading
2779	Secondary education
	Vocational education
2780	General works
2780.2	Agricultural education
2780.4	Business education
2780.5	Technical and industrial education
2780.8	Adult education
	Higher education
2781	General works
2781.5	Faculty
2781.7	Student life
2782	Teacher training
2785	Professional education
	Local
2802.A-Z	By region or state, A-Z
2803.A-Z	By city, A-Z
	Other regions or countries
	Canada
2804	General works
2804.2.A-Z	Provinces, A-Z
2804.3.A-Z	Cities, A-Z
	Other American regions or countries

Education of special classes of persons
Blacks. African Americans
Individual institutions
United States
Higher institutions
By name or place, A-Z -- Continued

2851.D59	Dillard University, New Orleans, La. (Table L7a)
2851.E5	Elizabeth City State University, Elizabeth City, N.C. (Table L7a)
	Formerly Elizabeth City State College
2851.F47-.F56	Fisk University, Nashville, Tenn. (Table L3)
2851.F59	Florida Agricultural and Mechanical University, Tallahassee, Florida (Table L7a)
2851.F7	Fort Valley State College, Fort Valley, Ga. (Table L7a)
2851.H27-.H36	Hampton University, Hampton, Va. (Table L3)
	Formerly Hampton Institute
2851.H77-.H86	Howard University, Washington, D.C. (Table L3)
2851.H89	Huston-Tillotson University, Austin, Tex. (Table L7a)
2851.K37-.K46	Kentucky State University, Frankfort, Ky. (Table L3)
2851.K5	Knoxville College, Knoxville, Tenn. (Table L7a)
	Lane College, Jackson, Tennessee see LD2935.L23
2851.L53	Lincoln University, Chester County, Pa. (Table L7a)
(2851.L55)	Lincoln University, Jefferson City, Mo. see LD3071.L79
2851.L58	Livingstone College, Salisbury, N.C. (Table L7a)
2851.L67	Louisiana. Southern University and A & M College, Baton Rouge, La. (Table L7a)
	Formerly Louisiana. Southern University and Agricultural and Mechanical College
2851.L68	Louisville Municipal College for Negroes, Louisville, Ky. (Table L7a)
2851.M36	Mary Allen College, Crockett, Tex. (Table L7a)
(2851.M57)	Mississippi Valley State University, Itta Bena, Mississippi see LD3428
2851.M72	Morehouse College, Atlanta, Ga. (Table L7a)
(2851.M8)	Morgan State University, Baltimore, Maryland see LD3541.M94
2851.M88	Morris Brown College, Atlanta, Ga. (Table L7a)
2851.N8	North Carolina Agricultural and Technical State University, Greensboro, N.C. (Table L7a)
	North Carolina Central University, Durham, North Carolina see LD3915

Education of special classes of persons
Blacks. African Americans
Individual institutions
United States
Higher institutions
By name or place, A-Z -- Continued

2851.P5	Philander Smith College, Little Rock, Ark. (Table L7a)
2851.P73	Prairie View A & M University, Prairie View, Tex. (Table L7a)
	Formerly Prairie View Agricultural and Mechanical College
2851.S226	Saint Paul's College, Lawrenceville, Va. (Table L7a)
2851.S575	Snow Hill Normal and Industrial Institute, Snow Hill, Ala. (Table L7a)
	Southern University and A & M College see LC2851.L58
2851.S685	Spelman College, Atlanta, Ga. (Table L7a)
2851.S69	Stillman College, Tuscaloosa, Ala. (Table L7a)
	Formerly Stillman Institute
2851.T3	Talladega College, Talladega, Ala. (Table L7a)
2851.T6	Tougaloo College, Tougaloo, Miss. (Table L7a)
2851.T77-.T86	Tuskegee University (Table L3)
	Formerly Tuskegee Normal and Industrial Institute, then Tuskegee Institute
2851.V5	Virginia State University, Petersburg, Va. (Table L7a)
2851.V7	Virginia Union University, Richmond, Va. (Table L7a)
(2851.V8)	Voorhees College, Denmark, S.C.
	see LD5701.V85
2851.W552	West Virginia. State College, Institute (Table L7a)
2851.W58	Wilberforce University, Wilberforce, Ohio (Table L7a)

Other schools

2852.A-Z	For men and boys. Coeducational. By place, A-Z
2853.A-Z	For women and girls. By place, A-Z

Other regions or countries
Other American regions or countries

2861.A-Z	Higher institutions. By name or place, A-Z

Other schools

2862.A-Z	For men and boys. Coeducational. By place, A-Z
2863.A-Z	For women and girls. By place, A-Z

Europe

2871.A-Z	Higher institutions. By name or place, A-Z

Other schools

	Education of special classes of persons
	Blacks. African Americans
	Individual institutions
	Other regions or countries
	Europe
	Other schools -- Continued
2872.A-Z	For men and boys. Coeducational. By place, A-Z
2873.A-Z	For women and girls. By place, A-Z
	Asia
2881.A-Z	Higher institutions. By name or place, A-Z
	Other schools
2882.A-Z	For men and boys. Coeducational. By place, A-Z
2883.A-Z	For women and girls. By place, A-Z
	Arab countries
2884.A-Z	Higher institutions. By name or place, A-Z
	Other schools
2885.A-Z	For men and boys. Coeducational. By place, A-Z
2886.A-Z	For women and girls. By place, A-Z
	Africa
2891.A-Z	Higher institutions. By name or place, A-Z
	Other schools
2892.A-Z	For men and boys. Coeducational. By place, A-Z
2893.A-Z	For women and girls. By place, A-Z
	Australia
2901.A-Z	Higher institutions. By name or place, A-Z
	Other schools
2902.A-Z	For men and boys. Coeducational. By place, A-Z
2903.A-Z	For women and girls. By place, A-Z
	New Zealand
2904.A-Z	Higher institutions. By name or place, A-Z
	Other schools
2905.A-Z	For men and boys. Coeducational. By place, A-Z
2906.A-Z	For women and girls. By place, A-Z
	Pacific islands
2911.A-Z	Higher institutions. By name or place, A-Z
	Other schools
2912.A-Z	For men and boys. Coeducational. By place, A-Z
2913.A-Z	For women and girls. By place, A-Z
	Asians
	For history of ancient Asian education see LA31+
	For general works on Asian Americans and Asians in the United States see LC2630+
3001	Collections
3015	General works
	Chinese
3051	Periodicals. Societies. Serials
3057	General works

	Education of special classes of persons
	Asians
	Chinese -- Continued
3059	General special
3065	Elementary
3067	Higher
	By region or country
	United States
3071	General works
3073.A-.W	States, A-W
3075.A-Z	Cities, A-Z
	Canada
3079	General works
3080.A-Z	Provinces, A-Z
3080.5.A-Z	Cities, A-Z
3081.A-Z	Other American regions or countries, A-Z
	Europe
3084	General works
3085.A-Z	By region or country, A-Z
3089.A-Z	Other regions or countries, A-Z
	Individual institutions
3091.A-Z	United States. By city, A-Z
3093.A-Z	Other countries. By country and city, A-Z
	Assign two Cutter numbers, the first for the country, and the second for the city
	Japanese
3151	Periodicals. Societies. Serials
3157	General works
3159	General special
3165	Elementary
3167	Higher
	By region or country
	United States
3171	General works
3173.A-.W	States, A-W
3175.A-Z	Cities, A-Z
	Canada
3179	General works
3180.A-Z	Provinces, A-Z
3180.5.A-Z	Cities, A-Z
3181.A-Z	Other American regions or countries, A-Z
	Europe
3184	General works
3185.A-Z	By region or country, A-Z
3189.A-Z	Other regions or countries, A-Z
	Individual institutions
3191.A-Z	United States. By city, A-Z

	Education of special classes of persons
	Asians
	Japanese
	Individual institutions -- Continued
3193.A-Z	Other countries. By country and city, A-Z
	Assign two Cutter numbers, the first for the country, and the second for the city
3301	Filipinos
	East Indians
3451	Periodicals. Societies. Serials
3457	General works
3459	General special
3465	Elementary
3469	Higher
	By region or country
	United States
3471	General works
3473.A-.W	States, A-W
3475.A-Z	Cities, A-Z
	Canada
3479	General works
3480.A-Z	Provinces, A-Z
3480.5.A-Z	Cities, A-Z
3481.A-Z	Other American regions or countries, A-Z
	Europe
3484	General works
3485.A-Z	By region or country, A-Z
3489.A-Z	Other regions or countries, A-Z
	Individual institutions
3491.A-Z	United States. By city, A-Z
3493.A-Z	Other countries. By country and city, A-Z
	Assign two Cutter numbers, the first for the country, and the second for the city
3501.A-Z	Other Asian and Pacific groups, etc., A-Z
3501.A3	Aboriginal Australians
3501.A7	Arabs
3501.B35	Bangladeshis
3501.H34	Hakka (Chinese people)
3501.H38	Hawaiians
3501.H56	Hmong (Asian people)
3501.I54	Indochinese
3501.J3	Javanese
3501.K35	Karen
3501.K6	Koreans
3501.M26	Malaysians
3501.M3	Maori
3501.M65	Mongols

Education of special classes of persons
Asians
Other Asian and Pacific groups, etc., A-Z -- Continued

3501.P33	Pacific Islanders
3501.P36	Panjabis (South Asian people)
3501.S54	Sikhs
3501.T26	Taiwan aboriginal peoples
3501.T28	Taiwanese
3501.T32	Tamil (Indic people)
3501.T4	Thais
3501.T5	Tibetans
3501.V53	Vietnamese
3501.Y5	Yi (Chinese people)

Romanies. Gypsies

3503	General works
3511-3520.4	By region or country, A-Z (Table L22)

Lapps

3530	General works

By region or country
United States

3531	General works
3532.A-Z	By region or state, A-Z
3533.A-Z	By city, A-Z

Canada

3534	General works
3534.2.A-Z	Provinces, A-Z
3534.3.A-Z	Cities, A-Z

Other American regions or countries

3535.A2	Latin America (General)
3535.A3-Z	By region or country, A-Z
	Subarrange each by Table L19

Europe

3536.A2	General works
3536.A3-Z	By region or country, A-Z
	Subarrange each by Table L19

Asia

3537.A2	General works
3537.A3-Z	By region or country, A-Z
	Subarrange each by Table L19
3537.3	Arab countries

Africa

3538.A2	General works
3538.A3-Z	By region or country, A-Z
	Subarrange each by Table L19

Australia

3539	General works
3539.3.A-Z	Local, A-Z

	Education of special classes of persons
	Lapps
	By region or country -- Continued
	New Zealand
3539.6	General works
3539.9.A-Z	Local, A-Z
3540.A-Z	Pacific islands, A-Z
	Subarrange each by Table L19
	Arctic regions
3540.4	Greenland
	Jews
	Cf. BM70+ Study and teaching of Judaism
	Cf. LA102 History of medieval Jewish education
	Cf. LC701+ Jewish education
3551	Periodicals. Societies. Serials
3557	General works
3559	General special
3565	Elementary
3567	Higher
	By region or country
	United States
3571	General works
3573.A-.W	States, A-W
3575.A-Z	Cities, A-Z
	Canada
3579	General works
3580.A-Z	Provinces, A-Z
3580.5.A-Z	Cities, A-Z
3581.A-Z	Other American regions or countries, A-Z
	Europe
3584	General works
3585.A-Z	By region or country, A-Z
3589.A-Z	Other regions or countries, A-Z
	Individual institutions
3591.A-Z	United States. By city, A-Z
3593.A-Z	Other countries. By country and city, A-Z
	Assign two Cutter numbers, the first for the country, and the second for the city
	Racially mixed people
3601	Periodicals. Societies. Serials
3607	General works
3609	General special
3615	Elementary
3617	Higher
	By region or country
	United States
3621	General works

	Education of special classes of persons
	Racially mixed people
	By region or country
	United States -- Continued
3623.A-.W	States, A-W
3625.A-Z	Cities, A-Z
	Canada
3629	General works
3630.A-Z	Provinces, A-Z
3630.5.A-Z	Cities, A-Z
3631.A-Z	Other American regions or countries, A-Z
	Europe
3634	General works
3635.A-Z	By region or country, A-Z
3639.A-Z	Other regions or countries, A-Z
	Individual institutions
3641.A-Z	United States. By city, A-Z
3643.A-Z	Other countries. By country and city, A-Z
	Assign two Cutter numbers, the first for the country, and the second for the city
3650.A-Z	Other ethnic groups, A-Z
3650.I74	Irish Travellers
3650.S35	Scandinavian Americans
	Children of nomads
3653	General works
	By region or country
	United States
3654	General works
3654.5.A-Z	By region or state, A-Z
3655.A-Z	Other regions or countries, A-Z
	Children of refugees
3663	General works
	By region or country
	United States
3664	General works
3664.5.A-Z	By region or state, A-Z
3665.A-Z	Other regions or countries, A-Z
	Immigrants or ethnic and linguistic minorities. Bilingual schools and bilingual education
	Cf. LC201.5+ Native language and education
3701	Periodicals. Societies. Collections
3705	Congresses, conferences, etc.
3707	Encyclopedias. Dictionaries
3715	General works
3719	General special
3723	Preschool education. Nursery schools
3725	Elementary and public school education

	Education of special classes of persons
	Immigrants or ethnic and linguistic minorities. Bilingual schools and bilingual education -- Continued
3726	Secondary education
3727	Higher education
3728	Teacher training
3731-3740.4	By region or country, A-Z (Table L22)
	Children of immigrants (First generation)
3745	General works
	By region or country
	United States
3746	General works
3746.5.A-Z	By region or state, A-Z
3747.A-Z	Other regions or countries, A-Z
	Ethnic schools
	Class here general works on ethnic schools
	For works on the schools of particular ethnic groups, see LC701+, LC2667+, etc.
3800	General works
	By region or country
	United States
3802	General works
3804.A-Z	By region or state, A-Z
3806.A-Z	Other regions or countries, A-Z
	Exceptional children and youth. Special education
	Including gifted children and children with disabilities
	For works on specific groups, see the group, e.g. LC3991+ Gifted children; LC4001+ Children with disabilities; etc.
	Cf. LC1200+ Inclusive education
3950	Periodicals. Societies
3951	Collections
3955	Congresses. Conferences, etc.
3957	Encyclopedias. Dictionaries
3965	General works
3969	General special
3969.4	Secondary education
3969.45	Teacher training
3969.48	Counseling
3969.5	Computer-assisted instruction
	Special topics
3970	Art. The arts
	Language arts
3973	General works
3973.5	Reading
3976	Vocational education
	By region or country
	United States

	Education of special classes of persons
	Exceptional children and youth. Special education
	By region or country
	United States -- Continued
3981	General works
3982.A-Z	By region or state, A-Z
3983.A-Z	By city, A-Z
	Canada
3984	General works
3984.2.A-Z	Provinces, A-Z
3984.3.A-Z	Cities, A-Z
	Other American regions or countries
3985.A2	Latin America (General)
3985.A3-Z	By region or country, A-Z
	Subarrange each by Table L19
	Europe
3986.A2	General works
3986.A3-Z	By region or country, A-Z
	Subarrange each by Table L19
	Asia
3987.A2	General works
3987.A3-Z	By region or country, A-Z
	Subarrange each by Table L19
3987.3	Arab countries
	Africa
3988.A2	General works
3988.A3-Z	By region or country, A-Z
	Subarrange each by Table L19
	Australia
3989	General works
3989.3.A-Z	Local, A-Z
	New Zealand
3989.6	General works
3989.9.A-Z	Local, A-Z
3990.A-Z	Pacific islands, A-Z
	Subarrange each by Table L19
	Arctic regions
3990.4	Greenland
	Gifted children and youth
3991	Periodicals. Societies
3992	Congresses, conferences, etc.
3993	General works
3993.2	General special
3993.218	Preschool education
3993.22	Elementary and public school education
3993.23	Secondary education
3993.25	Teacher training

Education of special classes of persons
Exceptional children and youth. Special education
Gifted children and youth -- Continued
Special topics

3993.265	Art. The arts
3993.27	Language arts
3993.3	Literature
3993.5	Reading
	By region or country
	United States
3993.9	General works
3994.A-Z	By region or state, A-Z
3995.A-Z	By city, A-Z
	Canada
3995.3	General works
3995.4.A-Z	Provinces, A-Z
3995.5.A-Z	Cities, A-Z
	Other American countries
3996.A1	Latin American (General)
3996.A3-Z	By region or country, A-Z
	Europe
3997.A1	General works
3997.A3-Z	By region or country, A-Z
	Asia
3998.A1	General works
3998.A3-Z	By region or country, A-Z
3998.3	Arab countries
	Africa
3999.A1	General works
3999.A3-Z	By region or country, A-Z
3999.4	Australia
3999.7	New Zealand
4000.A-Z	Pacific islands, A-Z
	Children and youth with disabilities
	For transportation see LB2864.2
	Cf. HV873+ Children's homes, etc.
4001-4043	General (Table L24 modified)
	Special topics
4026	Games. Crafts
	Cf. GV183.6 Recreation
	Cf. GV445 Physical training
	Children and youth with social disabilities. The destitute
	(Orphans, outcasts, paupers, etc.). Ragged schools
	Cf. HV873+ Children's homes, etc.
	Cf. HV959+ Orphanages
	Cf. LC4822+ Adults with social disabilities
4051	Periodicals. Societies

Education of special classes of persons
Exceptional children and youth. Special education
Children and youth with disabilities
Children and youth with social disabilities. The destitute
(Orphans, outcasts, paupers, etc.). Ragged schools --
Continued

4055	Congresses
4065	General works
4069	General special
4069.2	Early childhood education
4069.3	Elementary and public school education
4069.4	Secondary education
4069.6	Higher education
4069.8	Teacher training
	Special topics
4075	Art. The arts
4078	Drama
	Language arts
4085	General works
4086	Reading
4087	Mathematics
4088	Social science
4091-4100.4	By region or country (Table L22)
	Mentally ill children and youth
4165	General works
4169	General special
	By region or country
	United States
4181	General works
4182.A-.W	States, A-W
4184.A-Z	Other regions or countries, A-Z
4201-4243	Children and youth with physical disabilities (Table L24)
	Cf. LC4819+ Adults with physical disabilities
	Deaf-blind see HV1597.2
	Blind see HV1617.2+
	Deaf see HV2416.2+
	Chronically ill children and youth
	Cf. LB3401+ School hygiene
4545	General works
4549	General special
	By region or country
	United States
4561	General works
4562.A-.W	States, A-W
4564.A-Z	Other regions or countries, A-Z
	Brain-damaged children and youth
	Including cerebral palsied children and youth

	Education of special classes of persons
	Exceptional children and youth. Special education
	Children and youth with disabilities
	Brain-damaged children and youth -- Continued
4580	General works
4584	General special
	By region or country
	United States
4596	General works
4597.A-.W	States, A-W
4599.A-Z	Other regions or countries, A-Z
	Children and youth with mental disabilities
	Cf. LB1091 Educational psychology
	Cf. LC4815+ Adults with mental disabilities
	Periodicals. Collections
	see LC4001
4601	General works
4602	General special
4602.5	Preschool education
4603.3	Elementary and public school education
4604	Secondary education
4605	Audiovisual aids
	Special topics
4606	Arts. The arts (General)
4611	Games and exercises
4612	Geography
4613	Health education
	Language arts
4616	General works
4620	Reading
4621	Mathematics
4621.5	Natural history
4621.7	Social sciences
4622	Vocational education
4625	Teacher training
	By region or country
	United States
4631	General works
4632.A-Z	By region or state, A-Z
4633.A-Z	By city, A-Z
	Canada
4634	General works
4634.2.A-Z	Provinces, A-Z
4634.3.A-Z	Cities, A-Z
	Other American regions or countries
4635.A2	Latin America (General)

	Education of special classes of persons
	Exceptional children and youth. Special education
	Children and youth with disabilities
	Children and youth with mental disabilities
	By region or country
	Other American regions or countries -- Continued
4635.A3-Z	By region or country, A-Z
	Subarrange each by Table L19
	Europe
4636.A2	General works
4636.A3-Z	By region or country, A-Z
	Subarrange each by Table L19
	Asia
4637.A2	General works
4637.A3-Z	By region or country, A-Z
	Subarrange each by Table L19
4637.3	Arab countries
	Africa
4638.A2	General works
4638.A3-Z	By region or country, A-Z
	Subarrange each by Table L19
	Australia
4639	General works
4639.3.A-Z	Local, A-Z
	New Zealand
4639.6	General works
4639.9.A-Z	Local, A-Z
4640.A-Z	Pacific islands, A-Z
	Subarrange each by Table L19
	Arctic regions
4640.4	Greenland
4661	Slow learning children and youth
	Cf. LC4818+ Slow learning adults
	By region or country
	United States
4691	General works
4692.A-Z	By region or state, A-Z
4693.A-Z	By city, A-Z
	Canada
4694	General works
4694.2.A-Z	Provinces, A-Z
4694.3.A-Z	Cities, A-Z
	Other American regions or countries
4695.A2	Latin America (General)
4695.A3-Z	By region or country, A-Z
	Subarrange each by Table L19
	Europe

Education of special classes of persons
Exceptional children and youth. Special education
Children and youth with disabilities
Slow learning children and youth
By region or country
Europe -- Continued

4696.A2	General works
4696.A3-Z	By region or country, A-Z
	Subarrange each by Table L19

Asia

4697.A2	General works
4697.A3-Z	By region or country, A-Z
	Subarrange each by Table L19
4697.3	Arab countries

Africa

4698.A2	General works
4698.A3-Z	By region or country, A-Z
	Subarrange each by Table L19

Australia

4699	General works
4699.3.A-Z	Local, A-Z

New Zealand

4699.6	General works
4699.9.A-Z	Local, A-Z
4700.A-Z	Pacific islands, A-Z
	Subarrange each by Table L19

Arctic regions

4700.4	Greenland

Learning disabled children and youth
Cf. LC4818+ Learning disabled adults

4704	General works
4704.5	General special
4704.6	Directories
4704.73	Elementary and public school education
4704.74	Secondary education
(4704.75)	Higher education
	see LC4818.38
4704.8	Teacher training
4704.82	Computer-assisted instruction
	Special topics
4704.825	Art. The arts
4704.83	History
	Language arts
4704.85	General works
4704.87	Reading

By region or country
United States

Education of special classes of persons
Exceptional children and youth. Special education
Learning disabled children and youth
By region or country
United States -- Continued

4705	General works
4705.5.A-Z	By region or state, A-Z
4706.A-Z	Other regions or countries, A-Z
	Subarrange each by Table L19

Dyslexic children and youth

4708	General works
4708.5	General special
4708.6	Directories
4708.8	Teacher training
	Special topics
4708.85	Language arts
	By region or country
	United States
4709	General works
4709.5.A-Z	By region or state, A-Z
4710.A-Z	Other regions or countries, A-Z
	Subarrange each by Table L19

Hyperactive children and youth

4711.5	General special
4711.6	Directories
4711.8	Teacher training
	By region or country
	United States
4712	General works
4712.5.A-Z	By region or state, A-Z
4713.A-Z	Other regions or countries, A-Z
	Subarrange each by Table L19

Attention-deficit-disordered children and youth

4713.2	General works
	By region or country
	United States
4713.4	General works
4713.42.A-Z	By region or state, A-Z
4713.5.A-Z	Other regions or countries, A-Z
	Subarrange each by Table L19
4714	Aphasic children and youth
4714.5	General special
4714.6	Directories
4714.8	Teacher training
	By region or country
	United States
4715	General works

Education of special classes of persons
Exceptional children and youth. Special education
Learning disabled children and youth
Aphasic children and youth
By region or country
United States -- Continued

4715.5.A-Z	By region or state, A-Z
4716.A-Z	Other regions or countries, A-Z
	Subarrange each by Table L19
4717	Autistic children and youth
4717.5	General special
4717.6	Directories
4717.8	Teacher training
	Special topics
4717.85	Language arts
	By region or country
	United States
4718	General works
4718.5.A-Z	By region or state, A-Z
4719.A-Z	Other regions or countries, A-Z
	Subarrange each by Table L19
	Problem children and youth
	Including truants, delinquents, incorrigibles
	Cf. HV9081 Reformatories
	Cf. LB3081+ Truancy
4801	General works
4801.5	General special
4801.6	Directories
4801.8	Teacher training
	By region or country
	United States
4802	General works
4802.5.A-Z	By region or state, A-Z
4803.A-Z	Other regions or countries, A-Z
	Subarrange each by Table L19
	Children of prenatal substance abuse
4806	General works
	By region or country
	United States
4806.4	General works
4806.42.A-Z	By region or state, A-Z
4806.5.A-Z	Other regions or countries, A-Z
	Subarrange each by Table L19
	Adults with disabilities
	Cf. LC4001+ Children with disabilities
4812	General works
4812.6	Directories

	Education of special classes of persons
	Adults with disabilities -- Continued
4812.8	Teacher training
	By region or country
	United States
4813	General works
4813.5.A-Z	By region or state, A-Z
4814.A-Z	Other regions or countries, A-Z
	Subarrange each by Table L19
	Adults with mental disabilities
	Cf. LC4600.2+ Children with mental disabilities
4815	General works
	By region or country
	United States
4815.4	General works
4815.42.A-Z	By region or state, A-Z
4815.5.A-Z	Other regions or countries, A-Z
	Learning disabled adults. Slow learning adults
	Cf. LC4661 Slow learning children
	Cf. LC4704+ Learning disabled children
4818	General works
4818.3	Directories
4818.38	Higher education
4818.4	Teacher training
	By region or country
	United States
4818.5	General works
4818.52.A-Z	By region or state, A-Z
4818.53.A-Z	Other regions or countries, A-Z
	Subarrange each by Table L19
	Adults with physical disabilities
	Cf. LC4201+ Children with physical disabilities
4819	General works
4819.5	General special
4819.6	Directories
4819.8	Teacher training
	By region or country
	United States
4820	General works
4820.5.A-Z	By region or state, A-Z
4821.A-Z	Other regions or countries, A-Z
	Subarrange each by Table L19
	Adults with social disabilities
	Cf. LC4051+ Children with social disabilities
4822	General works
4822.5	General special
4822.6	Directories

	Education of special classes of persons
	Adults with disabilities
	Adults with social disabilities -- Continued
4822.8	Teacher training
	By region or country
	United States
4823	General works
4823.5.A-Z	By region or state, A-Z
4824.A-Z	Other regions or countries, A-Z
	Subarrange each by Table L19
	Mentally ill adults
4825	General works
4825.6	Directories
4825.8	Teacher training
	By region or country
	United States
4826	General works
4826.5.A-Z	By region or state, A-Z
4827.A-Z	Other regions or countries, A-Z
	Subarrange each by Table L19
4929	Upper classes
	Including royalty, aristocracy, nobility
	Cf. JC393 Education of princes
4931	General special
	By region or country
	United States
4941	General works
4942.A-Z	By region or state, A-Z
4942.2.A-Z	By city, A-Z
	Canada
4943	General works
4943.2.A-Z	Provinces, A-Z
4943.3.A-Z	Cities, A-Z
	Other American regions or countries
4944.A1	Latin America (General)
4944.A3-Z	By region or country, A-Z
	Subarrange each by Table L20
	Europe
4945.A1	General works
4945.A3-Z	By region or country, A-Z
	Subarrange each by Table L20
	Asia
4946.A1	General works
4946.A3-Z	By region or country, A-Z
	Subarrange each by Table L20
4946.3	Arab countries
	Africa

	Education of special classes of persons
	Upper classes
	By region or country
	Africa -- Continued
4947.A1	General works
4947.A3-Z	By region or country, A-Z
	Subarrange each by Table L20
	Australia
4948	General works
4948.3.A-Z	Local, A-Z
	New Zealand
4948.6	General works
4948.9.A-Z	Local, A-Z
4949.A-Z	Pacific islands, A-Z
	Subarrange each by Table L20
	Middle class
4959	General works
4961	General special
	By region or country
	United States
4971	General works
4972.A-Z	By region or state, A-Z
4972.2.A-Z	By city, A-Z
	Canada
4973	General works
4973.2.A-Z	Provinces, A-Z
4973.3.A-Z	Cities, A-Z
	Other American regions or countries
4974.A1	Latin America (General)
4974.A3-Z	By region or country, A-Z
	Subarrange each by Table L20
	Europe
4975.A1	General works
4975.A3-Z	By region or country, A-Z
	Subarrange each by Table L20
	Asia
4976.A1	General works
4976.A3-Z	By region or country, A-Z
	Subarrange each by Table L20
4976.3	Arab countries
	Africa
4977.A1	General works
4977.A3-Z	By region or country, A-Z
	Subarrange each by Table L20
	Australia
4978	General works
4978.3.A-Z	Local, A-Z

	Education of special classes of persons
	Middle classes
	By region or country -- Continued
	New Zealand
4978.6	General works
4978.9.A-Z	Local, A-Z
4979.A-Z	Pacific islands, A-Z
	Subarrange each by Table L20
	Working classes
	Cf. LC1041+ Vocational education
	Cf. LC1081+ Industrial education
	Cf. LC5201+ Education extension
	Cf. T61+ Technical education
	Cf. TT161+ Manual training
5001	Periodicals. Societies
5015	General works
	By region or country
	United States
5051	General works
5052.A-Z	By region or state, A-Z
5053.A-Z	By city, A-Z
	Canada
5054	General works
5054.2.A-Z	Provinces, A-Z
5054.3.A-Z	Cities, A-Z
	Other American regions or countries
5055.A2	Latin America (General)
5055.A3-Z	By region or country, A-Z
	Subarrange each by Table L19
	Europe
5056.A2	General works
5056.A3-Z	By region or country, A-Z
	Subarrange each by Table L19
	Asia
5057.A2	General works
5057.A3-Z	By region or country, A-Z
	Subarrange each by Table L19
5057.3	Arab countries
	Africa
5058.A2	General works
5058.A3-Z	By region or country, A-Z
	Subarrange each by Table L19
	Australia
5059	General works
5059.3.A-Z	Local, A-Z
	New Zealand
5059.6	General works

Education of special classes of persons
Working classes
By region or country
New Zealand -- Continued

5059.9.A-Z	Local, A-Z
5060.A-Z	Pacific islands, A-Z
	Subarrange each by Table L19
	Arctic regions
5060.4	Greenland

Other special classes
Nonmilitary education in armies see U715+
Nonnaval education in navies see V697+
Children of military personnel. Military post schools. "Army" schools

5081	General works, and United States
5082.A-Z	Other regions or countries, A-Z
	By country maintaining the schools

Children of merchant mariners

5091	General, and United States
5092.A-Z	Other regions or countries, A-Z
	By country maintaining the schools

Children of missionaries

5096	General works
5096.2	General special
5096.25	Teacher training
	By region or country
	United States
5097	General works
5097.5.A-Z	By region or state, A-Z
5098.A-Z	Other regions or countries, A-Z
5101-5143	Children in large cities. Urban education (Table L24)
	Cf. HT206+ Urban sociology
5144	Children of homeless parents. Homeless students
	By region or country
	United States
5144.2	General works
5144.22.A-Z	By region or state, A-Z
5144.3.A-Z	Other regions or countries, A-Z
	Children in suburban areas. Suburban education. Suburban schools
5145	General works
	By region or country
	United States
5145.2	General works
5145.22.A-Z	By region or state, A-Z
5145.3.A-Z	Other regions or countries, A-Z

Education of special classes of persons

Other special classes -- Continued

Children in rural areas. Rural education. Rural schools

Cf. HT453 Rural sociology

5146	General works
	By region or country
	United States
5146.5	General works
5147.A-Z	By region or state, A-Z
5148.A-Z	Other regions or countries, A-Z
	Subarrange each by Table L19
	Children of migrant workers
	Cf. KF4217.M5 United States law
5151	General works, and United States
5152.A-Z	By United States region or state, A-Z
5153.A-Z	Other regions or countries, A-Z
	Subarrange each by Table L19
	Children of illegal aliens
5155	General works
	By region or country
	United States
5155.2	General works
5155.22.A-Z	By region or state, A-Z
5155.3.A-Z	Other regions or countries, A-Z
	Children of foreign workers
5156	General works
5156.2	General special
5156.25	Teacher training
	By region or country
	United States
5157	General works
5157.5.A-Z	By region or state, A-Z
5158.A-Z	Other regions or countries, A-Z
	Adopted children
5158.5	General works
5158.7.A-Z	By region or country, A-Z
	Children of divorced or single parents
5159	General works
5159.3.A-Z	By region or country, A-Z
	Children of gay parents
5159.5	General works
5159.7.A-Z	By region or country, A-Z
	Children of entertainers
5160	General works
	By region or country
	United States
5160.2	General works

Education of special classes of persons

Other special classes

Children of entertainers

By region or country

United States -- Continued

5160.22.A-Z	By region or state, A-Z
5160.3.A-Z	Other regions or countries, A-Z

Fundamental education

5161	General works

By region or country

United States

5162	General works
5162.5.A-Z	By region or state, A-Z
5163.A-Z	Other regions or countries, A-Z

Subarrange each by Table L19

Education extension. Adult education. Continuing education

Including continuation schools

For general theoretical works on the principles of training
see LB1025+

Cf. LC148.5 Attendance and enrollment

Cf. LC1072.C56 Professional education

Cf. LC1660+ Women

Cf. LC4812+ Adults with disabilities

5201	Periodicals. Societies
5209	Congresses. Conferences
5211	Encyclopedias. Dictionaries
5215	General works
5219	General special

Including curriculum, methods of instruction

5225.A-Z	Special topics, A-Z
5225.A34	Administration
5225.A36	Adult education and state

For individual regions or countries see LC5251+

5225.A75	Assessment. Testing
5225.A83	Audiovisual aids
5225.C68	Counseling
5225.D38	Data processing
5225.E25	Economic aspects
5225.E57	Employment training

Class here works on occupational training provided by a
general education system

5225.F56	Finance
5225.L42	Learning
5225.M37	Marketing
5225.M45	Mentoring
5225.M47	Methods of study
5225.M67	Moral and ethical aspects

	Education extension. Adult education. Continuing education
	Special topics, A-Z -- Continued
5225.P78	Psychological aspects
5225.R4	Reading
5225.R47	Research
5225.S64	Socialization, social aspects, etc.
5225.T4	Teacher training
5225.T44	Television
	Testing see LC5225.A75
	By region or country
	United States
5251	General works
5252.A-Z	By region or state, A-Z
5253.A-Z	By city, A-Z
	Canada
5254	General works
5254.2.A-Z	Provinces, A-Z
5254.3.A-Z	Cities, A-Z
	Other American regions or countries
	Latin America
5255.A2	General works
5255.A3-Z	By region or country, A-Z
	Subarrange each by Table L19
	Europe
5256.A2	General works
5256.A3-Z	By region or country, A-Z
	Subarrange each by Table L19
	Asia
5257.A2	General works
5257.A3-Z	By region or country, A-Z
	Subarrange each by Table L19
5257.3	Arab countries
	Africa
5258.A2	General works
5258.A3-Z	By region or country, A-Z
	Subarrange each by Table L19
	Australia
5259	General works
5259.3.A-Z	Local, A-Z
	New Zealand
5259.6	General works
5259.9.A-Z	Local, A-Z
5260.A-Z	Pacific islands, A-Z
	Subarrange each by Table L19
	Arctic regions
5260.4	Greenland
5261	Developing countries

Education extension. Adult education. Continuing education --
Continued

5301-5401	Individual institutions (Table L25)
	Including mechanics' institutes
	Older adult education. Elderhostels
5451	Periodicals. Societies. Serials
5457	General works
	By region or country
	United States
5471	General works
5473.A-.W	States, A-W
5475.A-Z	Cities, A-Z
	Canada
5479	General works
5480.A-Z	Provinces, A-Z
5480.5.A-Z	Cities, A-Z
5481.A-Z	Other American regions or countries, A-Z
	Europe
5484	General works
5485.A-Z	By region or country, A-Z
5489.A-Z	Other regions or countries, A-Z
	Individual institutions
5491.A-Z	United States. By city, A-Z
5493.A-Z	Other countries. By country and city, A-Z
	Assign two Cutter numbers, the first for the country, and the second for the city
	Evening schools
5501	Collections
5515	General works
5519	General special
5551-5560.4	By region or country (Table L22)
	Vacation schools. Summer schools
	For summer sessions in teacher training see LB1740
	Cf. BV1585 Religious education
	Cf. LB1047 School excursions, fieldwork, etc.
5701	Collections
5715	General works
5719	General special
5751-5760.4	By region or country (Table L22)
	Traveling schools
5765	American
5767	Other
	Vacation colonies
5770	General works
5771.A-Z	By region or country, A-Z
	Distance education
5800	General works

	Education extension. Adult education. Continuing education
	Distance education -- Continued
5803.A-Z	Special topics, A-Z
5803.A33	Accreditation
5803.C65	Computer-assisted instruction
5803.L43	Learning
5803.M37	Marketing
5803.P5	Planning
5803.R46	Research
5803.V53	Videoconferencing
	By region or country
	United States
5805	General works
5806.A-Z	By region or state, A-Z
5808.A-Z	Other regions or countries, A-Z
	Subarrange each by Table L19
	Correspondence schools
5900	Periodicals. Societies
5901	Collections
5915	General works
5919	General special
5951-5959	By region or country (Table L23)
6001-6101	Individual schools (Table L25)
	University extension
6201	Periodicals. Societies
6206	Conferences
6211	Handbooks and manuals
6219	General works
6223	General special
	Including curriculum
6231	History and description
6251-6260.4	By region or country (Table L22)
6301-6401	Individual institutions (Table L25)
	Lyceums and lecture courses. Forums
	Including discussion groups, debates
	For technique of debating see PN4177+
	Cf. LC6601+ Group reading and discussion
6501	Periodicals. Societies
6503	Collections
6509	Directories
	Cf. PN4007 Public speaking
6515	General works
6519	General special
	Including the planning, organization and conduct of meetings, discussion groups, etc., their psychological and rhetorical aspects, leadership, etc.
6551-6560.4	By region or country (Table L22)

	Education extension. Adult education. Continuing education -- Continued
	Workshop classes
6562	General works
	By region or country
6562.2	United States
6562.3.A-Z	Other regions or countries, A-Z
	Radio and television extension courses. Instruction by radio and television
	Cf. LB1044.5+ Theory of radio in education
6571	Periodicals. Societies. Collections
6571.5	Congresses, conferences, etc.
6573	General works
6574	General special
(6575.A-Z)	By subject, A-Z
	Prefer classification in classes B - Z
	By region or country
	United States
6576	General works
6577.A-.W	States, A-W
6578.A-Z	Cities, A-Z
6579.A-Z	Schools or companies, A-Z
	e.g.
6579.M55	Mind Extension University
6579.S3	School of the Air of the Americas
6581.A-Z	Other regions or countries, A-Z

	Under each country:	
.x	*General works*	
.x2A-.x2Z	*Local, A-Z*	
.x3A-.x3Z	*Schools or companies, A-Z*	

	Reading circles and correspondence clubs
	Including group reading
	For Catholic see LC461+
	For Chautauqua literary circles see LC6501+
6601	Collections
6615	General works
6619	General special
6631	Juvenile reading circles, etc.
6635	Storytelling
	Cf. LB1042 Principle and practice of teaching
6651-6660.4	By region or country (Table L22)
6681	Education and travel
	Cf. LC5765+ Traveling schools
6691	Traveling educational exhibits
	e. g. Routzahn, Traveling publicity campaign
	Cf. L797+ Routzahn, Traveling publicity campaign

LD

Individual institutions
    United States
        For individual institutions limited to education in a special field,
            see the topic, e.g. KF292.A+ U.S. law schools, R747.A+ U.S.
            medical schools, S537.A+ U.S. agricultural colleges, T171.A+
            U.S. technical schools
        For teachers colleges see LB1805+
        For colleges for Blacks see LC2851+
        For summer schools see LC5751+
        For University extension see LC6301+
        For Junior colleges see LD6501.A+
        For colleges for women see LD7020+

13	Abilene Christian College, Abilene, Texas (Table L7)
15.A37-.A46	Abingdon College, Abingdon, Illinois (Table L3)
20-39.5	Adelphi University, Garden City, New York (Table L4)
	Formerly Adelphi College
51.A37-.A46	Adrian College, Adrian, Michigan (Table L3)
51.A57-.A66	Akron, Ohio. University (Table L3)
56	Alabama A&M University, Normal, Ala. (Table L7)
58	Alabama College, Montevallo, Alabama (Table L7)
59	Alabama State University, Montgomery, Alabama (Table L7)
59.13	Alabama. University of Alabama at Birmingham (Table L7)
	Earlier name: University of Alabama in Birmingham
59.3	Alabama. University of Alabama in Huntsville (Table L7)
59.5	Alabama. University of North Alabama, Florence, Alabama (Table L7)
	Alabama. University of West Alabama, Livingston, Alabama see LD3071.L967+
60-79.5	Alabama. University of Alabama (Table L4)
	Located in Tuscaloosa, Ala.
91.A4	Alaska. University of Alaska (System) Fairbanks, Alaska (Table L7a)
91.A487-.A496	Alaska. University. Fairbanks, Alaska (Table L3)
91.A497-.A506	Alatennga College, Bridgeport, Alabama (Table L3)
	Albany College, Albany, Oregon see LD3061.L4565
91.A55	Albany State College, Albany, Georgia (Table L7a)
91.A57-.A66	Albany University, Albany, New York (Table L3)
	In 1873 merged to form Union University, LD5481.U567+
91.A67-.A76	Albert Lea College, Albert Lea, Minnesota (Table L3)
100-119.5	Albion College, Albion, Michigan (Table L4)
131.A227-.A236	Albright College, Reading, Pennsylvania (Table L3)
131.A24	Alcorn State University, Lorman, Miss. (Table L7a)
131.A25	Alderson-Broaddus College, Philippi, West Virginia (Table L7a)
131.A27-.A36	Alfred University, Alfred, New York (Table L3)
131.A3657-.A3666	Algona College, Algona, Iowa (Table L3)
131.A37-.A46	All Hallows' College, Salt Lake City, Utah (Table L3)

United States -- Continued

131.A47-.A56	Allegheny College, Meadville, Pennsylvania (Table L3)
131.A5627-.A5636	Alliance College, Alliance, Ohio (Table L3)
131.A565	Alliance College, Cambridge Springs, Pennsylvania (Table L7a)
131.A57-.A66	Alma College, Alma, Michigan (Table L3)
131.A6627-.A6636	Alma White College, Zarephath, New Jersey (Table L3)
	Almira College, Greenville, Illinois see LD2051.G37+
131.A67-.A76	American International College, Springfield, Massachusetts (Table L3)
131.A767	American International Open University, St. Louis, Missouri (Table L7a)
131.A77-.A86	American University, Washington, D.C. (Table L3)
140-159.5	Amherst College, Amherst, Massachusetts (Table L4)
171.A27-.A36	Amity College, College Springs, Iowa (Table L3)
171.A37-.A46	Andalusia College, Andalusia, Pennsylvania (Table L3)
171.A465	Anderson University, Anderson, Ind. (Table L7a)
171.A467	Andrews University, Berrien Springs, Michigan (Table L7a)
	Formerly Battle Creek College, Battle Creek, Mich.; Emmanuel Missionary College, Berrien Springs, Mich.
171.A468	Angelo State University, San Angelo, Texas (Table L7a)
	Formerly San Angelo, Texas College; Angelo State College
171.A4685	Anna Maria College, Paxton, Massachusetts (Table L7a)
171.A47-.A56	Antioch College, Yellow Springs, Ohio (Table L3)
173	Appalachian State University, Boone, North Carolina (Table L7)
	Formerly Appalachian State Teachers' College (N.C.)
177	Aquinas College, Grand Rapids, Michigan (Table L7)
178	Arizona State College, Flagstaff, Arizona (Table L7)
	Formerly Arizona State Teachers College, Flagstaff
179	Arizona. State University, Tempe (Table L7)
180-199.5	Arizona. University. Tucson, Arizona (Table L4)
211.A67-.A76	Arkadelphia Methodist College, Arkadelphia, Arkansas (Table L3)
220-239.5	Arkansas. University. Fayetteville, Arkansas (Table L4)
	Arkansas. University. Pine Bluff, Ark. see LC2851.A75
239.7	Arkansas. University of Central Arkansas, Conway, Arkansas (Table L7)
(241)	Arkansas College, Batesville, Arkansas see LD3141.L98
	Arkansas Cumberland College, Clarksville, Arkansas see LD4445.O47+
243	Arkansas Polytechnic College, Russellville, Arkansas (Table L7)
245	Arkansas State University (Table L7)
	Formerly Arkansas. State College, Jonesboro, Arkansas

LD

United States -- Continued

246	Armand Hammer United World College of the American West, Montezuma, N.M. (Table L7)
247	Armstrong College, Berkeley, California (Table L7)
247.5	Armstrong State University, Savannah, Georgia (Table L7) Formerly Armstrong Atlantic State University; joined University System of Georgia in 1959
258	Asbury College, Wilmore, Kentucky (Table L7)
261.A47-.A56	Ashland College, Ashland, Ohio (Table L3)
261.A565	Associated Colleges of Upper New York (ACUNY) (Table L7a)
261.A567	Assumption College, Worcester, Massachusetts (Table L7a)
261.A568	Athens, Alabama. College (Table L7a)
261.A6	Atkinson Literary and Industrial College, Madisonville, Kentucky (Table L7a)
	Atlanta University, Atlanta, Ga. see LC2851.A82
(271.A6)	Atlantic Christian College, Wilson, North Carolina see LD331.B6695
271.A661	Atlantic Union College, South Lancaster, Massachusetts (Table L7a)
271.A6615	Auburn University, Auburn, Alabama (Table L7a)
271.A6617	Auburn University, Montgomery, Alabama (Table L7a)
271.A662	Augsburg College, Minneapolis, Minnesota (Table L7a) Including college, seminary, etc.
271.A6625	Augusta College, Augusta, Georgia (Table L7a)
271.A663	Augusta College, Augusta, Kentucky (Table L7a)
271.A6636	Augustana College, Canton, South Dakota (Table L7a)
271.A664	Augustana College, Sioux Falls, South Dakota (Table L7a)
271.A665	Augustana College, Rockville, Illinois (Table L7a) Formerly Augustana College and Theological Seminary, Rock Island, Illinois
	Augustinian College, Villanova, Pennsylvania see LD5651.V27+
271.A667	Aurora College, Aurora, Illinois (Table L7a)
271.A67	Austin College, Effingham, Illinois (Table L7a)
271.A7	Austin College, Sherman, Texas (Table L7a)
271.A77	Austin Peay State University (Table L7a)
271.A82	Avalon College, Trenton, Missouri (Table L7a)
271.A83	Averette College, Danville, Virginia (Table L7a)
271.A98	Azusa Pacific University, Azusa, California (Table L7a)
285	Bacone College, Muscogee, Oklahoma (Table L7) Formerly Indian University, the Bacone Indian University
300-319.5	Baker University, Baldwin, Kansas (Table L4)
331.B27-.B36	Baldwin-Wallace College, Berea, Ohio (Table L3)
331.B47-.B56	Baltimore City College, Baltimore, Maryland (Table L3)
331.B5637-.B5646	Baltimore College, Baltimore, Maryland (Table L3) Merged into University of Maryland

United States -- Continued

331.B565	Barclay College, Haviland, Kan. (Table L7a)
331.B5667-.B5676	Bard College, Annandale-on-Hudson, New York (Table L3)
331.B57-.B66	Bardstown Coeducational College, Bardstown, Kentucky (Table L3)
331.B668	Barrington College, Barrington, Rhode Island (Table L7a)
331.B669	Barry University, Miami, Florida (Table L7a)
331.B6695	Barton College, Wilson, North Carolina (Table L7a)
	Formerly Atlantic Christian College
331.B67-.B76	Bates College, Lewiston, Maine (Table L3)
	Battle Creek College, Battle Creek, Michigan see LD171.A467
340-359.5	Baylor University, Waco, Texas (Table L4)
371.B4	Beauvoir College, Wilmar, Arkansas (Table L7a)
371.B5	Bellarmine College, Louisville, Kentucky (Table L7a)
371.B6	Bellevue College, Bellevue, Nebraska (Table L7a)
371.B6647-.B6656	Belmont Abbey College, Belmont, North Carolina (Table L3)
371.B6659	Belmont College, Nashville, Tennessee (Table L7a)
371.B67-.B76	Beloit College, Beloit, Wisconsin (Table L3)
372	Bemidji State University, Bemidji, Minnesota (Table L7)
	Formerly Bemidji State College
	Benedict College, Columbia, S.C. see LC2851.B3
373	Benedictine College, Atkinson, Kansas (Table L7)
375	Bennington, Vermont School of the Arts (Table L7)
376	Bentley College, Waltham, Mass. (Table L7)
380-399.5	Berea College, Berea, Kentucky (Table L4)
401	Berkshire Christian College, Lenox, Massachusetts (Table L7)
405.B17-.B26	Berry Schools, Mount Berry, Georgia (Table L3)
411.B67-.B76	Bethany College, Bethany, West Virginia (Table L3)
420-439.5	Bethany College, Lindsborg, Kansas (Table L4)
443	Bethany-Peniel College, Bethany, Oklahoma (Table L7)
451.B27-.B36	Bethel College, McKenzie, Tennessee (Table L3)
451.B417-.B426	Bethel College, Newton, Kansas (Table L3)
451.B47-.B56	Bethel College, Russellville, Kentucky (Table L3)
451.B562	Bethel College, St. Paul, Minnesota (Table L7a)
451.B564	Biola College, La Mirada, California (Table L7a)
451.B5657-.B5666	Birmingham-Southern College, Birmingham, Alabama (Table L3)
451.B5673	Black Hawk College, Moline, Illinois (Table L7a)
451.B5677-.B5686	Black Mountain College, Black Mountain, North Carolina (Table L3)
451.B57-.B66	Blackburn College, Carlinville, Illinois (Table L3)
451.B747-.B756	Blinn Memorial College, Brenham, Texas (Table L3)
455.B57-.B66	Bloomington College, Bloomington, Tennessee (Table L3)
455.B686	Bloomsburg State College, Bloomsburg, Pennsylvania (Table L7a)

United States -- Continued

455.B8	Bluefield State College, Bluefield, W.Va. (Table L7a)
456.B57-.B66	Bluffton College, Bluffton, Ohio (Table L3)
456.B9	Bob Jones College, College Point, Florida (Table L7a)
457	Bob Jones University, Greenville, South Carolina (Table L7)
458	Boise State University, Boise, Idaho (Table L7)
	1932-1965, Boise Junior College; 1965-1969, Boise College;
	1969-1974, Boise State College
460-479.5	Boston College, Boston, Massachusetts (Table L4)
500-519.5	Boston University, Boston, Massachusetts (Table L4)
540-559.5	Bowdoin College, Brunswick Maine (Table L4)
571.B227-.B236	Bowdon College, Bowdon, Georgia (Table L3)
571.B245	Bowie State College, Bowie, Maryland (Table L7a)
571.B25	Bradford College, Bradford, Massachusetts (Table L7a)
571.B27-.B36	Bradley University, Peoria, Illinois (Table L3)
571.B37-.B46	Brandeis University, Waltham, Massachusetts (Table L3)
571.B463	Brewton-Parker College, Mount Vernon, Ga. (Table L7a)
	1904-1912, Union Baptist Institute; 1912-1948, Brewton-Parker
	Institute; 1948-1957, Brewton-Parker Junior College
571.B467	Bridgeport, Connecticut. University (Table L7a)
571.B47-.B56	Bridgewater College, Bridgewater, Virginia (Table L3)
571.B57-.B66	Brigham Young College, Logan, Utah (Table L3)
571.B667-.B676	Brigham Young University, Provo City, Utah (Table L3)
571.B75	Brigham Young University- Hawaii Campus (Table L7a)
	Formerly Church College of Hawaii
578.B29	Bronx Community College (Table L7a)
578.B37-.B46	Brooklyn College, Brooklyn, New York (Table L3)
580-599.5	Brooklyn Institute of Arts and Sciences, Brooklyn, New York (Table L4)
620-649.5	Brown University, Providence, Rhode Island (Table L5)
649.7	Bryan College, Dayton, Tenn. (Table L7)
649.8	Bryant College, Smithfield, Rhode Island (Table L7)
649.9	Bryn Athyn College of New Church, Bryn Athyn, Pennsylvania (Table L7)
650	Bryson College, Fayetteville, Tennessee (Table L7)
661.B37-.B46	Buchanan College, Troy, Missouri (Table L3)
661.B47-.B56	Buchtel College, Akron, Ohio (Table L3)
670-689.5	Bucknell University, Lewisburg, Pennsylvania (Table L4)
701.B237-.B246	Buckner College, Witcherville, Arkansas (Table L3)
701.B27-.B36	Buena Vista College, Storm Lake, Iowa (Table L3)
701.B37-.B46	Buffalo. University. Buffalo, New York (Table L3)
	Changed in 1962 to New York (State). State University, Buffalo
701.B657-.B666	Burleson College, Greenville, Texas (Table L3)
701.B717-.B726	Burlington College, Burlington, Vermont (Table L3)
701.B737-.B746	Burritt College, Spencer, Tennessee (Table L3)
701.B77-.B86	Butler University, Indianapolis, Indiana (Table L3)
721.C317-.C326	Calhoun College, Kingston, Texas (Table L3)

United States -- Continued

721.C347-.C356	California Christian College, Los Angeles, California (Table L3)
721.C37-.C46	California College, Oakland, California (Table L3)
	In 1912, reorganized and known as Berkeley Baptist Divinity School
729.C87-.C96	California, College of. Oakland, California (Table L3)
	Merged into University of California
729.C966	California. San Fernando Valley College, Los Angeles (Table L7a)
	California. State College of Applied Arts and Sciences, Los Angeles see LD729.6.L7
729.C9845	California State College, California, Pennsylvania (Table L7a)
729.C985	California State College at Palos Verdes (Table L7a)
	California State University (System)
	Formerly California State University and Colleges
729.5	General works (Table L7)
729.6.A-Z	Individual institutions. By place, A-Z
729.6.A6	Arcata. Humboldt State University (Table L7a)
729.6.B4	Bakersfield. California State College (Table L7a)
729.6.C5	Chico. California State University (Table L7a)
729.6.D7	Dominguez Hills. California State College (Table L7a)
729.6.F7	Fresno. California State University (Table L7a)
729.6.F8	Fullerton. California State University (Table L7a)
729.6.H3	Hayward. California State University (Table L7a)
729.6.L6	Long Beach. California State University (Table L7a)
729.6.L7	Los Angeles. California State University (Table L7a)
729.6.N6	Northridge. California State University (Table L7a)
729.6.P5	Pomona. California State Polytechnic University (Table L7a)
729.6.S2	Sacramento. California State University (Table L7a)
729.6.S25	San Bernardino. California State University, San Bernardino (Table L7a)
	Formerly San Bernardino-Riverside State College; then California State College, San Bernardino
729.6.S3	San Diego State University (Table L7a)
729.6.S35	San Francisco State University (Table L7a)
729.6.S4	San Jose State University (Table L7a)
729.6.S5	San Luis Obispo. California Polytechnic State University (Table L7a)
729.6.S6	Sonoma. California State College (Table L7a)
729.6.S8	Stanislaus. California State College (Table L7a)
729.8	University of California (System), Berkeley, California (Table L7)
730-779.5	California. University. Berkeley, California (Table L6)
781.A-Z	Branches

	United States
	California. University. Berkeley, California
	Branches -- Continued
781.D3	Davis (Table L7a)
781.I7	Irvine (Table L7a)
781.L67-.L76	University at Los Angeles. University of California, Los Angeles (Table L3)
	Formerly Southern Branch at Los Angeles
781.R5	Riverside (Table L7a)
781.S2	San Diego (Table L7a)
781.S24	San Francisco (Table L7a)
781.S27-.S36	Santa Barbara College (Table L3)
781.S4	Santa Cruz (Table L7a)
785	Calvin College, Grand Rapids, Michigan (Table L7)
786	Cameron University, Lawton, Oklahoma (Table L7)
788	Campbell College, Buies Creek, North Carolina (Table L7)
791.C37-.C46	Campbell College, Holton, Kansas (Table L3)
791.C4613	Campbellsville College, Campbellsville, Kentucky (Table L7a)
791.C4617-.C4626	Campion College of the Sacred Heart, Prairie du Chien, Wisconsin (Table L3)
791.C4637-.C4646	Cane Hill College, Canehill, Arkansas (Table L3)
791.C47-.C56	Canisius College, Buffalo, New York (Table L3)
791.C57-.C66	Capital University, Columbus, Ohio (Table L3)
791.C67-.C76	Carleton College, Farmington, Missouri (Table L3)
791.C77-.C86	Carleton College, Northfield, Minnesota (Table L3)
791.C88	Carlow College, Oakland, Pittsburgh, Pennsylvania (Table L7a)
	Before 1968 named Mount Mercy College
791.C89	Carnegie-Mellon University, Pittsburgh, Pennsylvania (Table L7a)
801.C117-.C126	Carroll College, Helena, Montana (Table L3)
801.C217-.C226	Carroll College, Waukesha, Wisconsin (Table L3)
801.C247-.C256	Carson-Newman College, Jefferson City, Tennessee (Table L3)
801.C297-.C306	Carthage College, Carthage, Illinois (Table L3)
	Formerly Illinois State University, LD2341.I57
801.C347-.C356	Carthage Collegiate Institute, Carthage, Missouri (Table L3)
801.C36	Cascade College, Portland, Oregon (Table L7a)
	Case Western Reserve University, Cleveland, Ohio see LD5950+
801.C37-.C46	Catawba College, Salisbury, North Carolina (Table L3)
810-859.5	Catholic University of America, Washington, D.C. (Table L6)
860.C57-.C66	Catholic University of Oklahoma, Shawnee, Oklahoma (Table L3)
871.C247-.C256	Cedarville College, Cedarville, Ohio (Table L3)

United States -- Continued

871.C27-.C36	Centenary College of Louisiana, Shreveport, Louisiana (Table L3)
	Central ... and Centre ...
	Cutter numbers and alphabetical arrangment are based on the city where the individual institution is located
881.A47-.A56	Central Christian College, Albany, Missouri (Table L3)
881.C47-.C56	Central YMCA College, Chicago, Illinois (Table L3)
881.D37-.D46	Centre College of Kentucky, Danville, Kentucky (Table L3)
	From 1901-1918, Central University, Danville, Kentucky
881.E35	Central State University, Edmond, Oklahoma (Table L7a)
881.E45	Central Washington University, Ellensburg, Wash. (Table L7a)
	Formerly Washington State Normal School, Central Washington College of Education, Central Washington State College
881.F27-.F36	Central College, Fayette, Missouri (Table L3)
881.H77-.H86	Central College, Huntington, Indiana (Table L3)
881.M45	Central College, McPherson, Kansas (Table L7a)
881.M68	Central Michigan University, Mount Pleasant, Michigan (Table L7a)
	Formerly Central Michigan Normal School and Business Institute, Central Michigan Normal School, Central State Normal School, Central State Teachers College, Central Michigan College of Education, Central Michigan College
881.P47-.P56	Central College, Pella, Iowa (Table L3)
	Formerly Central University of Iowa
881.R37-.R46	Central University, Richmond, Kentucky (Table L3)
	In 1901 merged with Centre College, Danville, Kentucky
	Central Missouri State University, Warrensburg, Mo. see LD3429.8
881.W27-.W36	Central Wesleyan College, Warrenton, Missouri (Table L3)
881.W54	Central State University, Wilberforce, Ohio (Table L7a)
891.C4	Chaddock College, Quincy, Illinois (Table L7a)
891.C42	Chadron State College (Table L7a)
891.C44	Champlain College, Plattsburg, New York (Table L7a)
891.C466	Chapman College, Orange, California (Table L7a)
891.C5	Charles City College, Charles City, Iowa (Table L7a)
891.C57-.C66	Charleston, College of, Charleston, South Carolina (Table L3)
891.C67-.C76	Chattanooga, Tennessee. University (Table L3)
891.C78	Chestnut Hill College, Philadelphia, Pennsylvania (Table L7a)

United States -- Continued

891.C8	Cheyney University, Cheyney, Pennsylvania (Table L7a)
	1903-1913, Institute for Colored Youth at Cheyney; 1914-1933, Cheyney Training School for Teachers; 1933-1959, State Teachers College at Cheyney; 1959-1983, Cheyney State College
891.C85	Chicago. Northeastern Illinois University (Table L7a)
891.C9	Chicago State University, Chicago, Illinois (Table L7a)
	Formerly Chicago State College
900-949.5	Chicago. University. Chicago, Illinois (Table L6)
961.C27-.C36	Christian Brothers College, Memphis, Tennessee (Table L3)
961.C47-.C56	Christian Brothers College, St. Louis, Missouri (Table L3)
	Christian University, Canton, Missouri see LD1401.C7637+
961.C65	Christopher Newport University, Newport News, Virginia (Table L7a)
	Formerly Christopher Newport College
970-989.5	Cincinnati. University. Cincinnati, Ohio (Table L4)
995	Claflin College, Orangeburg, South Carolina (Table L7)
1015.C37-.C46	Claremont Colleges. Claremont University Center, California (Table L3)
	An association comprising Claremont Men's College, Harvey Mudd College, Pitzer College, Pomona College, and Scripps College
1015.C47-.C56	Claremont Men's College, Claremont, California (Table L3)
1015.C75	Clarion State College, Clarion, Pennsylvania (Table L7a)
	Clark College, Atlanta Ga. see LC2851.C7
1015.C85	Clarke College, Dubuque, Iowa (Table L7a)
1020-1039.5	Clark University, Worcester, Massachusetts (Table L4)
1061.C23	Clarksburg College, Clarksburg, Missouri (Table L7a)
	Clarksville, Arkansas. College of the Ozarks see LD4445.O47+
1061.C24	Claverack College and Hudson River Institute, Claverack, New York (Table L7a)
1061.C3	Clemson University, Clemson, South Carolina (Table L7a)
1061.C35	Cleveland State University (Table L7a)
	Clifton College, Clifton, Texas see LD5311.T57+
1061.C382	Coastal Carolina University, Conway, S.C. (Table L7a)
1061.C4	Coe College, Cedar Rapids, Iowa (Table L7a)
1061.C62	Coker College, Hartsville, South Carolina (Table L7a)
1061.C67-.C76	Colby College, Waterville, Maine (Table L3)
1061.C79	Colegio Cesar Chavez, Mount Angel, Oregon (Table L7a)
1061.C8	Colfax College, Colfax, Washington (Table L7a)
1070-1089.5	Colgate University, Hamilton, New York (Table L4)
	College of Charleston, Charleston, South Carolina see LD891.C57+
(1100-1119.5)	College of Mount Saint Vincent, Riverdale, New York, N.Y. see LD3561.M697

United States -- Continued

College of Philadelphia, Philadelphia, Pennsylvania see
LD4561.P434

College of Saint James, Breathedsville, Maryland see
LD4807.S37+

College of Saint Joseph on the Rio Grande, Albuquerque,
New Mexico see LD4813.S5

College of Saint Rose, Albany, New York see LD4834.S22

1119.7	College of San Mateo, San Mateo, California (Table L7)

College of Santa Fe, Santa Fe, New Mexico see
LD4881.S39

College of Staten Island, Staten Island, New York see
LD5171.S49

College of the Ozarks, Clarksville, Arkansas see
LD4445.O47+

College of the Sacred Heart, Denver, Colorado see
LD4785.S27+

Colleges of the Seneca, Geneva, New York see LD2250+

1120-1139.5	Colorado College, Colorado Springs, Colorado (Table L4)
1150	Colorado. State University, Fort Collins, Colorado (Table L7)
	Colorado. University of Colorado (System)
1155	General works
1160-1189.5	University of Colorado, Boulder (Table L5)
1192	University of Colorado at Denver (Table L7)
1193	University of Colorado at Denver and Health Sciences Center (Table L7)
	University of Colorado Health Sciences Center see R747.A+
1205	Columbia College, Columbia, South Carolina (Table L7)
	Columbia College, Dubuque, Iowa see LD3081.L37+
1211.C87-.C96	Columbia University, Kittanning, Pennsylvania (Table L3)
1220-1269.5	Columbia University, New York, New York (Table L6)
	Saint Stephen's College, Annandale, New York see LD331.B5667+
1271.C17-.C26	Seth Low Junior College, Brooklyn, New York (Table L3)
1271.C37-.C46	Columbia University, Portland, Oregon (Table L3)
1273	Columbus State University, Columbus, Georgia (Table L7)
	Formerly Columbus College
1276	Commonwealth College, Mena, Arkansas (Table L7)
1281.C237-.C246	Conception College, Conception, Missouri (Table L3)
1281.C272	Concord College, Athens, West Virginia (Table L7a)
1281.C297-.C306	Concordia College, Conover, North Carolina (Table L3)
1281.C30647-.C30656	Concordia College, Fort Wayne, Indiana (Table L3)
1281.C30667-.C30676	Concordia College, Moorhead, Minnesota (Table L3)
1281.C307-.C316	Concordia Teachers College, River Forest, Illinois (Table L3)

United States -- Continued

1281.C318	Concordia Teachers College, Seward, Neb. (Table L7a)
1281.C322	Connecticut College, New London, Connecticut (Table L7a)
1281.C325	Connecticut. Connecticut State University (System) (Table L7a)
1281.C327-.C336	Connecticut. University. Storrs, Connecticut (Table L3)
1281.C337-.C346	Cooper College, Moundville, Missouri (Table L3)
	Cooper College, Sterling, Kansas see LD5171.S53
1300-1319.5	Cornell College, Mount Vernon, Iowa (Table L4)
1340-1389.5	Cornell University, Ithaca, New York (Table L6)
1401.C57-.C66	Cotner College, Lincoln, Nebraska (Table L3)
1401.C697-.C706	Creal Springs College, Creal Springs, Illinois (Table L3)
1401.C747-.C756	Creighton University, Omaha, Nebraska (Table L3)
1401.C7637-.C7646	Culver-Stockton College, Canton, Missouri (Table L3)
1401.C7687-.C7696	Cumberland College, Princeton, Kentucky (Table L3)
1401.C7698	Cumberland College, Williamsburg, Kentucky (Table L7a)
1401.C77-.C86	Cumberland University, Lebanon, Tennessee (Table L3)
1405	Dakota State College, Madison, South Dakota (Table L7)
1411.D237-.D246	Dakota Wesleyan University, Mitchell, South Dakota (Table L3)
1411.D2477	Dallas Baptist University, Dallas, Texas (Table L7a)
1411.D257-.D266	Dallas College, Dallas, Oregon (Table L3)
1411.D37-.D46	Dallas, Texas. University (Table L3)
1411.D47-.D56	Dana College, Blair, Nebraska (Table L3)
1420-1449.5	Dartmouth College, Hanover, New Hampshire (Table L5)
1451	Darton College, Albany, Ga. (Table L7)
	Formerly Albany Junior College
1455	David Lipscomb College, Nashville, Tennessee (Table L7)
1461.D27-.D36	Davidson College, Davidson, North Carolina (Table L3)
1461.D37-.D46	Davis and Elkins College, Elkins, West Virginia (Table L3)
1461.D47-.D56	Dayton University, Dayton, Ohio (Table L3)
	Deer Lodge, Montana. College of Montana see LD3501.M837+
1461.D57-.D66	Defiance College, Defiance, Ohio (Table L3)
1466	Del Mar College, Corpus Christi, Texas (Table L7)
1470-1489.5	Delaware University, Newark, Delaware (Table L4)
1492.D4	Delta State College, Cleveland, Mississippi (Table L7a)
1510-1529.5	Denison University, Granville, Ohio (Table L4)
1550-1569.5	Denver. University. Denver, Colorado (Table L4)
1580-1599.5	DePaul University, Chicago, Illinois (Table L4)
1600-1629.5	DePauw University, Greencastle, Indiana (Table L5)
1641.D27-.D36	Des Moines University, Des Moines, Iowa (Table L3)
	Formerly Des Moines College
1641.D3677-.D3686	Detroit. College of the City of Detroit (Table L3)
1641.D37-.D46	Detroit. University. Detroit, Michigan (Table L3)
1643	Diablo Valley College, Pleasant Hill, California (Table L7)
1650-1669.5	Dickinson College, Carlisle, Pennsylvania (Table L4)

United States -- Continued

1671	Dickinson State University, Dickinson, North Dakota (Table L7)
1675	District of Columbia, University of the, Washington, D.C. (Table L7)
1678	Dixie University, Cookeville, Tennessee (Table L7)
1681.D47-.D56	Doane College, Crete, Nebraska (Table L3)
1686	Dordt College, Sioux Center, Iowa (Table L7)
1688	Dowling College, Oakdale, New York (Table L7)
1700-1719.5	Drake University, Des Moines, Iowa (Table L4)
1725.D47-.D56	Drew University, Madison, New Jersey (Table L3)
1725.D62	Drexel University, Philadelphia, Pennsylvania (Table L7a)
1731.D67-.D76	Drury College, Springfield, Missouri (Table L3)
1731.D7647-.D7656	Dubuque, Iowa. University (Table L3)
1732.D77-.D86	Duke University, Durham, North Carolina (Table L3)
1733.D77-.D86	Duquesne University, Pittsburgh, Pennsylvania (Table L3)
1741.E4	Earlham College, Richmond, Indiana (Table L7a)
1741.E44	East Carolina University, Greenville, North Carolina (Table L7a)
1741.E4616	East Stroudsburg State College, East Stroudsburg, Pennsylvania (Table L7a)
1741.E4618	East Texas State University, Commerce, Texas (Table L7a)
1741.E462	Eastern College, St. Davids, Pennsylvania (Table L7a) Formerly Eastern Baptist College
1741.E4627	Eastern Illinois University, Charleston, Illinois (Table L7a)
1741.E463	Eastern Kentucky University, Richmond, Kentucky (Table L7a)
1741.E464	Eastern Mennonite College, Harrisonburg, Virginia (Table L7a)
1741.E465	Eastern Michigan University, Ypsilanti, Michigan (Table L7a)
1741.E466	Eastern Montana College, Billings, Montana (Table L7a)
1741.E467	Eastern Nazarene College, Quincy, Massachusetts (Table L7a)
1741.E47-.E56	Eastern Oklahoma College, Wilburton, Oklahoma (Table L3)
1741.E57	Eastern Oregon University, La Grande, Oregon (Table L7a) Formerly Eastern Oregon State College
1741.E62	Eisenhower College, Seneca Falls, New York (Proposed) (Table L7a)
	Elizabeth City State University, Elizabeth City, N.C. see LC2851.E5
1741.E697-.E706	Elizabeth College, Charlotte, North Carolina (Table L3)
1741.E727-.E736	Elizabethtown College, Elizabethtown, Pennsylvania (Table L3)
1741.E737-.E746	Elmhurst College, Elmhurst, Illinois (Table L3)
1741.E757-.E766	Elon College, Elon College (Durham), North Carolina (Table L3)

United States -- Continued

	Emmanuel Missionary College, Berrien Springs, Michigan see LD171.A467
1751.E367-.E376	Emory and Henry College, Emory, Virginia (Table L3)
1751.E3766	Emory College, Oxford, Georgia (Table L7a)
1751.E377-.E386	Emory University, Emory University, Georgia (Table L3)
1751.E397-.E406	Emporia State University, Emporia, Kansas (Table L3) Formerly College of Emporia
1761.E457-.E466	Erskine College, Due West, South Carolina (Table L3)
1761.E47-.E56	Eureka College, Eureka, Illinois (Table L3)
1761.E57-.E66	Evansville, University of, Evansville, Indiana (Table L3) 1854-1887, Moores Hill Male and Female Collegiate Institute; 1887-1919, Moores Hill College; 1919-1967, Evansville College
1761.E68	Evergreen State College, Olympia, Washington (Table L7a)
1761.E7	Ewing College, Ewing, Illinois (Table L7a)
1765.F35	Fair View College, Traphill, North Carolina (Table L7a)
1771.F2	Fairfield, Connecticut. University (Table L7a)
1771.F25	Fairfield College, Fairfield, Nebraska (Table L7a)
1771.F26	Farley Dickinson University, Rutherford, New Jersey (Table L7a) Formerly Farleigh Dickinson College
	Fairmount College, Wichita, Kansas see LD2667
1771.F37-.F46	Fargo College, Fargo, North Dakota (Table L3)
1771.F4617-.F4626	Farmers' College, College Hill, Ohio (Table L3)
1771.F4637-.F4646	Farmington College, West Farmington, Ohio (Table L3)
1771.F4667-.F4676	Fenn College, Cleveland, Ohio (Table L3) Formerly YMCA School of Technology. Merged into Cleveland State University in September, 1965
1771.F469	Ferris State College, Big Rapids, Michigan (Table L7a)
1771.F47-.F56	Findlay College, Findlay, Ohio (Table L3)
	Fisk University, Nashville, Tennessee see LC2851.F47+
1771.F64	Flagler College, St. Augustine, Fla. (Table L7a)
	Florida Agricultural and Mechanical University, Tallahassee, Fla. see LC2851.F59
1771.F73	Florida International University, Miami, Florida (Table L7a) Member of State University System of Florida For System see LD1771.F862
1771.F77-.F86	Florida Southern College, Lakeland, Florida (Table L3) Formerly Florida Conference College, Leesburg, Florida, then Florida Seminary, Sutherland, Florida
1771.F862	Florida. State University System of Florida (Table L7a)
1771.F865	Florida Atlantic University (Table L7a)
1771.F867	Florida Gulf Coast University (Table L7a)
1771.F87-.F96	Florida State University (Table L3)
1775	University of Central Florida (Table L7)
1780-1799.5	University of Florida (Table L4)

United States
    Florida. State University System of Florida -- Continued

1799.7	University of North Florida (Table L7)
1799.8	University of South Florida (Table L7)
1800	University of West Florida (Table L7)
1811.F47-.F56	Fordham University, New York, New York (Table L3)
1816	Fort Lewis College, Durango, Colorado (Table L7)
	Fort Valley State College, Fort Valley, Ga. see LC2851.F7
1820-1839.5	Fort Worth University, Fort Worth, Texas (Table L4)
	Formerly Texas Wesleyan College (Founded 1881)
1851	Francis Marion College, Florence, South Carolina (Table L7)
1861.F37-.F46	Franklin College, Franklin, Indiana (Table L3)
1861.F47-.F56	Franklin College, New Athens, Ohio (Table L3)
1871.F17-.F26	Franklin and Marshall College, Lancaster, Pennsylvania (Table L3)
1871.F285	Franklin Pierce College, Rindge, New Hampshire (Table L7a)
1871.F357-.F366	Frederick College, Frederick, Maryland (Table L3)
1871.F377-.F386	Fredericksburg College, Fredericksburg, Virginia (Table L3)
1871.F47-.F56	Friends' University, Wichita, Kansas (Table L3)
1871.F62	Frostburg State College, Frostburg, Maryland (Table L7a)
1871.F67-.F76	Furman University, Greenville, South Carolina (Table L3)
1891.G247-.G256	Gainesville College, Gainesville, Georgia (Table L3)
	Gallaudet University see HV2561.A+
1891.G267-.G276	Gardner-Webb University, Boiling Springs, North Carolina (Table L3)
1891.G297-.G306	Garrard College, Lancaster, Kentucky (Table L3)
1891.G8	Genesee Community College, Batavia, New York (Table L7a)
1891.G857-.G866	Geneva College, Beaver Falls, Pennsylvania (Table L3)
	Geneva, New York. Colleges of the Seneca see LD2250+
1893	George Fox College, Newberg, Oregon (Table L7)
	Formerly Pacific College
1894	George Mason University, Fairfax, Virginia (Table L7)
	Prior to 1972, George Mason College of Northern Virginia
1895.G27-.G36	George Pepperdine College, Los Angeles, California (Table L3)
1900-1949.5	George Washington University, Washington, D. C. (Table L6)
1961.G27-.G36	Georgetown College, Georgetown, Kentucky (Table L3)
1961.G47-.G56	Georgetown University, Washington, D.C. (Table L3)
1961.G63	Georgia. University system of Georgia (Table L7a)
1961.G67-.G76	Georgia. South Georgia College, College, Georgia (Table L3)
1961.82	Georgia College, Milledgeville, Ga. (Table L7)
	1889-1922, Georgia Normal and Industrial College; 1922-1961, Georgia State College for Women; 1961-1967, Woman's College of Georgia
1963	Georgia Southern University, Statesboro, Georgia (Table L7)
	Formerly Georgia Southern College

United States -- Continued

1965	Georgia State University, Atlanta, Georgia (Table L7)
1970-1989.5	Georgia. University. Athens, Georgia (Table L4)
2001.G297-.G306	German College, Mount Pleasant, Iowa (Table L3)
2001.G377-.G386	German Wallace College, Berea, Ohio (Table L3)
2001.G397-.G406	Gettysburg College, Gettysburg, Pennsylvania (Table L3)
2001.G407-.G416	Gladeville College, Wise, Virginia (Table L3)
2001.G4165	Glassboro State College, Glassboro, N.J. (Table L7a)
2001.G417-.G426	Glen Rose Collegiate Institute, Glen Rose, Texas (Table L3)
2001.G43	Glenville State College, Glenville, West Virginia (Table L7a)
2001.G447-.G456	Goddard College, Plainfield, Vermont (Table L3)
2001.G47-.G56	Gonzaga College, Washington, D.C. (Table L3)
2001.G57-.G66	Gonzaga University, Spokane, Washington (Table L3)
2001.G67	Gordon College, Wenham, Massachusetts (Table L7a)
2001.G747-.G756	Goshen College, Goshen, Indiana (Table L3)
2001.G77	Goucher College, Towson, Maryland (Table L7a)
	Formerly Goucher College, Baltimore
2011.G397-.G406	Graceland College, Lamoni, Iowa (Table L3)
	Grambling College, Grambling, Louisiana see LD3091.L367
2011.G57-.G66	Grand Island College, Grand Island, Nebraska (Table L3)
2011.G67-.G76	Grand River College, Gallatin, Missouri (Table L3)
2011.G767	Grand Valley State University, Michigan (Table L7a)
2011.G77-.G86	Grand View College, Des Moines, Iowa (Table L3)
	Grant Memorial University, Athens, Tennessee see LD5305.T47+
	Grant University, Chattanooga, Tennessee see LD891.C67+
2011.92	Green Mountain College, Poultney, Vermont (Table L7)
2030	Greensboro College, Greensboro, North Carolina (Table L7)
	Merged 1948 with Davenport College
	Greenville and Tusculum College see LD5457.T67+
2051.G37-.G46	Greenville College, Greenville, Illinois (Table L3)
	Formerly Almira College
2055.G47-.G56	Grinnell College, Grinnell, Iowa (Table L3)
2057.G47-.G56	Griswold College, Davenport, Iowa (Table L3)
2060-2079.5	Grove City College, Grove City, Pennsylvania (Table L4)
2091.G37-.G46	Guilford College, Guilford College, North Carolina (Table L3)
2091.G57-.G56	Gustavus Adolphus College, St. Peter, Minnesota (Table L3)
2091.G89	Gwynedd-Mercy College, Gwynedd Valley, Pennsylvania (Table L7a)
	Formerly Gwynedd-Mercy Junior College
2101.H17-.H26	Hamilton College, Clinton, New York (Table L3)
2101.H37-.H46	Hamline University, St. Paul, Minnesota (Table L3)
2101.H57-.H66	Hampden-Sydney College, Hampden-Sydney, Virginia (Table L3)
2101.H662	Hampshire College, Amherst, Massachusetts (Table L7a)
	Hampton University, Hampton, Virginia see LC2851.H27+
2101.H6637-.H6646	Hancock College, Hancock County, Mississippi (Table L3)

United States -- Continued

2101.H77-.H86	Hanover College, Hanover, Indiana (Table L3)
2101.H8637-.H8646	Hardin-Simmons University, Abilene, Texas (Table L3)
	Formerly Abilene Baptist College, then Simmons College
2101.H8657-.H8666	Harding University, Searcy, Arkansas (Table L3)
	Formerly Harding College
2101.H87-.H96	Harperville Collegiate Institute, Harperville, Mississippi (Table L3)
2101.H962	Harpur College, Endicott, New York (Table L7a)
2101.H963	University of Hartford (Table L7a)
2101.H9637-.H9646	Hartsville College, Hartsville, Indiana (Table L3)
2101.H977-.H986	Hartwick College, Oneonta, New York (Table L3)
	Harvard University, Cambridge, Massachusetts
2110	Charter. By imprint date
2111	Constitution and government
2111.3	University statutes
	Including rules and by-laws of overseers
2111.4	Report of nomination of overseers
2111.5	Report on rights and duties of president and fellows
2111.7	By-laws and regulations
	Administration
	General. Official reports
2111.8-.85	Board of Overseers
2111.8	Visiting committees (General)
2111.85	Special committees
2111.9	Other committees
2112	President
2114	Treasurer
	Special
	Finance
2115	Endowment
2116	Appropriations and grants
2117	Bequests, donations, etc.
2119	Scholarships
2120	Policy and organization
	Catalogs
	Cf. LD2144 Alumni
2121	General
2121.5	Calendar
2122	Announcements, circulars, etc.
2123	Directory of officers and students
2124	Harvard University register
2125	Other directories
	Requirements for admission
2126	General works
2127	Entrance examinations
	Curriculum. System. Method

United States
  Harvard University, Cambridge, Massachusetts
    Curriculum. System. Method -- Continued

2129	General works
2131	Graduate work and courses
2133	Degrees and honors
2134	Miscellaneous publications
	Biography
2135	Collective
2136	Presidents
2136.3	Portraits
2137	Faculty
	Alumni
2138	Directories
2139	General histories
2141	Obituary record
2142	General special
2144	General catalogs, triennial, quinquennial, etc.
2146	Other catalogs
2147	By classes
	Individual
2148	Presidents, chronologically, by date of inauguration
	e.g., 1869 William Charles Eliot
2149.A-Z	Other, A-Z
2150	Reminiscences
	History and description
	History
2151	General
	By period
2152	Early to 1800
2153	1801-
2153.9	Comic histories, etc.
	Description
2154	Guidebooks
2155	General
2156	Pamphlets
2157	Pictorial works
2159.A-Z	Buildings, places, etc., A-Z
	Student life and customs
2160	General works
2162	Minor works
	Special
2163	History of student publications
2164	Student expenses
	Student clubs
2165	General works
2166.A-Z	Special, A-Z

United States
  Harvard University, Cambridge, Massachusetts
    Student life and customs
      Special -- Continued
        Class Day or events

2168	Freshmen
2169	Sophomore
2170	Junior
2171	Senior
	Commencement
2172	General works
	Addresses. Orations. Sermons
2173	President
2174	Orator
2175	Presidential inaugurations
2176	Other inaugurations
2177	Special days and events. Anniversaries, etc. By date
	Undergraduate publications
	Periodicals see LH1+
2180	Annuals (Harvard class album)
2181	Nonserial
2182	Calendars
	Alumni activities
2184	Graduate class publications. By date of graduation
	Including exercises
2185	Alumni associations and graduate clubs
2185.A1-.A4	General
2195.H37-.H46	Hastings College, Hastings, Nebraska (Table L3)
2200-2219.5	Haverford College, Haverford, Pennsylvania (Table L4)
2221	Hawaii. University of Hawaii (System). Honolulu (Table L7)
2222.3	Hawaii. University of Hawaii at Hilo (Table L7)
2222.35	Hawaii. University of Hawaii at Manoa (Table L7)
2222.4	Hawaii. Honolulu Community College, Honolulu (Table L7)
2222.45	Hawaii. Kapiolani Community College, Honolulu (Table L7)
2222.5	Hawaii. Kauai Community College, Lihu Kauai (Table L7)
2222.55	Hawaii. Leeward Community College, Pearl City (Table L7)
2222.6	Hawaii. Maui Community College, Kahului (Table L7)
2222.65	Hawaii. West Oahu College, Pearl City (Table L7)
2222.7	Hawaii. Windward Community College, Kaneohe (Table L7)
2231.H197-.H206	Hawthorne College, McKinney, Texas (Table L3)
	Healdsburg College, Healdsburg, California see LD4461.P37
2231.H347-.H356	Hedding College, Abingdon, Illinois (Table L3)
2231.H37-.H46	Heidelberg College, Tiffin, Ohio (Table L3)
2231.H517-.H526	Henderson College, Arkadelphia, Arkansas (Table L3)
2231.H57-.H66	Hendrix College, Conway, Arkansas (Table L3)
2231.H817-.H826	Henry College, Campbell, Texas (Table L3)
2235	Hesston, Kansas. College and Bible School (Table L7)

United States -- Continued

2241.H17-.H26	High Point College, High Point, North Carolina (Table L3)
2241.H37-.H46	Highland College, Highland, Kansas (Table L3)
2241.H477-.H486	Hillsdale College, Hillsdale, Michigan (Table L3)
2241.H52	Hillyer College, Hartford, Connecticut (Table L7a)
2241.H57-.H66	Hiram College, Hiram, Connecticut (Table L3)
2241.H747-.H756	Hiwassee College, Madisonville, Tennessee (Table L3)
2250-2269.5	Hobart and William Smith Colleges, Geneva, New York (Table L4)
	Formerly Hobart College. Colleges of the Seneca
2276	Hofstra College, Hempstead, New York (Table L7)
2281.H17-.H26	Holy Cross College, New Orleans, Louisiana (Table L3)
2281.H27-.H36	Holy Cross College, Worcester, Massachusetts (Table L3)
2281.H45	Holy Names College, Oakland, California (Table L7a)
2281.H57-.H66	Hope College, Holland, Michigan (Table L3)
2281.H727-.H736	Houghton College, Houghton, New York (Table L3)
2281.H737-.H746	Houston, Texas. University (Table L3)
2281.H767-.H776	Houston, Texas. University of Houston System (Table L3)
	Howard College, Birmingham, Alabama see LD4881.S1563
2281.H817-.H826	Howard Payne College, Brownwood, Texas (Table L3)
2281.H89	Huntingdon College, Montgomery, Alabama (Table L7a)
2291.H57-.H66	Huron College, Huron, South Dakota (Table L3)
2301.I17-.I26	Iberia College, Iberia, Ohio (Table L3)
2301.I37-.I46	Idaho. Albertson College of Idaho, Caldwell, Idaho (Table L3)
	Formerly College of Idaho
2308.I57-.I66	Idaho. State College. Pocatello, Idaho (Table L3)
2310-2329.5	Idaho. University. Moscow, Idaho (Table L4)
	Idaho. University. Southern Branch, Pocatello, Idaho see LD2308.I57+
2341.I47-.I56	Illinois College, Jacksonville, Illinois (Table L3)
2341.I565	Illinois. Northern Illinois University, DeKalb, Illinois (Table L7a)
	1895-1921, Northern Illinois State Normal School; 1921-1955, Northern Illinois State Teachers College; 1955-1957, Northern Illinois State College
2341.I57-.I66	Illinois State University, Springfield, Illinois (Table L3)
	In 1870, rechartered as Carthage College, LD801.C297+
2347	Illinois. State University, Normal, Illinois (Table L7)
	Formerly Illinois State Normal University
2350-2399.5	Illinois. University. Urbana, Illinois (Table L6)
2420-2439.5	Illinois Wesleyan University, Bloomington, Illinois (Table L4)
2443	Illinois. Western Illinois University, Macomb (Table L7)
	1899-1921, Western Illinois Normal School; 1921-1947, Western Illinois State Teachers College; 1947-1957, Western Illinois State College
2451.I47-.I56	Immaculate Conception, College of the, New Orleans, Louisiana (Table L3)

United States -- Continued

2475   Incarnate Word, University of the, San Antonio, Texas (Table L7)

      Formerly a women's college; became co-educational in 1971

   Indian University see LD285

(2481.I37-.I46)   Indiana Central College, Indianapolis, Indiana

      see LD2534

2481.I47-.I56   Indiana College, Marion, Indiana (Table L3)

2485   Indiana University of Pennsylvania, Indiana, Pennsylvania (Table L7)

      1875-1920, Indiana Normal School (Pa.); 1920-1927, State Normal School at Indiana, Pa.; 1927-1959, Indiana State Teachers College (Pa.); 1959-1965, Indiana State College (Pa.)

2489   Indiana. Ball State University, Muncie, Indiana (Table L7)

      1929-1961, Ball State Teachers College

2500-2529.5   Indiana. University. Bloomington, Indiana (Table L5)

2530.3   Indiana University at Kokomo (Table L7)

2530.4   Indiana University at South Bend (Table L7)

2530.5   Indiana University East (Table L7)

2530.6   Indiana University Northwest (Table L7)

2530.7   Indiana University Southeast (Table L7)

2530.8   Indiana University-Purdue University at Fort Wayne (Table L7)

2530.9   Indiana University-Purdue University at Indianapolis (Table L7)

2533.I47-.I56   Indiana Wesleyan University, Marion, Ind. (Table L3)

      Formerly Marion College

2534   Indianapolis, University of (1986-), Indianapolis, Indiana (Table L7)

      Formerly Indiana Central University, also known as Indiana Central College

2535.I27-.I36   Institute for Advanced Study, Princeton, New Jersey (Table L3)

2535.I47-.I56   Intermountain Union College, Helena, Montana (Table L3)

      A merger of College of Montana, Deer Lodge, Montana, and Montana Wesleyan College, Helena, Montana

2545   Iona College, New Rochelle, New York (Table L7)

   Iowa College, Grinnell, Iowa see LD2055.G47+

2547   Iowa State University, Ames, Iowa (Table L7)

2550-2579.5   Iowa. University. Iowa City, Iowa (Table L5)

2583   Iowa. University of Northern Iowa (Table L7)

2591.I27-.I36   Iowa Wesleyan University, Mount Pleasant, Iowa (Table L3)

2594   Ithaca College, Ithaca, New York (Table L7)

2596   Jackson State University, Jackson, Mississippi (Table L7)

2598   Jacksonville, Florida. University (Table L7)

United States -- Continued

2599	Jacksonville State University, Jacksonville, Alabama (Table L7)
	Formerly Jacksonville State Teachers College
2600	James Madison University, Harrisonburg, Virginia (Table L7)
2601.J247-.J256	James Milliken University, Decatur, Illinois (Table L3)
2601.J257-.J266	Jamestown, College, Jamestown, North Dakota (Table L3)
2601.J27-.J36	Jefferson College, Canonsburg, Pennsylvania (Table L3)
2601.J37-.J46	Jefferson College, Convent, Louisiana (Table L3)
2601.J47-.J56	Jersey City, New Jersey. College of Jersey City (Table L3)
2601.J57-.J66	Jewell Lutheran College, Jewell, Iowa (Table L3)
2601.J67-.J76	John B. Stetson University, Deland, Florida (Table L3)
2601.J8	John Brown University, Siloam Springs, Arkansas (Table L7a)
2601.J87-.J96	John Carroll University, Cleveland, Ohio (Table L3)
2610-2639.5	Johns Hopkins University, Baltimore, Maryland (Table L5)
2645	Johnson C. Smith University (Table L7)
2648	Jordan College, Cedar Springs, Michigan (Table L7)
2651.J47-.J56	Jubilee College, Peoria, Illinois (Table L3)
2651.J67-.J76	Juniata College, Huntington, Pennsylvania (Table L3)
2651.K27-.K36	Kalamazoo College, Kalamazoo, Michigan (Table L3)
2651.K37-.K46	Kansas. Fort Hays State University, Hays, Kansas (Table L3)
	Formerly Fort Hays State College
2667	Kansas. Wichita State University, Wichita, Kansas (Table L7)
	Formerly University of Wichita, Municipal University of Wichita, and Fairmount College
2668	Kansas. State University of Agriculture and Applied Science, Manhattan (Table L7)
2670-2699.5	Kansas. University. Lawrence, Kansas (Table L5)
2711.K27-.K36	Kansas City University. Kansas City, Kansas (Table L3)
2715	Kansas City, Missouri. University (Table L7)
	Since 1963 one of the four campuses of Missouri. University. Kansas City, Missouri
2718	Kansas Newman College, Wichita, Kansas (Table L7)
	Kansas State College, Pittsburg see LD4561.P69
2720-2739.5	Kansas Wesleyan University, Salina, Kansas (Table L4)
2750.K42	Kean College of New Jersey, Union, New Jersey (Table L7a)
2750.K44	Keene State College, Keene, New Hampshire (Table L7a)
2755	Kennesaw College, Marietta, Georgia (Table L7)
	Formerly Kennesaw Junior College
	Kentucky State University, Frankfort, Kentucky see LC2851.K37+
	Kentucky State College, Lexington, Kentucky see LD2760+

	United States -- Continued
2760-2779.5	Kentucky. University of Kentucky, Lexington, Kentucky (Table L4)
	In 1908, Agricultural and Mechanical College of Kentucky separated from Kentucky University; from 1908-1916, State University of Kentucky
2790.K27-.K36	Kentucky University (1859-1908), Lexington, Kentucky (Table L3)
	1859-1865, moved to Lexington and merged with Transylvania University; 1908, name changed to Transylvania University
	For Transylvania University see LD5351.T67+
2791.K27-.K36	Kentucky Wesleyan College, Winchester, Kentucky (Table L3)
2791.K37-.K46	Kenyon College, Gambier, Ohio (Table L3)
2791.K4827-.K4836	Keuka College, Keuka Park, New York (Table L3)
2791.K52	Kilgore College, Kilgore, Texas (Table L7a)
2791.K537-.K546	King College, Bristol, Tennessee (Table L3)
2791.K56	King's College, Wilkes-Barre, Pennsylvania (Table L7a)
2800-2819.5	Knox College, Galesburg, Illinois (Table L4)
	Knoxville College, Knoxville, Tenn. see LC2851.K5
2860-2879.5	Lafayette College, Easton, Pennsylvania (Table L4)
2891.L17-.L26	Lafayette College, Lafayette, Alabama (Table L3)
2891.L27-.L36	La Grange College, La Grange, Missouri (Table L3)
2891.L37-.L46	La Grange Military Academy, La Grange, Alabama (Table L3)
	Formerly La Grange College
2891.L47-.L56	La Grange Synodical College, La Grange, Tennessee (Table L3)
2891.L65	LaGrange College, LaGrange, Ga. (Table L7a)
2897	Lake Erie College, Painesville, Ohio (Table L7)
2900-2929.5	Lake Forest College, Lake Forest, Illinois (Table L5)
	Formerly Lake Forest University
2931	Lakeland College, Sheboygan, Wisconsin (Table L7)
2932	Lamar University, Beaumont, Texas (Table L7)
2933	Lambuth University, Jackson, Tennessee (Table L7)
	Formerly Lambuth College
2935.L23	Lane College, Jackson, Tennessee (Table L7a)
2935.L27-.L36	Lane University, Lecompton, Kansas (Table L3)
2935.L45	Laredo State University, Laredo, Texas (Table L7a)
2935.L57-.L66	La Salle College, Philadelphia, Pennsylvania (Table L3)
2935.L85	La Sierra College, Arlington, California (Table L7a)
2937.L47-.L56	Latter Day Saints University, Salt Lake City, Utah (Table L3)
2940.L37-.L46	La Verne College, La Verne, California (Table L3)
	Formerly Lordsburg College, Lordsburg, California
2941.L37-.L46	Lawrence College, Appleton, Wisconsin (Table L3)
2951.L227-.L236	Leander Clark College, Toledo, Iowa (Table L3)
2951.L247-.L256	Lebanon University, Lebanon, Ohio (Table L3)

United States -- Continued

2951.L257-.L266	Lebanon Valley College, Annville, Pennsylvania (Table L3)
2955	Lee College, Baytown, Texas (Table L7)
2958.L37-.L46	Le Grand Christian College, Le Grand, Iowa (Table L3)
2960-2979.5	Lehigh University, Bethlehem, Pennsylvania (Table L4)
3000-3049.5	Leland Stanford Junior University, Stanford University, California (Table L6)
	Le Mars, Iowa. Western Union College see LD6031.W37+
3061.L347-.L356	Lenoir Rhyne College, Hickory, North Carolina (Table L3)
3061.L447-.L456	Lenox College, Hopkinton, Iowa (Table L3)
3061.L4563	LeTourneau University, Longview, Tx. (Table L7a)
3061.L4565	Lewis and Clark College, Portland, Oregon (Table L7a)
	Formerly Albany College
3061.L4566	Lewis-Clark State College, Lewiston, Idaho (Table L7a)
3061.L4567	Lewis University, Lockport, Illinois (Table L7a)
3061.L457-.L466	Lewis Institute, Chicago, Illinois (Table L3)
3061.L477-.L486	Liberal University, Silverton, Oregon (Table L3)
3071.L247-.L256	Liberty College, Glasgow, Kentucky (Table L3)
3071.L33	Liberty University, Lynchburg, Virginia (Table L7a)
	Formerly Lynchburg Baptist College, 1971-1976; Liberty Baptist College, 1976-1984
3071.L47-.L56	Lima College, Lima, Ohio (Table L3)
3071.L58	Limestone College, Gaffney, S.C. (Table L7a)
3071.L647-.L656	Lincoln College, Lincoln, Illinois (Table L3)
3071.L67-.L76	Lincoln Memorial University, Harrogate, Tennessee (Table L3)
	Lincoln University, Chester Co., Pa. see LC2851.L53
3071.L79	Lincoln University, Jefferson City, Missouri (Table L7a)
3071.L917-.L926	Lineville College, Lineville, Alabama (Table L3)
3071.L957-.L966	Linfield College, McMinnville, Oregon (Table L3)
3071.L9665	Little Rock University, Little Rock, Arkansas (Table L7a)
3071.L967-.L976	Livingston University, Livingston, Alabama (Table L3)
	Name changed in 1995 to University of West Alabama
	Livingstone College, Salisbury, N.C. see LC2851.L58
3071.L995	Loma Linda University, Loma Linda, California (Table L7a)
3081.L347-.L356	Lombard College, Galesburg, Illinois (Table L3)
3081.L358	Lone Mountain College, San Francisco, California (Table L7a)
	Formerly San Francisco College for Women
3081.L36	Long Island University, Brooklyn, New York (Table L7a)
3081.L365	Longwood College, Farmville, Virginia (Table L7a)
3081.L37-.L46	Loras College, Dubuque, Iowa (Table L3)
	Formerly St. Joseph's College, Dubuque College, Columbia College
	Lordsburg College, Lordsburg, California see LD2940.L37+
3081.L53	Loretto Heights College, Denver, Colorado (Table L7a)

United States -- Continued

Los Angeles. University of Southern California see
    LD5101.S27+

3091.L27-.L36	Louisiana College, Pineville, Louisiana (Table L3)
3091.L365	Louisiana. Francis T. Nicholls State College, Thibodaux (Table L7a)
3091.L367	Louisiana. Grambling College, Grambling (Table L7a)
3091.L368	Louisiana. Northwestern State College of Louisiana, Natchitoches (Table L7a)
3091.L37-.L46	Louisiana. Louisiana Tech University, Ruston, Louisiana (Table L3)

Formerly Louisiana Polytechnic Institute

3091.L47-.L56	Louisiana. Southeastern Louisiana University, Hammond, Louisiana (Table L3)

Formerly Louisiana. Southeastern Louisiana College

3091.L57-.L66	Louisiana. University of Southwestern Louisiana, Lafayette, Louisiana (Table L3)

Formerly Southwestern Louisiana Institute of Liberal and
    Technical Training

3098	Louisiana. State University. Alexandria, Louisiana (Table L7)
3100-3119.5	Louisiana. State University. Baton Rouge, Louisiana (Table L4)
3120.L58	Louisiana. University of New Orleans (Table L7a)

Louisiana Tech University, Ruston, Louisiana see
    LD3091.L37+

3131.L37-.L46	Louisville, Kentucky. University (Table L3)

Louisville Municipal College for Negroes, Louisville, Ky. see
    LC2851.L68

(3131.L52)	Lowell State College, Lowell, Massachusetts

see LD3234.M32

3131.L57-.L66	Loyola College, Baltimore, Maryland (Table L3)
3131.L67-.L76	Loyola University, Chicago, Illinois (Table L3)
3131.L763	Loyola Marymount University, Los Angeles, Calif. (Table L7a)

Formerly Loyola University

3141.L7657-.L7666	Loyola University, New Orleans, Louisiana (Table L3)
3141.L77-.L86	Luther College, Decorah, Iowa (Table L3)
3141.L865	Lycoming College, Williamsport, Pennsylvania (Table L7a)
3141.L87-.L96	Lynchburg College, Lynchburg, Virginia (Table L3)
3141.L98	Lyon College, Batesville, Arkansas (Table L7a)

Formerly Arkansas College

3141.M217-.M226	Macalester College, St. Paul, Minnesota (Table L3)
3141.M237-.M246	McCune College, Louisiana, Missouri (Table L3)

McDaniel College see LD5941.W57+

3141.M257-.M266	McGee College, College Mound, Missouri (Table L3)
3141.M27-.M36	McKendree College, Lebanon, Illinois (Table L3)
3141.M38	Mackinac College, Mackinac Island, Michigan (Table L7a)

United States -- Continued

3141.M4	McKinley-Roosevelt, Inc., Chicago, Illinois (Table L7a)
3141.M47-.M56	McLean College, Hopkinsville, Kentucky (Table L3)
3141.M562	McLemoresville Collegiate Institute, McLemoresville, Tennessee (Table L7a)
	McMinnville College, McMinnville, Oregon see LD3071.L957+
3141.M5635	McMurry College, Abilene, Texas (Table L7a)
3141.M564	McNeese State University, Lake Charles, Louisiana (Table L7a)
3141.M565	McPherson College, McPherson, Kansas (Table L7a)
3141.M566	Madison College, Madison College, Tennessee (Table L7a)
3141.M567	Madison College, Sharon, Mississippi (Table L7a)
3141.M568	Madison College, Spring Creek, Tennessee (Table L7a)
3141.M57-.M66	Madison College, Uniontown, Pennsylvania (Table L3)
3150-3169.5	Maine. University. Orono, Maine (Table L4)
3172	Maine, University of, at Farmington (Table L7)
3181.M27-.M36	Maine Wesleyan Seminary, Kent's Hill, Maine (Table L3)
3181.M43	Malone College, Canton, Ohio (Table L7a)
3181.M47-.M56	Manchester College, North Manchester, Indiana (Table L3)
3200-3219.5	Manhattan College, New York, New York (Table L4)
3221	Manhattanville College, Purchase, New York (Table L7)
	Mankato State University see LD3375
3225	Mansfield State College, Mansfield, Pennsylvania (Table L7)
3231.M37-.M46	Marietta College, Marietta, Ohio (Table L3)
(3231.M4897-.M4906)	Marion College, Marion, Indiana see LD2533.I47+
3231.M4927-.M4936	Marion College, Marion County, Missouri (Table L3)
3231.M517-.M526	Marist College, Atlanta, Georgia (Table L3)
3231.M537-.M546	Marquette College, Milwaukee, Wisconsin (Table L3)
3231.M557-.M566	Mars Hill College, Mars Hill, North Carolina (Table L3)
3231.M627-.M636	Marshall College, Huntington, West Virginia (Table L3)
3231.M647-.M656	Marshall College, Mercersburg, Pennsylvania (Table L3)
3231.M667-.M676	Marvin College, Clinton, Kentucky (Table L3)
3231.M678	Mary Hardin-Baylor, University of, Belton, Texas (Table L7a)
3231.M68	Mary Washington College, Fredericksburg, Virginia (Table L7a)
3231.M685	Marygrove College, Detroit, Michigan (Table L7a)
3231.M695	Maryland. University of Maryland (System), Adelphi, Maryland (Table L7a)
3231.M6954	Maryland. University of Maryland, Baltimore (County) (Table L7a)
3231.M697-.M706	Maryland. University of Maryland, College Park (Table L3)
3231.M837	Marylhurst University, Marylhurst, Oregon (Table L7a)
3231.M847-.M856	Maryville College, Maryville, Tennessee (Table L3)
3231.M858	Marywood College, Scranton, Pennsylvania (Table L7a)

	United States -- Continued
3231.M87	Massachusetts. Massachusetts State College (System) (Table L7a)
3232	Massachusetts. State College, Boston (Table L7)
3234	Massachusetts. University of Massachusetts (System) (Table L7)
3234.M17-.M26	Massachusetts. University of Massachusetts at Amherst (Table L3)
	Formerly Massachusetts Agricultural College, 1863-1931; Massachusetts State College, 1931-1937
3234.M27	Massachusetts. University of Massachusetts at Boston (Table L7a)
3234.M32	Massachusetts. University of Massachusetts at Lowell (Table L7a)
	Formerly Lowell State College
	Massachusetts. University of Massachusetts Medical School, Worcester, Massachusetts see R747.A+
3238	Memphis, University of, Memphis, Tennessee (Table L7)
	Formerly Memphis State University
3241.M247-.M256	Mendota College, Mendota, Illinois (Table L3)
3241.M27	Menlo College, Atherton, California (Table L7a)
3241.M297-.M306	Mercer University, Macon, Georgia (Table L3)
3241.M310	Mercyhurst College, Erie, Pennsylvania (Table L7a)
3241.M317-.M326	Meridian College, Meridian, Mississippi (Table L3)
	Successor to Meridian Male College and Meridian Women's College
3241.M327	Meridian College, Meridian, Texas (Table L7a)
	Merom, Indiana. Union Christian College see LD5471.U47+
3241.M33	Merrimack College, Andover, Massachusetts (Table L7a)
3241.M34	Mesa State College, Grand Junction, Colo. (Table L7a)
	Formerly Mesa College
3241.M35	Messiah College, Grantham, Pennsylvania (Table L7a)
3241.M37-.M46	Miami, University of, Coral Gables, Florida (Table L3)
3241.M47-.M56	Miami University, Oxford, Ohio (Table L3)
3248.M5	Michigan. State University, East Lansing (Table L7a)
	1857-1909, Michigan State Agricultural College; 1905-1925, Michigan Agricultural College; 1925-1955, Michigan State College of Agriculture and Applied Science; 1955-1964, Michigan. State University of Agriculture and Applied Science
3250-3299.5	Michigan. University. Ann Arbor, Michigan (Table L6)
3303	Michigan. Western Michigan University, Kalamazoo (Table L7)
	1904-1927, Western State Normal School; 1927-1941, Western State Teachers College; 1941-1955, Western Michigan College of Education; 1955-1957, Western Michigan College

United States -- Continued

3306	Mid-American Nazarene College, Olathe, Kansas (Table L7)
3309	Middle Tennessee State University, Murfreesboro, Tennessee (Table L7)
3311.M17-.M26	Middle Tennessee, University of, Tullahoma, Tennessee (Table L3)
3311.M27-.M36	Middlebury College, Middlebury, Vermont (Table L3)
3311.M547-.M556	Midland College, Freemont, Nebraska (Table L3) Formerly located at Atchison, Kansas
3311.M56	Midwestern State University, Wichita Falls, Texas (Table L7a)
3311.M5627-.M5636	Milligan College, Milligan, Tennessee (Table L3) Milliken University, Decatur, Illinois see LD2601.J247+
3311.M57-.M66	Millsaps College, Jackson, Mississippi (Table L3)
3311.M717-.M726	Milton College, Milton, Wisconsin (Table L3)
3318	Minnesota. University of Minnesota, Duluth (Table L7)
3319	Minnesota. University of Minnesota, Morris (Table L7)
3320-3369.5	Minnesota. University. Minneapolis, Minnesota (Table L6)
3375	Minnesota State University, Mankato (Table L7) Formerly Mankato State University, Mankato State College Mission House College, Plymouth, Wisconsin see LD2931
3381.M47-.M56	Mississippi College, Clinton, Mississippi (Table L3)
3381.M57-.M66	Mississippi. State University. State College, Mississippi (Table L3) Formerly Mississippi State College
3381.M67-.M76	Mississippi Synodical College, Holly Springs, Mississippi (Table L3)
3400-3419.5	Mississippi. University. University (Oxford), Mississippi (Table L4)
3425	Mississippi. University of Southern Mississippi, Hattiesburg (Table L7)
3428	Mississippi Valley State University, Itta Bena, Mississippi (Table L7) Formerly Mississippi Valley State College
3429.8	Missouri. Central Missouri State University (Table L7) Missouri. Southeast Missouri State University, Cape Girardeau, Missouri see LD5090
3430	Missouri. Southwest Missouri State College, Springfield (Table L7)
3440-3489.5	Missouri. University. Columbia, Missouri. University of Missouri (Table L6) Missouri. University. Kansas City, Missouri see LD2715
3500	Missouri Southern State University, Joplin, Mo. (Table L7) Formerly Missouri Southern State College
3501.M27-.M36	Missouri Valley College, Marshall, Missouri (Table L3)
3501.M37-.M46	Missouri Wesleyan College, Cameron, Missouri (Table L3)
3501.M57-.M66	Monmouth College, Monmouth, Illinois (Table L3)

United States -- Continued

3501.M837-.M846	Montana, College of, Deer Lodge, Montana (Table L3)
	Merged to form Intermountain Union College, LD2535.I47
3508	Montana. State University, Bozeman (Table L7)
3510-3529.5	Montana. University. Missoula, Montana (Table L4)
3541.M27-.M36	Montana Wesleyan College, Helena, Montana (Table L3)
	Merged to form Intermountain Union College, LD2535.I47+
3541.M37-.M46	Montezuma College, Montezuma, New Mexico (Table L3)
3541.M47-.M56	Moores Hill College, Moores Hill, Indiana (Table L3)
3541.M77-.M86	Moravian College, Bethlehem, Pennsylvania (Table L3)
3541.M89	Morehead State University, Morehead, Kentucky (Table L7a)
	Morehouse College, Atlanta, Ga. see LC2851.M72
3541.M94	Morgan State University, Baltimore, Maryland (Table L7a)
3551.M37-.M46	Morningside College, Sioux City, Iowa (Table L3)
	Morris Brown College, Atlanta, Ga. see LC2851.M88
3551.M5	Morris College, Sumter, S.C. (Table L7a)
3551.M57-.M66	Morris Harvey College, Charleston, West Virginia (Table L3)
	Morrisville College see LD4881.S67+
3551.M77-.M86	Mossy Creek Baptist College, Mossy Creek, Tennessee (Table L3)
3561.M37-.M46	Mount Hope College, Mount Hope, Maine (Table L3)
3561.M487-.M496	Mount Lebanon College, Mount Lebanon, Louisiana (Table L3)
	Formerly Mount Lebanon University, 1853-1861; Mount Lebanon High School, 1871-1873; Mount Lebanon Male and Female High School, 1883-1885; Mount Lebanon Male College, 1899-1906; Mount Lebanon Academy, 1906-1912
3561.M547-.M556	Mount Morris College, Mount Morris, Illinois (Table L3)
3561.M58	Mount Olive College, Mount Olive, N.C. (Table L7a)
3561.M627-.M636	Mount St. Joseph's College, Baltimore, Maryland (Table L3)
3561.M657-.M666	Mount St. Mary's College, Emmitsburg, Maryland (Table L3)
3561.M697	Mount St. Vincent, College of, Riverdale, New York, N.Y. (Table L7a)
3561.M77-.M86	Mount Union College, Alliance, Ohio (Table L3)
3561.M868	Mount Vernon College, Washington, D.C. (Table L7a)
3561.M87	Mount Vernon Nazarene College, Mount Vernon, Ohio (Table L7a)
3561.M887-.M896	Mountain Home Baptist College, Mountain Home, Arkansas (Table L3)
3571.M27-.M36	Muhlenberg College, Allentown, Pennsylvania (Table L3)
3571.M4	Mundelein College, Chicago, Ill. (Table L7a)
3571.M47	Murray State College, Tishomingo, Oklahoma (Table L7a)
3571.M5	Murray State University, Murray, Kentucky (Table L7a)
	Formerly Murray State Teachers College
3571.M57-.M66	Muskingum College, New Concord, Ohio (Table L3)
	Nampa, Idaho. Northwest Nazarene College see LD4013.N557+

United States -- Continued

3581.N47-.N56	Nannie Low Warthen Institute, Wrightsville, Georgia (Table L3)
3600-3619.5	Nashville. University. Nashville, Tennessee (Table L4)
3624	Nasson College, Springvale, Maine (Table L7)
3626	Nathaniel Hawthorne College, Antrim, New Hampshire (Table L7)
3631.N37-.N46	National University, Washington, D.C. (Table L3)
3638.N47-.N56	Nebraska Central College, Central City, Nebraska (Table L3)
3639.N5	Nebraska. Nebraska State College System (Table L7a)
3640-3689.5	Nebraska. University of Nebraska-Lincoln (Table L6)
	Nebraska. University at Omaha see LD4341.O57+
3695	Nebraska. University of Nebraska (Central administration) (Table L7)
3710-3729.5	Nebraska Wesleyan University, Lincoln, Nebraska (Table L4)
3731	Nebraska Western College, Scottsbluff, Nebraska (Table L7)
3740	Nevada. University and Community College System of Nevada (Table L7)
	Formerly University of Nevada System
3745	Nevada. University. Las Vegas, Nevada (Table L7)
3750-3769.5	Nevada. University. Reno, Nevada (Table L4)
3774	New Britain, Connecticut. Central Connecticut State College (Table L7)
3775	New College, Sarasota, Florida (Table L7)
3778	New Hampshire. University System of New Hampshire (Table L7)
3779.N37-.N46	New Hampshire. University. Durham, New Hampshire (Table L3)
	Cf. S537.A+ New Hampshire College of Agriculture and Mechanic Arts
3780.N28	New Haven. University, West Haven, Connecticut (Table L7a)
3780.N3	New Jersey. State College. Montclair, New Jersey (Table L7a)
3781.N3	New Mexico. Eastern New Mexico University, Portales (Table L7a)
3781.N35	New Mexico Highlands University (Table L7a)
3781.N4	New Mexico State University, Las Cruces, New Mexico (Table L7a)
3781.N47-.N56	New Mexico. University. Albuquerque, New Mexico (Table L3)
	New Orleans. College of the Immaculate Conception see LD2451.I47+
	New Orleans. Holy Cross College see LD2281.H17+
3781.N65	New Rochelle, New York. College of New Rochelle (Table L7a)
3781.N77-.N86	New Windsor College, New Windsor, Maryland (Table L3)

United States -- Continued

3800-3829.5	New York. City College. New York, New York (Table L5)
3835	New York. City University of New York (Table L7)
	Cf. LD578.B29 Bronx Community College (component college)
	Cf. LD578.B37+ Brooklyn College (component college)
	Cf. LD3800+ City College (component college)
	Cf. LD4685 Queens College (component college)
	Cf. LD5171.S49 College of Staten Island (component college)
	Cf. LD6371.Y54 York College (component college)
	Cf. LD7251.A+ Hunter College (component college)
3837	New York (City). New School for Social Research (Table L7)
3838	New York City Technical College (Table L7)
3839	New York (State). State University (SUNY) (Table L7)
	For central administrative offices of the state system of higher education see LB2341.6.N7
3841	New York (State). State University, Albany (Table L7)
3842	New York (State). State University at Binghamton (Table L7)
	New York (State). State University, Buffalo see LD701.B37+
3844	New York (State). State University at Stony Brook (Table L7)
3848.A-Z	New York (State). State University colleges. By place, A-Z
3848.B76	Brockport (Table L7a)
3848.C36	Canton (Table L7a)
3848.C6	Cortland (Table L7a)
3848.F7	Fredonia (Table L7a)
3848.G5	Geneseo (Table L7a)
3848.O85	Oswego (Table L7a)
3848.P53	Plattsburgh (Table L7a)
3848.P8	Purchase (Table L7a)
	New York (State). Community colleges, A-Z see LD6501.A+
	New York (State). University (i.e., New York State Education Department) see L182+
3850-3899.5	New York University, New York, New York (Table L6)
3905.N17-.N26	Newark, New Jersey. University. Newark, New Jersey (Table L3)
3905.N27-.N36	Newberry College, Newberry, South Carolina (Table L3)
3911.N47-.N56	Niagara University, Niagara Falls, New York (Table L3)
3913	Nicholls State University. Thibodaux, Louisiana (Table L7)
3913.N54	Nichols College, Dudley, Massachusetts (Table L7a)
3914.N48	Nichols School, Buffalo, New York (Table L7a)
3914.N5	Norfolk State University, Norfolk, Virginia (Table L7a)
	Formerly Norfolk State College, Norfolk, Virginia
	North Carolina Agricultural and Technical State University, Greensboro, N.C. see LC2851.N8
3915	North Carolina Central University, Durham, North Carolina (Table L7)

United States -- Continued

3921.N37-.N46	North Carolina College, Mount Pleasant, North Carolina (Table L3)
3928	North Carolina. State University, Raleigh (Table L7)
3929	North Carolina. University of North Carolina (System) (Table L7)
3929.5	North Carolina. University of North Carolina at Asheville (Table L7)
3930-3949.5	North Carolina. University. Chapel Hill, North Carolina (Table L4)
3950	North Carolina. University at Charlotte (Table L7)
3952	North Carolina. University. Greensboro, North Carolina (Table L7)
	Formerly North Carolina. University Woman's College, Greensboro
3953	North Carolina Wesleyan College, Rocky Mount, North Carolina (Table L7)
3954	North Carolina. Western Carolina University, Cullowhee (Table L7)
	Formerly Western Carolina Teachers College; Western Carolina College
3961.N57-.N66	North Central College, Naperville, Illinois (Table L3)
	Formerly North-Western College
3963	North Dakota. North Dakota University (System), Bismarck, North Dakota (Table L7)
	For Dickinson State University, Dickinson, North Dakota see LD1671
3967	North Dakota. North Dakota State University, Fargo, North Dakota (Table L7)
	Formerly North Dakota State University of Agriculture and Applied Science
3970-3989.5	North Dakota. University of North Dakota, Grand Forks, North Dakota (Table L4)
	For Valley City State University see LD5560
3991	North Georgia College, Dahlonega, Georgia (Table L7)
3992	North Greenville College, Tigerville, South Carolina (Table L7)
3993	North Idaho College, Coeur d'Alene, Idaho (Table L7)
3998.N17-.N26	North Park College, Chicago, Illinois (Table L3)
	North Texas State University see LD5312
4005	Northeast Louisiana University, Monroe, Louisiana (Table L7)
4008	Northeast Missouri State University, Kirksville, Missouri (Table L7)
	Name changed in 1996 to Truman State University
4011.N17-.N26	Northeastern University, Boston, Massachusetts (Table L3)
4011.N268	Northern Arizona University, Flagstaff, Arizona (Table L7a)

United States -- Continued

4011.N269	Northern Colorado, University of, Greeley, Colorado (Table L7a)
4011.N27-.N36	Northern Illinois College, Fulton, Illinois (Table L3)
4011.N375	Northern Kentucky University, Highland Heights, Ky. (Table L7a)
4011.N39	Northern Michigan University, Marquette, Michigan (Table L7a)
4011.N42	Northern State College, Aberdeen, South Dakota (Table L7a)
4011.N547-.N556	Northland College, Ashland, Wisconsin (Table L3)
4011.N7	Northrup University, Inglewood, California (Table L7a)
4013.N27-.N36	Northwest Missouri State University, Maryville, Missouri (Table L3)
4013.N557-.N566	Northwest Nazarene College, Nampa, Idaho (Table L3)
4013.N577-.N586	North-western Christian University, Indianapolis, Indiana (Table L3)
4015	Northwestern College, Minneapolis, Minnesota (Table L7)
4016	Northwestern College, Orange City, Iowa (Table L7)
4020-4069.5	Northwestern University, Evanston, Illinois (Table L6)
4081.N227-.N236	Northwestern College, Watertown, Wisconsin (Table L3)
4081.N47-.N56	Norwich University, Northfield, Vermont (Table L3)
4088	Notre Dame, College of, Belmont, California (Table L7)
4100-4119.5	Notre Dame University, Notre Dame, Indiana (Table L4)
4130	Nova University, Fort Lauderdale, Fla. (Table L7)
4141.O27-.O36	Oakland City College, Oakland City, Indiana (Table L3)
4143	Oakland College, Huntsville, Alabama (Table L7)
4145	Oakland University, Rochester, Michigan (Table L7)
4150-4179.5	Oberlin College, Oberlin, Ohio (Table L5)
4191.O3417-.O3426	Occidental College, Los Angeles, California (Table L3)
4191.O347-.O356	Odessa College, Odessa, Missouri (Table L3)
4191.O427-.O436	Ogden College, Bowling Green, Kentucky (Table L3)
4191.O457-.O466	Oglethorpe University, Atlanta, Georgia (Table L3)
4191.O468	Ohio Dominican College, Columbus, Ohio (Table L7a)
4191.O47-.O56	Ohio Northern University, Ada, Ohio (Table L3)
4191.O57-.O66	Ohio. State University. Bowling Green, Ohio (Table L3)
4191.O67-.O76	Ohio. State University. Kent, Ohio (Table L3)
4191.O77-.O86	Ohio, University, Athens, Ohio (Table L3)
4200-4249.5	Ohio. State University. Columbus, Ohio (Table L6)
4270-4289.5	Ohio Wesleyan University, Delaware, Ohio (Table L4)
4291.O67-.O76	Oklahoma Baptist University, Shawnee, Oklahoma (Table L3)
4291.5	Oklahoma Christian University, Oklahoma City, Oklahoma (Table L7)
	Formerly Central Christian College (1950-1959); Oklahoma Christian College (1950-1990); and Oklahoma Christian University of Science and Arts (1990-2000)
4292	Oklahoma City. University (Table L7)

United States -- Continued

4292.3	Oklahoma College of Liberal Arts, Chickasha, Oklahoma (Table L7)
	1909, Industrial Institute and College; 1916-1965, Oklahoma College for Women
4293.O67-.O76	Oklahoma. Northeastern State College. Tahlequah, Oklahoma (Table L3)
4297	Oklahoma. Oklahoma State University, Stillwater, Oklahoma (Table L7)
	Formerly Oklahoma State University of Agriculture and Applied Science, Stillwater, Oklahoma
4297.5	Oklahoma State University at Oklahoma City (Table L7)
4297.6	Oklahoma State University. Technical Branch, Okmulgee (Table L7)
4310-4329.5	Oklahoma. University. Norman, Oklahoma (Table L4)
4331	Old Dominion University, Norfolk, Virginia (Table L7)
4341.O17-.O26	Olivet College, Olivet, Illinois (Table L3)
	In 1940 the college moved to Bourbonnais, Illinois and changed its name to Olivet Nazarene College
4341.O27-.O36	Olivet College, Olivet, Michigan (Table L3)
	Omaha. Municipal University. Omaha, Nebraska see LD4341.O57+
	Omaha, University of, Bellevue, Nebraska see LD371.B6
4341.O57-.O66	Omaha University, Omaha, Nebraska (Table L3)
	Founded 1908. Merged into Municipal University of Omaha in 1931. July 1, 1968 name changed to University of Nebraska at Omaha
4344	Oral Roberts University, Tulsa, Oklahoma (Table L7)
	Oregon. State College, Portland see LD4571.P4
4345	Oregon. Oregon State System of Higher Education (Table L7)
4346.O37-.O46	Oregon State University, Corvallis, Oregon (Table L3)
4350-4369.5	Oregon. University. Eugene, Oregon (Table L4)
4375.O37-.O46	Oriental University, Washington, D.C. (Table L3)
4400-4419.5	Ottawa University, Ottawa, Kansas (Table L4)
4431.O37-.O46	Otterbein University, Westerville, Ohio (Table L3)
4431.O67-.O76	Ouachita Baptist University, Arkadelphia, Arkansas (Table L3)
4431.O87	Our Lady of Holy Cross College, New Orleans, Louisiana (Table L7a)
4445.O47-.O56	Ozarks, College of the. Clarksville, Arkansas (Table L3)
4450	Ozarks, College of the, Point Lookout, Missouri (Table L7)
	Formerly School of the Ozarks
4455	Pace University, New York, New York (Table L7)
4461.P227-.P236	Pacific, College, of the. Stockton, California (Table L3)
	Formerly at San Jose

United States -- Continued

Pacific, University of the. San Jose, California see
LD4461.P227+

Pacific College, Newberg, Oregon see LD1893

4461.P317-.P326	Pacific Lutheran University, Parkland, Washington (Table L3)
	Formerly Pacific Lutheran College
4461.P347-.P356	Pacific Methodist College, Santa Rosa, California (Table L3)
4461.P37	Pacific Union College, Angwin, California (Table L7a)
4461.P47-.P56	Pacific University, Forest Grove, Oregon (Table L3)
4471.P697-.P706	Palmer College, Albany, Missouri (Table L3)
	Formerly at Le Grand, Iowa
4471.P727-.P736	Palmer University, Muncie, Indiana (Table L3)
4471.P74	Pan American College, Edinburg, Texas (Table L7a)
	Formerly Edinburgh, Texas Junior College; Edinburgh, Texas Regional College
4471.P747-.P756	Park College, Parkville, Missouri (Table L3)
4471.P757-.P766	Park Region Luther College, Fergus Falls, Minnesota (Table L3)
4471.P767-.P776	Parker College, Winnebago, Minnesota (Table L3)
4471.P797-.P806	Parsons College, Fairfield, Iowa (Table L3)
4472.P37-.P46	Pasadena College, Pasadena, California (Table L3)
4472.P48	Patrick Henry College, Purcellville, Va. (Table L7a)
4473	Paul Smith's College, Paul Smiths, New York (Table L7)
4481.P447-.P456	Peirce City Baptist College, Peirce City, Missouri (Table L3)
	Penn College, Oskaloosa, Iowa see LD6054
	Pennsylvania College, Gettysburg, Pennsylvania see LD2001.G397+
4481.P67	Penn State Altoona, Altoona (Table L7)
4481.P77-.P86	Pennsylvania. State University. University Park, Pennsylvania (Table L3)
4500-4549.5	Pennsylvania. University. Philadelphia, Pennsylvania (Table L6)
4561.P417-.P426	People's College, Montour Falls, New York (Table L3)
4561.P428	Pepperdine University, Malibu, California (Table L7a)
4561.P429	Peru State College, Peru, Nebraska (Table L7a)
4561.P432	Pfeiffer College, Misenheimer, North Carolina (Table L7a)
4561.P434	Philadelphia, College of, Philadelphia, Pennsylvania (Table L7a)
	Philadelphia, Pennsylvania. Temple College see LD5275.T47+
	Philander Smith College, Little Rock, Ark. see LC2851.P5
4561.P4357-.P4366	Phillips University, Enid, Oklahoma (Table L3)
4561.P447-.P456	Philomath College, Philomath, Oregon (Table L3)
4561.P46	Phoenix, Ariz. University of Phoenix (Table L7a)
4561.P477-.P486	Piedmont College, Demorest, Georgia (Table L3)
4561.P497-.P506	Pierce Christian College, College City, California (Table L3)

United States -- Continued

4561.P55	Pine Manor College, Wellesley, Massachusetts (Table L7a)
	Formerly Pine Manor Junior College
4561.P57-.P66	Pio Nono College, Macon, Georgia (Table L3)
4561.P69	Pittsburg State University, Pittsburg, Kansas (Table L7a)
	Also known as Kansas. State College, Pittsburg
	Pittsburgh. University see LD6000+
	Pittsburgh College of the Holy Ghost see LD1733.D77+
4561.P77-.P86	Pleasant View Luther College, Ottawa, Illinois (Table L3)
4561.P94	Point Park College, Pittsburgh, Pennsylvania (Table L7a)
4571.P27-.P36	Pomona College, Claremont, California (Table L3)
	Affiliated with Associated Colleges at Claremont
4571.P4	Portland State University, Portland, Oregon (Table L7a)
	Formerly Extension Center, Vanport City, Oregon., 1946-1952; Portland State Extension Center, 1952-1955; Portland State College, 1955-1969
4571.P47-.P56	Portland, Oregon. University (Table L3)
	Potomac University, Washington, D.C. see LC6001+
4571.P64	Pratt Institute, Brooklyn, New York (Table L7a)
	Founded 1887; educated on nonbaccalaureate levels prior to 1938
4571.P67-.P76	Presbyterian College of South Carolina, Clinton, South Carolina (Table L3)
4571.P787-.P796	Presbyterian College of the Southwest, Del Norte, Colorado (Table L3)
4580-4629.5	Princeton University, Princeton, New Jersey (Table L6)
	Founded 1746 as the College of New Jersey; in 1896, changed to present name
4637.P17-.P26	Principia College of Liberal Arts, Elsah, Illinois (Table L3)
4651.P27-.P36	Pritchett College, Glasgow, Missouri (Table L3)
4651.P5	Providence, Rhode Island. College (Table L7a)
4651.P84	Puget Sound University, Tacoma, Washington (Table L7a)
4660-4679.5	Purdue University, Lafayette, Indiana (Table L4)
4683	Queens University, Charlotte, North Carolina (Table L7)
	Formerly Queens College; Queens-Chicora College
4685	Queens College, Flushing, New York (Table L7)
4695	Quincy, Illinois. College (Table L7)
	Formerly St. Francis Solanus College
	Quincy, Massachusetts. Eastern Nazarene College see LD1741.E467
4698	Quinnipiac, Hampden, Connecticut (Table L7)
4701.R17-.R26	Racine College, Racine, Wisconsin (Table L3)
4701.R33	Radford University, Radford, Va. (Table L7)
	Formerly State Normal and Industrial School for Women at Radford; State Teachers College at Radford; and Radford College
4701.R37-.R46	Randolph-Macon College, Ashland, Virginia (Table L3)

United States -- Continued

4701.R57-.R66	Redfield College, Redfield, South Dakota (Table L3)
4701.R6637-.R6646	Redlands, University of, Redlands, California (Table L3)
4701.R67-.R76	Reed College, Portland, Oregon (Table L3)
4701.R7657-.R7666	Regis College, Denver, Colorado (Table L3)
4701.R77	Reinhardt College, Waleska, Georgia (Table L7a)
4701.R8	Research University, Washington, D.C. (Table L7a)
4706	Rhode Island. University, Kingston, Rhode Island (Table L7)
4707	Rhodes College, Memphis, Tennessee (Table L7)
	Formerly Southwestern Presbyterian University
	Rice Institute, Houston, Texas see LD6053
4711.R37-.R46	Richmond, Virginia. University (Table L3)
4711.R5	Ricker College, Houlton, Maine (Table L7a)
4711.R52	Ricks College, Rexburg, Idaho (Table L7a)
4711.R54	Rider College, Trenton, New Jersey (Table L7a)
4711.R57-.R66	Ridgeville College, Ridgeville, Indiana (Table L3)
4711.R72	Rio Grande, Ohio. University of Rio Grande (Table L7a)
	Formerly Rio Grande College
4711.R737-.R746	Ripon College, Ripon, Wisconsin (Table L3)
4721.R27-.R36	Roanoke College, Salem, Virginia (Table L3)
4721.R42	Robert Morris University, Moon Township, Pa. (Table L7a)
4721.R47-.R56	Rochester. University. Rochester, New York (Table L3)
4721.R597-.R606	Rock Hill College, Ellicott City, Maryland (Table L3)
4721.R607-.R616	Rock Island University, Rock Island, Illinois (Table L3)
4721.R627-.R636	Rock River University, Dixon, Illinois (Table L3)
4721.R65	Rockford College, Rockford, Illinois (Table L7a)
	Formerly Rockford Female Seminary
4721.R6547-.R6556	Rockhurst College, Kansas City, Missouri (Table L3)
4721.R67-.R76	Rollins College, Winter Park, Florida (Table L3)
4724.R57-.R66	Roosevelt College, Chicago, Illinois (Table L3)
4724.R68	Rosary College, River Forest, Illinois (Table L7a)
4731.R67-.R76	Ruskin University, Glen Ellyn, Illinois (Table L3)
4737.R37-.R46	Russell Sage College, Troy, New York (Table L3)
	Formerly a women's college
4740-4759.5	Rutgers University, New Brunswick, New Jersey (Table L4)
4771.R17-.R26	Rutgers Scientific School, New Brunswick, New Jersey (Table L3)
4785.S27-.S36	Sacred Heart, College of the. Denver, Colorado (Table L3)
	Sacred Heart College, Shawnee, Oklahoma see LD4802.S6
4785.S47-.S56	Sacred Heart College, Watertown, Wisconsin (Table L3)
4785.S59	Sacred Heart University, Fairfield, Connecticut (Table L7a)
4791.S47-.S56	Saint Ambrose University, Davenport, Iowa (Table L3)
	Earlier name: Saint Ambrose College
4791.S57-.S66	Saint Anselm College, Manchester, New Hampshire (Table L3)
4792.S27-.S36	Saint Basil's College, Stamford, Connecticus (Table L3)
4794.S27-.S36	Saint Bede College, Peru, Illinois (Table L3)

United States -- Continued

4794.S37-.S46	Saint Benedict's College, Atchison, Kansas (Table L3)
4794.S57-.S66	Saint Benedict's College, Newark, New Jersey (Table L3)
4794.S717-.S726	Saint Bernard College, Saint Bernard, Alabama (Table L3)
4794.S77-.S86	Saint Bonaventure's College, Saint Bonaventure, New York (Table L3)
4797.S37-.S46	Saint Charles College, Catonsville, Maryland (Table L3)
4797.S47-.S56	Saint Charles College, Grand Coteau, Louisiana (Table L3)
4797.S60	Saint Cloud State University, Saint Cloud, Minn. (Table L7a)
4797.S67-.S76	Saint Edward's University, Austin, Texas (Table L3)
4801.S157-.S166	Saint Fidelis College, Herman, Pennsylvania (Table L3)
4801.S27-.S36	Saint Francis College, Brooklyn, New York (Table L3)
4801.S363	Saint Francis College, Burlington, Wisconsin (Table L7a)
4801.S37-.S46	Saint Francis College, Loretto, Pennsylvania (Table L3)
	Saint Francis Solanus College, Quincy, Illinois see LD4695
4801.S67-.S76	Saint Francis Xavier, College of. New York, New York (Table L3)
4802.S6	Saint Gregory's College, Shawnee, Oklahoma (Table L7a)
	Formerly Sacred Heart College, and until 1964 affiliated with Saint Gregory's High School
4804.S27-.S36	Saint Ignatius College, Chicago, Illinois (Table L3)
	Loyola University, Chicago, Illinois
	Cf. LD3131.L67+ Loyola University, Chicago, Illinois
	Saint Ignatius College, Cleveland, Ohio see LD2601.J87+
	Saint Ignatius College, San Francisco, California see LD4881.S157+
4807.S37-.S46	Saint James College, Breathedville, Maryland (Table L3)
4807.S847-.S856	Saint James College, Vancouver, Washington (Table L3)
4811.S17-.S26	Saint John's College, Annapolis, Maryland (Table L3)
	Saint John's College, Brooklyn, New York see LD4811.S847+
	Saint John's College, Fordham, New York see LD1811.F47+
4811.S57-.S66	Saint John's College, Toledo, Ohio (Table L3)
4811.S67-.S76	Saint John's College, Washington, D.C. (Table L3)
4811.S797-.S806	Saint John's Lutheran College, Winfield, Kansas (Table L3)
4811.S847-.S856	Saint John's University, Brooklyn, New York (Table L3)
4811.S857-.S866	Saint John's University, Collegeville, Minnesota (Table L3)
4813.S5	Saint Joseph on the Rio Grande, College of, Albuquerque, New Mexico (Table L7a)
4814.S17-.S26	Saint Joseph's College, Bardstown, Kentucky (Table L3)
4814.S27-.S36	Saint Joseph's College, Cincinnati, Ohio (Table L3)
4814.S37-.S46	Saint Joseph's College, Colledgeville, Indiana (Table L3)
	Saint Joseph's College, Dubuque, Iowa see LD3081.L37+
4814.S57-.S66	Saint Joseph's College, Emmitsburg, Maryland (Table L3)
4814.S67-.S76	Saint Joseph's College, Philadelphia, Pennsylvania (Table L3)

United States -- Continued

4817.S247-.S256	Saint Lawrence College, Mount Calvary, Wisconsin (Table L3)
4817.S27-.S36	Saint Lawrence University, Canton, New York (Table L3)
4817.S38	Saint Leo College, Saint Leo, Florida (Table L7a)
4817.S447-.S456	Saint Louis College, San Antonio, Texas (Table L3)
4817.S47-.S56	Saint Louis University, Saint Louis, Missouri (Table L3)
4819.S43	Saint Margaret's-McTernan (School), Waterbury, Connecticut (Table L7a)
4819.S57-.S66	Saint Martin's College, Lacey, Washington (Table L3)
	Saint Martin's College, Olympia, Washington see LD4819.S57+
4821.S197-.S206	Saint Mary's College, Belmont, North Carolina (Table L3)
4821.S25	Saint Mary's College, Orchard Lake, Michigan (Table L7a)
4821.S277-.S286	Saint Mary's College, Saint Mary's College, California (Table L3)
4821.S317-.S326	Saint Mary's College, Saint Mary, Kentucky (Table L3)
4821.S47-.S56	Saint Mary's College, Saint Mary's, Kansas (Table L3)
4821.S86	Saint Mary's College, Van Buren, Maine (Table L7a)
4821.S868	Saint Mary's College, Saint Mary's, Maryland (Table L7a)
4821.S871	Saint Mary's College, Winona, Minnesota (Table L7a)
	Saint Mary's Institute, Dayton, Ohio see LD1461.D47+
4821.S877-.S886	Saint Mary's University, Galveston, Texas (Table L3)
4821.S887-.S896	Saint Mary's University, San Antonio, Texas (Table L3)
4821.S917-.S926	Saint Michael's College, Colchester, Vermont (Table L3)
4821.S927-.S936	Saint Norbert College, West De Pere, Wisconsin (Table L3)
4827.S57-.S66	Saint Olaf College, Northfield, Minnesota (Table L3)
4831.S27-.S36	Saint Paul's College, College Point, New York (Table L3)
4831.S37-.S46	Saint Paul's College, Concordia, Missouri (Table L3)
4831.S57-.S66	Saint Peter's College, Jersey City, New Jersey (Table L3)
4833	Saint Procopius College, Lisle, Illinois (Table L7)
4834.S22	Saint Rose, College of, Albany, New York (Table L7a)
4834.S257-.S266	Saint Stanislaus College, Bay Saint Louis, Mississippi (Table L3)
4834.S27-.S36	Saint Stanislaus' College, Chicago, Illinois (Table L3)
	Saint Stephen's College, Annandale, New York see LD331.B5667+
4834.S47-.S56	Saint Thomas, College of, Saint Paul, Minnesota (Table L3) Since 1991, University of St. Thomas
4834.S57-.S66	Saint Thomas College, Scranton, Pennsylvania (Table L3) Since 1938, University of Scranton, LD4925.S37
	Saint Thomas College, Villanova, Pennsylvania see LD5651.V27+
4836.S47	Saint Thomas, University of, Houston, Texas (Table L7a)
4837.S37-.S46	Saint Viator College, Bourbonnais, Illinois (Table L3)
4837.S527-.S536	Saint Vincent College, Latrobe, Pennsylvania (Table L3)
4837.S647-.S656	Saint Vincent's College, Los Angeles, California (Table L3)

United States -- Continued

4840-4859.5	Saint Xavier College, Cincinnati, Ohio (Table L4)
	Since 1930, Xavier University
4865.S27-.S36	Saint Xavier University, Chicago, Ill. (Table L3)
4871.S27-.S36	Saint Xavier's College, Louisville, Kentucky (Table L3)
4881.S147-.S156	Salem College, Salem, West Virginia (Table L3)
	Salt Lake City, Utah. All Hallows' College see LD131.A37+
	Salt Lake City, Utah. Latter Day Saints University see LD2937.L47+
4881.S1561	Salve Regina College, Newport, Rhode Island (Table L7a)
4881.S1562	Sam Houston State University, Huntsville, Texas (Table L7a)
4881.S1563	Samford University, Birmingham, Alabama (Table L7a)
	Formerly Howard College
4881.S1565	University of San Diego (Table L7a)
4881.S157-.S166	San Francisco. University. San Francisco, California (Table L3)
	Formerly Ignatius College
4881.S1677	Sangamon State University, Springfield, Illinois (Table L7a)
4881.S17-.S26	San Joaquin Valley College, Woodbridge, California (Table L3)
4881.S27-.S36	Santa Clara, California. University (Table L3)
	Formerly Santa Clara College, Santa Clara, California
4881.S39	Santa Fe, College of, Santa Fe, New Mexico (Table L7a)
4881.S45	Sara Lawrence College, Bronxville, New York (Table L7a)
4881.S46	Savannah State College, Savannah, Georgia (Table L7a)
4881.S47-.S56	Savoy Male and Female College, Savoy, Texas (Table L3)
4881.S57-.S66	Scarritt Collegiate Institute, Neosho, Missouri (Table L3)
4881.S67-.S76	Scarritt-Morrisville, College, Morrisville, Missouri (Table L3)
4881.S85	Schreiner College, Kerrville, Texas (Table L7a)
4900-4919.5	Scio College, Scio, Ohio (Table L4)
4925.S37-.S46	Scranton. University. Scranton, Pennsylvania (Table L3)
4927.S57-.S66	Seattle University, Seattle, Washington (Table L3)
	Formerly Seattle College, Seattle, Washington
4928	Seattle Pacific University, Seattle, Washington (Table L7)
	Formerly Seattle Pacific College
4931.S27-.S36	Seton Hall College, South Orange, New Jersey (Table L3)
	Sewanee, Tennessee. University of the South see LD4980+
4931.S37	Shaw University, Raleigh, North Carolina (Table L7a)
4931.S387-.S396	Shelbina Collegiate Institute, Shelbina, Missouri (Table L3)
4931.S42	Sheldon Jackson College, Sitka, Alaska (Table L7a)
4931.S45	Shenandoah University, Winchester, Virginia (Table L7a)
	Formerly Shenandoah College and Conservatory of Music
4931.S517-.S526	Shoemaker College, Gate City, Virginia (Table L3)
4931.S55	Shorter College, Rome, Georgia (Table L7a)
4931.S57-.S66	Shurtleff College, Upper Alton, Illinois (Table L3)
4933	Siena College, Loudonville, New York (Table L7)
	Simmons University, Abilene, Texas see LD2101.H8637+

United States -- Continued

4940-4959.5	Simpson College, Indianola, Iowa (Table L4)
4960.S42	Simpson College, San Francisco, California (Table L7a)
4960.S47-.S56	Sinclair College, Dayton, Ohio (Table L3)
4961.S27-.S36	Sioux Falls College, Sioux Falls, South Dakota (Table L3)
4963	Skidmore College, Saratoga Springs, New York (Table L7)
4964	Slippery Rock State College, Slippery Rock, Pennsylvania (Table L7)
4971.S37-.S46	Soule College, Dodge City, Kansas (Table L3)
4980-4999.5	South, University of the. Sewanee, Tennessee (Table L4)
5015	South Carolina State University, Orangeburg, S.C. (Table L7) Formerly South Carolina State College
5020-5039.5	South Carolina. University. Columbia, South Carolina (Table L4)
5050	South Dakota State University, Brookings, South Dakota (Table L7)
5060-5079.5	South Dakota. University. Vermillion, South Dakota (Table L4)
	South Georgia College, College, Georgia see LD1961.G67+
5090	Southeast Missouri State University, Cape Giradeau, Missouri (Table L7)
	Southeastern Louisiana College see LD3091.L47+

5095	Southern Arkansas University, Magnolia, Ark. (Table L7)
	      Formerly Agricultural and Mechanical College; Southern State
	      College

5101.S27-.S36	Southern California, University of. Los Angeles, California (Table L3)
	Southern College, Sutherland, Florida see LD1771.F77+
5101.S362	Southern Connecticut State University, New Haven, Conn. (Table L7a)
5101.S363	Southern Illinois University, Carbondale, Illinois (Table L7a)
5101.S364	Southern Illinois University, Edwardsville, Illinois (Table L7a)
5101.S3647-.S3656	Southern Methodist University, Dallas, Texas (Table L3)
5101.S367	Southern Missionary College, Collegedale, Tennessee (Table L7a)
5101.S3675	Southern Nazarene University, Bethany, Okla. (Table L7a)
5101.S368	Southern Oregon College (Table L7a)

5101.S37-.S46	Southern University, Greensboro, Alabama (Table L3)
	      Merged with Birmingham College in 1918 to form the
	      Birmingham-Southern College, LD451.B5657+

5101.S52	Southern University System, Baton Rouge, La. (Table L7a)
	      Southern University and A & M College, Baton Rouge, La.
	      see LC2851.L67

5101.S53	Southern University in New Orleans (Table L7a)
5101.S55	Southern Utah University, Cedar City, Utah (Table L7a) Formerly Southern Utah State College
5101.S75	Southern Wesleyan University, Central, S.C. (Table L7a)

United States -- Continued

5111.S37-.S46	Southwest Baptist College, Bolivar, Missouri (Table L3)
	Southwest Kansas College see LD5125
5115	Southwest Minnesota State College, Marshall, Minnesota (Table L7)
5120	Southwest Texas State University, San Marcos, Texas (Table L7)
	Formerly, Southwest Texas State College
5125	Southwestern College, Winfield, Kansas (Table L7)
5130-5149.5	Southwestern University, Georgetown, Texas (Table L4)
5157.S67-.S76	Southwestern University, Los Angeles, California (Table L3)
5161.S27-.S36	Southwestern Baptist University, Jackson, Alabama (Table L3)
(5161.S67-.S76)	Southwestern Presbyterian University, Memphis, Tennessee
	Formerly at Clarksville, Tennessee. Name changed in 1984 to Rhodes College
	see LD4707
5171.S27-.S36	Spokane College, Spokane, Washington (Table L3)
5171.S37-.S46	Spring Hill College, Spring Hill, Alabama (Table L3)
5171.S48	Springfield College, Springfield, Massachusetts (Table L7a)
	St. ...
	see LD4791+
	Stanford University see LD3000+
5171.S49	Staten Island. College of Staten Island, New York (Table L7a)
5171.S517	Stefan University, La Jolla, California (Table L7a)
5171.S52	Stephen F. Austin State University, Nacogdoches, Texas (Table L7a)
5171.S524	Stephens College, Columbia, Missouri (Table L7a)
5171.S53	Sterling, Kansas. College (Table L7a)
	Formerly Cooper College
	Stetson University, Deland, Florida see LD2601.J67+
5171.S58	Stockton State College, Pomona, New Jersey (Table L7a)
5171.S62	Stonehill College, North Easton, Massachusetts (Table L7a)
5171.S7	Suffolk University, Boston, Massachusetts (Table L7a)
5171.S84	Suomi College and Theological Seminary, Hancock, Michigan (Table L7a)
5171.S847-.S856	Susquehanna University, Selinsgrove, Pennsylvania (Table L3)
5180-5199.5	Swarthmore College, Swarthmore, Pennsylvania (Table L4)
5220-5239.5	Syracuse University, Syracuse, New York (Table L4)
5270.T37-.T46	Tabor College, Hillsboro, Kansas (Table L3)
5271.T2	Tabor College, Tabor, Iowa (Table L7a)
	Tacoma, Washington. University of Puget Sound see LD4651.P84
	Talladega College, Talladega, Ala. see LC2851.T3
5271.T25	Tampa, Florida. University (Table L7a)

United States -- Continued

5271.T3	Tarkio College, Tarkio, Missouri (Table L7a)
5271.T33	Tarleton State University, Stephenville, Texas (Table L7a)
	Formerly Tarleton State College
5271.T37-.T46	Taylor University, Upland, Indiana (Table L3)
5271.T487-.T496	Taylorsville Collegiate Institute, Taylorsville, North Carolina (Table L3)
5275.T47-.T56	Temple University, Philadelphia, Pennsylvania (Table L3)
5278	Tennessee. East Tennessee State University, Johnson City, Tennessee (Table L7)
5278.5	Tennessee Technological University, Cookeville, Tenn. (Table L7)
5279	Tennessee. University of Tennessee (System) (Table L7)
	Tennessee. University. Chattanooga, Tenn. see LD891.C67+
5280-5299.5	Tennessee. University. Knoxville, Tennessee (Table L4)
5300	Tennessee. University of Tennessee at Martin (Table L7)
5305.T47-.T56	Tennessee Wesleyan College, Athens, Tennessee (Table L3)
5308	Texas A & I University, Kingsville, Texas (Table L7)
5309	Texas A & M University, College Station, Texas (Table L7)
5310	Texas A & M University, Corpus Christi, Tex. (Table L7)
	Opened 1947 as Arts and Technological College. Name changed in Dec. 1947 to University of Corpus Christi; changed to Texas A & I University in 1971; changed to Corpus Christi State University in 1977; changed to Texas A & M University--Corpus Christi in 1993
5311.T377-.T386	Texas Christian University, Fort Worth, Texas (Table L3)
5311.T3937-.T3946	Texas College of Arts and Industries, Kingsville, Texas (Table L3)
5311.T397-.T406	Texas Holiness University, Greenville, Texas (Table L3)
5311.T57-.T66	Texas Lutheran College, Seguin, Texas (Table L3)
	Absorbed Clifton College, Clifton, Texas, in January 1954
5312	Texas. University of North Texas, Denton, Texas (Table L7)
	Formerly North Texas State University
5313	Texas. Southern University, Houston, Texas (Table L7)
5313.5	Texas State University (System) (Table L7)
	For Sam Houston State University, Huntsville, Texas see LD4881.S1562
	For Southwest Texas State University see LD5120
5314	Texas Tech University, Lubbock, Texas (Table L7)
	Cf. T171+ Texas Tech University before 1969
5315	Texas. University at Arlington (Table L7)
	Formerly Texas State College, Arlington
5316	Texas. University of Texas at El Paso (Table L7)
5318	Texas. University of Texas of the Permian Basin, Odessa, Tex. (Table L7)
5320-5339.5	Texas. University. Austin, Texas (Table L4)

United States -- Continued

5340	Texas. University of Texas System (Table L7)
	Texas Wesleyan College, Fort Worth, Texas (founded 1881) see LD1820+
5342	Texas Wesleyan College, Fort Worth, Texas (Table L7)
5351.T217-.T226	Thiel College, Greenville, Pennsylvania (Table L3)
5351.T235	Thomas More College, Crestview Hills, Kentucky (Table L7a)
	Formerly Villa Madonna College
5351.T247-.T256	Tobin College, Fort Dodge, Iowa (Table L3)
5351.T257-.T266	Toledo University, Toledo, Ohio (Table L3)
5351.T55	Towson University. Baltimore, Maryland (Table L7a)
	Formerly Maryland State Normal School, 1866-1935; State Teachers College at Towson, 1935-1963; Towson State University, 1976-1997
(5351.T57-.T66)	Transylvania College, Lexington, Kentucky see LD5351.T67+
5351.T67-.T76	Transylvania University, Lexington, Kentucky (Table L3)
	Formerly Transylvania College, 1915-1970; Transylvania University, 1908-1915
	For Kentucky University prior to 1908 see LD2790.K27+
5356.T67-.T76	Trevecca Nazarene College, Nashville, Tennessee (Table L3)
5358.T74	Tri-College University (Table L7a)
5361.T27-.T36	Tri-State College, Angola, Indiana (Table L3)
5361.T3647-.T3656	Tri-State Normal University, Scottsboro, Alabama (Table L3)
	Trinity College, Durham, North Carolina see LD1732.D77+
5361.T37-.T46	Trinity College, Hartford, Connecticut (Table L3)
5361.T57-.T66	Trinity University, San Antonio, Texas (Table L3)
	Formerly at Tehuacana, Texas, then Waxahachie, Texas
5361.T7	Troy University, Troy, Alabama (Table L7a)
	Formerly Troy State Normal School, Troy State Teachers College, Troy State College, Troy State University
5361.T77-.T86	Troy University, Troy, New York (Table L3)
	Truman State University see LD4008
5380-5399.5	Tufts University, Medford, Massachusetts (Table L4)
	Includes Tufts College
5420-5449.5	Tulane University of Louisiana, New Orleans, Louisiana (Table L5)
	Tullahoma, Tennessee. University of Middle Tennessee see LD3311.M17+
5457.T47-.T56	Tulsa, Oklahoma. University (Table L3)
5457.T67-.T76	Tusculum College, Greeneville, Tennessee (Table L3)
	Merged with Greeneville College to form Greeneville and Tusculum College; since 1908 known as Tusculum College
	Tuskegee University, Tuskegee, Alabama see LC2851.T77+
5461.T57-.T66	Twin Valley College, Germantown, Ohio (Table L3)
5463	Tyler State College, Tyler, Texas (Table L7)

United States -- Continued

5471.U47-.U56	Union Christian College, Merom, Indiana (Table L3)
5481.U27-.U36	Union College, Barbourville, Kentucky (Table L3)
5481.U47-.U56	Union College, Lincoln, Nebraska (Table L3)
5481.U564	Union Institute & University, Vermont (Table L7a)
5481.U567-.U576	Union University, Jackson, Tennessee (Table L3)
5481.U67-.U76	Union University, Schenectady, New York (Table L3)
	Includes Union College
5491.U347-.U356	Upper Iowa University, Fayette, Iowa (Table L3)
5491.U377-.U386	Upsala College, East Orange, New Jersey (Table L3)
5491.U47-.U56	Urbana University, Urbana, Ohio (Table L3)
	Since 1933, Urbana Junior College
5491.U67-.U76	Ursinus College, Collegeville, Pennsylvania (Table L3)
5491.U8	Ursuline College, Cleveland, Ohio (Table L7a)
5515	Utah. Utah State University, Logan, Utah (Table L7)
	Formerly State University of Agriculture and Applied Science
5520-5539.5	Utah. University. Salt Lake City, Utah (Table L4)
	Chartered as University of Deseret
5541	Utah Valley University, Orem, Utah (Table L7)
	Formerly Utah Valley State College; Utah Valley Community College; Utah Technical College at Provo
5555	Valdosta State University, Valdosta, Ga. (Table L7)
	Formerly Valdosta State College; Georgia State Womans College
5560	Valley City State University, Valley City, North Dakota (Table L7)
5565.V37-.V46	Valparaiso University, Valparaiso, Indiana (Table L3)
5570-5599.5	Vanderbilt University, Nashville, Tennessee (Table L5)
5611.V47-.V56	Vashon College, Burton, Washington (Table L3)
5620-5639.5	Vermont. University. Burlington, Vermont (Table L4)
	Villa Madonna College, Crestview Hills, Kentucky see LD5351.T235
5651.V27-.V36	Villanova University, Villanova, Pennsylvania (Table L3)
	Formerly Villanova College
5651.V57-.V66	Vincennes University, Vincennes, Indiana (Table L3)
	For post 1970 see LD6501.A+
5651.V85	Virginia Commonwealth University, Richmond, Virginia (Table L7a)
(5655)	Virginia Polytechnic Institute and State University, Blacksburg
	see T171
5660-5689.5	Virginia. University. Charlottesville, Virginia (Table L5)
	Virginia State University, Petersburg, Virginia see LC2851.V5
	Virginia Union University, Richmond, Virginia see LC2851.V7
5693	Virginia Wesleyan University, Norfolk, Virginia (Table L7)
5694	Viterbo College, La Crosse, Wisconsin (Table L7)
5701.V67-.V76	Volant College, Volant, Pennsylvania (Table L3)

	United States -- Continued
5701.V85	Voorhees College, Denmark, South Carolina (Table L7a)
5721.W27-.W36	Wabash College, Crawfordsville, Indiana (Table L3)
5721.W37-.W46	Wagner College, Grymes Hill, Staten Island, New York (Table L3)
	Formerly Wagner Memorial Lutheran College. Formerly at Rochester, New York
5721.W47-.W56	Wake Forest University, Winston-Salem, North Carolina (Table L3)
	Formerly Wake Forest College. Formerly at Wake Forest, North Carolina
5721.W57-.W66	Walla Walla College, College Place, Washington (Table L3)
5721.W67-.W76	Wartburg College, Clinton, Iowa (Table L3)
5731.W17-.W26	Washburn Municipal University, Topeka, Kansas (Table L3)
	Also known as Washburn University
5731.W2637-.W2646	Washington Christian College, Washington, D.C. (Table L3)
5731.W37-.W46	Washington College, Chestertown, Maryland (Table L3)
5731.W47-.W56	Washington College, Washington College, Tennessee (Table L3)
5731.W567	Washington Missionary College, Washington, D.C. (Table L7a)
5731.W57-.W66	Washington State University, Pullman, Washington (Table L3)
5740-5759.5	Washington (State). University of Washington, Seattle, Washington (Table L4 modified)
5759.5.A-Z	Special colleges, campuses, etc., A-Z
	e. g.
5759.5.B67	Bothell campus
5759.5.T32	Tacoma campus
5780-5799.5	Washington University, St. Louis, Missouri (Table L4)
5820-5839.5	Washington and Jefferson College, Washington, Pennsylvania (Table L4)
5860-5879.5	Washington and Lee University, Lexington, Virginia (Table L4)
	Watertown, Wisconsin. Sacred Heart College see LD4785.S47+
5887	Wayland College, Plainview, Texas (Table L7)
5888	Wayne State College, Wayne, Nebraska (Table L7)
5889.W37-.W46	Wayne State University, Detroit, Mich. (Table L3)
	Formerly Wayne University
5891.W37-.W46	Waynesburg College, Waynesburg, Pennsylvania (Table L3)
5891.W57-.W66	Weaverville College, Weaverville, North Carolina (Table L3)
5894.W47-.W56	Webster University (Table L3)
5901.W27-.W36	Wesleyan University, Middletown, Connecticut (Table L3)
	West Alabama, University of, Livingston, Alabama see LD3071.L967+

United States -- Continued

5901.W4	West Chester State College, West Chester, Pennsylvania (Table L7a)
	Formerly West Chester Academy; West Chester Normal School; State Teachers College
5901.W46	West Hartford, Connecticut. University of Hartford (Table L7a)
5901.W49	West Liberty State College, West Liberty, West Virginia (Table L7a)
5901.W67-.W76	West Plains College, West Plains, Missouri (Table L3)
5901.W717-.W726	West Tennessee College, Jackson, Tennessee (Table L3)
5905	West Texas State University, Canyon, Texas (Table L7)
	Formerly West Texas State College
	West Virginia. State College, Institute, W.Va. see LC2851.W552
5910-5929.5	West Virginia. University. Morgantown, West Virginia (Table L4)
5941.W247-.W256	West Virginia Wesleyan College, Buckhannon, West Virginia (Table L3)
	Western Carolina University, Cullowhee, North Carolina see LD3954
	Western College, Toledo, Iowa see LD2951.L227+
5941.W38	Western Connecticut State University, Danbury, Connecticut (Table L7a)
	Formerly Western Connecticut State College
5941.W45	Western Illinois University, Macomb, Illinois (Table L7a)
5941.W5	Western Kentucky University, Bowling Green, Kentucky (Table L7a)
5941.W57-.W66	Western Maryland College, Westminster, Maryland (Table L3)
	Name changed in 2002 to McDaniel College
5943	Western New England College, Springfield, Massachusetts (Table L7)
5946	Western Oregon University, Monmouth, Oregon (Table L7)
5950-5969.5	Western Reserve University, Cleveland, Ohio (Table L4)
	For Flora Stone Mather College see LD7251.A+
5980	Western State College of Colorado, Gunnison, Colorado (Table L7)
	Western Union College, Le Mars, Iowa see LD6031.W27+
6000-6019.5	Western University of Pennsylvania, Pittsburgh, Pennsylvania (Table L4)
6024	Western Washington University, Bellingham, Wash. (Table L7)
6031.W27-.W36	Westfield College, Westfield, Illinois (Table L3)
6031.W363	Westhampton College, Richmond, Virginia (Table L7a)
6031.W37-.W46	Westmar College, Le Mars, Iowa (Table L3)
6031.W47-.W56	Westminster College, Fulton, Missouri (Table L3)

United States -- Continued

6031.W5647-.W5656	Westminster College, New Wilmington, Pennsylvania (Table L3)
6031.W568	Westminster College, Salt Lake City, Utah (Table L7a)
6031.W57-.W66	Westminster College, Tehuacana, Texas (Table L3)
6031.W75	Westmont College, Santa Barbara, California (Table L7a)
6040	Wheaton College, Norton, Massachusetts (Table L7)
6041.W557-.W566	Wheaton College, Wheaton, Illinois (Table L3)
6041.W57-.W66	Whitman College, Walla Walla, Washington (Table L3)
6041.W717-.W726	Whittier College, Whittier, California (Table L3)
6041.W727-.W736	Whitworth College, Spokane, Washington (Table L3)
	Wichita, Kansas. Municipal University see LD2667
	Wilberforce University, Wilberforce, Ohio see LC2851.W58
6051.W337-.W346	Willamette University, Salem, Oregon (Table L3)
6051.W47-.W56	William and Mary, College of, Williamsburg, Virginia (Table L3)
6051.W57-.W66	William and Vashti College, Aledo, Illinois (Table L3)
6051.W67	William Carey College, Hattiesburg, Mississippi (Table L7a)
	Formerly Mississippi Woman's college
6051.W687-.W696	William Jennings Bryan University, Dayton, Tennessee (Table L3)
6051.W77-.W86	William Jewell College, Liberty, Missouri (Table L3)
6053	William Marsh Rice University, Houston, Texas (Table L7)
	Formerly Rice Institute
6054	William Penn College, Oskaloosa, Iowa (Table L7)
	Formerly Penn College
6055.W55	William Woods University, Fulton, Missouri (Table L7a)
6058	Williams Baptist College, Walnut Ridge, Arkansas (Table L7)
6060-6079.5	Williams College, Williamstown, Massachusetts (Table L4)
6091.W327-.W336	Wilmington College, Wilmington, Ohio (Table L3)
6091.W37-.W46	Wilson College, Wilson, North Carolina (Table L3)
6091.W55	Wingate College, Wingate, North Carolina (Table L7a)
6092	Winona State University, Winona, Minnesota (Table L7)
6093	Winston-Salem State University, Winston-Salem, North Carolina (Table L7)
6094	Winthrop College, Rock Hill, South Carolina (Table L7)
	Formerly a women's college
6096	Wisconsin. University of Wisconsin System (Table L7)
6100-6149.5	Wisconsin. University of Wisconsin, Madison (Table L6)
6150.3	Wisconsin. University of Wisconsin, Eau Claire (Table L7)
6150.35	Wisconsin. University of Wisconsin, Green Bay (Table L7)
6150.4	Wisconsin. University of Wisconsin, La Crosse (Table L7)
6150.45	Wisconsin. University of Wisconsin, Milwaukee (Table L7)
6150.5	Wisconsin. University of Wisconsin, Oshkosh (Table L7)
6150.55	Wisconsin. University of Wisconsin, Parkside (Table L7)
6150.6	Wisconsin. University of Wisconsin, Platteville (Table L7)
6150.65	Wisconsin. University of Wisconsin, River Falls (Table L7)

	United States
	Wisconsin. University of Wisconsin System -- Continued
6150.7	Wisconsin. University of Wisconsin, Stevens (Table L7)
6150.75	Wisconsin. University of Wisconsin, Stout (Table L7)
6150.8	Wisconsin. University of Wisconsin, Superior (Table L7)
6150.85	Wisconsin. University of Wisconsin, Whitewater (Table L7)
6170-6189.5	Wittenberg University, Springfield, Ohio (Table L4)
	Formerly Wittenburg College
6201.W27-.W36	Wofford College, Spartanburg, South Carolina (Table L3)
6205	Woodbury University, Los Angeles, California (Table L7)
6210-6229.5	Wooster, Ohio. College of Wooster (Table L4)
6240	Wright State University, Dayton, Ohio (Table L7)
6250-6269.5	Wyoming. University. Laramie, Wyoming (Table L4)
	Xavier University, Cincinnati, Ohio see LD4840+
6280	Xavier University, New Orleans, Louisiana (Table L7)
6291.Y27-.Y36	Yadkin College, Davidson County, North Carolina (Table L3)
	Yale University, New Haven, Connecticut
6300	Charter
6300.5	Constitution and government
6301	Statutes. Rules and by-laws
	Administration
	General works. Official reports
6302	President
6303	Treasurer
	Special
	Finance
6305	Endowment
6306	Appropriations and grants
6307	Requests, donations, etc.
6308	Scholarships
	Policy and organization
6309	General works
6309.5	Early pamphlets (to 1800)
6310	Catalogs
	Sheffield Scientific School
6310.S5	Report
6310.S6	Catalog
6310.S7-.S9	Other reports, programmes, etc.
6311	Announcements, circulars, etc.
6312	Directories
	Requirements for admission
6313	General works
6314	Entrance examinations
	Curriculum
6315	General works
6316	Graduate work and courses
6318	Degrees and honors

	United States
	Yale University, New Haven, Connecticut
	Undergraduate publications -- Continued
	Periodicals see LH1+
6357	Annuals
6357.3	Nonserial (Yale handbook)
6357.5	Calendars
	Alumni activities
6358	Graduate class publications
	Including exercises
	Alumni associations and graduate clubs
6359.A1-.A4	Resident
6359.A5-Z	Nonresident. By place, A-Z
6368	Yampa Valley College, Steamboat Springs, Colorado (Table L7)
6371.Y27-.Y36	Yankton College, Yankton, South Dakota (Table L3)
6371.Y43	Yeshiva University, New York (Table L7a)
6371.Y54	York College, Queens, New York (Table L7a)
6371.Y57-.Y66	York College, York, Nebraska (Table L3)
6371.Y67-.Y76	York College of Pennsylvania, York, Pennsylvania (Table L3)
6372	Young Harris College, Young Harris, Georgia (Table L7)
	Formerly Young Harris Institute, 1881-1891; Young L. G. Harris College, 1891-1957
6373	Youngstown University (Table L7)
	Formerly Youngstown College
6501.A-Z	Community colleges. Junior colleges. By college, A-Z
	For women's colleges see LD7251.A+
	Cf. LD13+ Some junior and community colleges that were formerly four-year institutions or are administered by universities
6501.C37	Cascadia Community College, Bothell, Washington (Table L7a)
6501.H3	Harrisburg Area Community College, Harrisburg, Pennsylvania (Table L7a)
	Women's colleges
7020-7039.5	Barnard, New York, New York (Table L4)
7045	Bennett College, Greensboro, North Carolina (Table L7)
7047	Bessie Tift College, Forsyth, Ga. (Table L7)
7050-7069.5	Bryn Mawr, Bryn Mawr, Pennsylvania (Table L4)
7071	Caldwell College, Caldwell, New Jersey (Table L7)
7071.5	Douglass College, New Brunswick, New Jersey (Table L7)
7072	Georgian Court College, Lakewood, New Jersey (Table L7)
7073	Mills College, Oakland, California (Table L7)
7080-7099.5	Mount Holyoke, South Hadley, Massachusetts (Table L4)
7102	Mount Ida College, Newton, Massachusetts (Table L7)

	United States
	Women's colleges -- Continued
7105	Newcomb College, New Orleans, Louisiana (Table L7)
	In 2005, merged with Tulane University of Louisiana, LD5420+
7110-7129.5	Radcliffe, Cambridge, Massachusetts (Table L4)
7140-7159.5	Smith, Northampton, Massachusetts (Table L4)
7165	St. Catherine University, Saint Paul, Minnesota (Table L7)
	Formerly College of St. Catherine
7170-7189.5	Vassar, Poughkeepsie, New York (Table L4)
7200-7219.5	Wellesley, Wellesley, Massachusetts (Table L4)
7251.A-Z	Other women's colleges and girls' schools. By city, A-Z
7251.B48954	Binghamton, N.Y. Binghamton Female Seminary (Table L7a)
7251.C45	Chambersburg, Pa. Wilson College (Table L7a)
7251.C564	Clinton, N.Y. Kirkland College (Table L7a)
	Merged with Hamilton College in 1978
7251.D44	Denton, Tex. Texas Woman's University (Table L7a)
7251.E426	Ellicott City, Md. Patapsco Female Institute (Table L7a)
7251.G73	Greenville, S.C. Greenville Woman's College (Table L7a)
	Hattiesburg, Miss. Mississippi Woman's College see LD6051.W67
7251.M564	Meridian, Miss. East Mississippi Female College (Table L7a)
7251.M92	Murfreesboro, N.C. Chowan College (Table L7a)
7251.R3675	Richmond, Va. Mr. LeFebvre's School (Table L7a)
	San Antonio, Texas. University of the Incarnate Word see LD2475
7501.A-Z	Secondary schools, elementary schools, and preschools. By place, A-Z
	Subarrange each by Table L7a
	For institutions that originated as secondary schools and evolved into postsecondary institutions, see LD13+
(7501.B8)	Pratt Institute, Brooklyn, New York
	see LD4571.P64

Individual institutions
America (except United States)
For individual institutions limited to education in a special field,
see the topic, e.g. class K, law schools, R741+ medical
schools, S536.5+ agricultural colleges, T171+ technical
schools
Canada

3.A-Z	Universities and colleges. By name or place, A-Z
3.A27-.A36	Acadia University, Wolfville, Nova Scotia (Table L3)
3.A57-.A66	Alberta. University. Edmonton, Alberta (Table L3)
3.A75	Athabasca, Alberta. Athabasca University (Table L7a)
3.B47-.B56	Bishop's College, University of, Lennoxville, Quebec (Table L3)
3.B67-.B76	Bourget College, Montreal (Table L3)
3.B765	Brandon, Manitoba. College (Table L7a)
3.B77-.B86	British Columbia. University. Vancouver, British Columbia (Table L3)
3.B865	British Columbia. University of Northern British Columbia (Table L7a)
3.B88	British Columbia. University of Victoria (Table L7a)
3.C32	Calgary, Alberta. University (Table L7a)
3.C33	Capilano College, North Vancouver, British Columbia (Table L7a)
3.C37-.C46	Carleton University, Ottawa, Ontario (Table L3)
3.C53	Collège du Sacre-Coeur, Caraquet, N.B. (Table L7a)
3.C55	Collège du Sacré-Coeur, Sainte-Anne-de-la Pérade, Quebec (Table L7a)
3.D27-.D36	Dalhousie University, Halifax, Nova Scotia (Table L3)
3.G7	Guelph, Ontario. University of Guelph (Table L7a)
3.H77-.H86	Huron College, London, Ontario (Table L3)
3.K57-.K66	King's College, University of, Halifax, Nova Scotia (Table L3)
3.L14	Lakehead University, Port Arthur, Ontario (Table L7a)
3.L15	La Pocatière, Québec. Collège de Pocatière (Table L7a) Formerly Collège de Sainte-Anne-de-la-Pocatière
3.L17-.L26	L'Assomption, Quebec. Collège (Table L3)
3.L267	Laurentian University of Sudbury, Ontario (Table L7a)
3.L27-.L36	Université Laval, Québec (Table L3)
3.L4	Lethbridge, Alberta. University (Table L7a)
	London, Ontario. University of Western Ontario see LE3.W37+
3.L67-.L76	Loyola College, Montreal (Table L3)
3.M147-.M156	Macdonald College, Sainte Anne de Bellevue, Quebec (Table L3)
3.M17-.M26	McGill University, Montreal (Table L3)
3.M27-.M36	McMaster University, Hamilton, Ontario (Table L3)
3.M3827-.M3836	Manitoba. University. Winnipeg, Manitoba (Table L3)

America (except United States)
  Canada
    Universities and colleges -- Continued

3.M65	Montreal. College (Table L7a)
3.M66	Montreal. Concordia University (Table L7a)
3.M67-.M76	Montreal. Université (Table L3)
	Formerly Université Laval
3.M8	Montreal. Vanier College (Table L7a)
3.M87-.M96	Mount Allison University, Sackville, New Brunswick (Table L3)
3.M98	Mount Saint Vincent University. Halifax, Nova Scotia (Table L7a)
3.N27-.N36	New Brunswick. University. Fredericton, New Brunswick (Table L3)
3.N45	Newfoundland. Memorial University College, St. John's (Table L7a)
3.N57-.N66	Nicolet, Quebec. Séminaire (Table L3)
3.N72	Notre Dame College, Wilcox, Saskatchewan (Table L7a)
3.N74	Nova Scotia. Université Sainte-Anne (Table L7a)
3.O38	Okanagan College, Kelowna, British Columbia (Table L7a)
3.O77-.O86	Ottawa. University. Ottawa, Ontario (Table L3)
	Prince Edward Island
3.P75	Prince of Wales College, Charlottetown (Table L7a)
3.P77	University of Prince Edward Island (Table L7a)
	Québec (Province). Université du Québec (System)
3.Q25	General works (Table L7a)
3.Q254	Université du Québec à Montréal (Table L7a)
3.Q255	Université du Québec à Rimouski (Table L7a)
3.Q256	Université du Québec à Trois-Rivières (Table L7a)
3.Q27-.Q36	Queen's University. Kingston, Ontario (Table L3)
3.R44	Regina. University of Regina (Table L7a)
	Formerly University of Saskatchewan. Regina Campus
3.R55	Rimouski. Université du Québec à Rimouski (Table L7a)
3.R64	Rochdale College, Toronto, Ontario (Table L7a)
3.R67	Rosthern Junior College. Rosthern, Saskatchewan (Table L7a)
3.S2	Saint Dunstan's University, Charlottetown (Table L7a)
3.S47-.S56	Saint Laurent, Quebec. Collège (Table L3)
3.S5737-.S5746	Saint Mary's College, Montreal (Table L3)
3.S59	Saint Mary's University, Halifax, Nova Scotia (Table L7a)
	Sainte Anne de la Pocatière, Quebec (Province). Collège de la Pocatière see LE3.L15
3.S67-.S76	Saskatchewan. University. Saskatoon, Saskatchewan (Table L3)
3.S8	Sherbrooke, Quebec. Université (Table L7a)

America (except United States)
  Canada
    Universities and colleges -- Continued

3.S82	Simon Fraser University, Burnaby, British Columbia (Table L7a)
3.S85	Sir George Williams University, Montreal (Table L7a)
3.S89	St. Francis Xavier University, Antigonish, Nova Scotia (Table L7a)
3.S894	St. John's College, Winnepeg, Manitoba (Table L7a)
3.T47-.T56	Toronto. University (Table L3)
3.T57-.T66	Victoria College (Table L3)
3.T668	Toronto. University College (Table L7a)
3.T67-.T76	Trinity College, University of, Toronto (Table L3)
3.U67-.U76	Upper Canada College, Toronto (Table L3)
3.V37-.V46	Victoria University, Toronto (Table L3)
3.W25	Waterloo, Ontario. University (Table L7a)
3.W37-.W46	Western Ontario, University of. London, Ontario (Table L3)
3.W47	Windsor, Ontario. University (Table L7a)
3.W57-.W66	Winnipeg, University of (Table L3)

  Formed by union of Wesley College and Manitoba College, both situated in Winnipeg. July 1967, named changed from Winnipeg. United College

3.Y6	York University, Toronto (Table L7a)
3.5.A-Z	Community colleges. Junior colleges. By college, A-Z

  Subarrange each by Table L7a

4.A-Z	Women's colleges and girls' schools. By place, A-Z
5.A-Z	Schools. By place, A-Z

  Mexico

7.A-Z	Universities and colleges. By place, A-Z, i.e., by city, state, etc., as the case may be
7.A4	Acapulco. Universidad de América (Table L7a)
7.A47	Aguascalientes. Universidad Autónoma de Aguascalientes (Table L7a)
7.B4	Baja California Norte (Mexico). Universidad Autónoma de Baja California (Table L7a)
7.B5	Baja California Sur (Mexico). Universidad Autónoma de Baja California Sur (Table L7a)
7.C3	Campeche, Mexico (City). Universidad (Table L7a)

  Formerly known as Universidad del Sudeste

7.C43	Chapingo. Universidad Autónoma Chapingo (Table L7a)
7.C46	Chihuahua. Universidad Autónoma de Chihuahua (Table L7a)
7.C48	Chilpancingo de los Bravos. Universidad Autónoma de Guerrero (Table L7a)
7.C5	Ciudad Juárez. Universidad Autónoma de Ciudad Juárez (Table L7a)

America (except United States)
    Mexico
        Universities and colleges -- Continued

7.C62	Coahuila. Universidad Autónoma de Coahuila (Table L7a)
7.C636	Colima. Colegio de Colima (Table L7a)
7.C64	Colima. Universidad de Colima (Table L7a)
7.C83	Cuernavaca. Universidad Autónoma del Estado de Morelos (Table L7a)
7.C85	Culiacán. Universidad Autónoma de Sinaloa (Table L7a)
7.D85	Durango. Universidad Juárez del Estado de Durango (Table L7a)
7.G63	Guadalajara. Colegio de Jalisco (Table L7a)
7.G67-.G76	Guadalajara. Seminario Conciliar (Table L3)
7.G7657-.G7666	Guadalajara. Universidad (Table L3)
	Formerly Nueva Galicia (Mexico) Real Universidad Literaria de Guadalaxara
7.G7667-.G7676	Guadalajara. Universidad Autónoma de Guadalajara (Table L3)
7.G77-.G86	Guanajuato. Universidad (Table L3)
	Formerly known as Colegio de la Purísima Concepción and also as Colegio del Estado
7.H47-.H56	Hermosillo. Universidad de Sonora (Table L3)
7.L65	Los Mochis. Universidad de Occidente (Table L7a)
7.M17-.M26	Mérida. Universidad Autónoma de Yucatán (Table L3)
	Formerly Universidad Nacional del Sureste and Universidad de Yucatán
7.M27-.M36	Mexico (City). Colegio de México (Table L3)
7.M3667-.M3676	Mexico (City). Colegio de Santa Cruz de Tlatelolco (Table L3)
7.M368	Mexico (City). College (Table L7a)
	Name changed in 1963 to Mexico (City). University of the Americas
7.M37-.M46	Mexico (City). Escuela Nacional de Altos Estudios (Table L3)
7.M47-.M56	Mexico (City). Escuela Nacional Preparatorio (Table L3)
	Formerly Real Colegio de San Pedro, San Pablo y San Ildefonso, then Colegio de San Ildefonso
7.M563	Mexico (City). Universidad Autónoma Metropolitana (Table L7a)
7.M564	Mexico (City). Universidad Iberoamericana (Table L7a)
7.M57-.M66	Mexico (City). Universidad Nacional Autónoma de México (Table L3)
	Formerly Real y Pontificia Universidad de México, then Universidad Nacional de México
7.M67-.M76	Mexico (City). Universidad Obrera (Table L3)
	Mexico (City). University of the Americas see LE7.M368

America (except United States)
  Mexico
    Universities and colleges -- Continued

7.M765	Monterrey. Instituto Tecnológico y de Estudios Superiores de Monterrey (Table L7a)
7.M77-.M86	Morelia. Universidad Michoacana de San Nicolás de Hidalgo (Table L3)
7.N38	Nayarit. Universidad Autónoma de Nayarit, Tepic (Table L7a)
	Nueva Galicia (Mexico) Real Universidad Literaria de Guadalaxara see LE7.G7657+
7.N77-.N86	Nuevo León. Universidad Autónoma de Nuevo León (Table L3)
	Formerly Universidad de Nuevo León
7.O38	Oaxaca. Universidad Benito Juárez de Oaxaca (Table L7a)
7.P32	Pachuca. Universidad Autónoma de Hidalgo (Table L7a)
	Formerly Instituto Científico y Literario
7.P8	Puebla, Mexico (State). Benemérita Universidad Autónoma de Puebla (Table L7a)
	Formerly Universidad Autónoma de Puebla
7.P83	Puebla, Mexico (State). Universidad Popular Autónoma del Estado de Puebla (Table L7a)
7.Q45	Querétaro, Mexico (State). Universidad Autónoma de Querétaro (Table L7a)
7.S16	Saltillo. Universidad Autonoma Autónoma Agraria "Antonio Narro" (Table L7a)
7.S17	Saltillo. Universidad Autónoma del Noreste (Table L7a)
7.S2	Saltillo. Universidad de Coahuila (Table L7a)
7.S3	San Luis Potosí (City). Universidad (Table L7a)
7.T36	Tamaulipas. Universidad Autónoma de Tamaulipas (Table L7a)
7.T55	Tijuana. Colegio de la Frontera Norte (Table L7a)
	Formerly Centro de Estudios Fronterizos del Norte de México
7.T64	Toluca. Universidad Autónoma del Estado de México (Table L7a)
7.T88	Tuxtla Gutíerrez. Universidad Autónoma de Chiapas (Table L7)
7.V55	Villahermosa. Universidad Juárez Autónoma de Tabasco (Table L7a)
7.X34	Xalapa. Universidad Veracruzana (Table L7a)
7.Z34	Zacatecas. Universidad Autónoma de Zacatecas (Table L7a)
8.A-Z	Women's colleges and girls' schools. By place, A-Z
9.A-Z	Schools. By place, A-Z

  Central America

	America (except United States)
	Central America -- Continued
11.A-Z	Universities and colleges. By place, A-Z
11.C47-.C46	Costa Rica. Colegio de San Luis Gonzaga, Cartago (Table L3)
11.C64	Costa Rica. Universidad Autónoma de Centro América, San José (Table L7a)
11.C67-.C76	Costa Rica. Universidad de Costa Rica, San Pedro (Table L3)
11.C85	Costa Rica. Universidad de Santo Tomás, San José (Table L7a)
11.C87	Costa Rica. Universidad Nacional (Table L7a)
11.G77-.G86	Guatemala (City). Universidad de San Carlos (Table L3) Known also as Universidad Nacional and Universidad Autónoma
11.G872	Guatemala (City). Universidad Francisco Marroquín (Table L7a)
11.G88	Guatemala (City). Universidad Rafael Landivar (Table L7a)
11.H67-.H76	Honduras. Universidad Nacional Autónoma, Tegucigalpa (Table L3) Formerly Universidad Central
11.N35	Nicaragua. Instituto Nacional de Oriente (Table L7a)
11.N37-.N46	Nicaragua. Universidad Central, Managua (Table L3)
11.N48	Nicaragua. Universidad Centroamericana (Table L7a)
11.N6	Nicaragua. Universidad Nacional, León (Table L7a)
11.P55	Panama (City) Canal Zone College (Table L7a)
11.P67-.P76	Panama (City). Universidad (Table L3) Formerly Universidad Nacional and Universidad Interamericana
11.P77-.P86	Panama (City). Universidad Bolivariana (Table L3)
11.P88	Panama (City). Universidad Santa María La Antigua (Table L7a)
	San José, Costa Rica. Universidad de Santo Tomás see LE11.C85
11.S35	San Salvador. Universidad Centroamericana José Simeōn Cañas (Table L7a)
11.S37-.S46	San Salvador. Universidad de El Salvador (Table L3) Formerly Universidad Nacional Autónoma (El Salvador)
11.S49	San Salvador. Universidad Politecnica de El Salvador (Table L7a)
12.A-Z	Women's colleges and girls' schools. By place, A-Z
13.A-Z	Schools. By place, A-Z
	West Indies
15.A-Z	Universities and colleges. By place, A-Z, i.e., by city, province, island, etc., as the case may be

	America (except United States)
	West Indies
	Universities and colleges -- Continued
15.C38	Cave Hill, Barbados. University of the West Indies (Table L7a)
	Formerly Campus of the University of the West Indies
15.C87	Curaçao. Universiteit van de Nederlandse Antillen (Table L7a)
15.D65	Dominican Republic. Universidad Católica Madre y Maestra (Table L7a)
15.G73	Grand Turk Island (Turks and Caicos Islands). Mellen University (Table L7a)
15.H3	Port-au-Prince, Haiti (Republic). Université d'Etat d'Haiti (Table L7)
	Formerly Université, Port-au-Prince
15.H37-.H46	Havana. Universidad (Table L3)
15.H47-.H56	Havana. Universidad de Santo Tomás de Villanueva (Table L3)
15.H6	Havana. Universidad Masónica de Cuba (Table L7a)
15.K55	Kingston, Jamaica. Kingston College (Table L7a)
15.M37	Martinique. Académie des Antilles et de la Guyane (Table L7a)
15.M67-.M76	Mona, Jamaica. University of the West Indies (Table L3)
	Main campus of the University of the West Indies
15.P6	Santa María, Catholic University, Ponce, Puerto Rico (Table L7a)
	Puerto Rico. Sistema Universitario Ana G. Méndez
15.P718	General works (Table L7a)
15.P72	Universidad del Este (Table L7a)
	Formerly Puerto Rico Junior College, 1950-1992; Colegio Universitario del Este, 1992-2001
15.P725	Puerto Rico. Universidad Católica de Puerto Rico (Table L7a)
15.P73	Puerto Rico. Universidad del Sagrado Corazon (Table L7a)
15.P75	Puerto Rico. University. Mayagüez University Campus (Table L7a)
15.P77-.P86	Puerto Rico. University, Rio Pedras (Table L3)
15.S32	Santiago de Cuba. Universidad de Oriente (Table L7a)
15.S37-.S46	Santo Domingo. Universidad Autónoma de Santo Domingo (Table L3)
	Formerly Universidad de Santo Tomás, then Universidad de Santo Domingo
15.S48	Santo Domingo. Universidad Nacional Pedro Henríquez Ureña (Table L7a)
15.S7	St. Augustine, Trinidad. University of the West Indies (Table L7a)

	America (except United States)
	West Indies
	Universities and colleges -- Continued
15.S74	St. Lucia. University of the West Indies (Table L7a)
	University center of the University of the West Indies
15.S76	St. Vincent. University of the West Indies (Table L7a)
	University center of the University of the West Indies
15.V57	Virgin Islands of the United States. University of the Virgin Islands (Table L7a)
	Formerly College of the Virgin Islands
15.W47	West Indies. University of the West Indies (System) (Table L7a)
16.A-Z	Women's colleges and girls' schools. By place, A-Z
17.A-Z	Schools. By place, A-Z
	South America
	Argentina
21.A-Z	Universities and colleges. By place, A-Z, i.e., by city, province, county, etc., as the case may be
21.B22	Bahía Blanca. Universidad Nacional del Sur (Table L7a)
21.B27-.B36	Buenos Aires. Universidad del Salvador (Table L3)
	Formerly Colegio del Salvador
21.B47-.B56	Buenos Aires. Colegio Libre de Estudios Superiores (Table L3)
21.B6	Buenos Aires. Colegio Nacional (Table L7a)
21.B7	Buenos Aires. Pontificia Universidad Católica Argentina Santa María (Table L7a)
21.B77-.B86	Buenos Aires. Universidad (Table L3)
21.B88	Buenos Aires. Universidad de Belgrano (Table L7a)
21.B9	Buenos Aires. Universidad Nacional del Centro de la Provincia de Buenos Aires (Table L7a)
21.B95	Buenos Aires (Province). Universidad Nacional de General Sarmiento (Table L7a)
21.C5	Chubut (Ter.). Universidad de la Patagonia San Juan Bosco (Table L7a)
21.C57-.C66	Concepción del Uruguay. Colegio Nacional del Uruguay (Table L3)
21.C665	Córdoba. Universidad Católica de Córdoba (Table L7a)
21.C67-.C76	Córdoba. Universidad Nacional (Table L3)
21.C85	Corrientes (City). Universidad Nacional del Nordeste (Table L7a)
21.L32	La Pampa (Province). Universidad (Table L7a)
21.L37-.L46	La Plata. Universidad Nacional (Table L3)
21.L85	Luján (Buenos Aires). Universidad Nacional (Table L7a)
21.M25	Mar del Plata. Colegio National (Table L7a)
	Mendoza (City)

	America (except United States)
	South America
	Argentina
	Universities and colleges
	Mendoza (City) -- Continued
21.M35	Universidad de Mendoza (Table L7a)
21.M37-.M46	Universidad Nacional de Cuyo (Table L3)
21.N48	Neuquén. Universidad Nacional del Comahue (Table L7a)
21.R67-.R76	Rosario (Santa Fe). Universidad Nacional del Litoral (Table L3)
21.S25	Salta. Universidad Nacional de Salta (Table L7a)
21.S35	San Juan. Universidad Nacional de San Juan (Table L7a)
21.S42	San Luis. Universidad Nacional de San Luis (Table L7a)
21.T67-.T76	Tucumán. Universidad Nacional (Table L3)
	Formerly known as Colegio San Miguel and also as Colegio Nacional
21.V54	Villa María. Universidad Nacional de Villa María (Table L7a)
22.A-Z	Women's colleges and girls' schools. By place, A-Z
23.A-Z	Schools. By place, A-Z
	Bolivia
27.A-Z	Universities and colleges. By place, A-Z
27.B4	Beni. Universidad Autónoma (Table L7a)
27.C57-.C66	Cochabamba. Universidad Mayor de San Simón (Table L3)
	Formerly Cochabamba. Universidad Autónoma Simón Bolívar
27.L317	La Paz. Unviersidad Boliviana (System) (Table L7a)
27.L37-.L46	La Paz. Universidad Mayor de "San Andres" (Table L3)
27.L48	La Paz. Universidad Nuestra Señora de La Paz (Table L7a)
27.O77-.O86	Oruro. Universidad Técnica (Table L3)
27.P6	Potosí. Universidad Autónoma Tomás Frías (Table L7a)
27.S3	Santa Cruz. Universidad Autónoma "Gabriel René Moreno" (Table L7a)
	Formerly Universidad Mayor Gabriel René Moreno
27.S35	Santa Cruz. Universidad Privada de Santa Cruz de la Sierra (Table L7a)
27.S8	Sucre. Universidad Mayor de San Francisco Xavier (Table L7a)
27.T3	Tarija. Universidad Autónoma Juan Misael Saracho (Table L7a)
	Formerly Universidad "Juan Misael Saracho"

	America (except United States)
	South America
	Bolivia -- Continued
28.A-Z	Women's colleges and girls' schools. By place, A-Z
29.A-Z	Schools. By place, A-Z
	Brazil
31.A-Z	Universities and colleges. By place, A-Z, i.e., by city, province, county, etc., as the case may be
	Acre. Universidade see LE31.R37
31.A55	Alagoas, Brazil (State). Universidade Federal (Table L7a)
31.A58	Alta Floresta. UNIFLOR (União das Faculdades de Alta Floresta) (Table L7a)
31.A72	Aracaju. Universidade Federal de Sergipe (Table L7a)
	Bahia (State)
31.B28	Universidade Estadual de Santa Cruz (Table L7a)
31.B3	Universidade Federal (Table L7a)
31.B37	Bauru. Faculdade de Filosofia, Ciências e Letras do Sagrado Coração de Jesus (Table L7a)
	Bauru. Faculdades do Sagrado Coração see LE31.B38
	Bauru. Federação das Faculdades do Sagrado Coração see LE31.B38
31.B38	Bauru. Universidade do Sagrado Coração (Table L7a)
	Earlier names: Federação das Faculdades do Sagrado Coração; Faculdades do Sagrado Coração
31.B39	Belo Horizonte. Pontifícia Universidade Católica de Minas Gerais (Table L7a)
31.B4	Belo Horizonte. Universidade de Minas Gerais (Table L7a)
	Name changed in 1969 to Minas Gerais, Brazil. Universidade Federal
31.B55	Blumenau. Universidade Regional de Blumenau (Table L7a)
31.B7	Brasília. Universidade (Table L7a)
31.C2	Campina Grande. Universidade Regional do Nordeste (Table L7a)
31.C24	Campinas. Universidade Estadual de Campinas (Table L7a)
31.C25	Canoas. Universidade Luterana do Brasil (Table L7a)
31.C27-.C36	Colégio do Caraca (Table L3)
31.C38	Caxias do Sul. Universidade (Table L7a)
	Ceará
31.C39	Universidade Estadual do Ceará (Table L7a)
31.C4	Universidade Federal (Table L7a)
	Formerly Fortaleza. Universidade do Ceará
31.C65	Curitiba. Universidade Católica (Table L7a)
31.C77-.C86	Curitiba. Universidade do Paraná (Table L3)

	America (except United States)
	South America
	Brazil
	Universities and colleges -- Continued
31.E5	Espírito Santo. Universidade Federal (Table L7a)
	Formerly Vitória (Espírito Santo). Universidade Federal
31.F33	Feira de Santana. Universidade Estadual de Feira de Santana (Table L7a)
	Fortaleza
31.F45	Universidade de Fortaleza (Table L7a)
	Universidade do Ceará see LE31.C4
31.F77-.F86	Friburgo. Colégio Anchieta (Table L3)
31.G6	Goiás, Brazil (State). Universidade Federal (Table L7a)
31.G8	Guanabara. Universidade (Table L7a)
	Name changed to Rio do Janeiro (State). Universidade do Estado
31.I83	Itajaí. Universidade do Vale do Itajaí (Table L7a)
31.J8	Juiz de Fora. Universidade Federal (Table L7a)
31.L65	Londrina. Universidade Estadual (Table L7a)
	Mackenzie College see LE31.S27+
	Manaus
31.M315	Universidade de Manáos (Table L7a)
31.M32	Universidade do Amazonas (Table L7a)
31.M34	Maranhão. Universidade Estadual do Maranhão (Table L7a)
31.M35	Marílla. Faculdade de Filosofia, Ciência e Letras (Table L7a)
31.M36	Maringá. Universidade Estadual de Maringá (Table L7a)
31.M38	Mato Grosso, Brazil (State). Universidade Federal de Mato Grosso (Table L7a)
31.M55	Minas Gerais, Brazil. Universidade Católica (Table L7a)
	Minas Gerais, Brazil. Universidade Federal see LE31.B4
31.M62	Mogi das Cruzes, Brazil. Universidade (Table L7a)
31.M65	Mossoró. Colégio Diocesano Santa Luzia (Table L7a)
31.N5	Niteroi. Universidade Federal Fluminense (Table L7a)
31.O44	Olinda. Faculdade de Ciências Humanas de Olinda (Table L7a)
31.P24	Palmas. Faculdade de Filosofia Ciências e Letras de Palmas (Table L7a)
31.P3	Pará (State). Universidade Federal (Table L7a)
31.P32	Paraíba, Brazil (State). Universidade Federal (Table L7a)
31.P34	Paraná (State). Universidade Federal (Table L7a)
31.P35	Passo Fundo. Universidade de Passo Fundo (Table L7a)

	America (except United States)
	South America
	Brazil
	Universities and colleges -- Continued
31.P37	Pelotas, Brazil. Universidade Católica (Table L7a)
	Pernambuco
31.P4	Universidade Federal (Table L7a)
31.P5	Universidade Federal Rural (Table L7a)
31.P55	Piracicaba. Universidade Metodista de Piracicaba (Table L7a)
31.P67-.P76	Pôrto Alegre. Pontifícia Universidade Católica do Rio Grande do Sul (Table L3)
	Formerly Universidade Católica do Rio Grande do Sul
31.P8	Pôrto Alegre. Universidade Federal do Rio Grande do Sul (Table L7a)
31.R3	Recife. Universidade (Table L7a)
31.R33	Recife. Universidade Católica de Pernambuco (Table L7a)
31.R37	Rio Branco. Universidade Federal do Acre (Table L7a)
	Formerly Universidade do Acre
31.R4	Rio de Janeiro. Colégio Cruzeiro (Table L7a)
31.R47-.R56	Rio de Janeiro. Colégio Pedro II (Table L3)
31.R563	Rio de Janeiro. Colégio Santo Inácio (Table L7a)
31.R566	Rio de Janeiro. Pontífícia Universidade Católica (Table L7a)
31.R57-.R66	Rio de Janeiro. Universidade Federal (Table L3)
	Rio de Janeiro (State). Universidad do Estado see LE31.G8
31.R7	Rio Grande do Norte (State). Universidade Federal (Table L7a)
	Formerly Rio Grande do Norte (State)
31.R75	Rio Grande do Sul (State). Universidade Federal (Table L7a)
31.S2	Salvador. Universidade (Table L7a)
	Santa Catarina
31.S22	Universidade Federal (Table L7a)
31.S23	Universidade para o Desenvolvimento do Estado de Santa Catarina (Table L7a)
31.S235	Santa Cruz do Sul. Universidade de Santa Cruz do Sul (Table L7a)
31.S24	Santa Maria (Rio Grande do Sul). Universidade Federal (Table L7a)
31.S246	São Carlos. Universidade Federal de São Carlos (Table L7a)
31.S248	São José dos Campos (São Paulo). Universidade do Vale do Paraíba (Table L7a)

	America (except United States)
	South America
	Brazil
	Universities and colleges -- Continued
31.S25	São Luis. Universidade Federal do Maranhão (Table L7a)
	Formerly Universidade do Maranhão
31.S26	São Paulo. Fundação Armando Alvares Penteado (Table L7a)
31.S27-.S36	São Paulo. Instituto Mackenzie (Table L3)
	Formerly Mackenzie College
31.S363	São Paulo. Pontifícia Universidade Católica de São Paulo (Table L7a)
	Formerly Universidade Católica
31.S365	São Paulo. Universidade Cruzeiro do Sul (Table L7a)
31.S37-.S46	São Paulo. Universidade de São Paulo (Table L3)
31.S57	São Paulo. Universidade Estadual Paulista Julio de Mesquita (Table L7a)
31.S58	São Paulo. Universidade Federal de São Paulo (Table L7a)
31.S62	São Paulo. Universidade Metodista de São Paulo (Table L7a)
	Sergipe (State). Universidade Federal de Sergipe, Aracaju see LE31.A72
31.S73	Seropédica. Universidade Federal Rural do Rio de Janeiro (Table L7a)
31.T63	Tocantins. Universidade do Tocantins (Table L7a)
31.U23	Uberlândia. Universidade (Table L7a)
31.U55	União da Vitória. Faculdade Estadual de Filosofia, Ciências e Letras (Table L7a)
31.V5	Viọsa. Universidade Federal (Table L7a)
	Vitória (Espírito Santo). Universidade Federal see LE31.E5
32.A-Z	Women's colleges and girls' schools. By place, A-Z
33.A-Z	Schools. By place, A-Z
	Chile
36.A-Z	Universities and colleges. By place, A-Z
36.A5	Antofagasta. Universidad del Norte (Table L7a)
(36.C47-.C56)	Chile. Universidad, Santiago de Chile
	see LE36.S27+
	Concepción (City)
36.C64	Universidad del Bío-Bío (Table L7a)
36.C67-.C76	Universidad de Concepción (Table L3)
36.S27-.S36	Santiago. Universidad de Chile (Table L3)
36.S37-.S46	Santiago de Chile. Universidad Católica (Table L3)
36.T34	Talca. Universidad de Talca (Table L7a)

	America (except United States)
	South America
	Chile
	Universities and colleges -- Continued
36.V25	Valdivia (City). Universidad Austral de Chile (Table L7a)
36.V3	Valparaiso (City). Universidad Católica (Table L7a)
37.A-Z	Women's colleges and girls' schools. By place, A-Z
38.A-Z	Schools. By place, A-Z
	Colombia
41.A-Z	Universities and colleges. By place, A-Z
	Barranquilla
41.B17-.B26	Colegio de San José (Table L3)
41.B3	Universidad del Atlántico (Table L7a)
41.B34	Universidad del Norte (Table L7a)
	Bogotá
41.B47-.B56	Colegio Mayor de Nuestra Senora de Rosario (Table L3)
41.B58	Fundación Universidad Central (Table L7a)
41.B59	Fundación Universitaria Autónoma de Colombia (Table L7a)
41.B6	Real Colegio Mayor y Seminario de San Bartolomé (Table L7a)
41.B63	Universidad Antonio Nariño (Table L7a)
	Formerly Universidad Independiente de Colombia "Antonio Nariño," 1976-1980; Corporación Universitaria Antonio Nariño, 1980-1994.
41.B65	Universidad de La Salle (Table L7a)
41.B7	Universidad de los Andes (Table L7a)
41.B715	Universidad de San Buenaventura (Table L7a)
41.B72	Universidad de Santo Tomas (Bogotá, Colombia) (Table L7a)
41.B73	Universidad Distrital Francisco José de Caldas (Table L7a)
41.B76	Universidad Externado de Colombia (Table L7a)
41.B77-.B86	Universidad Javeriana (Table L3)
	Universidad Nacional see LE41.C67+
41.B87	Universidad Pedagógica Nacional (Table L7a)
41.B887-.B896	Bucaramanga. Colegio de Santander (Table L3)
	Cali
41.C2	Universidad del Valle (Table L7a)
41.C24	Universidad Santiago de Cali (Table L7a)
41.C27-.C36	Cartagena. Universidad (Table L3)
41.C47-.C56	Cauca (Dept.). Universidad Popayán (Table L3)
41.C63	Chia (Cundinamarca). Universidad de la Sabana (Table L7a)
41.C67-.C76	Colombia. Universidad, Bogotá (Table L3)

America (except United States)
South America
Colombia
Universities and colleges. By place, A-Z -- Continued
41.C78   Colombia. Universidad Libre, Bogotá (Table L7a)
41.C85   Córdoba, Colombia (Dept.). Universidad (Table L7a)
41.I2   Ibagué. Universidad del Tolima (Table L7a)
41.M27-.M36   Manizales. Universidad de Caldas (Table L3)
41.M47-.M56   Medellín. Colegio de San Ignacio de Loyola (Table L3)
41.M5677-.M5686   Medellín. Universidad Pontificia Bolivariana (Table L3)
    Formerly Universidad Católica Bolivariana
41.M57-.M66   Medellín. Universidad de Antioquia (Table L3)
41.M67   Medellín. Universidad EAFIT (Table L7a)
    Formerly Escuela de Administración y Finanzas y Tecnologías; Escuela de Administración y Finanzas e Instituto Tecnologías
41.P47-.P56   Pasto. Universidad de Nariño (Table L3)
41.P64   Pereira. Universidad Católica Popular del Risaralda (Table L7a)
    Formerly Fundación Autónoma Popular del Risaralda
41.Q49   Quindío. Universidad del Quindío (Table L7a)
41.T8   Tunja. Colegio de Boyacá (Table L7a)
41.T83   Tunja. Universidad Pedagógica y Tecnológica de Colombia (Table L7a)
    Formerly Escuela Normal Superior de Colombia
42.A-Z   Women's colleges and girls' schools. By place, A-Z
43.A-Z   Schools. By place, A-Z
Ecuador
46.A-Z   Universities and colleges. By place, A-Z
46.C87-.C96   Cuenca (City). Universidad del Cuenca (Table L3)
    Formerly Universidad del Azuay
46.G77-.G86   Guayaquil. Colegio Nacional Vicente Rocafuerte (Table L3)
46.G868   Guayaquil. Universidad Catlíca (Table L7a)
    Formerly Universidad Católica de Santiago de Guayaquil
46.G87-.G96   Guayaquil. Universidad de Guayaquil (Table L3)
46.Q27-.Q36   Quito. Instituto Nacional "Mejía" (Table L3)
46.Q365   Quito. Universidad Andina Simón Bolívar (Table L7a)
46.Q37-.Q46   Quito. Universidad Católica del Ecuador (Table L3)
46.Q47-.Q56   Quito. Universidad Central (Table L3)
47.A-Z   Women's colleges and girls' schools. By place, A-Z
    Subarrange each by Table L7a
48.A-Z   Schools. By place, A-Z
    Subarrange each by Table L7a
Guianas
Guyana
51.A-Z   Universities and colleges. By name, A-Z

	America (except United States)
	South America
	Guianas
	Guyana
	Universities and colleges. By name, A-Z -- Continued
51.Q37-.Q46	Queen's College, Georgetown (Table L3)
53.A-Z	Schools. By place, A-Z
	Suriname
54.A-Z	Universities and colleges. By place, A-Z, i.e., by city, province, county, etc., as the case may be
56.A-Z	Schools. By place, A-Z
	French Guiana
57.A-Z	Universities and colleges. By place, A-Z, i.e., by city, province, county, etc., as the case may be
59.A-Z	Schools. By place, A-Z
	Paraguay
61.A-Z	Universities and colleges. By place, A-Z
61.A75	Asunción. Universidad Católica Nuestra Señora de la Asunción (Table L7a)
61.A77-.A86	Asunción. Universidad Nacional (Table L3)
62.A-Z	Women's colleges and girls' schools. By place, A-Z
63.A-Z	Schools. By place, A-Z
	Peru
66.A-Z	Universities and colleges. By place, A-Z, i.e., by city, province, county, etc., as the case may be
66.A77-.A86	Arequipa (City). Universidad Nacional de Agustín (Table L3)
	Known also as Universidad Nacional and Universidad del Gran Padre San Agustín
66.A863	Arequipa (City). Universidad Popular Municipal de Arequipa (Table L7a)
66.A87-.A96	Ayachuco (City). Universidad de San Cristóbal de Huamanga (Table L3)
	Cajamarca
66.C24	Colegio Central de Ciencias y Artes de Cajamarca (Table L7a)
66.C27-.C36	Colegio Nacional "San Ramón" (Table L3)
66.C37-.C46	Caras. Colegio Nacional (Table L3)
66.C77-.C86	Cuzco. Universidad (Table L3)
66.H8	Huancayo. Universidad Nacional del Centro del Perú (Table L7a)
66.I3	Ica, Peru (City). Colegio San Luis Gonzaga (Table L7a)
66.L3	Lima. Colegio de la Inmaculada (Table L7a)
66.L4	Lima. Colegio Nacional de Nuestra Señora de Guadalupe (Table L7a)
66.L47-.L56	Lima. Universidad Católica del Perú (Table L3)

America (except United States)
  South America
    Peru
      Universities and colleges. By place, A-Z -- Continued

66.L67-.L76	Lima. Universidad de San Marcos (Table L3)
	Known also as Universidad Nacional Mayor de San Marcos de Lima
66.L78	Lima. Universidad del Pacífico (Table L7a)
66.L85	Lima. Universidad "Inca Garcilaso de la Vega" (Table L7a)
66.L89	Lima. Universidad Ricardo Palma (Table L7a)
66.P58	Piura. Universidad de Piura (Table L7a)
66.T77-.T86	Trujillo. Universidad de la Libertad (Table L3)
	Known also as Universidad Nacional
66.T89	Trujillo. Universidad Privada "Antenor Orrego" (Table L7a)
67.A-Z	Women's colleges and girls' schools. By place, A-Z
68.A-Z	Schools. By place, A-Z

    Uruguay

71.A-Z	Universities and colleges. By place, A-Z
71.M57-.M66	Montevideo. Universidad de la República (Uruguay) (Table L3)
	Formerly Montevideo. Universidad
71.M67-.M76	Montevideo. Universidad Central Americana (Table L3)
	Formerly Montevideo. Universidad
72.A-Z	Women's colleges and girls' schools. By place, A-Z
73.A-Z	Schools. By place, A-Z

    Venezuela

76.A-Z	Universities and colleges. By place, A-Z
76.B37	Barquisimeto. Universidad Centro Occidental Lisandro Alvarado (Table L7a)
76.C3	Caracas. Universidad Católica Andrés Bello (Table L7a)
76.C32	Caracas. Universidad Metropolitana (Table L7a)
76.C33	Caracas. Universidad Simon Bolivar (Table L7a)
76.C34	Caracas. Universidad Simón Rodriquez (Table L7a)
76.C37-.C46	Venezuela. Universidad Central, Caracas (Table L3)
76.C8	Cumaná. Universidad de Oriente (Table L7a)
	Name changed in 1946 to Zulia. Universidad
76.M27-.M36	Maracaibo. Universidad de Zulia (Table L3)
	Name changed in 1946 to Zulia. Universidad
76.M47-.M56	Mérida (City). Universidad de los Andes (Table L3)
	Name changed in 1946 to Zulia. Universidad
76.T33	Táchira. Universidad Experimental del Táchira (Table L7a)
76.V3	Valencia. Universidad de Carabobo (Table L7a)
	Zulia. Universidad see LE76.M27+

LE

America (except United States)
South America
Venezuela
77.A-Z Women's colleges and girls' schools. By place, A-Z
78.A-Z Schools. By place, A-Z

Individual institutions
For individual institutions limited to education in a special field, see
the topic, e.g. class K, law schools, R741+ medical schools,
S536.5+ agricultural colleges, T171+ technical schools
Great Britain
England
Bath (Avon)

14	University of Bath (Table L7)
	Birmingham
20-29.5	Mason College (Table L9)
29.8	University of Aston in Birmingham
30-39.5	University of Birmingham (Table L9)
	Brighton
55	University of Sussex (Table L7)
60-69.5	University College (Table L9)
	Bristol
75	Buckingham. University College at Buckingham (Table L7)
	Cambridge
98.5	Anglia Ruskin University (Table L7)
	University
101.A3	Charters. Constitution, etc.
101.A7	Regulations. Statutes
	Administration. Official publications
101.B1	Council
101.B3	Chancellor
101.B5	Financial Board
101.B6-.B9	Other
101.C5-.C6	Calendars. Catalogs. Registers
	Cf. LF124.A+ General biographical catalogs,
	registers of alumni
101.C7	Announcements
101.C8	Students' handbooks
101.C9	Directories
102.A-Z	Finance
	Cf. LF101.B5 Financial Board
102.F3	General
	Special
103.F5	Appropriations
103.F6	Endowments
103.F7	Bequests, etc.
103.F8	Fellowships, scholarships, etc.
103.F9	Prizes
	Organization. Policy
104.A3	Early works to 1800
104.A5-Z	Later works, 1801-
105	Curriculum
	Including entrance requirements

LF

	Great Britain
	England
	Cambridge
	University
	Colleges -- Continued
150-159.5	Clare (Table L9)
160-169.5	Corpus Christi (Table L9)
169.8	Darwin College (Table L7)
170-179.5	Downing (Table L9)
180-189.5	Emanuel (Table L9)
190-199.5	Jesus (Table L9)
200-209.5	King's (Table L9)
210-219.5	Magdalene (Table L9)
	New Hall see LF797.A+
	Newnham College see LF797.C34
220-229.5	Pembroke (Table L9)
229.8	Peterhouse (Table L7)
230-239.5	Queen's (Table L9)
240-249.5	St. Catherine's (Table L9)
250-259.5	St. John's (Table L9)
260-269.5	St. Peter's (Peterhouse) (Table L9)
270-279.5	Selwyn (Table L9)
280-289.5	Sidney Sussex (Table L9)
290-299.5	Trinity (Table L9)
300-309.5	Trinity Hall (Table L9)
	Colchester
309.55	University of Essex (Table L7)
	Coventry
309.6	University of Warwick (Table L7)
	Durham
310-319.5	Durham University (Table L9 modified)
319.5.A-Z	Special colleges, A-Z
	Subarrange each by Table L7a
	Cf. LF470+ Armstrong College
	Exeter
321	University of Exeter (Table L7)
	Formerly Royal Albert Memorial College, then University College of the South West of England
	Hackney
325	New College (Table L7)
	Hull
330	University College (Table L7)
332	Humberside. University of Lincolnshire and Humberside (Table L7)
	Formerly Hull College of Higher Education; Humberside College of Higher Education; Humberside Polytechic
	Keele

LF

	Great Britain
	England
	Keele -- Continued
335	University College of North Staffordshire (Table L7)
338	Lancaster University (Table L7)
	Leeds
340-349.5	University and Yorkshire College (Table L9)
	Cf. LF450+ Victoria University, Manchester, after 1903
	Leicester
355	University (Table L7)
	Liverpool
360	South Mersey College (Table L7)
370-379.5	Liverpool. University of Liverpool (Table L9)
	Formerly University College, Liverpool
	Cf. LF450+ Victoria University, Manchester, after 1903
	London
400-419.5	University of London (Table L8 modified)
419.5.A-Z	Special colleges, A-Z
	e.g.
419.5.B5	Birkbeck (Table L7a)
420-429.5	University College (Table L9)
430-439.5	King's College (Table L9)
449.A-Z	Other colleges, A-Z
	Manchester
450-459.5	Victoria University (Table L9)
460-469.5	Owens College (Table L9)
	University College see LF360+
	Yorkshire College see LF339.92+
	Newcastle
470-479.5	Armstrong College (Table L9)
479.9	University (Table L7)
479.95	Norwich. University of East Anglia (Table L7)
	Nottingham
480-489.5	University (Table L9)
495	Old Windsor Beaumont College (Table L7)
	Oxford
	University
501.A3	Charters. Constitutions, etc.
501.A7	Regulations. Statutes
	Administration. Official publications
501.B1	Council
501.B3	Chancellor
501.B5	Treasurer
501.B6-.B9	Other
501.C3	Oxford University gazette

	Great Britain
	England
	Oxford
	University -- Continued
	Calendars. Registers. Yearbooks
	Cf. LF524 General biographical catalogs, registers of alumni
501.C4	Early to 1800
501.C5	1801-
501.C7	Announcements
501.C8	Students' handbooks
501.C9	Directories
502	Finance
	Cf. LF501.B5 Treasurer or the university
502.F3	General
	Special
503.F5	Appropriations
503.F6	Endowments
503.F7	Bequests
503.F8	Fellowships, scholarships, etc.
	Including Rhodes scholarships
503.F9	Prizes
	Organization. Policy
504.A3	Early works to 1800
504.A5-Z	Later works, 1801-
505	Curriculum
	Including entrance requirements
506	Degrees and honors
507	Examinations
	History and description
508	Collections. Documents. Sources
509	General works
510	General special. Description. Architectural histories
	Medieval
511	General
513	Special
	16th-18th centuries
514	Early works
	Modern works
515	General
516	General special. Policy
517	Reminiscences
	19th century
518	General
519	General special. Policy
520	Reminiscences
	20th century

	Great Britain
	England
	Oxford
	University
	History and description
	16th-18th centuries
	20th century -- Continued
521	General
522	General special. Policy
523	Reminiscences
523.2	21st century
	Biography
524	General catalogs. Registers of alumni
524.A2	Official
525	Other collections
526.A-Z	Individual, A-Z
527	Guidebooks
528	Other descriptive works
	Student life
	Cf. LA637.7 University student life in England
529	General works
529.5.A-Z	Student societies, A-Z
	e.g.
529.5.O7	Oxford Union Society
	Colleges
530-539.5	All Souls (Table L9)
540-549.5	Balliol (Table L9)
550-559.5	Brasenose (Table L9)
560-569.5	Christ Church (Table L9)
570-579.5	Corpus Christi (Table L9)
580-589.5	Exeter (Table L9)
590-599.5	Hertford (Table L9)
600-609.5	Jesus (Table L9)
610-619.5	Keble (Table L9)
620-629.5	Lincoln (Table L9)
630-639.5	Magdalen (Table L9)
640-649.5	Merton (Table L9)
650-659.5	New College (Table L9)
659.55	Nuffield College (Table L7)
660-669.5	Oriel (Table L9)
670-679.5	Pembroke (Table L9)
680-689.5	Queen's (Table L9)
690-699.5	St. John's (St. John the Baptist) (Table L9)
700-709.5	Trinity (Table L9)
710-719.5	University College (Table L9)
720-729.5	Wadham (Table L9)
730-739.5	Worcester (Table L9)

	Great Britain
	England
	Oxford
	University
	Colleges -- Continued
741.A-Z	Other. Noncomformist, etc., A-Z
741.M21	Manchester College (Table L7a)
741.M35	Mansfield College (Table L7a)
750	Reading. University (Table L7)
755	Salford (Lancashire) University (Table L7)
760-769.5	Sheffield. University College (Table L9)
775	Southampton. University (Table L7)
	Springhill College, Birmingham see LF741.M35
780	Surry, England. University (Table L7)
787	York. University College of Ripon and York St. John (Table L7)
790	York University (Table L7)
795.A-Z	Schools. By place, A-Z
	Subarrange each by Table L7a
	e.g.
795.R92	Rugby School (Table L7a)
797.A-Z	Women's colleges and girls' schools. By place, A-Z
	Subarrange each by Table L7a
797.C337	Cambridge, England. New Hall (Table L7a)
797.C34	Cambridge, England. Newnham College (Table L7a)
	Ireland
800-809.5	Belfast. Queen's College (Table L9)
	Later (1908-) Queen's University
830-839.5	Cork. University College (Table L9)
	Formerly Queen's College
	Dublin
	Catholic University of Ireland see LF910+
850-859.5	Queen's University in Ireland (Table L9)
860-869.5	Royal University of Ireland (Table L9)
870-879.5	National University of Ireland (Table L9)
900-909.5	University of Dublin (Trinity College) (Table L9)
910-919.5	University College (Table L9)
	Including Catholic University of Ireland
930-939.5	Galway. University College (Table L9)
953.A-Z	Other universities and colleges. By place, A-Z
	Subarrange each by Table L7a
955.A-Z	Schools. By place, A-Z
957.A-Z	Womens' colleges and girls' schools. By place, A-Z
	Scotland
960-979.5	Aberdeen. University of Aberdeen (Table L8)
1000-1009.5	Dundee. University College (Table L9)
	Edinburgh

	Great Britain
	Scotland
	Edinburgh -- Continued
1020-1029.5	New College (Table L9)
1030-1049.5	University of Edinburgh (Table L8)
	Glasgow
1070-1089.5	University of Glasgow (Table L8)
1095	University of Strathclyde (Table L7)
1100-1119.5	St. Andrew's. University of St. Andrew's (Table L8)
1134.A-Z	Other universities and colleges, A-Z
1135.A-Z	Schools. By place, A-Z
1137.A-Z	Women's colleges and girls' schools. By place, A-Z
	Wales
1140-1149.5	University of Wales (Table L9)
1150-1159.5	University College of Wales, Aberystwith (Table L9)
1170-1179.5	University College of North Wales, Bangor (Table L9)
1200-1209.5	University College of South Wales and Monmouthshire, Cardiff (Table L9)
1210-1219.5	University College of Swansea (Table L9)
1223	Carmarthen. Trinity College (Table L7)
1225	Harlech. Coleg Harlech (Table L7)
1230-1239.5	Lampeter. St. David's College (Table L9)
1255.A-Z	Schools. By place, A-Z
1257.A-Z	Women's colleges and girls' schools. By place, A-Z
	Continental Europe
	Austria-Hungary (Former)
	Austria
(1311-1330)	Chernivets'kyĭ derz͡havnyĭ see LF4449.25
1341-1360.5	Graz. Universität Graz (Table L10)
1371-1380.5	Innsbruck. Universität Innsbruck (Table L11) Formerly Leopold-Franzens Universität
(1401-1420)	Uniwersytet Jagielloński see LF4203
(1431-1450)	L'vivs'skyĭ derz͡havnyĭ universytet im. Iv. Franka see LF4449.23
(1451-1460)	Univerzita Palackého v Olomouci see LF1543
(1461-1480)	Universita Karlova see LF1545
(1481-1500)	Deutsche Universität see LF1546
1511-1530.5	Vienna. Universität Wien (Table L10)
1533.A-Z	Other universities. By place, A-Z Subarrange each by Table L13a
1535.A-Z	Schools. By place, A-Z

Continental Europe
  Austria-Hungary (Former)
    Austria -- Continued
1537.A-Z   Women's colleges and girls' schools. By place, A-Z
                    Subarrange each by Table L13a
    Czech Republic
1541   Brno. Masarykova universita v Brně (Table L13)
1543   Olomouc. Univerzita Palackého v Olomouci (Table L13)
      Prague
1545   Universita Karlova (Table L13)
1546   Deutsche Universität (Table L13)
1546.2   Universita 17. listopadu v Praze (Table L13)
1547.A-Z   Other universities. By place, A-Z
                    Subarrange each by Table L13a
1548.A-Z   Schools. By place, A-Z
1549.A-Z   Women's colleges and girls' schools. By place, A-Z
                    Subarrange each by Table L13a
    Slovakia
1550   Bratislava. Univerzita Komenského v Bratislave (Table
                    L13)
                    Formerly Bratislava. Univerzita
1550.2.A-Z   Other universities. By place, A-Z
                    Subarrange each by Table L13a
1550.5.A-Z   Schools. By place, A-Z
1550.8.A-Z   Women's colleges and girls' schools. By place, A-Z
                    Subarrange each by Table L13a
    Hungary
(1551-1560.5)   Agram (Zagreb). Univerzitet
                    see LF5523
      Budapest
1561-1570.5   Central European University (Table L11)
1581-1600.5   Eőtvős Lorand Tudományegyetem (Table L10)
                    Formerly Tudományegyetem
1611-1630.5   Debrecen. Kossuth Lajos Tudományegyetem (Table L10)
                    Formerly Todományegyetem
(1631-1650)   Magyar Királyi Ferenc József Tudományegyetem
                    see LF5143.C5
(1651-1670)   Universita Komenského v Bratislave
                    see LF1550
1693.A-Z   Other universities. By place, A-Z
                    Subarrange each by Table L13a
1695.A-Z   Schools. By place, A-Z
1697.A-Z   Women's colleges and girls' schools. By place, A-Z
                    Subarrange each by Table L13a
    Finland

	Continental Europe
	Finland -- Continued
1705	Helsingfors (Helsinki). Universitet. Yliopisto (Table L13)
	Formerly Åbo akademi (1640-1827), then Keisarillinen Aleksanterin yliopisto
1707.A-Z	Other universities. By place, A-Z
1707.J64	Joensuu. Korkeakoulu (Table L13a)
	Jyvaskyla
(1707.J94)	Kasvatusopillinen Korkeakoulu
	see LB2100.5
1707.J97	Yliopisto (Table L13a)
1707.O946	Oulu. Yliopisto (Table L13a)
1707.T34	Tampere. Yliopisto (Table L13a)
	Turku
1707.T878	Åbo akademi (1918-) (Table L13a)
1707.T9	Yliopisto (Table L13a)
1708.A-Z	Schools. By place, A-Z
1709.A-Z	Women's colleges and girls' schools. By place, A-Z
	Subarrange each by Table L13a
	France
1711-1730.5	Aix-Marseille. Université de Provence (Table L10)
	Formerly Université d'Aix-Marseille
1735	Amiens. Université de Picardie (Table L13)
	Formerly Université d'Amiens
1741-1750.5	Angers. Université catholique (Table L11)
1757	Avignon. Université (Table L13)
	1303-1791
1771-1790.5	Besançon. Université (Table L10)
1801-1820.5	Bordeaux (Aquitaine). Université (Table L10)
1822	Bourges. Université (Table L13)
1831-1850.5	Caen. Université (Table L10)
1861-1880.5	Clermont-Ferrand. Université (Table L10)
1891-1900.5	Dijon. Université (Table L11)
1921-1940.5	Université de Grenoble (Table L10)
	Replaced in 1970 by Université scientifique et médicale de Grenoble (Grenoble 1), Université des sciences sociales de Grenoble (Grenoble 2), and Université Stendhal-Grenoble 3, see LF1945
	Grenoble
1945	Université Stendhal-Grenoble 3 (Table L13)
	Haute Bretagne. Université see LF2305
1949	Le Havre. Université du Havre (Table L13)
	Lille
1951-1970.5	Université (Table L10)
1971-1990.5	Facultés catholiques (Table L10)
	Lyons
2021-2040.5	Université (Table L10)

	Continental Europe
	France
	Lyons -- Continued
2046	Université Claude Bernard (Table L13)
2051-2070.5	Facultés catholiques (Table L10)
	Marseilles see LF1711+
2101-2120.5	Montpelier. Université (Table L10)
2121	Mulhouse. Universite de Haute-Alsace (Table L13)
2131-2150.5	Nancy. Université (Table L10)
2151	Nantes. Université (Table L13)
2151.5	Orange. Université d'Orange (Table L13)
2152	Orleans. Université (Table L13)
2153	Orthez. Université (Table L13)
	Paris
2161-2180.5	Université (Table L10)
2191-2210.5	Sorbonne (Table L10)
2211-2230.5	Collège de France (Table L10)
2231-2250.5	École pratique des hautes études (Table L10)
2251-2270.5	Institut catholique (Table L10)
2275.A-Z	Other universities. By place, A-Z
	Subarrange each by Table L13a
2275.C41	Cité Universitaire (Table L13a)
2279	Pau. Université de Pau et des pays de l'Ardour (Table L13)
2280	Perpignan. Université (Table L13)
2281-2300.5	Poitiers. Université (Table L10)
	Rennes
2303	Université de Rennes (Rennes I) (Table L13)
2305	Université de Haute Bretagne (Rennes II) (Table L13)
	Founded in 1970 as one of 3 universites replacing the former Université de Rennes
	Strasbourg. Université see LF3101+
	Toulouse
2341-2360.5	Université (Table L10)
2365	Université de Toulouse-Le Mirail (Table L13)
2371-2390.5	Institut catholique (Table L10)
2393	Tours. Université Franois Rabelais (Table L13)
2395.A-Z	Schools. By place, A-Z
2397.A-Z	Women's colleges and girls' schools. By place, A-Z
	Subarrange each by Table L13a
	Germany
	Altdorf. Universität Altdorf see LF3194.A44
2402	Augsburg. Universität Augsburg (Table L13)
	Albertus-Universität zu Königsberg i. Pr. see LF2901+
	Aschaffenburg. Karls-Universität see LF3194.A85
	Bayreuth. Universität Bayreuth see LF3194.B35
	Baltic University see LF3194.P54

	Continental Europe
	Germany -- Continued
	Bayerische Julius-Maximilians-Universität Würzburg see LF3161+
	Berlin
2405	Freie Universität Berlin (Table L13)
2411-2430.5	Humboldt-Universität zu Berlin (Table L10)
	Formerly Berlin. Universität
	Bielefeld. Universität Bielefeld see LF3194.B5
2441-2460.5	Bonn. Universität Bonn (Table L10)
2471-2490.5	Braunsberg. K. Lyceum Hosianum (Table L10)
	Bremen
	Gesamthochschule Bremen see LF3194.B75
	Universität Bremen see LF3194.B8
2501-2520.5	Breslau. Schlesische Friedrich-Wilhelms Universität zu Breslau (Table L10)
	Formerly Königliche Universität zu Breslau, formed in 1811 by the consolidation of the Academia Leopoldina and the Universität Frankfurt an der Oder
2525	Cologne. Universität zu Köln (Table L13)
	Collegium Carolinum see LF3194.M77
2530	Dillinger. Universität (Table L13)
	Existed 1549-1804
	Dortmund
	Gesamthochschule Dortmund see LF3194.D6
	Universität Dortmund see LF3194.D65
2548	Duisburg. Universität Duisburg (Table L13)
	Formerly Gesamthochschule Duisburg
	Düsseldorf. Universität Düsseldorf see LF3194.D8
	Eichstätt. Katholische Universität Eichstätt see LF3194.E35
2558	Erfurt. Universität Erfurt (Table L13)
2561-2580.5	Erlangen. Friedrich-Alexander-Universität Erlangen-Nürnberg (Table L10)
	Universität Altdorf (see LF3194.A44) merged in 1809 with Universität Erlangen, in 1961 Universität Erlangen merged with Hochschule für Wirtschafts- und Sozialwissenschaften, Nuremberg to form Friedrich-Alexander-Universität Erlangen
	Ernst-Moritz-Arndt-Universität Greifswald see LF2731+
	Essen. Universität Essen see LF3194.E84
	Fernuniversität-Gesamthochschule-Hagen see LF3194.H3
2583	Frankfurt am Main. Universität Frankfurt am Main (Table L13)
	Frankfurt an der Oder

	Continental Europe
	Germany
	Frankfurt an der Oder -- Continued
2585	Universität Frankfurt an der Oder (Table L13)
	In 1811 merged with Academia Leopoldina to form Königliche Universität zu Breslau; name changed 1911 to Schlesische Friedrich-Wilhelms-Universität zu Breslau LF2501+
2587	Europa-Universität Viadrina Frankfurt an der Oder (Table L13)
2601-2620.5	Freiburg. Universität Freiburg im Breisgau (Table L10)
	Freie Universität Berlin see LF2405
	Friedrich-Alexander-Universität Erlangen-Nürnberg see LF2561+
	Friedrich-Schiller-Universität Jena see LF2831+
2661-2680.5	Giessen. Justus Liebig-Universität Giessen (Table L10)
	Formerly Universität Giessen
2701-2720.5	Göttingen. Universität Göttingen (Table L10)
2731-2750.5	Greifswald. Ernst-Moritz-Arndt-Universität Greifswald (Table L10)
	Formerly Universität Greifswald
	Hagen. Fernuniversität-Gesamthochschule-Hagen see LF3194.H3
2761-2780.5	Halle. Martin-Luther-Universität Halle-Wittenberg (Table L10)
	Formerly Universität Halle-Wittenberg (1817-1933) which joined Universität Halle (founded 1694) and Universität Halle-Wittenberg, LF3157
2782	Halle. Universität Halle (Table L13)
	Founded 1694; merged with Universität Wittenberg in 1817; name changed in 1933 to Martin-Luther-Universität Halle-Wittenberg see LF2761+
2786	Hamburg. HWP - Hamburger Universität für Wirtschaft und Politik (Table L13)
	Formerly Hochschule für Wirtschaft und Politik Hamburg, Akademie für Wirtschaft und Politik, and Akademie für Gemeinwirtschaft Hamburg
2791	Hamburg. Universität Hamburg (Table L13)
	Handelshochschule Köln see LF3194.C63
	Hannover. Universität Hannover see LF3194.H4
2801-2820.5	Heidelberg. Universität Heidelberg (Table L10)
2825	Helmstedt. Universität Helmstedt (Table L13)
	Herborn. Hohe Schule see LF3194.H47
	Hildesheim. Gesamthochschule see LF3194.H5
	Humboldt-Universität zu Berlin see LF2411+
2831-2850.5	Jena. Friedrich-Schiller-Universität Jena (Table L10)
	Formerly Universität Jena

Continental Europe
  Germany -- Continued
    Johannes Gutenberg-Universität see LF2955
    Justus Liebig-Universität Giessen see LF2661+
    Kaiser-Wilhelms-Universität Strassburg see LF3101+
    Kaiserslautern. Universität Kaiserslautern see LF3194.K27
    Karl-Marx -Universität Leipzig see LF2931+
    Karls-Universität Aschaffenburg see LF3194.A85
    Kassel. Gesamthochschule Kassel see LF3194.K3
    Katholische Universität Eichstätt see LF3194.E35

2861-2880.5	Kiel. Universität Kiel (Table L10)
2885	Koblenz. Universität Koblenz-Landau (Table L13)

    Köln
      Handelshochschule Köln see LF3194.C63
      Universität Köln see LF2525

2901-2920.5	Königsberg. Albertus-Universität zu Königsberg i. Pr. (Table L10)

        Formerly Universität Königsberg
    Konstanz. Universität Konstanz see LF3194.C65
    Kurfürstliche Universität Bonn see LF3194.B65

2931-2950.5	Leipzig. Universität Leipzig (Table L10)

        During the period 1953-1991, the university was named Karl-Marx-Universität Leipzig
    Mainz

2955	Johannes Gutenberg-Universität (Table L13)

        Formerly Universität Mainz
      Universitas Moguntina see LF3194.M33

2961-2980.5	Marburg. Philipps-Universität Marburg (Table L10)

        Formerly Universität Marburg
    Martin-Luther-Universität Halle-Wittenberg see LF2761+
    München
      Collegium Carolinum see LF3194.M77
      Ukraïns'kyï vil'nyï universytet (Ukrainian Free University) see LF3194.M8

3001-3020.5	Universität München (Table L10)

        Formerly Universität Landshut

3031-3050.5	Münster. Universität Münster (Table L10)

    Nürnberg. Hochschule für Wirtschafts- und Sozialwissenschaften see LF2561+
    Oldenberg. Universität Oldenburg see LF3194.O4
    Osnabrück. Universität Osnabrück see LF3194.O8

3057	Passau. Universität Passau (Table L13)

    Paderborn. Universität-Gesamthochschule Paderborn see LF3194.P3
    Philipps-Universität Marburg see LF2961+
    Pinneberg. Baltic University see LF3194.P54

	Continental Europe
	Germany -- Continued
	Posen. Uniwersytet im. Adama Mickiewicza w Poznaniu
	see LF3194.P6
3065	Regensburg. Universität Regensburg (Table L13)
	Formerly Universität Ratisbon
	Rinteln. Universität Rinteln see LF3194.R5
3071-3090.5	Rostock. Universität Rostock (Table L10)
	From 1976 to 1990 Wilhelm-Pieck-Universität Rostock
3094	Ruhr-Universität Bochum (Table L13)
	Saarbrücken. Universität des Saarlandes see LF3194.S3
	Schlesische Friedrich-Wilhelms-Universität zu Breslau see
	LF2501+
	Siegen. Universität Siegen see LF3194.S55
3101-3120.5	Strassburg. Kaiser-Wilhelms-Universität Strassburg (Table
	L10)
	Formerly Universität Strassburg
3125	Stuttgart. Universität Stuttgart (Table L13)
	Trier. Universität Trier see LF3194.T76
3131-3150.5	Tübingen. Universität Tübingen (Table L10)
	Ulm. Universität Ulm see LF3194.U4
	Universitas Moguntina see LF3194.M33
	Ukraïns'kyĭ vil'nyĭ universytet (Ukrainian Free University)
	see LF3194.M8
	Uniwersytet im. Adama Mickiewicza w Poznaniu see
	LF3194.P6
	Wilhelm-Pieck-Universität Rostock see LF3071+
3157	Wittemberg. Universität Wittemberg (Table L13)
	Founded 1502; merged in 1817 with Universität Halle; name
	changed in 1933 to Martin-Luther-Universität Halle-
	Wittenberg, LF2761+
	Wuppertal. Universität-Gesamthochschule-Wuppertal see
	LF3194.W8
3161-3180.5	Würzburg. Bayerische Julius-Maximilians-Universität
	Würzburg (Table L10)
	Formerly Universität Würzburg
3194.A-Z	Other universities. By place, A-Z
3194.A44	Altdorf. Universität Altdorf (Table L13a)
	Merged with Universität Erlangen in 1809, in 1961
	Universität Erlangen merged with Hochschule für
	Wirtschafts- und Sozialwissenschaften, Nüremberg to
	form Friedrich-Alexander-Universität Erlangen-
	Nürnberg, LF2561+
3194.A85	Aschaffenburg. Karls-Universität (Table L13a)
3194.B28	Bamberg. Universität Bamberg (Table L13a)
	Formerly Gesamthochschule Bamberg
3194.B35	Bayreuth. Universität Bayreuth (Table L13a)

LF

Continental Europe

Germany

Other universities. By place, A-Z -- Continued

3194.B5	Bielefeld. Universität Bielefeld (Table L13a)
3194.B65	Bonn. Kurfürstliche Universität Bonn (Table L13a)
	Closed in 1798
	Bremen
3194.B75	Gesamthochschule (Table L13a)
3194.B8	Universität Bremen (Table L13a)
3194.B88	Bützow. Herzogliche Friedrichs-Universität zu Bützow (Table L13a)
	Closed in 1789
3194.C63	Cologne. Handelshochschule Köln (Table L13a)
3194.C65	Constance. Universität Konstanz (Table L13a)
	Dortmund
3194.D6	Gesamthochschule Dortmund (Table L13a)
3194.D65	Universität Dortmund (Table L13a)
3194.D8	Düsseldorf. Universität Düsseldorf (Table L13a)
(3194.D85)	Duisburg. Gesamthochschule Duisberg
	see LF2548
3194.E35	Eichstätt. Katholische Universität Eichstätt (Table L13a)
3194.E76	Erfurt. Europaische Universität Erfurt (Table L13)
3194.E84	Essen. Universität Essen (Table L13a)
3194.F73	Frankfurt an der Oder. Europa-Universität Viadrina Frankfurt an der Oder (Table L13a)
3194.H3	Hagen. Fernuniversität-Gesamthochschule-Hagen (Table L13a)
	Formerly Fernuniversität Hagen
3194.H4	Hannover. Universität Hannover (Table L13a)
3194.H47	Herborn. Hohe Schule (Table L13a)
	Now Evangelisch-Theologisches Seminar, see BV
3194.H5	Hildesheim. Gesamthochschule (Table L13a)
3194.H64	Hohenheim. Universität Hohenheim (Table L13a)
	Formerly Landwirtschaftliche Hochschule Hohenheim
3194.K27	Kaiserslautern. Universität Kaiserslautern (Table L13a)
	1975 Universität Trier-Kaiserslautern split and became the Universität Kaiserslautern and the Universität Trier, LF3194.T76
3194.K3	Kassel. Gesamthochschule Kassel (Table L13a)
	Köln see LF3194.C63
	Konstanz see LF3194.C65
3194.L84	Lüneburg. Universitet Lüneburg (Table L13a)
3194.M32	Magdeburg. Otto-von-Guericke-Universität Magdeburg (Table L13a)
3194.M33	Mainz. Universitas Moguntina (Table L13a)
	Ceased to exist in 1797
3194.M4	Mannheim. Universität Mannheim (Table L13a)

	Continental Europe
	Germany
	Other universities. By place, A-Z -- Continued
	Munich
3194.M77	Collegium. Carolinum (Table L13a)
3194.M8	Ukraïns'kyĭ vil'nyĭ universytet (Ukrainian Free University) (Table L13a)
	München see LF3194.M77+
3194.O4	Oldenburg. Universität Oldenburg (Table L13a)
3194.O8	Osnabrück. Universität Osnabrück (Table L13a)
3194.P3	Paderborn. Universität-Gesamthochschule Paderborn (Table L13a)
	Formerly Gesamthochschule Paderborn
3194.P54	Pinneberg. Baltic University (Table L13a)
3194.P6	Posen. Uniwersytet im. Adama Mickiewicza w Poznaniu (Table L13a)
	Formerly Reichsuniversität Posen
3194.P7	Potsdam. Universität Potsdam (Table L13a)
3194.R5	Rinteln. Universität Rinteln (Table L13a)
3194.S3	Saarbrücken. Universität des Saarlandes (Table L13a)
3194.S55	Siegen. Universität Siegen (Table L13a)
	Formerly Universität-Gesamthochschule-Siegen
	Treves see LF3194.T76+
	Trier
3194.T76	Universität Trier (Table L13a)
3194.T8	Universität Trier-Kaiserslautern (Table L13a)
	1975 Universität Trier-Kaiserslautern split and became Universität Trier, LF3194.T76, and Universität Kaiserslautern, LF3194.K27
3194.U4	Ulm. Universität Ulm (Table L13a)
3194.W8	Wuppertal. Universität-Gesamthochschule-Wuppertal (Table L13a)
	Formerly Gesamthochschule Wuppertal
3195.A-Z	Schools. By place, A-Z
3197.A-Z	Women's colleges and girls' schools. By place, A-Z
	Subarrange each by Table L13a
	Greece
3211-3230.5	Ethnikon kai Kapodistriakon Panepistēmion Athēnōn (Table L10)
	Formerly Ethnikon panepistemion
	Athens
3238.A-Z	Other universities and colleges. By place, A-Z
	Subarrange each by Table L13a
3245.A-Z	Other schools. By place, A-Z
	Subarrange each by Table L13a
3247.A-Z	Women's colleges and girls' schools. By place, A-Z
	Subarrange each by Table L13a

Continental Europe -- Continued
Italy

3248	Badia Fiesolana. European University Institute (Table L13)
3251-3270.5	Bari. Università di Bari (Table L10)
3271-3290.5	Bologna. Università di Bologna (Table L10)
3301-3320.5	Cagliari. Università di Cagliari (Table L10)
3321-3340.5	Camerino. Università di Camerino (Table L10)
3341-3360.5	Catania. Università di Catania (Table L10)
3361-3380.5	Ferrara. Università di Ferrara (Table L10)
	Formerly Università "Italo Balbo", Università libera di Ferrara
3401-3420.5	Florence. Università di Firenze (Table L10)
	Formerly R. Instituto di studi superiori
3451-3470.5	Genoa. Università di Genoa (Table L10)
3474	Lecce. Università degli studi di Lecce (Table L13)
3478	Macerata. Università di Macerata (Table L13)
3481-3500.5	Messina. Università di Messina (Table L10)
	Milan
3500.8	Università degli studi Milano-Bicocca (Table L13)
3501-3510.5	Università di Milano (Table L11)
3511-3520.5	Università cattolica del Sacro Cuore (Table L11)
3521-3540.5	Modena. Università (Table L10)
3541-3560.5	Naples. Università (Table L10)
3571-3590.5	Padua. Università (Table L10)
3601-3620.5	Palermo. Università (Table L10)
3631-3650.5	Parma. Università (Table L10)
3651-3670.5	Pavia. Università (Table L10)
	Perugia
3671-3690.5	Università (Table L10)
3691	R. Università italiana per stranieri (Table L13)
	Pisa
3700	Scuola normale superiore (Table L13)
3700.5	Scuola superiore di studi universitari e di perfezionamento Sant'Anna di Pisa (Table L13)
3701-3720.5	Università (Table L10)
3724	Potenza. Universita degli studi della Basilicata (Table L13)
	Rome
3731-3750.5	Università (Table L10)
3751-3770.5	Pontificia università gregoriana (Table L10)
3780.A-Z	Other colleges, A-Z
	Subarrange each by Table L13a
3801-3820.5	Sassari. Università (Table L10)
3821-3840.5	Siena. Università (Table L10)
3841-3860.5	Turin. Università (Table L10)
3871-3890.5	Urbino. Università libera (Table L10)
3893.A-Z	Other universities. By place, A-Z
3893.B47	Bergamo. Università di Bergamo (Table L13a)
3893.B67	Bolzano. Libera università di Bolzano (Table L13a)

	Continental Europe
	Italy
	Other universities. By place, A-Z -- Continued
3893.C37	Cassino. Università degli studi di Cassino (Table L13a)
3893.F47	Fermo. Università di Fermo (Table L13a)
3893.M36	Mantua. Pacifico ginnasio mantovano (Table L13a)
3893.T74	Trento. Università degli studi di Trento (Table L13a)
3893.U3	Udine. Università di Udine (Table L13a)
3895.A-Z	Schools. By place, A-Z
3897.A-Z	Women's colleges and girls' schools. By place, A-Z
	Subarrange each by Table L13a
	Malta
3899	Valleta. University of Malta (Table L13)
	Formerly Royal University of Malta
	Low Countries
	Belgium
	Brussels
3911-3930.5	Université libre (Table L10)
3941-3960.5	Université nouvelle (Table L10)
3965	Vrije Universiteit Brussel (Table L13)
	Until 1970 part of Université libre de Bruxelles
3971-3990.5	Ghent. Rijksuniversiteit. Rijksuniversiteit te Gent (Table L10)
	Formerly Ghent. Université
3991-4000.5	Leuven. Katholicke Universiteit te Leuven (1970-) (Table L11)
4001-4020.5	Liége. Université (Table L10)
4031-4050.5	Louvain. Université catholique (Table L10)
4053.A-Z	Other universities. By place, A-Z
4065.A-Z	Schools. By place, A-Z
4067.A-Z	Women's colleges and girls' schools. By place, A-Z
	Luxembourg
4069.A-Z	Colleges and schools, A-Z
	Netherlands
	Amsterdam
4071-4090.5	Universiteit (Table L10)
4091-4110.5	Vrije universiteit. Vrije universiteit te Amsterdam (Table L10)
4111-4130.5	Groningen. Rijksuniversiteit (Table L10)
4135	Harderwijk. Universiteit (Table L13)
4141-4160.5	Leyden. Rijksuniversiteit (Table L10)
4165	Nijmegen. Roomsch-katholieke universiteit (Table L13)
	Rotterdam
4166	Erasmus Universiteit (Table L13)
4167	Volks-Universiteit (Table L13)
4169	Sint Maartenscollege (Table L13)
4171-4190.5	Utrecht. Rijksuniversiteit (Table L10)

LF

Continental Europe
  Low Countries
    Netherlands -- Continued

4193.A-Z	Other universities. By place, A-Z
4195.A-Z	Schools. By place, A-Z
4197.A-Z	Women's colleges and girls' schools. By place, A-Z
	Poland
4203	Kraków. Uniwersytet Jagielloński (Table L13)
4206	Warsaw. Uniwersytet Warszawski (Table L13)
	Formerly Szkoła Głowna Warszawska; Cesarski Uniwersytet Warszawski
4207.A-Z	Other universities. By place, A-Z
4207.G38	Gdansk. Uniwersytet Gdanski (Table L13a)
4207.K37	Katowice. Uniwersytet Sląski w Katowicach (Table L13a)
4207.L6	Łódź. Uniwersytet Łodzki (Table L13a)
4207.L8	Lublin. Katolicki Uniwersyet Lubelski (Table L13a)
4207.L82	Lublin. Uniwersytet Marii Curie-Skłodowskiej (Table L13a)
4207.O65	Opole. Instytut Śląski w Opolu (Table L13a)
4207.O66	Opole. Uniwersytet Ludowy ZMU w Błotnicy Strzeleckiej (Table L13a)
4207.P6	Poznan. Uniwersytet im. Adama Mickiewicze w Poznaniu (Table L13a)
4207.R97	Rzeszów. Uniwersytet Rzeszowski (Table L13a)
4207.S93	Szczecin. Uniwersytet Szczeciński (Table L13a)
4207.T6	Torun. Uniwersytet Mikolaja Kopernika w Toruniu (Table L13a)
(4207.W377)	Warsaw. Szkoła Głowna Warszawska
	see LF4206
4207.W5	Warsaw. Wolna Wszechnica Polska (Table L13a)
4207.W76	Wrocław. Uniwersytet Wrocławski (Table L13a)
4208.A-Z	Schools. By place, A-Z
4209.A-Z	Women's colleges and girls' schools. By place, A-Z
	Subarrange each by Table L13a
	Russia (Federation)
	Siberia see LG310+
(4211-4230)	Tartu Ülikool
	see LF4440.A1+
4251-4260.5	Kazan. Kazanskiĭ gosudarstvennyĭ universitet im V.I. Ul'ĩanova-Lenina (Table L11)
(4271-4290)	Kharkivs'kyĭ derz̆havnyĭ universytet imeni O.M. Hor'koho
	see LF4449.2.A1+
(4291-4310)	Kyïvs'kyĭ derz̆havnyĭ universytet im. T.H. Shevchenka
	see LF4449.22.A1+
4311-4330.5	Moscow. Moskovskiĭ gosudarstvennyĭ universitet im. M.V. Lomonosova (Table L10)

	Continental Europe
	Russia (Federation) -- Continued
(4351-4370)	Odes'kyĭ derzhavnyĭ niversytet imeni I.I. Mechnykova
	see LF4449.24.A1+
4371-4390.5	Saint Petersburg (formerly Petrograd; Leningrad). Sankt-Peterburgskiĭ universitet (Table L10)
(4395)	T'bilisis saxelmcip'o universiteti
	see LG332.7
(4401-4420)	Uniwersytet Warszawski
	see LF4206
4425.A-Z	Other universities. By place, A-Z
(4425.A77)	A.M. Gor'kiĭ adyndaky Türkmen dövlet universiteti
	see LG305.2
4425.A8	Arkhangel'sk. Pomorskiĭ gosudarstvennyĭ universitet imeni M.V. Lomonosova (Table L13a)
4425.C3	Cheboksary. Chuvashskiĭ gosudarstvennyĭ universitet im. I.N. Ul'ianova (Table L13a)
(4425.C45)	Chernivets'kyĭ derzhavnyĭ universytet
	see LF4449.25.A1+
(4425.F78)	Kirgizskiĭ gosudarstvennyĭ universitet imeni 50-letiia SSSR
	see LG320.I74
(4425.I74)	Irkutskiĭ gosudarstvennyĭ universitet
	see LG320.I74
4425.I8	Ivanov. Ivanovskiĭ gosudarstvennyĭ universitet (Table L13a)
4425.I95	Izhevski. Udmurtskiĭ gosudarstvennyĭ universitet (Table L13a)
4425.K65	Kostroma. Kostromskoĭ gosudarstvennyĭ universitet im. N. A. Nekrasova (Table L13a)
4425.M597	Moscow. Moskovskiĭ eksternyĭ gumanitarnyĭ universitet (Table L13a)
4425.M598	Moscow. Moskovskiĭ gosudarstvennyĭ sotsialnyi universitet (Table L13a)
4425.M599	Moscow. Moskovskiĭ gosudarstvennyĭ universitet kul'tury i iskusstv (Table L13a)
4425.M5995	Moscow. Moskovskiĭ gumanitarnyĭ universitet (Table L13a)
4425.M6	Moscow. Sun Yat-sen University (Table L13a)
4425.M64	Moscow. Rossiĭskiĭ gosudarstvennyĭ gumanitarnyĭ universitet (Table L13a)
4425.M66	Moscow. Rossiiskiĭ universitet druzhby narodov (Table L13a)
4425.P4	Perm'. Permskiĭ gosudarstvennyĭ universitet imeni A.M. Gor'kogo (Table L13a)
4425.P43	Petrozavodsk. Petrozavodskiĭ gosudarstvennyĭ universitet (Table L13a)

Continental Europe
Russia (Federation)
Other universities. By place, A-Z -- Continued

4425.R65	Rostov. Rostovskiĭ gosudarstvennyĭ universitet im. M.A. Suslova (Table L13a)
4425.S27	Samara. Samarskiĭ gosudarstvennyĭ universitet (Table L13a)
4425.S3	Saratov. Saratovskiĭ gosudarstvennyĭ universitet im N.G. Chernyshevskogo (Table L13a)
4425.S7	Stavropol'. Stavropol'skiĭ gosudarstvennyĭ universitet (Table L13a)
4425.S97	Syktyvkar. Syktyvkarskiĭ universitet (Table L13a)
(4425.T65)	Tomskiĭ gosudarstvennyĭ universitet
	see LG310+
4425.T848	Tver'. Tverskoĭ gosudarstvennyĭ universitet (Table L13a)
(4425.U93)	Uzhhorods'kyĭ derzhavnyĭ universytet
	see LF4449.26.A1+
4425.V63	Vladimir. Vladimirskiĭ gosudarstvennyĭ universitet (Table L13a)
4425.V68	Volgograd. Volgogradskiĭ gosudarstvennyĭ universitet (Table L13a)
4425.V76	Voronezh. Voronezhskiĭ gosudarstvennyĭ universitet (Table L13a)
(4425.W3)	Wolna Wszechnical Polska
	see LF4207.W5
4435.A-Z	Schools. By place, A-Z
4437.A-Z	Women's colleges and girls' schools. By place, A-Z
	Subarrange each by Table L13a

The Baltic States
Estonia

4440	Tartu. Tartu Ülikool (Table L13)
	Formerly I͡Ur'evskiĭ universitet
4441.A-Z	Other universities, colleges, and schools. By place, A-Z
	Subarrange each by Table L13a

Latvia

4443	Riga. Latvijas universitāte
	Formerly Pētera Stučkas Latvijas Valsts universitāte; Riga. Universitāte
4444.A-Z	Other universities, colleges, and schools. By place, A-Z

Lithuania

4445	Kaunas (Kovno). Universitetas
	Moved in 1940 to Vilna and became Vilniaus Valstybinis V. Kapsuko vardo universiteta, LF4445.5
4445.5	Vilnius. Vilniaus Universitetas
	Formerly Vilniaus Valstybinis V. Kapsuko vardo universitetas
	Formerly Kaunas. Universitetas, LF4445

	Continental Europe
	The Baltic States
	Lithuania -- Continued
4446.A-Z	Other universities, colleges, and schools. By place, A-Z
	Belarus
4447.2	Minsk. Belaruski universitėt (Table L13)
4447.5.A-Z	Other universities, colleges, and schools. By place, A-Z
	Subarrange each by Table L13a
	Moldova
4448.A-Z	Universities, colleges, and schools. By place, A-Z
	Subarrange each by Table L13a
	Ukraine
4449.2	Kharkiv. Kharkivs′kyĭ derzhavnyĭ universytet imeni O.M. Har'koho (Table L13)
4449.22	Kiev. Kyïvs'kyĭ derzhavnyĭ universytet im. T.H. Shevchenka (Table L13)
4449.23	L'viv. L'vivs'kyĭ derzhavnyĭ universytet im. Iv. Franka (Table L13)
4449.24	Odesa. Odes'kyĭ derzhavnyĭ universtytet imeni I.I. Mechnykova (Table L13)
4449.25	Chernivtsi. Chernivets'kyĭ derzhavnyĭ universytet (Table L13)
4449.26	Uzhhorod. Uzhhorods'kyĭ derzhavnyĭ universytet (Table L13)
4449.27	Kiev. Universytet "Kyĭevo-Mohylïans'ka akademĭïa" (Table L13)
4449.5.A-Z	Other universities, colleges, and schools. By place, A-Z
	Subarrange each by Table L13a
	Scandinavia
	Denmark
4451-4470.5	Copenhagen. Universitet. Københavns universitet (Table L10)
4483.A-Z	Other universities. By place, A-Z
4483.A143	Ålborg. Aalborg universitetscenter (Table L13a)
4483.A2	Århus. Aarhus universitet (Table L13a)
4483.E77	Esbjerg. Sydjysk universitetscenter (Table L13a)
	In 1999 merged with Odense universitet and Handelshøjskole syd-Ingeniørhøjskole syd to form Syddansk universitet
4483.H455	Helsingør. International People's College (Table L13a)
	Odense
4483.O3	Odense universitet (Table L13a)
	In 1999 merged with Sydjysk universitetscenter and Handelshøjskole syd-Ingeniørhøjskole syd to form Syddansk universitet

Continental Europe
  Scandinavia
    Denmark
      Other universities. By place, A-Z
        Odense -- Continued
4483.O34   Syddansk universitet (Table L13a)
                    In 1999 Sydjysk universitetscenter, Odense universitet,
                      and Handelshøjskole syd-Ingeniørhøjskole syd
                      merged to form Syddansk universitet
4483.R67   Roskilde. Roskilde universitetscenter (Table L13a)
4485.A-Z   Schools. By place, A-Z
4487.A-Z   Women's colleges and girls' schools. By place, A-Z
      Faroe Islands
4488   Tórshavn. Fróðskaparsetur Føroya (Table L13)
4488.2.A-Z   Other colleges and schools. By place, A-Z
                    Subarrange each by Table L13a
    Finland see LF1705+
    Greenland
4488.4   Prinsesse Margrethe Skolen Kollegie (Table L13)
4488.5.A-Z   Other colleges and schools. By place, A-Z
                    Subarrange each by Table L13a
    Iceland
4489   Reykjavík. Háskóli Íslands (Table L13)
4491.A-Z   Other colleges and schools. By place, A-Z
                    Subarrange each by Table L13a
    Norway
4493   Bergen. Universitet
4501-4520.5   Oslo (Christiania). Universitet (Table L10)
4524   Tromsø. Universitetet (Table L13)
4525   Trondheim. Universitet (Table L13)
4535.A-Z   Schools. By place, A-Z
4537.A-Z   Women's colleges and girls' schools. By place, A-Z
                    Subarrange each by Table L13a
    Sweden
4539   Gothenburg. Högskola (Table L13)
4540   Gothenburg. Universitet (Table L13)
4541-4560.5   Lund. Universitet (Table L10)
4561-4580.5   Stockholm. Universitet (Table L10)
                    Formerly Stockholm. Högskola
4580.6   Umeå. Universitet (Table L13)
4580.7   Universitetet i Linköping (Table L13)
4581-4600.5   Uppsala. Universitet (Table L10)
4605.A-Z   Schools. By place, A-Z
4607.A-Z   Women's colleges and girls' schools. By place, A-Z
                    Subarrange each by Table L13a
  Spain
4610   Universidad de Almagro (Table L13)

	Continental Europe
	Spain -- Continued
4611-4630.5	Barcelona. Universidad (Table L10)
4630.5	Cartagena. Universidad Popular (Table L13)
4631-4650.5	Granada (City). Universidad (Table L10)
4650.8	Madrid. Universidad Autónoma (Table L13)
4650.9	Madrid. Universidad Carlos III de Madrid (Table L13)
4651-4670.5	Madrid. Universidad Complutense de Madrid (Table L10)
	Formerly Alcalá de Henares. Universidad (1508-1836);
	Madrid. Universidad Central (1836-1971)
4670.7	Olot. Universitat d'Olot (Table L13)
4670.8	Osuna. Universidad (Table L13)
4671-4690.5	Oviedo (City). Universidad (Table L10)
4691-4710.5	Salamanca. Universidad (Table L10)
4711-4730.5	Santiago de Compostela. Universidad (Table L10)
4731-4750.5	Saragossa. Universidad (Table L10)
4751-4770.5	Seville. Universidad (Table L10)
4771-4790.5	Valencia (City). Universidad (Table L10)
4801-4820.5	Valladolid. Universidad (Table L10)
	Zaragoza. Universidad see LF4731+
4823.A-Z	Other universities. By place, A-Z
4823.A37	Albacete. Universidad de la Mancha (Table L13a)
4823.A4	Alcalá de Henares. Universidad (Table L13a)
4823.A44	Almería. Universidad Laboral de Almería (Table L13a)
	Barcelona
4823.B37	Universidad Autónoma de Barcelona (Table L13a)
4823.B39	Universitat Pompeau Fabra (Table L13a)
	Bilbao
4823.B54	Universidad del País Vasco (Table L13a)
4823.B56	Universidad Popular de Rekaldeberri (Table L13a)
4823.B87	Burgos. Universidad (Table L13a)
4823.C25	Cáceres. Universidad de Extremadura (Table L13a)
	Cadiz
4823.C27	Colegio de San Felipe Neri (Table L13a)
4823.C275	Universidad (Table L13a)
4823.C4	Cervera. Universidad (Table L13a)
4823.C53	Cheste. Universidad Laboral de Cheste (Table L13a)
4823.C83	Cuenca. Colegio Mayor de Cuenca (Table L13a)
4823.G55	Gijon. Universidad Laboral José Antonio Girón (Table L13a)
4823.H77	Huelva. Universidad de la Rábida (Table L13a)
4823.H8	Huesca (City). Universidad (Table L13a)
4823.J33	Jaén. Universidade Jaén (Table L13a)
4823.L36	Laguna, Canary Islands. Universidad (Table L13a)
4823.L38	Las Palmas. Universidad de Las Palmas de Gran Canaria (Table L13a)
4823.L4	Lérida. Estudio General (Table L13a)

LF

	Continental Europe
	Spain
	Other universities. By place, A-Z -- Continued
4823.M3	Universidad de Málaga (Table L13a)
4823.M85	Murcia (City). Universidad (Table L13a)
4823.O54	Oñate. Antigua Universidad de Oñati (Table L13a)
4823.O56	Oñate. Universidad de Sancti Spiritus (Table L13a)
4823.O75	Orihuela. Universidad (Table L13a)
4823.P28	Palma Majorca. Real y Pontificia Universidad Literaria (Table L13a)
4823.P29	Palma Majorca. Universitat de les Illes Balears (Table L13a)
4823.P3	Pamplona. Universidad de Navarra (Table L13a)
4823.S29	Salamanca. Colegio Mayor del Arzobispo Fonseca (Table L13a)
4823.S292	Salamanca. Colegio Mayor Universitario de Carmelitas (Table L13a)
4823.S32	Santander. Universidad Internacional Menendez Pelayo (Table L13a)
	Formerly Universidad Internacional de Verano (Santander, Spain)
4823.S36	Santiago. Colegio de San Clemente (Table L13a)
4823.S5	Sigüenza. Universidad (Table L13a)
4823.S65	Solsona. Universidad Literaria de Solsona (Table L13a)
4823.V36	Valladolid. Colegio de San Gregorio (Table L13a)
4825.A-Z	Schools. By place, A-Z
4827.A-Z	Women's colleges and girls' schools. By place, A-Z
	Portugal
4831-4850.5	Coimbra. Universidade (Table L10)
4861-4880.5	Lisbon. Universidade (Table L10)
4883.A-Z	Other universities. By place, A-Z
4883.A94	Aveiro. Universidade de Aveiro (Table L13a)
4883.E935	Evora. Universidade de Evora (Table L13a)
4883.F376	Faro. Universidade do Algarve (Table L13a)
4883.F86	Funchal. Colégio dos Jesuítas do Funchal (Table L13a)
	Lisbon
4883.L515	Colegio Real dos Nobres (Table L13a)
4883.L54	English College of Lisbon (Table L13a)
4883.L55	Lusíada University (Table L13a)
4883.L58	Universidade do Real Convento de S. Domingos de Lisboa (Table L13a)
4883.L59	Universidade Livre (Table L13a)
	Oporto
4883.O63	Lusíada. University (Table L13a)
4883.O65	Universidade Porto (Table L13a)
4883.P65	Ponta Delgada. Universidade dos Açores (Table L13a)
4883.V55	Vila Nova de Famalicão. Lusíada University (Table L13a)

	Continental Europe
	Portugal -- Continued
4885.A-Z	Schools. By place, A-Z
4887.A-Z	Women's colleges and girls' schools. By place, A-Z
	Subarrange each by Table L13a
	Switzerland
4901-4920.5	Basel. Universität (Table L10)
4921-4940.5	Bern. Universität (Table L10)
4941-4960.5	Fribourg. Université (Table L10)
	Known also as Università di Friburgo, Universität Freiburg
4961-4980.5	Geneva. Université (Table L10)
4981-5000.5	Lausanne. Université (Table L10)
5001-5020.5	Neuchâtel. Université (earlier, Académie) (Table L10)
5021-5040.5	Zurich. Universität (Table L10)
5042.A-Z	Other universities. By place, A-Z
5042.S83	St. Gallen. Universität (Table L13a)
5045.A-Z	Schools. By place, A-Z
5047.A-Z	Women's colleges and girls' schools. By place, A-Z
	Subarrange each by Table L13a
	Turkey and the Balkan states
	Albania
5051.A-Z	Universities. By place, A-Z
	Subarrange each by Table L13a
5054.A-Z	Schools. By place, A-Z
5055.A-Z	Women's colleges and girls' schools. By place, A-Z
	Subarrange each by Table L13a
	Bulgaria
5061-5080.5	Sofia. Sofiiški universitet "Sv. Kliment Okhridski" (Table L10)
	Formerly Sofiiški universitet
5085.A-Z	Other universities. By place, A-Z
5085.P58	Plovdiv. Plovdivski universitet "Paisiĭ Khilendarksi" (Table L13a)
5085.V45	Veliko Tŭrnovo. Velikotŭrnovski universitet Kiril i Metodiĭ (Table L13a)
5095.A-Z	Schools. By place, A-Z
5097.A-Z	Women's colleges and girls' schools. By place, A-Z
	Subarrange each by Table L13a
	Romania
5101-5120.5	Bucharest. Universitatea din București (Table L10)
5120.8	Bucharest. Universitatea Populara București (Table L13)
5121-5140.5	Iași. Universitatea "Al. I. Cuza" din Iași (Table L10)
5143.A-Z	Other universities. By place, A-Z
	e.g.

	Continental Europe
	Turkey and the Balkan states
	Romania
	Other universities. By place, A-Z -- Continued
5143.C5	Cluj. Universitatea din Cluj-Napoca (Table L13a)
	Formerly Magyar Királyi Ferenc Jozsef Tudományegyetem; Universitatea "Babeș-Bolyai"; Universitatea din Cluj
5145.A-Z	Schools. By place, A-Z
	Serbia see LF5401+
	Turkey
	Ankara
5169	Hacettepe Üniversitesi (Table L13)
5170	Ankara Üniversitesi (Table L13)
5175	Erzurum (City). Atatürk Üniversitesi (Table L13)
	Istanbul. (Constantinople)
5181-5200.5	İstanbul Üniversitesi (Table L10)
5221-5240.5	Robert College (Table L10)
5245	Pandidaktērion (Table L13)
5250.A-Z	Other universities. By place, A-Z
	Subarrange each by Table L13a
5321.A-Z	Schools. By place, A-Z
5323.A-Z	Women's colleges and girls' schools. By place, A-Z
	Subarrange each by Table L13a
	Yugoslavia
5401-5420.5	Belgrade (Serbia). Universitet u Beogradu (Table L10)
(5451-5470)	Sveučilište u Zagrebu (Croatia) see LF5523
5475.A-Z	Other universities. By place, A-Z
(5475.B3)	Banja Luka (Bosnia and Hercegovina). Radnički univerzitet see LF5483
5475.B4	Belgrade (Serbia). Radnički univerzitet (Belgrade, Serbia) (Table L13a)
5475.B5	Belgrade (Serbia). Radnički univerzitet "Đuro salaj" (Table L13a) Formerly Radnički univerzitet (Belgrade, Serbia)
(5475.L383)	Ljubljana (Slovenia). Academia Operosorum Labacensium see LF5622
(5475.L5-.L59)	Ljubljana (Slovenia). Univerza v Ljubljani see LF5601+
5475.N5	Niš (Serbia). Univerzitet u Nišu (Table L13a)
5475.N6	Novi Sad (Serbia). Univerzitet u Novom Sadu (Table L13a)
(5475.O5)	Ohrid (Macedonia). Rabotnički univerzitet see LF5561

	Continental Europe
	Turkey and the Balkan states
	Yugoslavia
	Other universities. By place, A-Z -- Continued
5475.P75	Priština (Serbia). Univerzitet u Prištini (Table L13a)
(5475.S3)	Sarajevo (Bosnia and Hercegovina). Univerzitet u Sarajevu
	see LF5482
(5475.S45)	Skopje (Macedonia). Univerzitet "Kiril i Metodij"-Skopje
	see LF5562
(5475.S7)	Split (Croatia). Narodno sveučilište
	see LF5521
5476.A-Z	Schools. By place, A-Z
5477.A-Z	Women's colleges and girls' schools. By place, A-Z
	Subarrange each by Table L13a
	Bosnia and Hercegovina
5481	Banja Luka. Radnički univerzitet (Table L13)
	Sarajevo
5482	Univerzitet u Sarajevu (Table L13)
5483	Radnički univerzitet Đuro Đakovic (Table L13)
5485.A-Z	Other universities. By place, A-Z
	Subarrange each by Table L13a
5501.A-Z	Schools. By place, A-Z
5511.A-Z	Women's colleges and girls' schools. By place, A-Z
	Subarrange each by Table L13a
	Croatia
5521	Split. Narodno sveučilište (Table L13)
5523	Zagreb. Sveučilište u Zagrebu (Table L13)
5525.A-Z	Other universities. By place, A-Z
	Subarrange each by Table L13a
5541.A-Z	Schools. By place, A-Z
5551.A-Z	Women's colleges and girls' schools. By place, A-Z
	Subarrange each by Table L13a
	Macedonia (Republic)
5561	Ohrid. Rabotnički univerzitet (Table L13)
5562	Skopje. Univerzitet "Kiril i Metodij"-Skopje (Table L13)
5565.A-Z	Other universities. By place, A-Z
	Subarrange each by Table L13a
5581.A-Z	Schools. By place, A-Z
5591.A-Z	Women's colleges and girls' schools. By place, A-Z
	Subarrange each by Table L13a
	Montenegro
5592.A-Z	Universities. By place, A-Z
	Subarrange each by Table L13a
5595.A-Z	Schools. By place, A-Z
5596.A-Z	Women's colleges and girls' schools. By place, A-Z
	Subarrange each by Table L13a

LF

	Continental Europe
	Turkey and the Balkan states -- Continued
	Slovenia
	Ljubljana
5601-5620.5	Univerza v Ljubljani (Table L10)
5622	Academia Operosorum Labacensium (Table L13)
5625.A-Z	Other universities. By place, A-Z
	Subarrange each by Table L13a
5626.A-Z	Schools. By place, A-Z
5627.A-Z	Women's colleges and girls' schools. By place, A-Z
	Subarrange each by Table L13a

Individual institutions
    For individual institutions limited to education in a special field, see
       the topic, e.g. class K, law schools, R741+ medical schools,
       S536.5+ agricultural colleges, T171+ technical schools
  Asia, Africa, Oceania
    Asia

21.A-Z	Afghanistan
21.K3	Kābul Pohantūn (Table L13a)
(31.A-Z)	Arabia
	see LG359
(31.A24)	Abhā Kulliyat al-Sharī'ah wa-al-Lughah al-'Arabīyah
	see LG359.A24
(31.D35)	Dammam. Jami'at al-Malik Fayṣal
	see LG359.D35
	Hasa. Jāmi'at al-Malik Faysal see LG359.D35
(31.J35)	Jiddah. Jāmi'at al-Malik 'Abd al-'Azīz
	see LG359.J35
(31.K87)	Kuwait (City). Jāmi'at al-Kuwayt
	see LG347.K88
(31.R5)	Riyadh. Jāmi'at al-Riyād
	see LG359.R5
	China
51.A5	Amoy. University (Table L13a)
	Beijing
	Beijing da xue see LG51.P28
	Fu ren da xue see LG51.P275
	Qing hua da xue see LG51.P6
	Tong wen guan see LG51.P69
	Yanjing da xue see LG51.P95
	Zhongguo ke xue ji shu da xue see LG51.P264
	Zhongguo she hui ke xue yuan. Yan jiu sheng yuan see
	LG51.P266
	Zhongguo ren min da xue see LG51.P26
	Canton
	Kuang-chou ta hsüeh see LG51.G85
51.C27	Kuang-tung kuo min ta hsüeh (Table L13a)
51.C3	Ling-nan ta hsüeh (Table L13a)
	Formerly Christian College
51.C4	Sun Yat-sen University (Table L13a)
51.C48	Ch'ang-ch'un shih. Chien kuo ta hsüeh (Manchoukuo)
	(Table L13a)
	Chang-sha
51.C49	Hunan shi fan da xue (Table L13a)
51.C5	Yale Mission (Table L13a)
51.C53	Yüeh-lu shu yüan (Table L13a)
	Later names: Hunan gao deng xue tang; Hunan da xue
	Changchun (Jilin Sheng, China)

	Asia, Africa, Oceania
	Asia
	China
	Changchun (Jilin Sheng, China) -- Continued
	Jian guo da xue (Manchoukuo) see LG51.C48
51.C535	Jilin da xue (Table L13a)
	Changsha
	Hunan da xue see LG51.C53
	Hunan gao deng xue tang see LG51.C53
	Yale Mission see LG51.C5
	Yuelu shu yuan see LG51.C53
51.C547	Ch'eng-ku hsien. Hsi-pei ta hsüeh (Table L13a)
	Ch'eng-tu
51.C549	Ssu-ch'uan ta hsüeh (Table L13a)
51.C55	West China Union University (Table L13a)
	Chengdu
	Hua xi da xue see LG51.C55
	Sichuan da xue see LG51.C549
	Chenggu Xian. Xi bei da xue see LG51.C547
51.C57	Chi-mei. Chi-mei hsüeh hsiao (Table L13a)
	Chongqing
	She hui da xue see LG51.C6
51.C594	Xi nan da xue (Table L13a)
	Formerly Xi nan shi fan da xue
51.C6	Ch'ung-ch'ing shih. She hui ta hsüeh (Table L13a)
51.D34	Dalian li gong da xue (Table L13a)
51.F8	Foochow. Fukien Christian University (Table L13a)
	Fuzhou Shi (Fujian Sheng). Fujian xie he da xue see LG51.F8
	Guangzhou
	Guangdong guo min da xue see LG51.C27
51.G85	Guangzhou da xue (Table L13a)
51.G86	Ji nan da xue (Table L13a)
	Ling nan da xue see LG51.C3
	Zhongshan da xue see LG51.C4
51.H16	Hainan Sheng. Hainan da xue (Table L13a)
51.H18	Hangzhou. Zhejiang da xue (Table L13a)
51.H38	Harbin. Ha'erbin shi fan da xue (Table L13a)
51.H42	Hefei Shi. Anhui da xue (Table L13a)
51.H45	Hohhot. Nei Menggu gong ye da xue (Table L13a)
	Hong Kong
51.H47	Baptist College (Table L13a)
51.H5	Chinese University (Table L13a)
51.H52	City University (Table L13a)
51.H55	Queen's College (Table L13a)
51.H58	United College (Table L13a)
51.H6	University (Table L13a)

Asia, Africa, Oceania
Asia
China -- Continued

51.H78	Hsü-chou. Chiang-su hsüeh yüan (Table L13a)
51.H83	Hsüan-hua hsien. Chung yüan min chu chien kuo ta hsüeh (Table L13a)
	Jimei. Jimei xue xiao see LG51.C57
	Jinan (Shandong Sheng)
	Qi Lu da xue see LG51.T8
51.J56	Shandong da xue (Table L13a)
51.K33	Kaifeng Xian. Guo li Henan da xue (Table L13a)
51.K85	Kunming Shi. Xi nan lian he da xue (Table L13a)
51.L35	Lanzhou Shi. Xi bei min zu xue yuan (Table L13a)
	Macau
51.M3	Christian College in China (Table L13a)
51.M36	Colegio de Sao Paulo de Macau (Table L13a)
51.M53	Universidade de Macau (Table L13a)
51.M8	Mukden. Tung-pei shih fan ta hsüeh (Table L13a)
	Nanchang
51.N352	Jiangxi gong chan zhu yi lao dong da xue (Table L13a)
51.N353	Nanchang hang kong da xue (Table L13a)
	Nanjing (Jiangsu Sheng)
	Nanjing da xue see LG51.N4
	Nanjing Shi fan da xue see LG51.N38
51.N355	San jiang shi fan xue tang (Table L13a)
	Zhong yang da xue see LG51.N358
	Nanking
51.N358	Chung yang ta hsüeh (Table L13a)
51.N38	Nan-ching shih fan ta hsüeh (Table L13a)
51.N4	Nan-ching ta hsüeh (Table L13a)
	Formerly Chin-ling ta hsüeh
	Peking
	Ch'ing hua ta hsüeh see LG51.P6
51.P26	Chung-kuo jen min ta hsüeh (Table L13a)
	Formerly Hua bei da xue
51.P264	Chung-kuo k'o hsüeh chi shu ta hsüeh (Table L13a)
51.P266	Chung-kuo she hui k'o hsüeh yüan. Yen chiu sheng yüan (Table L13a)
51.P275	Fu jên ta hsüeh (Table L13a)
	Formerly Catholic University of Peking
51.P28	Pei-ching ta hsüeh (Table L13a)
	Formerly National University
51.P6	Tsing Hua University (Table L13a)
	Formerly Tsing hua University
51.P69	T'ung wen kuan (Table L13a)
51.P95	Yen-ching ta hsüeh (Table L13a)
	Formerly Yenching University

	Asia, Africa, Oceania
	Asia
	China -- Continued
	Shanghai
51.S2	Aurore, Université l' (Table L13a)
51.S33	Chi nan ta hsüeh (Table L13a)
51.S35	Chiao-tung University (Table L13a)
51.S37	Chung-kuo kung hsüeh (Table L13a)
	Da xia da xue see LG51.S54
51.S38	Fu dan da xue (Table L13a)
51.S382	Guang hua da xue (Table L13a)
	Guo li ji nan da xue see LG51.S33
51.S383	Hua dong shi fan da xue (Table L13a)
51.S385	Lao dong da xue (Table L13a)
51.S4	St. John's University (Table L13a)
51.S53	Shanghai da xue (Table L13a)
	Shanghai jiao tong da xue see LG51.S35
	Sheng Yüeh-han ta hsüeh see LG51.S4
51.S54	Ta hsia ta hsüeh (Table L13a)
51.S56	Tōa Dōbun Shoin Daigaku (Table L13a)
51.S57	Tong ji da xue (Table L13a)
	Zhen dan da xue see LG51.S2
	Zhongguo gong xue see LG51.S37
	Shenyang (Liaoning Sheng). Dongbei shi fan da xue see LG51.M8
51.S58	Shenzhen (Guangdong Sheng : East). Shenzhen da xue (Table L13a)
51.S6	Suzhou Shi (Jiangsu Sheng). Dong Wu da xue (Table L13a)
	Tianjin
51.T4	Anglo-Chinese College (Table L13a)
	Bei yang shi fan xue tang see LG51.T6
	Guo li bei yang da xue see LG51.T6
51.T57	Nan kai da xue (Table L13a)
51.T6	Pei Yang University (Table L13a)
	Name changed to Guo li bei yang da xue and later to Tianjin da xue
	Tianjin da xue see LG51.T6
51.T8	Tsinan. Ch'i Lu ta hsüeh (Table L13a)
	Formerly Shantung Christian University; Cheelo University
	Wuchang Qu (Wuhan Shi)
51.W8	Hua zhong da xue (Table L13a)
	Formerly Boone University; Wen hua da xue
51.W95	Wuhan da xue (Table L13a)
51.W96	Wuhan Shi. Hua zhong shi fan da xue (Table L13a)
	Xiamen (Xiamen Shi). Xiamen da xue see LG51.A5
	Xi'an Shi. Xi bei da xue see LG51.C547

	Asia, Africa, Oceania
	Asia
	China -- Continued
	Xuanhua Xian. Zhong yuan min zhu jian guo da xue see LG51.H83
	Xuzhou (Jiangsu Sheng)
	Jiangsu xue yuan see LG51.H78
51.X88	Zhongguo kuang ye da xue (Table L13a)
	Yan'an Shi
	Yan'an da xue see LG51.Y44
	Yan'an zhong yang yan jiu yuan see LG51.Y42
	Zhongguo ren min kang Ri jun zheng da xue see LG51.Y24
51.Y23	Yanji. Yanbian da xue (Table L13a)
	Yenan
51.Y24	Chung-kuo jen min k'ang Jih chün cheng ta hsüeh (Table L13a)
51.Y42	Yen-an chung yang yen chiu yüan (Table L13a)
51.Y44	Yen-an ta hsüeh (Table L13a)
52.A-Z	Schools. By place, A-Z
53.A-Z	Women's colleges and girls' schools. By place, A-Z
	Subarrange each by Table L13a
	Taiwan
55.C45	Chia-i T'ai-wan sheng li Chia-i shih fan chuan k'o hsüeh hsiao (Table L13a)
55.C48	Chung-li. Kuo li chung yang ta hsüeh (Table L13a)
55.H737	Hsin-chu. Kuo li chiao t'ung ta hsüeh (Table L13a)
55.H738	Hsin-chu. Kuo li ch'ing hua ta hsüeh (Table L13a)
55.H74	Hsin-chuang. Fu jen ta hsüeh (Table L13a)
55.K34	Kao-hsiung shih. Kuo li Chung-shan ta hsüeh (Table L13a)
55.M83	Mu-cha. Kuoli cheng chih ta hsüeh (Table L13a)
55.T25	T'ai-chung. Tung hai ta hsüeh (Table L13a)
55.T29	T'ai-nan. Kuo li Ch'eng-king ta hsüeh (Table L13a)
	Taipei
55.T315	Guo li Taiwan shi fan da xue (Table L13a)
55.T32	Kuo li chung hsing ta hsüeh. Fa shang hsüeh yuan (Table L13a)
55.T328	T'ai-wan sheng li T'ai-pei shih fan chuan k'o hsüeh hsiao (Table L13a)
55.T33	T'ai-wan ta hsüeh (Table L13a)
55.T34	Tung Wu ta hsüeh (Table L13a)
55.T37	Tan-shui. Tan-chiang ta hsüeh (Table L13a)
	Formerly Tan-chiang wen li hsüeh yüan
55.Y35	Yang-mīng-shan. Chung-Kuo wen hua hsüeh yüan (Table L13a)
56.A-Z	Schools. By place, A-Z

	Asia, Africa, Oceania
	Asia
	Taiwan -- Continued
57.A-Z	Women's colleges and girls' schools. By place, A-Z
	Subarrange each by Table L13a
	India. Pakistan. Bangladesh. Burma. Sri Lanka. Nepal
60-69.5	Allahabad. University (Table L12)
70-79.5	Banaras Hindu University (Table L12)
	Formerly Central Hindu College
80-89.5	Bombay. University (Table L12)
100-109.5	Calcutta. University (Table L12)
110-119.5	Dhaka. University of Dhaka (Table L12)
	Cf. LG169.D2 Dhaka. College
	Cf. LG169.D24 Dhaka. Madrasah-i-Alia
120-129.5	Punjab. University, Lahore (Table L12)
	Cf. LG169.P82 Punjab (State)
130-139.5	Lucknow. University (Table L12)
140-149.5	Madras. University (Table L12)
150-159.5	Rangoon. University (Table L12)
169.A-Z	Other universities and colleges. By place, A-Z
169.A22	Agra (City). Radhasoami Educational Institute (Table L13a)
169.A23	Agra (City). St. John's College (Table L13a)
169.A242	Agra (City). University (Table L13a)
169.A432	Ahmedabad. Gujarat University (Table L13a)
169.A446	Aligarh. Jāmi'ah Urdū (Table L13a)
169.A45	Aligarh. Muslim University (Table L13a)
169.A59	Allahabad. Ewing Christian College (Table L13a)
169.A62	Amritsar. Guru Nanak University (Table L13a)
169.A65	Andra. University (Table L13a)
169.A79	Aurangabad. Government College of Arts and Sciences (Table L13a)
169.A797	Aurangabad. Marathwada University (Table L13a)
169.A8	Aurangabad. Milind Maha Vidyalaya (Table L13a)
	Bangalore
169.B25	Central College (Table L13a)
169.B27	University of Bangalore (Table L13a)
169.B29	Barisāl. Brajamohan College (Table L13a)
169.B3	Baroda. Maharaja Sayajirao University (Table L13a)
169.B345	Batala. Baring Union Christian College (Table L13a)
169.B35	Batticotta, Jaffna. Jaffna College (Table L13a)
169.B5	Bhubaneswar. Utkal University (Table L13a)
169.B62	Bombay. St. Xavier's College (Table L13a)
169.B8	Burdwan (City). University (Table L13a)
	Calcutta
169.C24	Bangabasi College (Table L13a)

	Asia, Africa, Oceania
	Asia
	India. Pakistan. Bangladesh. Burma. Sri Lanka. Nepal
	Other universities and colleges. By place, A-Z
	Calcutta -- Continued
169.C245	Bethune College (Table L13a)
	Earlier name: Bethune School
169.C25	City College (Table L13a)
169.C26	College of Fort William (Table L13a)
169.C28	Jadavpur University (Table L13a)
169.C29	Presidency College (Table L13a)
169.C295	Rabindra Bharati University (Table L13a)
169.C297	Scottish Church College (Table L13a)
169.C3	Vidyasagar College (Table L13a)
169.C35	Calicut. University (Table L13a)
169.C452	Ceylon. University (Table L13a)
169.C5	Chidambvaram. Annamalai University (Table L13a)
169.C55	Chittagong. University (Table L13a)
169.C65	Coimbatore (City). Government Arts College (Table L13a)
	Colombo, Sri Lanka
169.C69	Methodist College (Table L13a)
169.C7	Musaeus College (Table L13a)
169.C75	Royal College (Table L13a)
169.C83	University of Colombo (Table L13a)
169.C85	Wesley College (Table L13a)
169.C86	Zahira College (Table L13a)
169.C87	Comilla. Kumillā Bhiktoriyā Kaleja (Table L13a)
	Dhaka, Bangladesh
169.D2	College (Table L13a)
169.D23	Independent University, Bangladesh (Table L13a)
169.D24	Madrasah-i-Alia (Table L13a)
(169.D25)	University of Dhaka
	see LG110+
169.D36	Darjeeling (City). St. Joseph's College (Table L13a)
169.D362	Daulatpur. Brajalāla Kaleja (Table L13a)
	Delhi. Delhi College see LG169.D45
169.D363	Delhi. Guru Gobind Singh Indraprastha University (Delhi, India) (Table L13a)
169.D364	Delhi. Hindu College (Table L13a)
169.D365	Delhi. Jamia Hamdard (New Delhi, India) (Table L13a)
169.D367	Delhi. Jamia Millia Islamia (Table L13a)
169.D37	Delhi. Jawaharlal Nehru University (Table L13a)
169.D393	Delhi. Lady Irwin College (Table L13a)
169.D397	Delhi. Ramjas College (Table L13a)
169.D3985	Delhi. St. Stephen's College (Table L13a)
169.D4	Delhi. University (Table L13a)

Asia, Africa, Oceania
Asia
India. Pakistan. Bangladesh. Burma. Sri Lanka. Nepal
Other universities and colleges. By place, A-Z --
Continued

169.D45	Delhi. Zakir Husain College (Table L13a)
	Formerly Delhi College
169.D5	Deoband. Dārul-'Ulūm (Table L13a)
169.D6	Dharwar. Karnatak University (Table L13a)
169.E7	Ernakulam. Sacred Heart College (Table L13a)
169.G24	Galle. St. Aloysius' College (Table L13a)
169.G3	Gauhati. University (Table L13a)
169.G52	Goa University (Table L13a)
169.G6	Gorakhpur. University (Table L13a)
169.G73	Gujrāt. Zamīndār Digrī Kālij (Table L13a)
169.G8	Guntur. Andhra Christian College (Table L13a)
169.G9	Gwalior. Jiraji University (Table L13a)
169.H27	Hampī. Kannada University (Table L13a)
169.H3	Hardwar. Gurukul Kangri Vishwavidyalaya (Table L13a)
169.H75	Hyderabad. Dr. B.R. Ambedkar Open University (Table L13a)
	Formerly Āndhrapradēśa Sārvatrika Viśvavidyālayaṃ
169.H8	Hyderabad. Maulana Azad National Urdu University (Table L13a)
169.H82	Hyderabad. Osmania University (Table L13a)
169.H83	Hyderabad. Osmania University. Nizam College (Table L13a)
169.H85	Hyderabad. Sind University (Table L13a)
	Islamabad
169.I68	Allama Iqbal Open University (Table L13a)
169.I7	University (Table L13a)
169.J26	Jaffna. Jaffna College (Table L13a)
169.J27	Jaffna. University of Jaffna (Table L13a)
169.J3	Jaipur (Rajasthan). University of Rajasthan (Table L13a)
169.J36	Jamshoro. University of Sind (Table L13a)
169.J45	Jessore (City). Michael Madhusudan College (Table L13a)
169.J6	Jodphur, India (City). University (Table L13a)
169.J8	Jubbulpore (City). University (Table L13a)
169.K17	Kanpur. University (Table L13a)
169.K23	Karachi. Sind Madressah-tul-Islam (Table L13a)
169.K24	Karachi. University (Table L13a)
169.K27	Karaikkudi. Alagappa Chettiar College (Table L13a)
169.K32	Kathmandu, Nepal. Tribhuban University (Table L13a)
169.K45	Kelaniya, Sri Lanka. University of Kelaniya (Table L13a)

Asia, Africa, Oceania
Asia
India. Pakistan. Bangladesh. Burma. Sri Lanka. Nepal
Other universities and colleges. By place, A-Z --
Continued

169.K6	Kilhapur. Shri Chhatrapati Shivaji University (Table L13a)
169.K65	Koch Bihar. Kocabihāra Bhiktoriẏā Kaleja (Table L13a)
169.K8	Kurukshetra. Chakravarty (B.N.) University (Table L13a)
169.L28	Lahore. Aitchison College (Table L13a)
169.L3	Lahore. Forman Christian College (Table L13a)
169.L32	Lahore. Government College (Table L13a)
169.L34	Lahore. Islāmiyah Kālij (Table L13a)
169.L67	Lucknow. Isabella Thoburn College (Table L13a)
169.L7	Lucknow. Reid Christian College (Table L13a)
169.M34	Madras. Pachaiyappa's College (Table L13a)
169.M38	Madurai (City). University (Table L13a)
169.M4	Mandalay. University College (Table L13a)
169.M427	Mangalore. St. Agnes College (Table L13a)
169.M43	Mangalore. St. Aloysius College (Table L13a)
169.M46	Manikganj. Sarakair Debendra Kaleja (Table L13a)
169.M67	Mount Lavinia. St. Thomas College (Table L13a)
169.M77	Multān. Bahauddin Zakariya University (Table L13a)
169.M78	Muzaffarabad. Khvushīd Naishnal Lā'brerī āf Āzād Jammūn o Kashmīr (Table L13a)
169.M8	Mysore. University (Table L13a)
169.N32	Nagpur (City). University (Table L13a)
169.N35	Naini Tāl. Kumaun University (Table L13a)
169.N85	Nugegoda. Śrī Jayavardhanapura Viśva Vidyālaya (Table L13a)
169.O72	Orissa. Berhampur University (Table L13a)
169.P3	Patna. University (Table L13a)
	Peradeniya. University see LG169.C452
169.P44	Periyanāyakkanapālayam. Sir Ramakrishna. Mission Vidyalaya (Table L13a)
169.P452	Peshawar (City). University (Table L13a)
169.P52	Pilamedu. P.S.G. Arts College (Table L13a)
169.P55	Pondicherry. Pondicherry University (Table L13a)
169.P555	Poona. Fergusson College (Table L13a)
169.P625	Poona. Sir Parashurambhau College (Table L13a)
169.P63	Poona. University (Table L13a)
169.P82	Punjab (State). University, Solan (Table L13a)
	Founded in 1947 following partition of Punjab University Cf. LG120+ Punjab. University, Lahore
169.R27	Rajputana. University (Table L13a)
169.R3	Rajshahi (City). University (Table L13a)

Asia, Africa, Oceania
Asia
India. Pakistan. Bangladesh. Burma. Sri Lanka. Nepal
Other universities and colleges. By place, A-Z --
Continued

169.R355	Ranchi. Ranchi University (Table L13a)
169.R36	Rangpur. Carmichael College (Table L13a)
169.R62	Roorkee. University (Table L13a)
169.S33	Santiniketan. Visva-Bharati (Table L13a)
169.S38	Saugor (City). University (Table L13a)
169.S4	Serampore. College (Table L13a)
169.S434	Shillong. North-Eastern Hill University (Table L13a)
169.S44	Sholapur (City). Dayanand Anglo-Vedic College (Table L13a)
169.S54	Simla. Himachal Pradesh University (Table L13a)
	Srinagar
169.S7	University of Jammu (Table L13a)
	University of Jammu and Kashmir reorganized in 1969 to form University of Jammu and University of Kashmir
169.S8	University of Kashmir (Table L13a)
169.S94	Sylhet. Murari Chand College (Table L13a)
169.T53	Tirupati. Sri Venkatesvara University (Table L13a)
169.T72	Trichinopoli. St. Joseph's College (Table L13a)
169.T87	Tripunithura. Sri Rama Varma Sanskrit College (Table L13a)
169.T88	Trivandrum. Mahatma Gandhi College (Table L13a)
169.T89	Trivandrum. University of Kerala (Table L13a)
169.U3	Udaipur (City). University (Table L13a)
169.U5	Ujjaina. Vikram University (Table L13a)
169.V37	Varanasi (City). Kashi Vidyapith (Table L13a)
169.V385	Varanasi (City). Sampūrṇānanda Saṃskṛta Viśvavidyālaya (Table L13a)
	Earlier names: Varanaseya Sanskrit Vishwavidyalaya; Government Sanskrit College; Benares Patshala
170.A-Z	Schools. By place, A-Z
170.2.A-Z	Women's colleges and girls' schools. By place, A-Z
	Subarrange each by Table L13a
	Indochina
171.C36	Cân Tho, Vietnam. Viên Dai-hoc (Table L13a)
171.D3	Da Lat, Vietnam. Viên Dai-Hoc (Table L13a)
171.H25	Hanoi, Vietnam. Đại học qûôc gia Hà Nôi (Table L13a)
	Saigon, Vietnam. Ho Chi Minh City, Vietnam
171.S3	Đại Hoc Minh đú'c (Table L13a)
171.S33	Đại học qûôc gia TP. Hô Chí Minh (Table L13a)
171.S35	Viện Đại Học Vạn Hạnh (Table L13a)

	Asia, Africa, Oceania
	Asia
	Indochina -- Continued
171.T54	Thái Nguyên. Vietnam, Đại học Thái Nguyên (Table L13a)
171.V53	Viangchan, Laos. Mahāvithayālai Hāengsāt (Table L13a)
172.A-Z	Schools. By place, A-Z
	Malaysia
173.K58	Kota Kinabalu (Table L13a)
173.K63	Kota Saramahan. Universiti Malaysia Sarawak (Table L13a)
173.K78	Kuala Kangsar. Malay College (Table L13a)
173.K8	Kuala Lipis. Clifford School (Table L13a)
	Kuala Lampur
173.K813	Kolej Tunka Abdul Rahman (Table L13a)
173.K82	Universiti Kebangsaan (Table L13a)
173.K83	Universiti Malaya (Table L13a)
	Formerly University of Malaya in Kuala Lumpur (1958-1962); University of Malaya (1962-1966)
173.K86	Victoria Institution (Table L13a)
	Melaka
173.M4	Anglo-Chinese College (Table L13a)
173.M45	Maktab Melayu Melaka (Table L13a)
173.N55	Nilai. Kolej Universiti Islam Malaysia (Table L13a)
	Penang
173.P4	Universiti Pulau Pinang (Table L13a)
173.P5	Universiti Sains Malaysia (Table L13a)
173.S45	Serdang. Universiti Putra Malaysia (Table L13a)
	Formerly Universiti Pertanian Malaysia
	Singapore
	Raffles College see LG395.S54
	University of Malaya (Singapore) see LG395.S58
	University of Singapore see LG395.S58
174.A-Z	Schools. By place, A-Z
175.A-Z	Women's colleges and girls' schools. By place, A-Z
	Subarrange each by Table L13a
	Indonesia
181.A-Z	Universities and colleges, A-Z
181.B2	Bandjarmasin. Universitas Lambung Mangkurat (Table L13a)
	Bandung
181.B23	Institut Agama Islam Negeri Sunan Gunung Djati (Table L13a)
181.B27	Universitas katolik Parahyangan (Table L13a)
181.B3	Universitas Negeri Padjadjaran (Table L13a)
181.B4	Bengkulu. Universitas Semarak Bengkulu (Table L13a)
181.D3	Darussalam. Universitas Syiah Kuala (Table L13a)

Asia, Africa, Oceania
  Asia
    Indonesia
      Universities and colleges, A-Z -- Continued

181.D4	Denpasar. Universitas Udayana (Table L13a)
181.D45	Djajapura. Universitas Tjenderawasih (Table L13a)
	Djakarta
181.D48	Pusat Penelitian Atma Jaya (Table L13a)
181.D485	Sekolah K.W. III (Table L13a)
181.D49	Sekolah Tinggi Ilmu Administrasi (Table L13a)
181.D5	Taman Siswa (Table L13a)
181.D52	Universitas Baperki (Table L13a)
181.D526	Universitas Ibnu Chaldun (Table L13a)
181.D53	Universitas Indonesia (Table L13a)
	Formerly Batavia. Universiteit van Indonesie
181.D533	Universitas Jayabaya (Table L13a)
181.D535	Universitas Katolik Indonesia Atma Jaya (Table L13a)
181.D538	Universitas Krisnadwipajana (Table L13a)
181.D54	Universitas Kristen Indonesia (Table L13a)
181.D544	Universitas Kristen Krida Wacana (Table L13a)
181.D55	Universitas Muhammadiyah Jakarta (Table L13a)
181.D77	Universitas Trisakti (Table L13a)
181.J22	Jayapura. Universitas Cenderawasih (Table L13a)
181.J23	Jember. Universitas Negeri Jember (Table L13a)
	Jogjakarta (City)
181.J55	Institut Agama Islam Negeri Sunan Kalidjaga (Table L13a)
181.J6	Universitas Gadjah Mada (Table L13a)
181.J62	Universitas Islam Indonesia (Table L13a)
181.J65	Universitas Sanata Dharma (Table L13a)
181.M3	Makasar. Universitas Hasanuddin (Table L13a)
181.M35	Malang. Universitas Brawijaya (Table L13a)
181.M357	Malang. Universitas Merdeka (Table L13a)
181.M36	Malang. Universitas Muhammadiyah (Table L13a)
181.M37	Manado. Universitas Sam Ratulangi (Table L13a)
	Medan
181.M392	Universitas Darma Agung (Table L13a)
181.M393	Universitas HKBP Nommensen (Table L13a)
181.M395	Perguan Tinggi Swadaya (Table L13a)
181.M397	Universitas Islam Sumatera Utara (Table L13a)
181.M4	Universitas Sumatera Utara (Table L13a)
181.M43	Warta Nommensen (Table L13a)
181.M48	Metro. Universitas Muhammadijah Metro Lampung (Table L13a)
181.P3	Padang. Universitas Andalas (Table L13a)
181.P33	Pakanbaru. Universitas Riau (Table L13a)
181.P34	Palembang. Universitas Sriwijaya (Table L13a)

	Asia, Africa, Oceania
	Asia
	Indonesia
	Universities and colleges, A-Z -- Continued
181.P66	Pontianak. Universitas Tanjungpura (Table L13a)
181.S25	Salatiga. Universitas/I.K.I.P. Kristen Satya Wacana (Table L13a)
181.S28	Samarinda. Universitas Mulawarman (Table L13a)
	Semarang (City)
181.S34	Institut Agama Islama Negeri Walisongo (Table L13a)
181.S37	Universitas Diponegoro (Table L13a)
181.S4	Universitas Islam Sultan Agung (Table L13a)
181.S75	Sukarnapura. Universitas Tjenderawasih (Table L13a)
	Subaraja (City)
181.S8	Universal Centre for Public Instruction (Table L13a)
181.S82	Universitas Airlangga (Table L13a)
181.S85	Universitas Surabaya (Table L13a)
181.S87	Universitas Widya Mandala (Table L13a)
	Ujung Pandang. Universitas Hasanuddin see LG271.S42
183.A-Z	Schools. By place, A-Z
184.A-Z	Women's colleges and girls' schools. By place, A-Z
	Subarrange each by Table L13a
	Papua-New Guinea (Ter.)
185.A-Z	Universities and colleges. By place, A-Z
185.B3	Boroko. University of Papua-New Guinea (Ter.) (Table L13a)
185.B6	Port Moresby. University (Table L13a)
186.A-Z	Schools. By place, A-Z
187.A-Z	Women's colleges and girls' schools. By place, A-Z
	Subarrange each by Table L13a
	Philippines
200-209.5	Manila. University of Santo Tomás (Table L12)
210-219.5	Quezon. University of the Philippines (Table L12)
221.A-Z	Other universities and colleges. By place, A-Z
221.A54	Angeles City. Holy Angel University (Table L13a)
221.B37	Baguio. Saint Louis University (Table L13a)
	Cebu City
221.C4	Southern College (Table L13a)
221.C43	University of San Carlos (Table L13a)
221.D8	Dumaguete. Silliman University (Table L13a)
	Iloilo (City)
221.I4	Central Philippine University (Table L13a)
221.I47	University San Agustín (Table L13a)
221.L43	Legazpi. Bicol University (Table L13a)
221.L67	Los Baños. University of the Philippines at Los Baños (Table L13a)

LG

	Asia, Africa, Oceania
	Asia
	Philippines
	Other universities and colleges. By place, A-Z -- Continued
	Manila
221.M26	Araneta University (Table L13a)
221.M27	De La Salle University (Table L13a)
221.M28	Far Eastern University (Table L13a)
221.M29	Philippine Christian College (Table L13a)
221.M294	Philippine Normal College (Table L13a)
221.M295	St. Scholastica's College (Table L13a)
221.M297	University of Asia and the Pacific (Table L13a)
221.M3	University of the East (Table L13a)
221.M36	Marawi City. Mindanao State University (Table L13a)
221.M385	Muñoz (Luzon). Central Luzon State University (Table L13a)
221.Q4	Quezon City. Ateneo de Manila University (Table L13a)
225.A-Z	Schools. By place, A-Z
227.A-Z	Women's colleges and girls' schools. By place, A-Z
	Subarrange each by Table L13a
	Japan
240-249.5	Kyōto Daigaku (Table L12)
	Formerly Kyōto Teikoku Daigaku
250-259.5	Tokyo Daigaku, Tokyo (Table L12)
	Formerly Tokyo Teikoku Daigaku
	For Daiichi Kōtō Gakkō, Tokyo see LG271.D3
271.A-Z	Other universities and colleges. By place, A-Z
	Tokyo institutions alphabetically, by name rather than by place
271.A37	Akita. Akita Daigaku (Table L13a)
271.A6	Aoyama Gakuin, Tokyo (Table L13a)
271.B8	Bunrika Daigaku, Tokyo (Table L13a)
271.C47	Chiba. Chiba Daigaku (Table L13a)
271.C5	Chūō Daigakū, Tokyo (Table L13a)
271.D3	Daiichi Koto Gakkó, Tokyo (Table L13a)
	Established in 1886; reorganized in 1949 to form Tōkyō Daigaku. Kyōyō
271.D34	Daitō Bunka Daigaku, Tokyo (Table L13a)
271.F8	Fukuoka. Kyūshū Daigaku (Table L13a)
	Formerly Kyushu Imperial University; Fukuoka University
271.F84	Fukushima. Fukushima Daigaku (Table L13a)
271.G3	Gakshūin Daigaku, Tokyo (Table L13a)
271.G54	Ginowan-shi. Okinawa Kokusai Daigaku (Table L13a)
	Hachiōji-shi
271.H3	Sōka Daigaku (Table L13a)
271.H33	Teikyō Daigaku (Table L13a)

Asia, Africa, Oceania
  Asia
    Japan
      Other universities and colleges. By place, A-Z --
        Continued

271.H35	Hikone-shi. Shiga Daigaku (Table L13a)
271.H36	Hikone-shi. Shiga Kenritsu Tanki Daigaku (Table L13a)
271.H37	Hino-shi. Meisei Daigaku (Table L13a)
271.H4	Hirosaki. Hirosaki Daigaku (Table L13a)
271.H46	Hiroshima. Hiroshima Daigaku (Table L13a)
271.H5	Hitotsubashi Daigaku, Tokyo (Table L13a)
271.H67	Hōsei Daigaku, Tokyo (Table L13a)
271.I8	Ise. Kōgakukan Daigaku (Table L13a)
271.J5	Jichi Daigaku, Tokyo (Table L13a)
271.J6	Jochi Daigaku, Tokyo (Table L13a)
271.K19	Kagoshima. Daishichi Kōtō Gakkō Zōshikan (Table L13a)

           Opened in 1901; merged to form Kagoshima Daigaku in 1949, LG271.K2

271.K2	Kagoshima. Kagoshima Daigaku (Table L13a)
271.K296	Kamakura Akademia (Table L13a)

           Established as Kamakura Daigakkō in 1946, name changed to Kamakura Akademia, closed in 1950

271.K33	Kanazawa. Kanazawa Daigaku (Table L13a)
271.K35	Kashiwagi. Hiroike Gakuen (Table L13a)
271.K44	Ke-io Gijuku Daigaku, Tokyo (Table L13a)
271.K48	Kitakyūshū. Kitakyūshū Daigaku (Table L13a)
271.K49	Kitakyūshū. Yahata Daigaku (Table L13a)
271.K495	Kitasato Daigaku, Tokyo (Table L13a)
	Kobe
271.K5	Kobe Daigaku (Table L13a)
271.K513	Kobe Gakuin Daigaku (Table L13a)
271.K52	Konan Daigaku (Table L13a)
271.K54	Kōchi. Kōchi Daigaku (Table L13a)
271.K545	Kōchi-shi. Kōchi Tanki Daigaku (Table L13a)
	Kōfu
271.K55	Yamanashi Daigaku (Table L13a)
271.K552	Yamanashi Gakuin Daigaku (Table L13a)
271.K556	Kokugakuin Daigaku, Tokyo (Table L13a)

           Formerly Kōten Kōkyūjo (Japan)

271.K56	Kokusai Kirisutokyō Daigaku, Tokyo (Table L13a)
271.K565	Kokushikan Daigaku, Tokyo (Table L13a)
271.K58	Komazawa Daigaku, Tokyo (Table L13a)

           Formerly Kōten Kōkyūjo (Japan)

271.K586	Kōya-chō. Kōyasan Daigaku (Table L13a)

LG

Asia, Africa, Oceania
Asia
Japan
Other universities and colleges. By place, A-Z --
Continued

271.K663	Kumamoto. Daigo Kōtō Gakkō (Table L13a)
	Established as Daigo Kōtō Chūgakkō in 1887; name changed to Daigo Kōtō Gakkō in 1894; merged to form Kumamoto Daigaku (Hōbungakubu) in 1950
271.K664	Kumamoto. Kumamoto Daigaku (Table L13a)
271.K665	Kumamoto. Kumamoto Kenritsu Daigaku (Table L13a)
271.K72	Kurume, Japan (Fukuoka Prefecture). Kurume Daigaku (Table L13a)
	Kyoto
271.K8	Bukkyō Daigaku (Table L13a)
271.K83	Dōshisha Daigaku (Table L13a)
271.K84	Hanazono Daigaku (Table L13a)
271.K86	Ōtani Daigaku (Table L13a)
271.K866	Ritsumeikan Daigaku (Table L13a)
271.K87	Ryūkoku Daigaku (Table L13a)
271.M29	Matsue. Shimane Daigaku (Table L13a)
271.M33	Matsumoto. Shinshu Daigaku (Table L13a)
	Formerly Shinshu Daigaku
271.M36	Meiji Daigaku, Tokyo (Table L13a)
271.M38	Meiji Gakuin Daigaku, Tokyo (Table L13a)
	Mito
271.M5	Ibaraki Daigaku (Table L13a)
271.M54	Mito Kōtō Gakkō (Table L13a)
	Established in 1920, closed in 1950
271.M65	Morioka-shi. Iwate Daigaku (Table L13a)
271.M7	Mu-cha, Formosa. Chêng chih ta hsüeh (Table L13a)
271.M76	Musashi Daigaku (Table L13a)
271.M78	Musashino-shi. Ajia Daigaku (Table L13a)
271.M84	Musashino-shi. Seikei Daigaku (Table L13a)
271.N27	Nagasaki-shi. Nagasaki Daigaku (Table L13a)
271.N28	Nagasaki-shi. Nagasaki Sḡ Kagaku Daigaku (Table L13a)
	Nagoya
271.N33	Aichi Gakuin Daigaku (Table L13a)
271.N35	Nagoya Daigaku (Table L13a)
271.N37	Naha. Ryukyu Daigaku (Table L13a)
271.N38	Nara-shi. Nara Daigaku (Table L13a)
271.N39	Nara-shi. Nara Kenritsu Tanki Daigaku (Table L13a)
271.N5	Nihon Daigaju, Tokyo (Table L13a)
271.N53	Niigata. Niigata Daigaku (Table L13a)
271.N57	Nishinomiya. Kwansei Gakuin Daigaku (Table L13a)
271.N65	Nishō Gakusha Daigaku, Tokyo (Table L13a)

Asia, Africa, Oceania
  Asia
    Japan
      Other universities and colleges. By place, A-Z --
        Continued

271.O35	Ōita. Ōita Daigaku (Table L13a)
271.O382	Okayama. Okayama Daigaku (Table L13a)
	Osaka
271.O67	Kaitokudō (Table L13a)
271.O78	Kansai Daigaku (Table L13a)
271.O79	Ōsaka Daigaku (Table L13a)
	Formerly Ōsaka Teikoku Daigaku
271.O8	Ōsaka Furitsu Daigaku (Table L13a)
271.O85	Ōsaka Shiritsu Daigaku (Table L13a)
271.R5	Rikkyō Daigaku, Tokyo (Table L13a)
271.R55	Risshō Daigaku, Tokyo (Table L13a)
271.S27	Sakura-mura. Tsukuba Daigaku (Table L13a)
	Formerly Tōkyō Kyōiku Daigaku, Tokyo, LG271.T59
	Sapporo
271.S3	Hokkaidō Daigaku (Table L13a)
	Formerly Hokkaido Imperial University
271.S34	Hokkaidō Kyōikui Daigaku (Table L13a)
	Formerly Hokkaidō Gakugei Daigaku
271.S366	Hokusei Gakuen Daigaku (Table L13a)
271.S37	Sapporo Daigaku (Table L13a)
271.S393	Seijō Daigaku, Tokyo (Table L13a)
271.S394	Seikei Daigaku, Tokyo (Table L13a)
271.S397	Sendai. Daini Kōtō Gakkō (Table L13a)
	Established in 1887, merged to form Tohoku Daigaku in 1950, LG271.S4
271.S4	Sendai. Tōhoku Daigaku (Table L13a)
271.S42	Sendai. Tohoku Gakuin Daigaku (Table L13a)
271.S45	Senshū Daigaku, Tokyo (Table L13a)
271.S55	Shizuoka. Shizuoka Daigaku (Table L13a)
271.S64	Sōka. Dokkyō Daigaku (Table L13a)
271.T357	Taishō Daigaku (Table L13a)
271.T36	Takamatsu. Kagawa Daigaku (Table L13a)
271.T37	Takushoku Daigaku, Tokyo (Table L13a)
271.T39	Tama-shi. Tama Daigaku (Table L13a)
271.T43	Tenri. Tenri Daigaku (Table L13a)
271.T58	Tōkai Daigaku, Tokyo (Table L13a)
271.T582	Tokushima-shi. Tokushima Daigaku (Table L13a)
271.T583	Tokuyama-shi. Tokuyama Daigaku (Table L13a)
271.T586	Tōkyō Gaikokugo Daigaku (Table L13a)
271.T588	Tōkyō Komyuniti Karejji (Table L13a)

LG

	Asia, Africa, Oceania
	Asia
	Japan
	Other universities and colleges. By place, A-Z -- Continued
271.T59	Tōkyō Kyōiku Daigaku, Tokyo (Table L13a)
	Closed in 1978, relocated and continued as Tsukuba Daigaku, LG271.S27
271.T597	Tōkyō Toritsu Daigaku (Table L13a)
271.T599	Tottori Daigaku (Table L13a)
271.T6	Toyama. Toyama Daigaku (Table L13a)
	A merger of Toyama Kōtō Gakkō (1923-1949); Toyama Yakugaku Semmon Gakkō (1920-1949), Takaoka Kōgyō Semmon Gakkō (1944-1949), Toyama Shihan Gakkō (1943-1949), and Toyama Seinen Shihan Gakkō (1944-1949)
271.T65	Toyama. Toyama Kōtō Gakkō (Table L13a)
	Merged to form Toyama Daigaku in 1949, LG271.T6
271.T67	Tōyō Daigaku (Tokyo, Japan) (Table L13a)
	Tsukuba. Tsukuba Daigaku see LG271.S27
271.T75	Tsuru-shi. Tsuru Bunka Daigaku (Table L13a)
271.T78	Tsu-shi. Mie Daigaku (Table L13a)
271.U54	United Nations University (Table L13a)
271.U77	Utsunomiya-shi. Utsunomiya Daigaku (Table L13a)
271.W22	Wakayama-shi. Wakayama Daigaku (Table L13a)
271.W25	Wako Daigaku, Tokyo (Table L13a)
271.W3	Waseda Daigaku, Tokyo (Table L13a)
	Formerly Tōkyō Semmon Gakkō
271.Y28	Yamagata. Yamagata Daigaku (Table L13a)
	Yamaguchi-shi
271.Y287	Yamaguchi Daigaku (Table L13a)
271.Y29	Yamaguchi Kōtō Gakkō (Table L13a)
	Yokohama-shi
271.Y62	Kanagawa Daigaku (Table L13a)
271.Y64	Kantō Gakuin Daigaku (Table L13a)
271.Y68	Yokohama Kokuritsu Daigaku (Table L13a)
271.Y73	Yokohama Shiritsu Daigaku (Table L13a)
274.A-Z	Junior colleges. By place, A-Z
	Tokyo institutions alphabetically, by name rather than by place
	Subarrange each by Table L13a
275.A-Z	Schools. By place, A-Z
277.A-Z	Women's colleges and girls' schools. By place, A-Z
	Subarrange each by Table L13a
	Korea
281.A-Z	Universities and colleges. By place, A-Z
	Subarrange each by Table L13a

Asia, Africa, Oceania
  Asia
    Korea -- Continued

283.A-Z	Women's colleges and girls' schools. By place, A-Z
	Subarrange each by Table L13a
285.A-Z	Schools. By place, A-Z
	Iran
291.A-Z	Universities and colleges. By place, A-Z
	Subarrange each by Table L13a
291.I8	Isfahan. Dānishgāh. Dānishkadah-i Adabīyāt (Table L13a)
291.S45	Shiraz. Dānishgāh-i Pahlavī (Table L13a)
291.T2	Tabriz. Dānishgāh. (Table L13a)
291.T4	Teheran. Dānishgāh. (Table L13a)
295.A-Z	Schools. By place, A-Z
	Subarrange each by Table L13a
	Former Soviet republics in Asia
	Central Asia
(301.A-Z)	General
(301.A44)	Alma-Ata (Kazakhstan). Qazaqtyñg S.M. Kirov atyndaghy memlekettīk universiteti
	see LG302.2
(301.D87)	Dushanbe (Tajikistan). Universitet davlatii Tojikiston be nomi V.I. Lenin
	see LG304.2
(301.T3)	Tashkent (Uzbekistan). V.I. Lenin nomidagi Toshkent davlat universiteti
	see LG306.2
	Kazakhstan
302.2	Alma-Ata. Qazaqtyñg S.M. Kirov atyndaghy memlekettīk universiteti (Table L13)
302.5.A-Z	Other colleges and schools. By place, A-Z
	Subarrange each by Table L13a
	Kyrgyzstan
303.2	Bishkek (formerly Frunze). Kirgizskiĭ gosudarstvennyĭ universitet imeni 50-letiīa SSSR (Table L13)
303.5.A-Z	Other colleges and schools. By place, A-Z
	Subarrange each by Table L13a
	Tajikistan
304.2	Dushanbe. Universiteti davlatii Tojikiston ba nomi V.I. Lenin (Table L13)
304.5.A-Z	Other colleges and schools. By place, A-Z
	Subarrange each by Table L13a
	Turkmenistan
305.2	Ashkhabad. A.M. Gor'kiĭ adyndaky Türkmen dóvlet universiteti (Table L13)

Asia, Africa, Oceania
Asia
Former Soviet republics in Asia
Central Asia
Turkmenistan -- Continued
305.5.A-Z   Other colleges and schools. By place, A-Z
Subarrange each by Table L13a
Uzbekistan
306.2   Tashkent. V.I. Lenin nomidagi Toshkent daviat universiteti (Table L13)
306.5.A-Z   Other colleges and schools. By place, A-Z
Subarrange each by Table L13a
Siberia
310-319.5   Tomsk. Tomskiĭ gosudarstvennyĭ universitet (Table L12)
320.A-Z   Other colleges and schools. By place, A-Z
320.C44   Cheliabinsk. IUzhno-Ural'skiĭ gosudarstvennyĭ universitet (Table L13a)
(320.D8)   Dushanbe (Tajikistan). Universiteti davlati Tojikiston ba nomi V.I. Lenin
see LG304.2
320.I25   IAkutsk. IAkutskiĭ gosudarstvennyĭ universitet im. M.K. Ammosova (Table L13a)
320.I56   Ioshkar-Ola. Mariĭskiĭ gosudarstvennyĭ universitet (Table L13a)
320.I74   Irkutsk. Irkutskiĭ gosudarstvennyĭ universitet (Table L13a)
320.K7   Krasnoiarsk. Muzhskaia gimnaziia (Table L13a)
320.K8   Kurgan. Kurganskiĭ gosudarstvennyĭ universitet (Table L13a)
320.O57   Omsk. Omskiĭ gosudarstvennyĭ universitet (Table L13a)
320.S27   Saransk. Mordovskoĭ gosudarstvennyĭ universitet (Table L13a)
320.T48   Tiumen'. Tiumenskiĭ gosudarstvennyĭ universitet (Table L13a)
320.U43   Ufa. Bashqort dăŭlăt universitety. Bashkirskiĭ gosudarstvennyĭ universitet (Table L13a)
320.V6   Vladivostok. Dal'nevostochnyĭ gosudarstvennyĭ universitet (Vladivostok, Russia) (Table L13a)
Middle East (Near East)
(321)   Asia Minor. Turkey
see LF5169+
Armenia (Republic)
331.A-Z   Universities. By place, A-Z
331.E73   Yerevan. Erevani Petakan Hamalsaran (Table L13a)

	Asia, Africa, Oceania
	Asia
	Middle East (Near East)
	Armenia (Republic) -- Continued
331.5.A-Z	Other colleges and schools. By place, A-Z
	Subarrange each by Table L13a
	Azerbaijan
332.2	Baku. M.Ă. Răsulzadă adyna Baky Dȯvlăt Universiteti (Table L13)
332.5.A-Z	Other colleges and schools. By place, A-Z
	Subarrange each by Table L13a
	Georgia (Republic)
332.7	T'bilisi. T'bilisi saxelmcip'o universiteti (Table L13)
332.9.A-Z	Other colleges and schools. By place, A-Z
	Subarrange each by Table L13a
333.A-Z	Bahrain
333.M34	Manama. Jāmi'at al-Baḥrayn (Table L13a)
338.A-Z	Iraq
338.B33	Bagdad. Jāmi'at Baghdād (Table L13a)
338.B35	Bagdad. al-Madrasah al-Mustanṣirīyah (Table L13a)
338.B36	Baghdad College (Table L13a)
338.B38	Basra. Jami'at al-Basrah (Table L13a)
	Jami'at al-Basrah see LG338.B38
338.M5	Mosul. Jāmi'at al-Mawṣil (Table L13a)
338.S5	Sulaymānīyah. Jāmi'at al-Sulaymānīyah (Table L13a)
338.S52	Sulaymānīyah. Zankoy Silêmanî (1992-) (Table L13a)
	Israel. Palestine
341.B4	Beersheba. Universitat Ben Guryon ba-Negev (Table L13a)
	Formerly Universitat ha-Negev
341.B48	Bethlehem. Jāmi'at Bayt Laḥm (Table L13a)
341.B57	Bīr Zayt. Jāmi'at Bīr Zayt (Table L13a)
	Formerly Kulliyat Bīr Zayt
341.G38	Gaza. Ma'had Filasṭīn al-Dīnī (al-Azhar) bi-Ghazzah (Table L13a)
341.H33	Haifa. Universitat Hefah (Table L13a)
	Jerusalem
341.J45	Hebrew University. Universitah ha-'Ivrit bi-Yerushalayim (Table L13a)
341.J497	Masjid a-Aqṣá (Table L13a)
341.M42	Mikhlalah ha-aḳademit 'Emeḳ Yizre'el (Table L13a)
341.M44	Mikhlalah ha-aḳademit Sapir (Table L13a)
341.M45	Mikhlalah ha-aḳademit Tel-Ḥai (Table L13a)
341.M46	Mikhlalah ha-aḳademit Yehudah ve-Shomron (Table L13a)
	Formerly Mikhlelet Yehudah ṿe-Shomron
341.N37	Nazareth. Jāmi'at al-Jalīl al-'Arabīyah (Table L13a)

Asia, Africa, Oceania
  Asia
    Middle East (Near East)
      Israel. Palestine -- Continued

341.N4	Neḥalim. Yeshivat Benei Akiva Nahal Yitzhak (Table L13a)
341.R33	Ramat Gan. Bar-Ilan University (Table L13a)
341.T38	Tel-Aviv. Open University (Table L13a)
341.T47	Tel-Aviv. University (Table L13a)
341.T7	Tsofit. Berl Katznelson Institute (Table L13a)
	Universiṭah ha-ivrit bi-Yerushalayim see LG341.J45
	Universiṭah ha-petuḥah see LG341.T38
	Universiṭat Bar-Ilan see LG341.R33
	Universiṭat Ben-Guryon ba-Negev see LG341.B4
	Universiṭat Tel-Aviv see LG341.T47
345.A-Z	Schools. By place, A-Z
346.A-Z	Jordan
	Amman
346.A45	Jāmi'ah al-Urdunīyah (Table L13a)
346.A47	Jāmi'at al-Quds al-Maftūḥah (Table L13a)
346.A53	Sharikat al-Batrā' lil-Ta'līm (Table L13a)
346.I73	Irbid. Jāmi'at al-Yarmūk (Table L13a)
347.A-Z	Kuwait
347.K88	Kuwait (City). Jāmi'at al-Kuwayt (Table L13a)
	Lebanon
351.A72	American University of Beirut (Table L13a)
	Formerly Syrian Protestant College
	Other universities and colleges
	Beirut
351.B25	Beirut University College (Table L13a)
	Formerly American Junior College for Women (Founded in 1924). In 1949 became Beirut College for Women until 1973
351.B32	École supérieure des lettres (Table L13a)
351.B34	International College (Table L13a)
351.B35	al-Jami'ah al-Lubnānīyah (Table L13a)
351.B36	al-Kullīyah al-Úthmñiyah al-Islāmīyah (Table L13a)
351.B37	al-Madrasah al-Kullīyah al-Sūrīyah al-Injīilīyah (Table L13a)
351.B4	Université Saint-Joseph (Table L13a)
355.A-Z	Schools. By place, A-Z
357.A-Z	Women's colleges and girls' schools. By place, A-Z
	Subarrange each by Table L13a
358.A-Z	Qatar
358.D38	Dawḥah. Jāmi'at Qaṭar (Table L13a)
359.A-Z	Saudi Arabia

Asia, Africa, Oceania
Asia
Middle East (Near East)
Saudi Arabia -- Continued

359.A24	Abhā. Kullīyat al-Sharī 'ah wa-al-Lughah al-'Arabīyah (Table L13a)
359.D35	Dammām. Jāmi'at al-Malik Fayṣal (Table L13a)
359.D47	Dhahran. Jāmiạt al-Malik Fahd lil-Batrūl Wa-al-Maạdin (Table L13a)
	Hasa. Jāmi'at al Malik Fayṣal see LG359.D35
359.J35	Jiddah. Jāmi'at al-Malik 'Abd al-'Azīz (Table L13a)
359.M45	Mecca. Jāmi'at Umm al-Qurá (Table L13a)
359.M47	Medina. Jāmi'ah al-Islāmīyah bi-al-Madīnah al-Munawwarah (Table L13a)
359.R4	Riyadh. Jāmi'at al-Imām Muḥammad ibn Sa'ūd al-Islāmīyah (Table L13a)
359.R5	Riyadh. Jāmi'at al-Riyād (Table L13a)

Syria
Universities and colleges

361.A43	Aleppo. Jāmi'at Halab (Table L13a)
361.D43	Damascus. Jāmi'at Dimashq (Table L13a)
365.A-Z	Schools. By place, A-Z
367.A-Z	Women's colleges and girls' schools. By place, A-Z
	Subarrange each by Table L13a

United Arab Emirates

368.A37	Abū Ẓaby. Jāmi'at Zāyid (Table L13a)
368.A45	Ajman. Ajman University of Science and Technology (Table L13a)
368.A92	'Ayn. Jāmi'at al-Imārāt al-'Arabīyah al-Muttaḥidah (Table L13a)
368.S53	Shāriqah. American University of Sharjah (Table L13a)
368.S56	Shāriqah. Jāmi'at al-Shāriqah (Table L13a)

Yemen (Yemen Arab Republic)

370.S26	Ṣan'ā'. Jāmi'at Ṣan'ā' (Table L13a)
370.T34	Ta'izz. Jāmi'at Ta'izz (Table L13a)
395.A-Z	Other places of Asia, A-Z
(395.A45)	Amman (Jordan). al-Jāmi'ah al Urdunīyah see LG346.A45
395.B26	Ban Bang Saen (Thailand). Mahāwitthayālai Sīnakharinwirōt Bāng Sǣn (Table L13a)
395.B28	Bandar Seri Begawan (Brunei). Universiti Brunei Darussalem (Table L13a)
	Bangkok (Thailand)
395.B3	Chulalongkon University (Table L13a)
395.B33	Mahāñulālongkōn Rātchawitthayālai (Table L13a)
395.B333	Mahāwitthayālai Mahidon (Table L13a)
395.B335	Mahāwitthayālai Rāmkhamhāeng (Table L13a)

	Asia, Africa, Oceania
	Asia
	Other places of Asia, A-Z
	Bangkok (Thailand) -- Continued
395.B337	Mahāwitthayālai Sinlapākōn (Table L13a)
395.B338	Rōngrīan Trīam Prinyā Mahāwitthayalāi Wichā Thammasāt lae Kānmūáng (Table L13a)
395.B3386	Sathāban Thēknōlōyī Rātchamongkhon (Table L13a)
395.B339	Sattrī Čhunlānak (Table L13a)
395.B34	Thammasat University (Table L13a)
395.B37	Witthayālai Khritsatīan (Table L13a)
(395.B57)	Bīr Zayt. Jāmi'at Bīr Zayt. Kullīyat Bīr Zayt see LG341.B57
395.C44	Ceylon University (Table L13a)
	Chiang Mai (Thailand)
395.C45	Mahawitthayalai Chiang Mai (Table L13a)
395.C55	Mahawitthayalai Phayap (Table L13a)
395.C57	Mongfot Witthayalai (Table L13a)
(395.D38)	Dawḥah (Qatar). Jāmi'at Qaṭar see LG358.D38
395.F35	Famagusta (Cyprus). Hellēniko Gymnasio Ammochōstou
(395.I73)	Irbid (Jordan). Jāmi'at al-Yarmūk see LG346.I73
395.K35	Kanchanaburi (Thailand). Moo Baan Dek (Table L13a)
395.K46	Khōn Kāen (Thailand). Mahāwitthayālai Khōn Kāen (Table L13a)
(395.K88)	Kuwait (Kuwait). Jāmi'at al-Kuwayt see LG347.K88
395.L48	Leukara (Cyprus). Gymnasio Leukarōn (Table L13a)
395.L56	Limassol (Cyprus). Gymnasio Katholikēs (Table L13a)
395.M87	Muscat (Oman). Jāmi'at al-Sulṭān Qābūs (Table L13a)
	Nicosia (Cyprus)
395.N52	Dēmotiko Scholeio Hagiōn Homologētōn (Table L13a)
395.N526	Melgonean Krt'akan Hastatut'iwn (Table L13a)
395.N53	Panepistemio Kyprou (Table L13a)
395.N54	Pankyprion Gymnasion (Table L13a)
395.P4	Penang. Anglo-Chinese School (Table L13a)
395.P44	Phetchaburi (Thailand) Sathāban Rātchaphat Phetchaburī (Table L13a)
395.P45	Phitsanulok (Thailand). Witthayālai Khrū Phibūnsongkhrām (Table L13a)
395.R38	Ratchaburi (Thailand). Mahāwitthayālai Rātchaphat Mūbān Čhọm Bứng (Table L13a)
395.R48	Réunion. Centre Universitaire de la Réunion (Table L13a)
395.S25	Sam Phran (Thailand). Rōngrīan Phō. Pō. Rō Rāt chawitthayālai (Table L13a)

	Asia, Africa, Oceania
	Asia
	Other places of Asia, A-Z -- Continued
395.S255	Samut Prakan (Thailand). Rōngrīan Samut Prākān (Table L13a)
(395.S26)	San'ā (Yemen). Jāmi'at Sab'ā
	see LG370.S26
	Singapore
395.S5	Anglo-Chinese School of the Methodist Mission (Table L13a)
395.S52	Institute of Education (Table L13a)
395.S53	Nanyang University (Table L13a)
	Formerly Nan-yang ta hsüeh; 1980 merged with University of Singapore, name changed to National University of Singapore, LG395.S58
395.S54	Raffles College (Table L13a)
	Founded 1929, merged in 1949 with King Edward VII College of Medicine to form University of Malaya (Singapore), LG395.S58
395.S55	Raffles Institution (Table L13a)
395.S56	St. Andrew's School (Table L13a)
395.S58	National University of Singapore (Table L13a)
	Founded 1980 by merger of University of Singapore and Nanyang University. the former had its origins in the King Edward College of Medicine, Raffles College and the University of Malaya (Singapore)
	University of Malaya (Singapore) see LG395.S58
	University of Singapore see LG395.S58
395.S59	Whampoa Secondary School (Table L13a)
395.S64	Songkhla (Thailand). Mahāwitthayālai Songkhlā Nakharin (Table L13a)
395.S84	Sukhothai (Thailand). Mahāwitthayālai Sukhōthaithammāthirāt (Table L13a)
	Africa
401.A-Z	Ethiopia
401.A4	Addis Ababa. Addis Ababa University (Table L13a)
	Formerly Haile Selassie I University; National University
401.A84	Asmara. 'Aśmarā yunivarsiti (Table L13a)
	British Africa. South Africa
405	South Africa. University, Pretoria (Table L13)
	Formerly the University of the cape of Good Hope. An examining university only
	Cf. LG411.H77-86, LG411.R57-66, LG431.N3, LG451.B5, LG471.P6, LG471.P7
	Cape of Good Hope. Cape Colony. Cape Province
411.B4	Bellville. University of Western Cape (Table L13a)

	Asia, Africa, Oceania
	Africa
	British Africa. South Africa
	Cape of Good Hope. Cape Colony. Cape Province -- Continued
411.B64	University of North-West (South Africa) (Table L13a)
	Formerly University of Bophuthatswana
411.C2	Cape Town, University of (Table L13a)
	Formerly South African College
411.C3	Cape Town. University of the Cape of Good Hope (Table L13a)
	Continued as University of South Africa, LG405
411.F6	Fort Hare, South Africa. University College (Table L13a)
	Formerly south African Native College
411.G7	Graeme College, Grahamstown (Table L13a)
411.H77	Huguenot University College, Wellington, South Africa (Table L13a)
	A constituent college of the University of South Africa, LG405
411.K55	Kingswood College, Grahamstown (Table L13a)
411.P63	Port Elizabeth, Cape of Good Hope. University (Table L13a)
411.R57	Rhodes University College, Grahamstown (Table L13a)
	A constituent college of the University of South Africa, LG405
411.S25	Selborne College, East London (Table L13a)
	South African Native College, Fort Hare see LG411.F6
411.S68	St. Andrew's College, Grahamstown (Table L13a)
411.S7	Stellenbosch. University (Table L13a)
414.A-Z	Schools. By place, A-Z
416.A-Z	Botswana
416.G32	Gaborone. University of Botswana (Table L13a)
	Central African Protectorate see LG441+
418.A-Z	Kenya
418.E43	Eldoret. Moi University (Table L13a)
	Cf. LG418.M37 Maseno University
418.M37	Maseno. Maseno University (Table L13a)
	Formerly Maseno University College
	A constituent college of Moi University
418.M65	Mombasa. Kenya Coast University (Table L13a)
	Nairobi
418.N18	Catholic University of Eastern Africa (Table L13a)
418.N2	Cooperative College of Kenya (Table L13a)
418.N23	East African Academy (Table L13a)
418.N24	Kenya Utalii College (Table L13a)

	Asia, Africa, Oceania
	Africa
	British Africa. South Africa
	Kenya
	Nairobi -- Continued
418.N25	Kenyatta University (Table L13a)
	Formerly Kenyatta University College
418.N3	University (Table L13a)
	Formerly Nairobi. University College
418.N55	Njoro. Egerton University (Table L13a)
418.5.A-Z	Schools. By place, A-Z
419.A-Z	Lesotho
419.R64	Roma. National University of Lesotho (Table L13a)
	Formerly University of Botswana, Lesotho, and Swaziland
420.A-Z	Schools. By place, A-Z
421.A-Z	Uganda
421.B8	Budo. King's College (Table L13a)
	Entebbe
421.E5	University of East Africa (Table L13a)
421.E78	Nkumba University (Table L13a)
	Kampala
421.K35	Makerere University College (Table L13a)
421.K37	University of East Africa (Table L13a)
421.T67	Tororo. St. Peter's College (Table L13a)
422.A-Z	Schools. By place, A-Z
423.A-Z	Women's colleges and girls' schools. By place, A-Z
	Subarrange each by Table L13a
431.A-Z	Natal
431.D87	Durban. University of Durban-Westville (Table L13a)
431.N3	Natal University College. Pietermaritzburg (Table L13a)
	A constituent college of the University of South Africa, LG405
438.A-Z	Schools. By place, A-Z
	Malawi
441.A-Z	Universities and colleges. By place, A-Z
441.M35	University of Malawi (Table L13a)
443.A-Z	Schools. By place, A-Z
451.A-Z	Orange Free State
451.B5	Bloemfontein. University College of the Orange Free State (Table L13a)
	Formerly Grey University College
	A constituent college of the University of South Africa, LG405
454.A-Z	Swaziland
454.S89	University College of Swaziland, Kwaluseni (Table L13a)

	Asia, Africa, Oceania
	Africa
	British Africa. South Africa
	Swaziland -- Continued
454.S93	University of Swaziland (Table L13a)
455.A-Z	Schools. By place, A-Z
457.A-Z	Transkei
457.U57	Umtata. University of Transkei (Table L13a)
459.A-Z	Venda
459.S53	Sibasa. University of Venda (Table L13a)
461.A-Z	Zimbabwe
461.B84	Bulawayo. St. George's College (Table L13a)
461.G86	Gweru. Midlands State University (Table L13a)
461.S3	University of Zimbabwe, Harare (Table L13a)
	Formerly University of Rhodesia, Salisbury
462.A-Z	Schools. By place, A-Z
	Tanzania
468.D3	Chou Kikuu cha Dar es Salaam (Table L13a)
	Formerly University College, Dar es Salaam
468.5.A-Z	Schools. By place, A-Z
469.A-Z	Zambia (Northern Rhodesia)
469.K23	Kabur. President's Citizenship College (Table L13a)
469.K58	Kitwe. Copperbelt University (Table L13a)
469.L8	Lusaka. University of Zambia (Table L13a)
469.N37	Ndola. University of Zambia at Ndola (Table L13a)
471.A-Z	Transvaal
	Johannesburg
471.J55	Randse Afrikaanse Universiteit (Table L13a)
471.J56	St. Stithians College (Table L13a)
471.J6	University of the Witwatersrand (Table L13a)
471.P6	Potchefstroom University for Christian Higher Education (Table L13a)
	Formerly Potchefstroom University College
	A constituent college of the University of South Africa, LG405
471.P7	Pretoria. University (Table L13a)
	A constituent college of the University of South Africa, LG405
	Cf. LG471.T8 Transvaal University College, its predecessor
471.T8	Transvaal University College, Pretoria (Table L13a)
	Cf. LG471.P7 University of Pretoria, its successor
471.U6	University of the North (Table L13a)
	From 1959-1970, under the supervision of the University of South Africa
475.A-Z	Schools. By place, A-Z
478.A-Z	Zululand

	Asia, Africa, Oceania
	Africa
	British Africa. South Africa
	Zululand -- Continued
478.K82	Kwa Dlangezwa. University of Zululand (Table L13a)
	West Africa
	Nigeria
480	Nigerian University System
481.A-Z	Universities and colleges. By place, A-Z
481.A28	Abuja. University of Abuja (Table L13a)
481.A36	Ado-Ekiti. University of Ado-Ekiti (Table L13a)
481.A38	Ago-Iwoye. Olabisi Onabanjo University (Table L13a)
	Formerly Ogun State University
481.A58	Akungba-Akoko. Adekunle Ajasin University (Table L13a)
	Formerly Ondo State University
481.A8	Awka. Nnamdi Azikiwe University (Table L13a)
481.B35	Bauchi. Abubakar Tafawa Balewa University (Table L13a)
481.B4	Benin City. University of Benin (Table L13a)
	Formerly Benin University
481.C34	Calabar. University of Calabar (Table L13a)
481.E46	Ekpoma. Edo State University (Table L13a)
481.E58	Enugu. Enugu State University of Science and Technology (Table L13a)
481.I2	Ibadan. University of Ibadan (Table L13a)
	Formerly University College
481.I422	Ife. Obafemi Awolowo University (Table L13a)
	Formerly University of Ife
481.I47	Ikere-Ekiti. College of Education, Ikere-Ekiti (Table L13a)
	Formerly Ondo State College of Education
481.I49	Ila-Orangun. Osun State College of Education (Ila-Orangun) (Table L13a)
	Formerly Oyo State College of Education (Ila-Orangun)
481.I52	Ilisan. Babcock University (Table L13a)
481.I527	Ilorin. Kwara State College of Arabic and Islamic Legal Studies (Table L13a)
481.I53	Ilorin. University of Ilorin (Table L13a)
481.I59	Imo State University, Etiti, Nigeria (Table L13a)
481.I74	Iree. Osun State Polytechnic (Table L13a)
481.J68	Jos. University of Jos (Table L13a)
481.K35	Kano. Bayero University (Table L13a)
	Formerly Abdullahi Bayero College; Bayero University College

LG

Asia, Africa, Oceania
Africa
British Africa. South Africa
West Africa
Nigeria
Universities and colleges. By place, A-Z -- Continued

481.K38	Katsina. Hassan Usman Katsina Polytechnic (Table L13a)
481.K39	Katsina. Umaru Musa Yar'adua University, Katsina (Table L13a)
481.L2	Lagos. University of Lagos (Table L13a)
481.L3	Lagos. Lagos Training College and Industrial Institute (Table L13a)
481.M34	Maiduguri. University of Maiduguri (Table L13a)
	Including the former North East College of Arts and Sciences
481.M35	Makurdi. Benue State University (Table L13a)
481.M56	Minna. Federal University of Technology, Minna (Table L13a)
(481.N45)	Nekede. Federal Polytechnic Nekede (Table L13a)
	see T173
481.N75	Nsugbe. Nwafor Orizu College of Education, Nsugbe (Table L13a)
481.N8	Nsukka. University of Nigeria, Nsukka (Table L13a)
	Obafemi Awolowo University see LG481.I422
481.O35	Ogbomoso. Ladoke Akintola University of Technology (Table L13a)
481.O37	Okigwe. Imo State University (Table L13a)
481.O38	Okija. Madonna University (Table L13a)
481.O83	Ota. Covenant University (Table L13a)
481.O94	Owerri. Alvan Ikoku College of Education (Table L13a)
481.O95	Owerri. Imo State University (Table L13a)
	Originally located in Etiti (1981); moved to Uturu in late 1980s, and to Owerri in early 1990s.
481.P65	Port Harcourt. University of Port Harcourt (Table L13a)
481.S68	Sokoto. Usmanu Danfodiyo University (Table L13a)
	Formerly University of Sokoto
481.U45	Uli. Anambra State University (Table L13a)
481.U68	Uturu. Abia State University (Table L13a)
481.U96	Uyo. University of Uyo (Table L13a)
481.Z3	Zaria. Ahmadu Bello University (Table L13a)
481.Z34	Zaria. Federal College of Education (Table L13a)
483.A-Z	Schools. By place, A-Z
	Cameroons see LG581+
	Gambia

	Asia, Africa, Oceania
	Africa
	British Africa. South Africa
	West Africa
	Gambia -- Continued
493.A-Z	Universities and colleges. By place, A-Z
	Subarrange each by Table L13a
493.K36	Kanifing. University of the Gambia (Table L13a)
495.A-Z	Schools. By place, A-Z
	Ghana. Gold Coast
497.A-Z	Universities and colleges. By place, A-Z
497.A25	Achimota. Prince of Wales College and School (Table L13a)
497.C34	Cape Coast, Ghana. University (Table L13a)
497.L43	Legon. University of Ghana (Table L13a)
	Formerly University College of Ghana
497.T36	Tamale. University for Development Studies (Table L13a)
499.A-Z	Schools. By place, A-Z
	Sierra Leone
503.A-Z	Universities and colleges. By place, A-Z
503.F73	Freetown. Fourah Bay College (Table L13a)
503.N53	Njala Njala University College (Table L13a)
505.A-Z	Schools. By place, A-Z
511.A-Z	Egypt
511.A57	Alexandria. al-Jāmi'at al-Iskandarīyah (Table L13a)
511.A6	American University at Cairo (Table L13a)
511.A74	Asyut. Jāmi'at Asyūṭ (Table L13a)
511.C42	Cairo. Collège de la Sainte Famille (Table L13a)
511.C45	Cairo. al-Jāmi'al Azhar (Table L13a)
511.C48	Cairo. Jāmi'at al-Qāhirah (Table L13a)
	Formerly Université égyptienne; Fouad I University
511.C5	Cairo. Jāmi'at 'Ayn Shams (Table L13a)
511.C54	Cairo. Kullīyat Dār al-'Ulūm (Table L13a)
511.M37	Mansūrah. Jāmīyat al Mansūrah (Table L13a)
511.T3	Tanta. Jāmīyat Tantā (Table L13a)
	Sudan
513.A-Z	Universities and colleges. By place, A-Z
513.G49	Gezira. Jāmi'at al-Jazīrah (Table L13a)
513.G6	Gordon Memorial College, Khartum (Table L13a)
	Merged September 1951 with Kitchener School of Medicine to form University College of Khartum (later University of Khartum)
513.J83	Juba. Jāmi'at Jūbā (Table L13a)

	Asia, Africa, Oceania
	Africa
	Sudan
	Universities and colleges. By place, A-Z -- Continued
513.K45	Khartum. University (Table L13a)
	September 1951 Gordon Memorial College and Kitchener School of Medicine merged to form the University College Khartum. Name changed in 1956 to University of Khartum
513.O45	Omdurman. Jāmiʻat Umm Durmān al-Islāmīyah. (Table L13a)
513.O46 (Table	Omdurman. Kullīyat al-Aḥfād al-Jāmiʻyah lil-Banāt
	L13a)
514.A-Z	Schools. By place, A-Z
	French Africa
521.A-Z	Algeria and Tunis
521.A4	Algiers (City). Université (Table L13a)
521.T8	Tunis. al-Jāmiʻah al-Tunisīyah (Table L13a)
521.T83	Tunis. al-Madrasah al-Ṣādiqīyah (Table L13a)
	Burundi
525	Bujumbura. Université du Burundi (Table L13)
	Formerly Université officielle de Bujumbura; Centre universitaire; Facultés universitaires d'Usumbura
528.A-Z	Schools. By place, A-Z
	French Equatorial Africa. French Congo
	Chad
531.A-Z	Universities and colleges. By place, A-Z
531.N4	N'Djamena. Université du Tchad (Table L13a)
532.A-Z	Schools. By place, A-Z
	Central African Republic
533.A-Z	Universities and colleges. By place, A-Z
534.A-Z	Schools. By place, A-Z
	Congo (Brazzaville). Moyen-Congo
535.A-Z	Universities and colleges. By place, A-Z
535.B7	Brazzaville. Université Marien Ngouabi (Table L13a)
	Formerly Université de Brazzaville; Centre d'enseignement supérieur de Brazzaville
536.A-Z	Schools. By place, A-Z
	Gabon
537.A-Z	Universities and colleges. By place, A-Z
537.L53	Libreville. Universite Omar Bongo (Table L13a)
	Formerly Université nationale El Hadj Omar Bongo
538.A-Z	Schools. By place, A-Z
	Madagascar
541.A-Z	Universities and colleges. By place, A-Z

	Asia, Africa, Oceania
	Africa
	French Africa
	Madagascar
	Universities and colleges. By place, A-Z -- Continued
541.A46	Antananarivo. Université d'Antananarivo (Table L13a)
	Formerly Université de Madagascar
543.A-Z	Schools. By place, A-Z
	Rwanda
545.A-Z	Universities and colleges. By place, A-Z
545.B88	Butare. Université nationale de Rwanda (Table L13a)
547.A-Z	Schools. By place, A-Z
	West Africa
	Senegal
551.A-Z	Universities and colleges. By place, A-Z
551.D33	Dakar. Université Cheikh Anta Diop de Dakar (Table L13a)
	Formerly Université de Dakar; Institut des hautes e études de Dakar
551.P55	Piré Goureye. Piroe Sagnakhôre (Table L13a)
552.A-Z	Schools. By place, A-Z
	Benin. Dahomey
553.A-Z	Universities and colleges. By place, A-Z
553.C66	Cotonou. Université nationale du Benin (Table L13a)
	Formerly Université du Dahomey
554.A-Z	Schools. By place, A-Z
	Burkina Faso. Upper Volta
555.A-Z	Universities and colleges. By place, A-Z
555.O93	Ouagadougou. Université de Ouagadougou (Table L13a)
556.A-Z	Schools. By place, A-Z
	Cameroun see LG581+
	Guinea
557.A-Z	Universities and colleges. By place, A-Z
558.A-Z	Schools. By place, A-Z
	Côte d'Ivoire. Ivory Coast
559.A-Z	Universities and colleges. By place, A-Z
	Abidjan
559.A23	Université catholique de l'Afrique de l'Ouest (Table L13a)
559.A24	Université nationale de Côte d'Ivoire (Table L13a)
	Formerly Université d'Abidjan
560.A-Z	Schools. By place, A-Z
	Mali. French Sudan
561.A-Z	Universities and colleges. By place, A-Z
562.A-Z	Schools. By place, A-Z

	Asia, Africa, Oceania
	Africa
	Congo (Democratic Republic). Zaire
615.K57	Kisangani. Université de Kisangani (1981-) (Table L13a)
	Formerly Université libre du Congo, 1963-1970. In 1971 merged to form Université nationale du Zaire LG615.K54. Separated from the Université nationale du Zaire in 1981.
	Leopoldville. Université Lovanium de Kinshasa see LG615.K53
615.L83	Lubumbashi. Université de Lubumbashi (Table L13a)
	Formerly Université officielle du Congo à Lubumbashi, 1955-1970. In 1971 merged to form Université nationale du Zaire LG615.K54. Separated from the Université nationale du Zaire in 1981.
617.A-Z	Schools. By place, A-Z
621.A-Z	Liberia
621.C28	Cuttington College and Divinity School (Table L13a)
621.L5	Liberia College, Monrovia (Table L13a)
621.M62	Monrovia. University of Liberia (Table L13a)
	Morocco
631.A-Z	Universities and colleges. By place, A-Z
631.F45	Fès. Jāmi'at al-Qarawīyīn (Table L13a)
632.A-Z	Schools. By place, A-Z
	Portuguese Africa (Former)
641.A-Z	Mozambique
641.L58	Laurenǫ Marquez (City). Universidade (Table L13a)
641.M367	Maputo. Universidade Eduardo Mondlane (Table L13a)
643.A-Z	Schools. By place, A-Z
651.A-Z	Angola
651.B45	Benguela. Lusíada University (Table L13a)
651.C25	Cabinda. Lusíada University (Table L13a)
	Luanda
651.L75	Lusíada University (Table L13a)
651.L77	Universidade Agostinho Neto (Table L13a)
651.L78	Universidade Catolica de Angola (Table L13a)
651.L8	Universidade de Luanda (Table L13a)
671	Spanish Africa (Table L13)
	Togo. Togoland
675.A-Z	Universities and colleges. By place, A-Z
675.L65	Lomé. Université du Benin (Table L13a)
677.A-Z	Schools. By place, A-Z
681.A-Z	Tripoli. Libya
681.B45	al-Jāmi'ah al-Lībīyah, Bengazi. Jāmi'at Banghāzī (Table L13a)
681.T75	Tripoli. Jāmi'at al-Fātih (Table L13a)
690.A-Z	Indian Ocean islands, A-Z

	Asia, Africa, Oceania
	Indian Ocean islands, A-Z -- Continued
	Mauritius
690.M38M64	Moka. Mahatma Gandhi Institute
690.M38R43	Réduit. University of Mauritius
690.M38.A-Z	Universities and colleges. By place, A-Z
690.M382A-.M382Z	Schools. By place, A-Z
690.M384A-.M384Z	Women's colleges and girl's schools. By place, A-Z
690.R48	Réunion. Université de la (Table L13a)
	Australia
715.A-Z	Universities and colleges. By place, A-Z
715.A2	Adelaide. University (Table L13a)
715.A7	Armidale. University of New England (Table L13a)
715.B35	Bathurst. All Saints' College (Table L13a)
	Brisbane
715.B64	Kelvin Grove College of Advanced Education (Table L13a)
715.B7	University of Queensland (Table L13a)
715.B8	Bundoora. La Trobe University (Table L13a)
	Canberra
715.C2	Australian National University (Table L13a)
	Canberra College of Advanced Education see LG715.C35
715.C3	University College (Table L13a)
715.C35	University of Canberra (Table L13a)
	Formerly Canberra College of Advanced Education
715.D37	Darwin. Northern Territory University (Table L13a)
715.E17	Eastwood. Macquarie University (Table L13a)
715.F6	Freemantle. Murdoch University (Table L13a)
715.G43	Geelong. Deakin University (Table L13a)
715.G64	Gold Coast. Bond University (Table L13a)
	Hobart
715.H4	Tasmanian College of Advanced Education (Table L13a)
715.H6	University of Tasmania (Table L13a)
715.K4	Kensington. New South Wales University (Table L13a)
	Melbourne
715.M34	Australian Catholic University (Table L13a)
715.M45	Monash University (Table L13a)
715.M46	Ormond College (Table L13a)
715.M5	University (Table L13a)
	Nedlands. Western Australia. University see LG715.P4
715.N34	Nathan. Griffith University (Table L13a)
715.N4	Newcastle. University of Newcastle (Table L13a)
	Perth. Western Australia
715.P36	Central Metropolitan College of TAFE (Table L13a)

	Asia, Africa, Oceania
	Australia
	Universities and colleges. By place, A-Z
	Perth. Western Australia -- Continued
715.P4	University of Western Australia (Table L13a)
	Moved to Nedlands in 1930
715.P42	Western Australian College of Advanced Education (Table L13a)
715.P67	Port Adelaide. Aboriginal Community College (Table L13a)
	Sydney
715.S78	Mcquarie University (Table L13a)
715.S82	Scots College (Table L13a)
715.S9	University of Sydney (Table L13a)
715.S95	University of Western Sydney (Table L13a)
715.T6	Townsville. James Cook University of North Queensland (Table L13a)
715.W64	Wollongong. University of Wollongong (Table L13a)
718.A-Z	Women's colleges and girls' schools. By place, A-Z
	Subarrange each by Table L13a
720.A-Z	Schools. By place, A-Z
	New Zealand
741.A-Z	Universities and colleges. By place, A-Z
	Auckland
741.A36	College of St. John the Evangelist (Table L13a)
741.A8	University of Auckland (Table L13a)
	Formerly Auckland University College
741.C3	Christchurch. University of Canterbury (Table L13a)
	Canterbury College (1873-1934); Canterbury University College (1935-1956)
741.D8	Dunedin. University of Otago (Table L13a)
741.H3	Hamilton. University of Waikato (Table L13a)
741.P34	Palmerston North. Massey University (Table L13a)
	Wellington
741.W4	New Zealand University (Table L13a)
	Established 1871; dissolved 1961
741.W5	Victoria University (Table L13a)
	Victoria College (1897-1914); Victoria University College (1915-1956)
743.A-Z	Women's colleges and girls' schools. By place, A-Z
	Subarrange each by Table L13a
745.A-Z	Schools. By place, A-Z
	Pacific islands, A-Z
	Fiji Islands
961.F5	Universities and colleges. By place, A-Z
961.F5S77	Suva. University of the South Pacific
961.F52.A-Z	Schools. By place, A-Z

	Asia, Africa, Oceania
	Pacific islands, A-Z
	Fiji Islands -- Continued
961.F54.A-Z	Women's colleges and girls' schools. By place, A-Z
	Subarrange each by Table L13a
	Guam
961.G8.A-Z	Universities and colleges. By place, A-Z
961.G8.A37	Guam. University, Agana
	Formerly Guam. Territorial College
961.G82.A-Z	Schools. By place, A-Z
961.G84.A-Z	Women's colleges and girls' schools. By place, A-Z
	Subarrange each by Table L13a
	Universities and colleges see LD1+
	Hawaii
	Hawaii. University, Honolulu see LD2221
	Oahu. Church College of Hawaii, Laie see LD571.B75
	Women's colleges and girls schools see LD7251.A+
961.M53	Micronesia. College of Micronesia (Table L13a)
961.N64	Northern Mariana Islands. Northern Marianas College (Table L13a)
	Palau
961.P24	Palau Community College (Table L13a)
961.P26A-.P26Z	Schools. By place, A-Z
	Papua New Guinea
961.P3	Universities and colleges. By place, A-Z
961.P3P38	Papua. University of Papua New Guinea
961.P32A-.P32Z	Schools. By place, A-Z
	Solomon Islands
961.S5A-.S5Z	Universities and colleges. By place, A-Z
961.S5H5	Honiara. Solomon Islands College of Higher Education (Table L13a)
961.S52A-.S52Z	Schools. By place, A-Z
961.S54A-.S54Z	Women's colleges and girls' schools. By place, A-Z
	Subarrange each by Table L13a
961.T65	Tonga. Tupou College (Table L13a)

College and school magazines and papers

> Arrange each magazine or paper, affiliated with a school, by assigning two Cutter numbers, the first for the school, by name, and the second for the title of the magazine or paper. Expand the second Cutter number for the magazine or paper as follows: x Original, x2 Selections. By date, x3-39 History. criticism, etc. By author
>
> Arrange each magazine or paper, not affiliated with a particular school, by assigning one Cutter number for the name of the magazine or paper. Expand the Cutter number for the magazine or paper as follows: x Original, x2 Selections. By date, x3A-Z History, criticism, etc. By author
>
> Class alumni magazines here
>
> For general works on history and criticism of school magazines and papers, see the institution in LD+
>
> Cf. LB3621 Editing and publishing

1	United States
3	American (except United States)
5	Europe
7	Asia
8	Africa
8.5	Indian Ocean islands
9	Oceania

	Textbooks
	Class here general textbooks (Textbooks covering several subjects)
	For general textbooks for women see LC1461+
6	Exhibitions
	Cf. L797+ General educational exhibitions
15	History
23	United States
25.A-Z	Other countries, A-Z
	Early through 1800
101	Latin
105	American
109	English
113	Dutch
117	French
121	German
125	Italian
127	Japanese
129	Scandinavian
133	Slavic
137	Spanish
141	Portuguese
	1801-1850/70
205	American
210	English
215	Dutch
220	French
225	German
230	Italian
	Scandinavian
235	Danish
240	Norwegian
245	Swedish
	Slavic
250	Russian
255	Polish
260.A-Z	Other, A-Z
265	Spanish
270	Portuguese
275	Celtic
280.A-Z	Other, A-Z
	1850/70-
305	American
310	English
315	Dutch
320	French
325	German
330	Italian

	1850/70- -- Continued
	Scandinavian
335	Danish
340	Norwegian
345	Swedish
	Slavic
350	Russian
355	Polish
360.A-Z	Other, A-Z
365	Spanish
370	Portuguese
375	Celtic
380.A-Z	Other, A-Z
501	Textbooks for radio
(1001)	Special subjects
	see the subject in classes B - Z

0	Periodicals. Collections
	History
	General, and general modern
1.A2	Sources. Documents
1.A4	Exhibitions (Reports, etc.)
1.A5-Z	General works
	Early and medieval
1.3.A2	Sources. Documents
1.3.A4	Exhibitions (Reports, etc.)
1.3.A5-Z	General works
	16th century. Period of the Reformation
1.4.A2	Sources. Documents
1.4.A4	Exhibitions (Reports, etc.)
1.4.A5-Z	General works
	Early modern. 17th and 18th centuries
1.5.A2	Sources. Documents
1.5.A4	Exhibitions (Reports, etc.)
1.5.A5-Z	General works
	19th century
1.7.A2	Sources. Documents
1.7.A4	Exhibitions (Reports, etc.)
1.7.A5-Z	General works
	20th century
1.8.A2	Sources. Documents
1.8.A4	Exhibitions (Reports, etc.)
1.8.A5-Z	General works
	1945-2000
1.82.A2	Sources. Documents
1.82.A4	Exhibitions (Reports, etc.)
1.82.A5-Z	General works
	21st century
1.83.A2	Sources. Documents
1.83.A4	Exhibitions (Reports, etc.)
1.83.A5-Z	General works
2	General works. Present situation, etc.
2.7	General special
	e.g. Student activities
	Primary and elementary education (Schools)
	History
3.A2	Sources and documents
3.A4	Exhibitions (Reports, etc.)
3.A5-Z	General works
4	General works. Present situation
4.7	General special
	e.g. Student activities
	Secondary education (Schools)

	Secondary education (Schools) -- Continued
	History
5.A2	Sources. Documents
5.A4	Exhibitions (Reports, etc.)
5.A5-Z	General works
6	General works. Present situation
6.7	General special
	e.g. Student life
	Higher or university education (Colleges and universities)
	History
7.A2	Sources. Documents
7.A4	Exhibitions (Reports, etc.)
7.A5-Z	General works
8	General works. Present situation
8.7	General special
	e.g. Student life
9.A-Z	Local, A-Z
	Individual schools and colleges
	see LE+

TABLES

0	Periodicals. Collections
	History
	General, and general modern
1.A2	Sources. Documents
1.A4	Exhibitions (Reports, etc.)
1.A5-Z	General works
	Early and medieval
1.3.A2	Sources. Documents
1.3.A4	Exhibitions (Reports, etc.)
1.3.A5-Z	General works
	16th century. Period of the Reformation
1.4.A2	Sources. Documents
1.4.A4	Exhibitions (Reports, etc.)
1.4.A5-Z	General works
	Early modern. 17th and 18th centuries
1.5.A2	Sources. Documents
1.5.A4	Exhibitions (Reports, etc.)
1.5.A5-Z	General works
	19th century
1.7.A2	Sources. Documents
1.7.A4	Exhibitions (Reports, etc.)
1.7.A5-Z	General works
	20th century
1.8.A2	Sources. Documents
1.8.A4	Exhibitions (Reports, etc.)
1.8.A5-Z	General works
	1945-2000
1.82.A2	Sources. Documents
1.82.A4	Exhibitions (Reports, etc.)
1.82.A5-Z	General works
	21st century
1.83.A2	Sources. Documents
1.83.A4	Exhibitions (Reports, etc.)
1.83.A5-Z	General works
2	General works. Present situation, etc.
2.7	General special
	e.g. Student activities
	Primary and elementary education (Schools)
	History
3.A2	Sources and documents
3.A4	Exhibitions (Reports, etc.)
3.A5-Z	General works
4	General works. Present situation
4.7	General special
	e.g. Student activities
	Secondary education (Schools)

	Secondary education (Schools) -- Continued
	History
5.A2	Sources. Documents
5.A4	Exhibitions (Reports, etc.)
5.A5-Z	General works
6	General works. Present situation
6.7	General special
	e.g. Student life
	Higher or university education (Colleges and universities)
	History
7.A2	Sources. Documents
7.A4	Exhibitions (Reports, etc.)
7.A5-Z	General works
8	General works. Present situation
8.7	General special
	e.g. Student life
	Individual schools and colleges
	see LE+

TABLES

0	Periodicals. Collections
	History
	General, and general modern
1.A2	Sources. Documents
1.A4	Exhibitions (Reports, etc.)
1.A5-Z	General works
	Early and medieval
1.3.A2	Sources. Documents
1.3.A4	Exhibitions (Reports, etc.)
1.3.A5-Z	General works
	16th century. Period of the Reformation
1.4.A2	Sources. Documents
1.4.A4	Exhibitions (Reports, etc.)
1.4.A5-Z	General works
	Early modern. 17th and 18th centuries
1.5.A2	Sources. Documents
1.5.A4	Exhibitions (Reports, etc.)
1.5.A5-Z	General works
	19th century
1.7.A2	Sources. Documents
1.7.A4	Exhibitions (Reports, etc.)
1.7.A5-Z	General works
	20th century
1.8.A2	Sources. Documents
1.8.A4	Exhibitions (Reports, etc.)
1.8.A5-Z	General works
	1945-2000
1.82.A2	Sources. Documents
1.82.A4	Exhibitions (Reports, etc.)
1.82.A5-Z	General works
	21st century
1.83.A2	Sources. Documents
1.83.A4	Exhibitions (Reports, etc.)
1.83.A5-Z	General works
2	General works. Present situation, etc.
2.7	General special
	e.g. Student activities
	Primary and elementary education (Schools)
	History
3.A2	Sources and documents
3.A4	Exhibitions (Reports, etc.)
3.A5-Z	General works
4	General works. Present situation
4.7	General special
	e.g. Student activities
	Secondary education (Schools)

	Secondary education (Schools) -- Continued
	History
5.A2	Sources. Documents
5.A4	Exhibitions (Reports, etc.)
5.A5-Z	General works
6	General works. Present situation
6.7	General special
	e.g. Student life
	Higher or university education (Colleges and universities)
	History
7.A2	Sources. Documents
7.A4	Exhibitions (Reports, etc.)
7.A5-Z	General works
7.5	General works. Present situation
7.7	General special
	e.g. Student life
	Individual schools and colleges
	see LE+

TABLES

0	Periodicals. Collections
	General works. History and present situation
1	General
2	Primary education. Secondary education
3	Higher education
3.7	General special
	e.g. Student life
4.A-Z	Local, A-Z
	Individual schools and colleges
	see LE+
	Educational biography
	see LA2301+

0	Periodicals. Collections
	General works. History and present situation
1	General
2	Primary education. Secondary education
3	Higher education
3.7	General special
	e.g. Student life
	Individual schools and colleges
	see LE+
	Educational biography
	see LA2301+

Each university or college to which this table applies has been assigned a span of Cutter numbers as shown in the classification schedule. To apply this table, drop the final digit from the first Cutter number of the institution's assigned span and substitute the remaining number for ".x1" in the table. Drop the final digit from the second Cutter number in the span and substitute the remaining number for ".x2" in the table.

For example, Canisius College, Buffalo, N.Y., has been assigned the span LD791.C47-.C56. Drop the final digit ("7") from the first Cutter number and substitute the remaining number (LD791.C4) for ".x1" in the table. Drop the final digit ("6") from the second Cutter number and substitute the remaining number (LD791.C5) for ".x2" in the table. This results in the following numbers for Canisius College: "Charter (and founding)" (.x17 in table) - LD791.C47; "Bequests, donations, etc. (.x197 in the table) - LD791.C497; "Personnel management (.x1995 in table) - LD791.C4995; etc. "Dormitories, residence halls, etc." (.x234 in the table) - LD791.C534; "Presidential inaugurations" (.x248) - LD791.C548; etc.

.x17	Charter (and founding)
.x173	Heraldry. Seal
.x175	College statutes, by-laws, etc.
	Administration
.x177	General works. Office reports
.x18	Board of regents, trustees, etc.
.x19	President (or head of the institution)
.x192	Other administrative reports
	Finance
.x193	General works
.x194	Endowment
.x195	Appropriations and grants
.x197	Bequests, donations, etc.
.x198	Scholarships
	Policy and organization
.x199	General works
	Personnel management
.x1995	General works
.x1996	Salaries, pensions, etc.
	Catalogs, registers, bulletins, etc.
.x2	Annual, semiannual, quarterly
.x2a	Announcements, circulars, etc.
.x2b	Directories
	Requirements for admission
.x2d	General works
.x2e	Entrance examinations and accredited schools
	Curriculum

	Curriculum -- Continued
.x2g	General works
.x2ga	Syllabi (Collected)
.x2gb	Honors courses
.x2h	Graduate work and courses
.x2j	Degrees and honors
.x2k	Miscellaneous publications
	Biography
.x21	Collective
	Alumni
.x21a	Directories
.x21b	General histories
.x21c	Obituary record
.x21d	General special
.x21f	General catalogs
.x21g	Other catalogs
.x21k	Individual classes. By date of class
	Subarrange by author
	Individual
.x213A-.x213Z	Founders, benefactors, etc.
.x217	Presidents, A-Z
.x218A-.x218Z	Other faculty members, A-Z
.x219	Reminiscences
	History and description
.x22	History (including early descriptions)
.x23	Description (including guidebooks)
.x233	Views. Pictorial works
.x2335	Campus planning
.x234	Dormitories, residence halls, etc.
	Laboratories
	see classes Q, T, etc.
	Libraries
	see class Z
	Museums
	see subclass AM, or special subject
.x238	Individual buildings and places, A-Z
	Student life and customs
.x24	General works
	Special
.x241	Student societies and clubs
	For fraternities, see LJ
	Class days or events
.x242	Freshman
.x243	Sophomore
.x244	Junior
.x245	Senior

TABLES

	Basketball
	see GV885.43
	Football
	see GV958
	Religion
	see BR561
	Commencement
.x246	General works
.x247	Addresses. Orations. Sermons. By date
.x248	Presidential inaugurations. By date
.x249	Other special days and events
	Undergraduate publications
	Periodicals
	see LH
.x25	Annuals
	Alumni activities
	Alumni magazines
	see LH
.x257	Graduate class publications (and exercises)
	Alumni associations and graduate clubs
.x26A1-.x26A4	Resident
.x26A5-.x26Z	Nonresident. By name of place
.x265A-.x265Z	Special colleges, campuses, etc., A-Z

0	Charter (and founding)
0.3	Heraldry. Seal
0.5	College statutes, by-laws, etc.
	Administration
0.7	General works. Office reports
1	Board of regents, trustees, etc.
2	President (or head of the institution)
2.5	Treasurer
2.7	Registrar
2.9	Other administrative reports
	Finance
3	General works
3.5	Endowment
4	Appropriations and grants. By date
5	Bequests, donations, etc.
5.5	Scholarships
	Policy and organization
5.8	General works
	Personnel management
5.9	General works
5.95	Salaries, pensions, etc.
	Catalogs, registers, bulletins, etc.
6	Annual, semiannual, quarterly
	Triennial, quinquennial
	see Biography
7	Announcements, circulars, etc.
8	Directories
	Requirements for admission
9	General works
10	Entrance examinations and accredited schools
	Curriculum
11	General works
11.2	Syllabi (Collected)
11.25	Honors courses
11.3	Graduate work and courses
11.7	Degrees and honors
11.8	Miscellaneous publications
	Biography
12	Collective
12.1	Presidents
12.2	Faculty or faculties
	Alumni
12.3	Directories
12.4	General histories
12.43	Obituary record
12.45	General special

TABLES

	Biography
	Collective
	Alumni -- Continued
12.49	General catalogs. Triennial etc.
12.5	Other catalogs
12.6	Individual classes. By date of class
	Subarrange by author
	Individual
12.65.A-Z	Founders, benefactors, etc., A-Z
	If founder is first president, prefer the latter classification
12.7.A-Z	Presidents, A-Z
12.8.A-Z	Other faculty members, A-Z
12.9	Reminiscences
	History and description
	History (including early descriptions)
13	General
14	Description (including guidebooks)
14.5	Views
14.6	Dormitories, residence halls, etc.
	Cf. NA6600+, Architecture
	Laboratories
	see classes Q, T, etc.
	Libraries
	see class Z
	Museums
	see subclass AM, or special subject
15.A-Z	Individual buildings and places, A-Z
	Student life and customs
16	General works
	Special
16.2	Student societies and clubs
	For fraternities, see LJ
	Class days or events
16.4	Freshman
16.5	Sophomore
16.6	Junior
16.7	Senior
	Basketball
	see GV885.43
	Football
	see GV958
	Religion
	see BR561
	Commencement
17	General works
17.2	Addresses. Orations. Sermons. By date

17.5	Presidential inaugurations. By date
17.7	Other special days and events. By date
	Undergraduate publications
	Periodicals
	see LH
18	Annuals
18.3	Handbooks
18.5	Calendars
	Alumni activities
	Alumni magazines
	see LH
18.7	Graduate class publications (and exercises)
	Alumni associations and graduate clubs
19.A1-.A4	Resident
19.A5-Z	Nonresident. By name of place
19.5.A-Z	Special colleges, campuses, etc., A-Z

0	Charter (and founding)
0.3	Heraldry. Seal
0.5	College statutes, by-laws, etc.
	Administration
0.7	General works. Office reports
1	Board of regents, trustees, etc.
2	President (or head of the institution)
2.5	Treasurer
2.7	Registrar
2.9	Other administrative reports
	Finance
3	General works
3.5	Endowment
4	Appropriations and grants. By date
5	Bequests, donations, etc.
6	Scholarships
	Policy and organization
6.5	General works
	Personnel management
6.7	General works
6.75	Salaries, pensions, etc.
	Catalogs, registers, bulletins, etc.
7	Annual, semiannual, quarterly
	Triennial, quinquennial
	see Biography
8	Announcements, circulars, etc.
9	Directories
	Requirements for admission
10	General works
11	Entrance examinations and accredited schools
	Curriculum
12	General works
12.5	Syllabi (Collected)
12.7	Honors courses
13	Graduate work and courses
14	Degrees and honors
14.5	Miscellaneous publications
	Biography
15	Collective
15.1	Presidents
15.2	Faculty or faculties
	Alumni
15.3	Directories
15.4	General histories
15.43	Obituary record
15.45	General special

	Biography
	Collective
	Alumni -- Continued
15.49	General catalogs. Triennial, etc.
15.5	Other catalogs
15.6	Individual classes. By date of class
	Subarrange by author
	Individual
15.8.A-Z	Founders, benefactors, etc., A-Z
	If founder is first president, prefer the latter classification
16.A-Z	Presidents, A-Z
17.A-Z	Other faculty members, A-Z
17.5	Reminiscences
	History and description
	History (including early descriptions)
18	General
	By period
18.3	Early
18.8	Recent
	Description
19	General (including guidebooks)
19.2	Y.M.C.A. handbooks
19.7	Views. Pictorial works
19.8	Dormitories, residence halls, etc.
	Cf. NA6600+, Architecture
	Laboratories
	see classes Q, T, etc.
	Libraries
	see class Z
	Museums
	see subclass AM, or special subject
20	Individual buildings and places, A-Z
	Student life and customs
21	General works
	Special
21.4	Student societies and clubs
	For fraternities, see LJ
	Class days or events
22	Senior
	Basketball
	see GV885.43
	Football
	see GV958
	Religion
	see BR561
	Commencement

TABLES

	Commencement -- Continued
23	General works
24	Addresses. Orations. Sermons. By date
25	Presidential inaugurations. By date
26	Other special days and events. By date
	Undergraduate publications
	Periodicals
	see LH
27	Annuals
	Alumni activities
	Alumni magazines
	see LH
28	Graduate class publications (and exercises)
	Alumni associations and graduate clubs
29.A1-.A4	Resident
29.A5-Z	Nonresident. By name of place
29.5.A-Z	Special colleges, campuses, etc., A-Z

0	Charter (and founding)
0.3	Heraldry. Seal
0.5	College statutes, by-laws, etc.
	Administration
0.7	General works. Office reports
1	Board of regents, trustees, etc.
2	President (or head of the institution)
2.5	Treasurer
2.7	Registrar
2.9	Other administrative reports
	Finance
3	General works
3.5	Endowment
4	Appropriations and grants
5	Bequests, donations, etc.
6	Scholarships
	Policy and organization
6.5	General works
	Personnel management
6.7	General works
6.75	Salaries, pensions, etc.
	Catalogs, registers, bulletins, etc.
7	Annual, semiannual, quarterly
	Triennial, quinquennial
	see Biography
9	Announcements, circulars, etc.
10	Directories
	Requirements for admission
11	General works
12	Entrance examinations and accredited schools
	Curriculum
13	General works
14	Syllabi (Collected)
14.5	Honors courses
15	Graduate work and courses
17	Degrees and honors
17.5	Miscellaneous publications
	Biography
18	Collective
19	Presidents
20	Faculty or faculties
	Alumni
21	Directories
22	General histories
23	General catalogs. Triennial, etc.
23.5	Other catalogs

TABLES

	Biography
	Collective
	Alumni -- Continued
24	Individual classes. By date of class
	Subarrange by author
	Individual
24.5.A-Z	Founders, benefactors, etc., A-Z
25.A-Z	Presidents, A-Z
26.A-Z	Other faculty members, A-Z
27	Reminiscences
	History and description
	History (including early descriptions)
28	General
	By period
29	Early
30	Recent
	Description
31	General (including guidebooks)
31.2	Y.M.C.A. handbooks
33	Views. Pictorial works
34	Dormitories, residence halls, etc.
	Laboratories
	see classes Q, T, etc.
	Libraries
	see class Z
	Museums
	see subclass AM, or special subject
35	Individual buildings and places, A-Z
	Student life and customs
36	General works
36.5	Student societies and clubs
	For fraternities, see LJ
	Class days or events
(37)	Freshman
(38)	Sophomore
(39)	Junior
40	Senior
	Basketball
	see GV885.43
	Football
	see GV958
	Religion
	see BR561
	Commencement
41	General works
42	Addresses. Orations. Sermons. By date

45	Presidential inaugurations. By date
46	Other special days and events. By date
	Undergraduate publications
	Periodicals
	see LH
47	Annuals
47.3	Handbooks
47.5	Calendars
47.7	Almanacs
	Alumni activities
	Alumni magazines
	see LH
48	Graduate class publications (and exercises)
	Alumni associations and graduate clubs
49.A1-.A4	Resident
49.A5-Z	Nonresident. By name of place
49.5.A-Z	Special colleges, campuses, etc., A-Z

	Official publications
.A1-.A4	Serial
.A5-.A7	Nonserial
.A8-.Z	Other works. By author
	Including student yearbooks, etc.

	Official publications
.xA1-.xA4	Serial
.xA5-.xA7	Nonserial
.xA8-.xZ	Other works. By author
	Including student yearbooks, etc.

0	Charter and statutes
0.5	Heraldry. Seal
1	Official reports
	Finance
2	General works
2.5	Special funds, etc., A-Z
3	Policy
4	Catalogs. Yearbooks
5	Announcements
6	Entrance requirements and examinations
7	Curriculum. Degrees. Examinations (in course)
	Biography
8	Collective
9	Individual
10	Reminiscences
	History
11	General
12	Early
13	Recent
	Description
15	Guidebooks
16	Other books
17	Student life
17.5	Rectorial addresses, etc. (Collected)
18	Special days and events. By date
	e.g. 1884 October 28
19	Other
19.5.A-Z	Special colleges or branches, A-Z

0	Charter and statutes
0.5	Heraldry. Seal
1	Official reports
2	Catalogs. Yearbooks
3	Curriculum. Degrees. Examinations (in course)
	Biography
	Collective
4.A2	General catalogs. Register of alumni. Faculty
4.A3	Other
4.A4-Z	Individual
5	History
	Including reminiscences
6	Description
7	Student life
7.5	Rectorial addresses, etc. (Collected)
8	Special days and events. By date
	e.g. 1884 October 28
9	Other
9.5.A-Z	Special colleges or branches, A-Z

TABLES

1.A3	Charters. Constitutions, etc.
	Assign second Cutter number for main entry (author or title)
1.A5	Heraldry. Seal
	Assign second Cutter number for main entry (author or title)
1.A7	Regulations. Statutes
	Assign second Cutter number for main entry (author or title)
1.A9	Administration (General works). Official publications
	Assign second Cutter number for main entry (author or title)
1.B1	Governing board. Reports
	Assign second Cutter number for main entry (author or title)
1.B3	President. Rector
	Assign second Cutter number for main entry (author or title)
1.B5	Treasurer
	Assign second Cutter number for main entry (author or title)
1.B6	Other
	Assign second Cutter number for main entry (author or title)
1.C5	Catalogs. Registers. Yearbooks ("Chronik")
	Assign second Cutter number for main entry (author or title)
1.C7	Announcements ("Verzeichnis der vorlesungen")
	Assign second Cutter number for main entry (author or title)
1.C9	Directories ("Personalbestand")
	Assign second Cutter number for main entry (author or title)
	Finance
	Cf. L10 1.B5 Treasurer
1.F3	General
	Assign second Cutter number for main entry (author or title)
	Special
1.F5	Appropriations
	Assign second Cutter number for main entry (author or title)
1.F6	Endowments
	Assign second Cutter number for main entry (author or title)
1.F7	Bequests, etc.
	Assign second Cutter number for main entry (author or title)
1.F8	Fellowships, scholarships, etc.
	Assign second Cutter number for main entry (author or title)
1.F9	Prizes
	Assign second Cutter number for main entry (author or title)
	Organization. Policy
	General works
2.A3	Early through 1800
2.A5	1801-
2.A6-Z	Special topics, A-Z
2.C8	Curriculum
2.D4	Degrees
2.E6	Entrance requirements

	Organization. Policy
	Special topics, A-Z -- Continued
2.E9	Examinations
2.F3	Faculty
2.P83	Public relations
2.5	Miscellaneous publications
	History
3.A1-.A29	Collections. Documents. Sources
3.A3-Z	General works
(3.5)	Anniversary celebrations, jubilees, commemorations of the
	founding
	see L10 19.5
4	General special. Descriptive
	e.g. Architectural histories
	Medieval
5	General
6	Special
	16th-18th centuries
7.A3	Early works
	Modern
7.A4-Z	General
8	General special. Policy
9	Reminiscences
	19th century
10.A-.Z3	General
10.Z4	Special. Policy
11	Reminiscences
12	20th century
12.2	21st century
	Biography
14	General catalogs. Registers of alumni. Faculty
	Official
14.A1	Serials
14.A2	Monographs. By title
14.A3-Z	Other
15	Other collections
16.A-Z	Individual, A-Z
17	Guidebooks
18	Other descriptive works
19	Student life
	For general, see LA
19.5	Special days and events. Anniversary celebrations, jubilees,
	commemorations, etc.
20	Other
20.5.A-Z	Special colleges or branches, A-Z

TABLES

1	Charter and statutes
1.5	Heraldry. Seal
2	Administration (General works). Official reports. Organization and policy
3	Catalogs. Yearbooks. Announcements
3.6	Entrance requirements and examinations
4	Curriculum
4.8	Miscellaneous publications
	Biography
	Collective
5.A2	General catalogs. Registers of alumni. Faculty
5.A3	Other
5.A4-Z	Invidvidual, A-Z
	History
6	General works
(6.5)	Anniversaries, jubilees, commemorations of the founding see subdivision 9
7	Description
8	Student life
9	Special days and events
10	Other
10.5.A-Z	Special colleges or branches, A-Z

0	Charters and statutes
0.5	Heraldry. Seal
1	Administration (General works). Official reports. Organization and policy
2	Catalogs. Yearbooks. Announcements
2.6	Entrance requirements and examinations
3	Curriculum
3.8	Miscellaneous publications
	Biography
	Collective
4.A2	General catalogs. Registers of alumni. Faculty
4.A3	Other
4.A4-Z	Individual, A-Z
	History
5	General works
(5.5)	Anniversaries, jubilees, commemorations of the founding see subdivision 8
6	Description
7	Student life
8	Special days and events
9	Other
9.5.A-Z	Special colleges or branches, A-Z

TABLES

	Official publications
.A1-.A4	Serial
.A5-.A7	Nonserial
.A8-.Z	Other works
	Including student yearbooks, etc.

	Official publications
.xA1-.xA4	Serial
.xA5-.xA7	Nonserial
.xA8-.xZ	Other works
	Including student yearbooks, etc.

.x date	Collected works. Selections. By date
.xA-.xZ	Individual works. By title
.x2	Biography and criticism

1	Periodicals. Societies. Collections
	History and present situation
2	General
4	Primary
5	Secondary
6	Higher
7	General special
	Including student life
8.A-Z	States or provinces, A-Z
9.A-Z	Cities, A-Z

TABLES

1	Periodicals. Societies. Collections
	History and present situation
2	General
4	Primary
5	Secondary
6	Higher
7	General special
	Including student life

1	General works
2.A-Z	Individual colleges and schools. By place, A-Z
3	Institutes

1	General
2.A-Z	States, provinces, counties, etc., A-Z
3.A-Z	Cities, A-Z

1	General
1.5	Higher education
2.A-Z	Counties or regions, A-Z
3.A-Z	Cities, A-Z

.x   General works
.x2A-.x2Z   Local, A-Z

.xA1-.xA5	Documents
.xA6-.xZ	General works
.x2A-.x2Z	Local, A-Z

TABLES

.x	General works
.x2A-.x2Z	By province, state, etc., A-Z
.x3A-.x3Z	By city, A-Z

	United States
1	General works
2.A-Z	By region or state, A-Z
3.A-Z	By city, A-Z
	Canada
4	General works
4.2.A-Z	Provinces, A-Z
4.3.A-Z	Cities, A-Z
	Other American regions or countries
5.A2	Latin America (General)
5.A3-Z	By region or country, A-Z
	Subarrange each by Table L19
	Europe
6.A2	General works
6.A3-Z	By region or country, A-Z
	Subarrange each by Table L19
	Asia
7.A2	General works
7.A3-Z	By region or country, A-Z
	Subarrange each by Table L19
7.3	Arab countries
	Africa
8.A2	General works
8.A3-Z	By region or country, A-Z
	Subarrange each by Table L19
	Australia
9	General works
9.3.A-Z	Local, A-Z
	New Zealand
9.6	General works
9.9.A-Z	Local, A-Z
10.A-Z	Pacific Islands, A-Z
	Subarrange each by Table L19
	Arctic regions
10.3	General works
10.4	Greenland

	United States
1	General works
2.A-Z	By region or state, A-Z
2.2.A-Z	By city, A-Z
	Canada
3	General works
3.2.A-Z	Provinces, A-Z
3.3.A-Z	Cities, A-Z
	Other American regions or countries
4.A1	Latin America (General)
4.A3-Z	By region or country, A-Z
	Subarrange each by Table L20
	Europe
5.A1	General works
5.A3-Z	By region or country, A-Z
	Subarrange each by Table L20
	Asia
6.A1	General works
6.A3-Z	By region or country, A-Z
	Subarrange each by Table L20
6.3	Arab countries
	Africa
7.A1	General works
7.A3-Z	By region or country, A-Z
	Subarrange each by Table L20
7.5.A-Z	Indian Ocean islands, A-Z
	Subarrange each by Table L20
	Australia
8	General works
8.3.A-Z	Local, A-Z
	New Zealand
8.6	General works
8.9.A-Z	Local, A-Z
9.A-Z	Pacific Islands, A-Z
	Subarrange each by Table L20

1	Periodicals. Societies. Collections
5	Congresses, conferences, etc.
7	Encyclopedias. Dictionaries
15	General works
19	General special
19.15	Home-based education
	Including portage and instruction by visiting teachers
19.2	Preschool education
19.3	Early childhood education
19.7	Vocational education
19.8	Teacher training
23	Audiovisual aids
24	Computer-assisted instruction
	Special topics
25	Art. The arts
25.4	Drama
26	Games. Crafts
27	Home economics
	Language arts
28	General works
28.5	Reading
29	Science
29.5	Social science
31-40.4	By region or country (Table L22)
	Individual institutions
41	United States
43.A-Z	Other countries, A-Z

1	United States
	Subarrange by city, A-Z
5	Canada
	Subarrange by city, A-Z
9	Mexico
	Subarrange by city, A-Z
13.A-Z	Central American regions or countries, A-Z
	Assign two Cutter numbers, the first for the country and the second for the city
17.A-Z	West Indian regions or countries, A-Z
	Assign two Cutter numbers, the first for the country and the second for the city
21.A-Z	South American regions or countries, A-Z
	Assign two Cutter numbers, the first for the country and the second for the city
25	Great Britain
	Subarrange by city, A-Z
29	Austria
	Subarrange by city, A-Z
33	France
	Subarrange by city, A-Z
37	Germany
	Subarrange by city, A-Z
41	Greece
	Subarrange by city, A-Z
45	Italy
	Subarrange by city, A-Z
	Low countries
49	Belgium
	Subarrange by city, A-Z
53	Netherlands
	Subarrange by city, A-Z
57	Russia. Former Soviet Union
	Subarrange by city, A-Z
	Scandinavia
61	Denmark
	Subarrange by city, A-Z
65	Norway
	Subarrange by city, A-Z
69	Sweden
	Subarrange by city, A-Z
73	Spain
	Subarrange by city, A-Z
77	Portugal
	Subarrange by city, A-Z

81	Switzerland
	Subarrange by city, A-Z
85	Turkey and the Balkans
	Subarrange by city, A-Z
87.A-Z	Other European regions or countries, A-Z
	Assign two Cutter numbers, the first for the country and the second for the city
89.A-Z	Asian regions or countries, A-Z
	Assign two Cutter numbers, the first for the country and the second for the city
90.A-Z	Arab regions or countries, A-Z
	Assign two Cutter numbers, the first for the country and the second for the city
93.A-Z	African regions or countries, A-Z
	Assign two Cutter numbers, the first for the country and the second for the city
97	Australia
	Subarrange by city, A-Z
98	New Zealand
	Subarrange by city, A-Z
101.A-Z	Pacific islands, A-Z
	Assign two Cutter numbers, the first for the country and the second for the city

TABLES

.x	General works
	By region or country
	United States
.x2	General works
.x24.A-Z	By region or state, A-Z
.x26.A-Z	Other regions or countries, A-Z
.x3	General special
	Training
	see LB1738.5
	Supply and demand. Turnover
.x4	General works
	By region or country
	United States
.x42	General works
.x44.A-Z	By region or state, A-Z
.x46.A-Z	Other regions or countries, A-Z
	Selection and appointment. Contractual status
	Including tenure and dismissal
.x5	General works
	By region or country
	United States
.x52	General works
.x54.A-Z	By region or state, A-Z
.x56.A-Z	Other regions or countries, A-Z
.x58	Time management
	Certification
	see LB1767+
	Efficiency. Rating
.x6	General works
	By region or country
	United States
.x62	General works
.x64.A-Z	By region or state, A-Z
.x66.A-Z	Other regions or countries, A-Z
	Salaries. Pensions
.x7	General works
	By region or country
	United States
.x72	General works
.x74.A-Z	By region or state, A-Z
.x76.A-Z	Other regions or countries, A-Z

| .A-.Z8 | General works |
| .Z9 | Catalogs |

Music rooms
  School architecture and equipment:
    LB3325.M84
MY Tests: LB3060.33.M54

N

National Association of School
  Superintendents: LB2804
National Competency Tests:
  LC1034.5.N38
National Merit Scholarship Qualifying
  Test: LB2353.66
National university (United States):
  LC174
Natural history (Curriculum)
  Children with mental disabilities:
    LC4621.5
Nature study
  Early childhood education:
    LB1139.5.S35
  Elementary education: LB1585+
  Kindergarten: LB1185
  Preschool education: LB1140.5.S35
  Primary education: LB1532
Necker de Saussure, Albertine-Adrinne:
  LB675.N3+
New Jerusalem Church (Education):
  LC586.N4
New teachers: LB2844.1.N4
New thought
  Moral education: LC287
Newspapers
  Instruction: LB1044.9.N4
Newspapers, Student: LB3621
  Colleges: LB3621.25
NMSQT: LB2353.66
Nobility, Education of: LC4929
Nomad's children, Education of:
  LC3653+
Non-professional personnel: LB2844.2+
  Higher education: LB2335.5
Nonformal education: LC45+
  Women: LC1496+
Nongraded schools
  Instruction: LB1029.N6

Nonverbal communication
  Instruction: LB1033.5
Norm-referenced tests: LB3060.32.N67
Normal school teachers: LB1737.5.A3+
Normal schools: LB1805+
Norms, Test: LB3060.82+
North Carolina Competency Test:
  LB3060.33.N65
Note taking
  Elementary education: LB1601.5
  Higher education: LB2395.25
Numbers (Kindergarten): LB1186
Nursery school teachers: LB1732.5
Nursery schools: LB1140+
  Administration: LB2822.7
  Ethnic minorities: LC3723
  School architecture and equipment:
    LB3325.N8
Nutrition
  Elementary education: LB1587.N8

O

Object teaching
  Instruction: LB1029.O3
Objective tests: LB3060.32.O35
Observation (Educational method):
  LB1731.6
  Teaching: LB1027.28
Occupational literacy: LC149.7
Occupational therapy
  Schools: LB3457
Office layout: LB3325.O35
Office of Education (United States):
  L111.A3+
Ohio Graduation Test: LC1034.5.O45
Older adult education: LC5451+
Open admission (Higher education):
  LB2351.45+
Open-air schools: LB3481+
Open plan schools
  Instruction: LB1029.O6
  Preschool education: LB1140.35.O63
Opening exercises in schools: LB3015
Oral reading (Elementary education):
  LB1573.5
Orientation, College: LB2343.3+

Women teachers: LB2837
  Higher education: LB2332.3+
  Salaries: LB2843.W7
Women's colleges (United States):
  LD7020+
Women's fraternities: LJ141+
Woodcock-Johnson Psycho-Educational
  Battery: LB1131.75.W66
Woodcock-Munoz Language Survey:
  LB3060.33.W66
Word recognition (Reading): LB1050.44
  Elementary education: LB1573.6
  Kindergarten: LB1181.4
Working classes, Education of:
  LC5001+
Workload (Teachers): LB2844.1.W6
  Higher education: LB2335.35
Workplace literacy: LC149.7
Workshop classes: LC6562+
Writing (Child study): LB1139.W7

Y

Yearbooks, College: LB3621.67
Yearbooks, School: LB3621.25
Yeshivah ketanah (Jewish education):
  LC723
Yi (Chinese people), Education of:
  LC3501.Y5
Yiddish school: LC724
Youth, African American
  Education: LC2701+
Youth, Cerebral palsied, Education of:
  LC4580+
Yüan, Yen: LB475.Y45+

Z

Zwingli, Ulrich: LB275.Z7+

GPO U.S. GOVERNMENT PRINTING OFFICE: 2012–372–396/40012